# THE FAST FORWARD MBA IN PROJECT MANAGEMENT

### FIFTH EDITION

ERIC VERZUH

WILEY

Cover image: ©iStock.com/marigold_88
Cover design: Wiley

This book is printed on acid-free paper.

Published by John Wiley & Sons, Inc., Hoboken, New Jersey
Published simultaneously in Canada

For general information about our other products and services, please contact our Customer Care Department within the United States at (800) 762-2974, outside the United States at (317) 572-3993 or fax (317) 572-4002.

Wiley publishes in a variety of print and electronic formats and by print-on-demand. Some material included with standard print versions of this book may not be included in e-books or in print-on-demand. If this book refers to media such as a CD or DVD that is not included in the version you purchased, you may download this material at http://booksupport.wiley.com. For more information about Wiley products, visit www.wiley.com.

***Library of Congress Cataloging-in-Publication Data:***

Verzuh, Eric.
    The fast forward MBAba in project management / Eric Verzuh. — Fifth edition.
      1 online resource. — (Fast forward mba series)
    Revised edition of the author's The fast forward MBAba in project management, 2011.
    Includes index.
      Description based on print version record and CIP data provided by publisher; resource not viewed.
      ISBN 978-1-119-08667-3 (pdf) — ISBN 978-1-119-08658-1 (epub) — ISBN 978-1-119-14822-7 (hardback); ISBN 978-1-119-08657-4 (paperback)
    1. Project management.  I. Title.
    HD69.P75
    658.4'04—dc23                                                   2015032111

Printed in the United States of America

10 9 8 7 6 5 4

# CONTENTS

## PART 1
## INTRODUCTION

## PART 2
## DEFINING THE PROJECT

**PART 3
THE PLANNING PROCESS**

**CHAPTER 7 — RISK MANAGEMENT: MINIMIZE THE THREATS TO YOUR PROJECT**  137

**CHAPTER 8 — WORK BREAKDOWN STRUCTURE: BREAK YOUR PROJECT INTO MANAGEABLE UNITS OF WORK**  164

**PART 4**
**CONTROLLING THE PROJECT**

**CHAPTER 13 — BUILDING A HIGH-PERFORMANCE PROJECT TEAM**

**CHAPTER 14 — CLEAR COMMUNICATION AMONG PROJECT STAKEHOLDERS**

## PART 5
## ADVANCING YOUR PRACTICE OF
## PROJECT MANAGEMENT

The following downloadable forms mentioned in the book are available online from www.VersatileCompany .com/FFMBAinPM. Original purchasers of this book can then open, edit, and print any of the documents using Microsoft Word or other word processing software.

Checklist for Successful Projects
Project Proposal
Stakeholder Analysis
Project Charter
Statement of Work
Small Project Statement of Work
Responsibility Matrix
Definition Checklist
Risk Analysis Template
Risk Log
Home Landscape Action Plan
Planning Checklist
Kickoff Checklist
Communication Plan
Task Assignment
Meeting Agenda
Status Report
Control Checklist
Closure Report
Change Log
Change Request
Issues Log

# ACKNOWLEDGMENTS

Project management remains a dynamic field, moving forward through the accumulated effort of many thousands of professionals who face new, interesting challenges and then generously share their lessons learned during conferences, at trade shows, through associations and over coffee with friends.

I have the privilege to both travel with the project management movement and to record the journey. To all of the project teams and project leaders who continue to innovate and move the state of the art forward, I wish to thank you for your example and the freedom with which you share what you learn.

There are, of course, particular friends and colleagues that made a direct contribution to this fifth edition, and to whom I owe particular recognition.

Don Kingsberry and The Bill & Melinda Gates Foundation, who do so much for improving lives around the world, will now be contributing to excellence in project management. Thank you for sharing the details of your Enterprise Project Management Office.

Robert Cooper is a world-renowned expert on new product development. For this edition he offered his insights on the most current practices for launching successful new products. Working with Dr. Cooper is a delight and an education.

Tim Creasey enthusiastically accepted my invitation to contribute his expertise on change management, the practices that motivate employees to change their behavior in support of project goals. Tim and his company, Prosci, are building a body of research in this field and are tireless advocates of the value of change management on projects. I appreciate his willingness to become involved in this book and to accept my editorial direction.

Mandy Dietz epitomizes the synthesis required to effectively lead projects. She long ago mastered the science of project management, and she is expert at integrating additional concepts from process management and leadership. I rely on her facilitation skills to delight our customers and appreciate her contribution to this edition with insights on stakeholder management.

Donna McEwen has a gift for translating her substantial leadership experience into practical advice in a manner that is constantly engaging. She has been a valued member of our team for well over a decade. Donna ensured the new content on Scrum and product development stayed relevant to project managers.

Both Sam Huffman and Tony Johnson examined and updated the chapters they had developed for previous editions, on Microsoft Project and PMP Exam Preparation, respectively. I appreciate the friendship and support of these two experts.

At the risk of missing other friends who spent time discussing this edition, I wish to recognize several who made valuable suggestions: Ernie Baker, Ralph Kliem, Robin Nicklas, Dale Christenson, Jeff Lynch, Jon Wagner, and Barry Otterholt.

Richard Narramore, my editor at John Wiley & Sons, excels at the role of catalyst, expanding my vision for this edition and providing the critical voice of the customer. Seventeen years ago, an editor at Wiley took a risk on an unpublished author. I am very grateful for the opportunity that Wiley provides and the partnership that continues.

My wife, Marlene Kissler, again played the critical role of sounding board and editor. This book is readable because she reads it first.

## ERIC VERZUH

Eric Verzuh is president of The Versatile Company, a project management training and consulting firm based in Seattle, Washington.

His company trains thousands of professionals every year in the fundamentals of successful project management, including how to get the most out of Microsoft Project. Versatile's consulting practice focuses on helping firms establish consistent, practical methods for managing their projects and implementing Microsoft's enterprise project management solution. The company's client list includes large corporations as well as government agencies, small companies, and nonprofit organizations.

Verzuh has been certified as a Project Management Professional (PMP) by the Project Management Institute, and he is a founding board member of PM4NGOs, a nonprofit organization committed to promoting project management in developing countries. His other publications include articles, conference papers, and *The Portable MBA in Project Management* (2003), also published by John Wiley & Sons, Inc.

Verzuh can be reached via his company's website at www.Versatile Company.com or you can e-mail Eric directly at EVerzuh@Versatile Company.com.

Economic upheavals have sharpened the need to effectively manage transformation and innovation. Project management remains critical but is no longer sufficient; project portfolio management is now widely embraced as a strategy for aligning resources with strategic direction and iterative development methods are spreading to new industries.

This fifth edition retains the book's primary focus on excellence in project management and continues to include the enterprise project management factors that influence project success.

Parts 1 through 4 have been refreshed to stay current, including a greater emphasis on stakeholder management and the introduction of change management. Industry is increasingly concerned with measuring projects by the value they contribute to the firm. This emphasis can be seen in many chapters, particularly Chapter 4, which describes the core questions related to authorizing a project.

The most substantial updates to this edition address iterative development and the reality that innovation continues to play a larger role for nearly all firms. Chapters 3 and 10 are completely new.

More than ever, organizations are in need of leaders who can synthesize facts and assumptions to set a direction. Many government, for-profit, and nonprofit organizations have less predictability about their future than at any time in the past 50 years. Project management continues to be a discipline for navigating through turbulent circumstances.

The basics of project management can be learned quickly from this book. True understanding comes only through practice. I wish you good luck as you learn and practice the art and science of project leadership.

—Eric Verzuh
Seattle, Washington

# Introduction

As the pace of change increases in every aspect of our societies, from government to health care to business, the ability to manage projects continues to grow in importance.

Why has project management become a strategic capability for organizations and a popular career track for individuals? In Part 1 of this book, you will find answers to these questions and more.

Every project has a start and finish, and every project is unique. That makes managing projects different from managing ongoing operations. The tools and techniques presented in this book have evolved over 60 years to deal with these challenges. Chapters 1 and 2 introduce the value of mastering project management and give an overview of the discipline.

Innovation is accomplished through projects. But it takes more than project management to create breakthrough products and services. Chapter 3 shows the connection that project management has to other important disciplines.

We live in a world where change—and the rate of change—is constantly increasing. In order to survive and prosper, organizations need to continually modify their products and services. Projects are the means by which these innovations are delivered.

Greater change = more innovations = more projects.

## CHAPTER 1

# Project Management: A Platform for Innovation

## INTRODUCTION

Projects dominate our headlines.

Reform—in health care, in education, on Wall Street—is accomplished through projects.

Electric cars are a reality. Biodiesel, solar, wave, and wind energy are supplying an increasing proportion of energy. And the gadget factory is in high gear. Devices you'd never have dreamed of five years ago are already out of style. The constant drive to innovate makes the ability to deliver new products a core asset of technology companies.

Projects dominate our workplace.

Our project-based workforce creates advertising campaigns, repairs freeways, remodels homes, writes articles, revises compensation plans, and connects the world with cellular communication networks. We grow our organizations as we open new stores, merge with rivals, and expand or consolidate distribution networks. We are constantly transforming our global civilization in tiny increments.

Projects help us react, survive, and thrive. A global economy on the rise or in recession creates constant change, and the pace is increasing. The changes are disruptive for some: those whose companies and industries have become irrelevant faster than they could imagine. For others, it is an endless opportunity. For everyone, it is a challenge to navigate and prosper in an environment in which we are forced to learn, to adapt, and to contribute our own changes.

In the past it was possible to leave the management and mastery of projects to innovation leaders like Boeing, Apple Computer, Ford, or Disney. But the new pace of change affects every organization, and those that don't adapt don't survive. Project management is a must-have capability for every organization and a personal job skill that will only become more valuable in the years ahead.

## Projects Drive Innovation

Project management is not new. The pyramids and aqueducts of antiquity certainly required the coordination and planning skills of a project manager. While supervising the building of St. Peter's Basilica in Rome, Michelangelo experienced all the torments of a modern-day project manager: incomplete specifications, insufficient labor, unsure funding, and a powerful customer. Michelangelo was the exception in his day. Now, 500 years later, our global economy is powered by innovation. Although not every project aspires to be innovative, every innovation is the result of one or more projects.

To connect project management and innovation, we must first understand projects. Projects are all the work we do *one time*. Whether it's designing an aircraft, building a bakery display case, or creating a business logo, every project produces an outcome and every project has a beginning and an end. Fundamental to understanding the importance of projects is realizing that each one produces something unique. Designing and tooling up to build a new sports car is a project (actually a lot of projects), but manufacturing thousands of sports cars is not. Manufacturing and other repetitive processes are defined as ongoing operations.

Project management techniques cover a range of topics:

- Communicating with team members and stakeholders from project conception through completion.
- Estimating the effort, cost, and time it will take to deliver a project, and evaluating whether the benefits of the project will justify the forecasted costs.
- Rapidly building cohesive project teams that are highly productive even though team members have not worked together before.
- Coordinating the actions of a diverse workforce, assembled specifically for a project, to achieve the goal for the least possible expense and in a reasonable time frame.
- Accounting for progress and productivity to provide accurate forecasts of project completion dates and budget amounts.

- Managing the varying staffing needs that result from continually running multiple projects concurrently, all of which share a common pool of personnel.

With that understanding of project management, it is easier to make the connection between projects and innovation. For our purposes, innovation is a fresh, new approach to solving a problem that is important to people. Apply that definition to education, transportation, or telecommunication, and you'll find many projects driving innovation. Clayton Christensen[1] classically identified two kinds of innovation: disruptive and sustaining. Disruptive innovation will destroy a current paradigm or market, in the way that online universities could change traditional on-campus college educations. Sustaining innovations make our current products and services better and more valuable to our customers.

The world is experiencing a fundamental shift from rewarding excellence in ongoing operations to rewarding the ability to chart an effective path of change and deliver on the goals. The discipline of project management provides the methods and techniques to meet the challenge.

## KEY CONCEPT    PROJECT MANAGEMENT IS KEEPING PACE WITH GLOBAL CHANGE

Project management is a discipline—a set of methods, theories, and techniques that have evolved to manage the complexities of work that is unique and temporary. Even as the discipline continues to evolve, it can claim a proven track record. Millions of projects around the globe routinely rely on the concepts found in this and other project management books. The Project Management Institute (PMI), headquartered in the United States; the International Project Management Association (IPMA), serving Europe, Asia, and Africa; and other standards organizations have formalized this discipline over the past 60 years.

The proliferation of projects has led to substantial growth in the number of people who call themselves project managers, and project manager is now a common role in nearly every kind of organization. The related phenomenon is the rise of the certified project manager. PMI and IPMA both offer professional certification programs to formally recognize skills, knowledge, or both.

Examples of how project management is spreading to new parts of our global workplace can be found in the profiles at the end of this chapter on two organizations, OrthoSpot and PM4NGOs. The first is a business start-up, and the second is a nonprofit that is promoting the use of project management in developing countries by aid agencies. In both cases, these organizations have used the proven project management framework as a starting point, and then adjusted it to meet the needs of their unique audience.

## PROJECT MANAGEMENT IS AN ESSENTIAL LEADERSHIP SKILLSET

Given the importance of thriving in a project-driven world, the people who lead projects—who turn visions of what might be into tangible products and services—stand out. But it has been proven that project managers alone can't carry the burden of creating mature organizations whose project management capability produces a strategic advantage. In fact, as the pace of change continues to increase, leaders at every level must be able to speak the language of project management.

- *Executives* select projects. They also stand behind projects as champions or sponsors, overseeing project progress and providing advice to the project manager and team. Every major project or program has an executive who is ultimately accountable for its success. Executives are also accountable for the project portfolio, the collection of all active projects that have been selected as the best way to achieve the organization's goals.
- *Functional managers* sponsor, lead, or oversee projects within their departments. They make decisions about project priorities as they assign their staff to project teams.
- *Team members* who understand project management make the entire project run more smoothly. They make the project manager more effective because they make better estimates, identify risks, and participate in planning and problem solving.

How does project management fit into your personal career goals? In an economy that is pushing each of us to learn and adapt, how much change do you expect in your job over the next decade? If the new normal is continuous transformation, isn't the ability to navigate new territory the most enduring skill?

## SUCCESSFUL PROJECTS DELIVER VALUE

Twenty years ago, the project management community could agree that a successful project was on time, on budget, and delivered to specification. But times change. Too many projects have "delivered to specification" without actually being valuable to the organization that paid for them. The most common offenders have been expensive information technology (IT) projects that produced reports or systems that didn't make a positive difference to the business, either because the system was rejected by the users or it didn't solve the real problem driving the project. But IT isn't alone. Any project team that focuses only on delivering the specified product or service, but loses sight of the context of the project can be guilty of failing to deliver value.

A more current definition of a successful project is one that delivers business value. The implication is that the project manager should understand the business case—why was this project approved? It has also broadened the perception of who is a project stakeholder. After all, if a solution to my part of the organization causes pain to your part of the organization, have we made things better or worse?

Another aspect of delivering value is the realization that if our solutions are not really accepted and used, they probably aren't achieving their potential impact. Therefore, the practice of change management has a growing role on project teams. Change management, as the term is used here, refers to assisting affected people to change their behaviors in support of the project goal. This should not be confused with change control, which addresses controlling changes to scope, schedule, budget, and other previous agreements.

When project managers see their job as *leading change that delivers business value*, they see the bigger picture and increase their contribution to their employer and to all stakeholders.

## THE ART AND SCIENCE OF PROJECT LEADERSHIP

Project management has been called both an art and a science. In these pages, you will see how mastering the science of project management provides a foundation for the art of leadership. The necessary skills are common to both. There is no question that the best project managers are also outstanding leaders. They have vision, they motivate, they bring people together, and, most of all, they accomplish great things.

Indeed, when we characterize the attributes of the great project managers, their skill can seem mysterious and magical, as though the good ones are born and not made. Fortunately, that is not the case. Through over 25 years of listening to many thousands of professionals and observing the most successful project leaders, it has become very clear to me that project management is a skill that can be taught and learned. Far from magical or mysterious, I've learned that certain characteristics are consistently found on successful projects in every industry. Boiled down, they consist of these five project success factors that drive the design of this book.

1. *Agreement among the project team, customers, and management on the goals of the project.* The importance of having clear goals seems so obvious that it's almost embarrassing to bring it up. Yet thousands of projects, at this very moment, do not have clear goals, and the results of this fuzziness can be devastating.

2. *A plan that shows an overall path and clear responsibilities and that can be used to measure progress during the project.* Since every project is unique, the only way to understand and execute it efficiently is with a plan. Not only does a good plan show who is responsible for what and when, but it also demonstrates what is possible. It contains the details for estimating the people, money, equipment, and materials necessary to get the job done. And because the plan is the basis for measuring progress, it can also act as an early warning system for tasks that are late or over budget.

3. *Constant, effective communication among everyone involved in the project.* People—not plans or software—complete projects. A successful project is a result of people agreeing on goals and then meeting them. From concept through implementation, success depends on the ability to come to agreement, coordinate action, recognize and solve problems, and react to changes.

4. *A controlled scope.* Success is in the eye of the beholder. This is why, from the very start, the successful project manager will ensure that everyone involved understands exactly what can be accomplished within a given time frame and budget. This is called managing stakeholder expectations, and it is an important, ongoing task throughout the project, especially if changes are introduced. Stakeholders must not only agree to the original scope of the project, but also understand any changes in scope.

5. *Management support.* Project managers rarely have enough formal authority to make all the decisions it takes to complete a project. They rely on people in traditional management roles to supply people and equipment, make policy decisions, and remove organizational obstacles. Even the most enthusiastic, creative, motivational project leaders will stumble if they do not enlist the people with authority to act on their behalf.

Far from being mysterious, these five essential factors can be achieved through the diligent, persistent use of the science of project management. That is not to say that success comes without art—on the contrary, art is immensely important. Art encompasses political and interpersonal skills, making creative decisions when complete information is lacking, knowing intuitively when to delegate work, and more. But learning the basic science is requisite to practicing this art.

That's important for all of us, because it means that success at leading projects is not reserved for the lucky few born with the skills; rather, it is a discipline that can be taught and learned.

### Processes Are Not Leadership

**DANGER!**

Project management can be viewed as a science composed of techniques and methods, and even software. It can also be viewed as the ability to inspire a team to achievement, to make tough choices, and to act with integrity when mistakes are made. In fact, project management can be all of these things. To grow, we must recognize the difference between knowing the science and practicing the art.

The art of project leadership embodies skills that are gained through experience, sensitivity, and a thorough knowledge of the basic science of management. Learning the basics of project management can be your first step on the road to becoming a skilled and inspiring leader. While developing all these skills will take time, the basic science can be learned fairly quickly; able students can read and practice the lessons in this book on their very next project.

### A PRACTICAL CHECKLIST FOR SUCCESSFUL PROJECTS: HOW THIS BOOK WILL HELP YOU

**KEY CONCEPT**

This book is written for people who need to understand the time-tested techniques of project management and how those methods are being put to use on projects every day. It is for people who need a complete foundation in the discipline, whether they are recent graduates, experienced executives, midlevel managers, or team members wanting to be team leaders. This book is primarily about *how*: how to get agreement on goals and how to reach them, how to enlist team members and project sponsors, how to negotiate schedules and budgets, and how to reduce risk and increase the odds of success.

The five project success factors introduced earlier in this chapter drive the content in this book. As the workplace has become more project-driven, other factors that influence projects also needed to be addressed. The following checklist expands on the five factors and shows you where to look in this book for practical advice.

1. Agreement among the project team, customers, and management on the goals of the project.

- It is apparent why this project is worthwhile. The benefits that will be realized from the project have been balanced against the costs, both tangible and intangible, and we understand the urgency. *Chapter 4 addresses the minimum content of a project proposal.*

- We know who needs to be satisfied and who will judge the success of the project. *Chapter 5 explains who our stakeholders are and how to find them.*

- What will be delivered, and the actions required to complete the project have been described at both the macro and micro level. *Chapter 6 explains how the statement of work establishes agreements on a common goal. Chapter 8 introduces the work breakdown structure, the detailed view of tasks and deliverables.*

2. A plan that shows an overall path and clear responsibilities and that can be used to measure progress during the project.

    - We have planned for the unexpected and for factors beyond our control. *Chapter 7 demonstrates how risk management techniques reveal potential threats and opportunities, allowing the team to proactively influence or prepare for these future events.*

    - The schedule is constructed using a detailed understanding of the work to be performed and the sequence relationships between the tasks. *Chapters 8 and 9 use a step-by-step approach to breaking down a project and building a realistic schedule.*

    - The schedule is based on work reasonably assigned and the people responsible for the work have not been over-burdened. *Chapter 9 provides task estimating guidelines and an explanation of resource levelling, the process of evaluating a schedule to find unrealistic assignments of work in any time period. Look for tips on communicating clear task assignments in Chapter 14.*

    - Progress against the plan is measured with a steady rhythm. *Chapter 16 contains formulas for calculating the progress against cost and schedule baselines. Chapter 10 provides an overview of the Scrum method of planning and monitoring a project.*

3. Constant, effective communication among everyone involved in the project.

    - We know who will be actively engaged in the project to accomplish the work and make decisions. *Chapter 5 gives us stakeholder identification techniques, and Chapter 6 describes the RACI matrix that clarifies project roles.*

    - Our project team has the trust and commitment to tell each other the truth and to work together to solve problems. *The attributes of cohesive project teams are described in Chapter 13.*

- We are prepared to assist those who will be affected by the changes that the project creates so that they contribute to achieving the project's goals. *Chapter 14 introduces the discipline of change management.*

- Our project infrastructure contains risk logs, issue logs, visible schedules, and other practical methods that team members can easily access and update. *Chapter 14 focuses on team communication and Chapter 22 introduces tips for leveraging Microsoft's Project and SharePoint tools.*

- We have established a rhythm of project reporting that is appropriate to the size and pace of the project and will keep our team and management synchronized. *Chapters 14 and 16 present a communication plan and guidelines for reporting status graphically. Every technique in this book promotes more effective communication among project stakeholders!*

4. A controlled scope.

- A practical approach to documenting and managing requirements has been adopted, so we deliver on the real business need. *Chapter 19 introduces the discipline of requirements engineering, explaining the different kinds of requirements and how each helps us move toward the goal.*

- We know who must approve changes to schedule and cost, and what authority the team has for accepting changes to specifications and scope. The people who will approve changes have agreed to the process, so that change requests will be processed in a timely manner. *Chapter 15 describes the steps for maintaining the proper balance between what is delivered, how much it costs, and when it arrives.*

- Cost and schedule estimates and commitments were created using reliable models developed from similar past projects. *Read about techniques for making accurate estimates in Chapter 11. Chapter 18 presents the role of a Project Management Office in creating repeatable project management practices.*

- We have realistic expectations about the potential for deviating from the plan when our assumptions turn out to be wrong. *Chapter 12 is full of strategies for catching up, cutting costs, and shifting the balance between cost, schedule, and quality. Chapter 17 contains classic project problems and reasonable responses.*

5. Management support.

- The project sponsor is accountable for project success and has planned to meet with the project manager on a regular basis to provide support and guidance. *Learn about the role and responsibility of a project sponsor in Chapter 5.*

- The people with the right skills and availability have been assigned to the project. *The planning process in Chapter 9, particularly task estimating, reveals the necessary skills. Functional managers are responsible for assigning people to the project, which is discussed in Chapter 5.*

- Our sponsor and management team has met with the customer and other key stakeholders. All are committed to regular communication. *Chapter 14 covers the project communication plan and team kickoff.*

- Escalation thresholds are in place to raise issues and risks up to the proper level of management. We know our allowance for cost and schedule variance before higher level management will intervene. *Chapter 16 shows how cost and schedule variance boundaries create escalation thresholds.*

6. Strategic alignment drives prioritization.

- This project is prioritized and sequenced relative to other projects in the firm, and therefore has been assigned resources that are sufficiently available to complete the project. *Chapter 18 and 20 address multi-project management factors, including portfolio management.*

7. Technical competence and mature development practices.

- Our team has up-to-date skills. *The techniques in Chapters 8, 9, and 11 on planning and estimating reveal the skills that are required to perform the work.*

- We use industry best practices to clarify our customers' goals and to design, build, test, and deliver great products and services. *Read about traditional and iterative development lifecycles and the benefits of a consistent development approach in Chapter 3.*

This checklist is available as a downloadable form at www .VersatileCompany.com/FFMBAinPM.

## BEYOND THE BOOK: TOOLS FOR APPLICATION AND CONTINUOUS LEARNING

In addition to practical advice applying proven techniques, this book has several additional features that make it easier to apply this advice:

- Access to webinars describing new developments in project management or expanding on topics within the book.
- Downloadable forms of common project management deliverables.

- Tips for using Microsoft Project, the most popular project management software application.
- Practice questions and advice for passing the Project Management Institute's Project Management Professional exam.

### Webinars to Explore New Topics or Learn in a New Way

Books are one medium for learning. Live, interactive webinars with the author and his team provide another medium to stay up-to-date on new trends or explore a new twist on topics within the book. Be notified of free webinars by registering for updates at www .VersatileCompany.com/FFMBAinPM.

### Downloadable Forms for Putting the Discipline to Work

The distance from concept to application can be shortened for all of us by using standard forms and templates. This book contains more than 20 checklists, forms, and templates for managing your own projects. We've titled these forms the *Fast Foundation in Project Management*, because together they form a basic project management methodology. Download these forms from www .VersatileCompany.com/FFMBAinPM. Look for them at the ends of Chapters 4, 5, 6, 7, 9, 11, 14, and 15. Since these forms were first included in the second edition of this book, many firms have used them, adjusted them to fit their own projects, and adopted them as their own standards.

### Microsoft Project Best Practice Tips

There are many effective project management software tools in the market, but by far the most common is Microsoft Project. This book has three resources to help you gain the most from Project: Chapter 22 contains recommended practices for getting the most value from Project with the least effort when planning and managing projects. In addition, purchasers of this book are entitled to download tutorials for the basic use of Project from www.VersatileCompany.com/ FFMBAinPM. The third resource is live webinars conducted by leading experts on Project.

### PMP Exam Preparation Guidelines and Test Questions

Many project managers benefit from earning PMI's Project Management Professional certification. One requirement for earning this certification is passing a lengthy exam. As an aid in exam preparation, sample exam questions are provided at the ends of Chapters 2 through 9, 11 through 16, and 18. These exam questions, along with Chapter 21, which contains general advice on preparing for the exam, have been contributed by Tony Johnson, author of a leading PMP exam preparation course series.

## END POINT

Every increment of change in our rapidly transforming economies and societies is brought about by a project. As projects dominate the way we work, it is critical to understand project management.

Projects are defined as work that happens one time only and has both a clear beginning and end. This kind of work may be contrasted with the ongoing operations of an organization that involve repetitive work—such as manufacturing or retail—with no defined end.

As our workplace becomes increasingly project-driven, organizations are investing in the ability to select and manage projects. Managers at every level play a role in creating successful projects. Project managers, in particular, must understand and practice the proven discipline of project management.

Innovation is created through projects, by project leaders that understand the real benefit the project brings to stakeholders. These leaders know their job is more than delivering to specification, they must be conscious of the original business goals that justified authorization of the project.

The purpose of this book is to help you gain these skills. Learn them and you will have every chance of steering a project from its planning stages through to its successful conclusion. For, while employing art and creativity are also important, the tools put forth in this book—the science of project management—provide the foundation for the success of any project.

## *Stellar Performer: OrthoSpot*
## Entrepreneurs Leverage
## Project Management

Entrepreneurs are the ultimate project managers. They start with an idea and create a company. The founders of OrthoSpot knew they were playing against the odds when they set up their company, which offers an Internet-based inventory management solution to orthopedic surgeons. But they made it. Within a few years they had hundreds of orthopedic practices across 44 states relying on OrthoSpot's distribution network to supply over 60,000 products.

CEO Bill Schafer attributes the company's survival and continued growth to using fundamental project management techniques from the start. "We didn't have any idea how to start a business—how to get funding or bring our product to market." So the prelaunch months were spent in planning, building a detailed picture of the work ahead of them.

They started with a fundamental question: "What do we have to do to make money?" They built an answer from the top down. "We needed a product, business infrastructure, and sales and marketing distribution structure. Our first three major tasks became: get a business model, raise money, and set up an office." Shari Cohen, vice president of customer relations, had offered her home's basement as the original offices. "The wall's were covered with sticky notes and string, showing all the tasks and what had to be done before what."

Venture capital is two-edged sword for a start-up, providing the means for growth but also giving away the future fruits of the founders' innovation. So OrthoSpot used venture capital sparingly, limiting the number of employees who could be brought on board. Schafer relied on the detailed plan to accomplish a lot with a small team. "The early-stage mentality of overcoming obstacles by intensity can lead you astray if you don't have focus and keep your eye on the objective and allocate resources appropriately."

Schafer also relied on the plan when making strategic decisions. He found that the new thinking OrthoSpot was bringing to orthopedic practices attracted other opportunities. "When you're changing the way business is done and you're making headway, a lot of opportunities present themselves—for example, do this for cardiologists. But we don't have enough people and hours to do it all, so a focus on the plan keeps energy directed. The payoff is that the team stayed incredibly energized. When they are focused they can do incredible things."

The early focus on executing against a plan has seeped into every operation at the firm. New product development efforts and system implementations for customers are driven from detailed work breakdown structures (WBSs). "It's in our DNA—project planning and accountability," says Schafer. As a result, he believes OrthoSpot is positioned to be incredibly competitive. "We compete and win against companies that have a hundred times our capital."

Orthopedic practices across the United States rely on OrthoSpot to bring efficiency and lower costs, enabling them to offer better value to their patients. OrthoSpot relies on fundamental project planning and execution to serve its growing customer base and enable the OrthoSpot founders to enjoy the fruits of their vision and hard work.

*Source:* Interview with Bill Schafer.

# *Stellar Performer: PM4NGOs*
# Extending the Practice of Project Management to Accomplish Social Change

"Let's not try to solve world hunger" is an oft-used warning about scope creep. Don't tell World Vision, Oxfam, Inter-America Development Bank, CARE, Catholic Relief Services, and the hundreds of other nongovernmental organizations (NGOs) working around the globe in developing countries to improve living conditions. Their efforts promote education and increase access to basic health care, clean drinking water, cheap solar energy, and other essentials that citizens of the developed world take for granted.

For those of us in the project management profession, it is easy to see this work as a never-ending series of projects. Key people in the NGO community have come to the same conclusion. Their passion for project management and development has created PM4NGOs.

PM4NGOs was launched in 2010. This nonprofit's stated mission is to maximize the impact of project investments for donors and beneficiaries. To do that, PM4NGOs pursues two primary strategies:

1. Promote and enable professional project management practices to be contextualized for the development and humanitarian environments.

2. Develop and maintain standards for project management in development and humanitarian agencies.

To meet these goals, PM4NGOs has created a certification based on a description of project management that bridges the gap between the realities of development projects and the existing standards such as PRINCE2 and the Project Management Institute. The certification is called Project Management for Development Professionals, but is usually referred to as PMD Pro. The accompanying standards document is called *A Guide to the PMD Pro*.

How do another standard and another certification make a difference? Mike Culligan is one of PM4NGOs founding board members and a principal author of the standard. He explains the genesis of PM4NGOs: "After 20 years of working on projects in the development sector I was introduced to the project management standards that were commonplace in industry. That was a revelation. But it wasn't easy to apply them. I found that they simply didn't connect with the way development workers were running their projects." Other seasoned development project managers felt the same way. Culligan and his PM4NGOs colleagues want to promote proven best practices, but know that to be accepted these practices must be contextualized, described in a way that makes sense to development projects. Culligan, along with all other PM4NGOs board members, is a volunteer. His full-time job is providing learning opportunities to 59 major NGOs around the world. "*The Guide to PMD Pro* creates a global standard that development workers will recognize. It can be adopted by international NGOs or small, local NGOs." The standard can also be promoted by independent training and consulting firms, just like the PMI and PRINCE2 certification.

PM4NGOs puts a special emphasis on serving its unique audience. One board member explained it this way, "A very important role of PM4NGOs is to make certain that access to the new certification is broad and the price affordable. We work in an environment where professional credentials are very important but not often available. We want to make sure the PMD Pro reaches all project managers that are interested."

The members of PM4NGOs have donated their time and money to write the standard, to develop the certification exam, and to have both translated into multiple languages. They also strive to make the certification accessible by keeping the cost of the exams to a minimum, as low as $20 per applicant in some cases.

By early 2015 PM4NGOs had certified over 9,000 people. The *Guide to the PMD Pro* has been translated into Spanish, Portuguese, French, Arabic, and Dari, with plans for Italian, Russian, and Mandarin later in the year.

Projects undertaken to achieve social change need proven project management practices, such as planning, risk management, and scope control. They also need optimism, persistence, passion, and imagination. The founders of PM4NGOs have a grand vision and the hard-won experience to make it a reality. To learn more, visit their website: www.pm4ngos.com.

# CHAPTER

# Foundation Principles of Project Management

## INTRODUCTION

Understanding project management begins with understanding the project environment. This environment is different from that of a traditional organizational environment. This chapter looks at the ways in which managing projects differs from managing ongoing operations and shows how the discipline of project management has evolved to address the challenges that are unique to projects. In addition, this chapter establishes the terminology used throughout the book, describes the project management process, and investigates the organizational challenges posed by projects.

## PROJECTS REQUIRE PROJECT MANAGEMENT

Why do we need a different discipline for managing projects? To answer this, we have to consider that the range of activities in any workplace can be broken down into two groups: projects and ongoing operations. To put it simply, *projects* are all the work that's done one time, and *ongoing operations* represent the work we perform over and over. By looking at each one separately, we'll see how they present different management challenges.

**17**

## How a Project Is Defined

All projects have two essential characteristics:

1. *Every project has a beginning and an end.* The date of the beginning may be somewhat fuzzy, as an idea evolves into a project. The end, however, must be clearly defined so that all project participants agree on what it means to be complete.

2. *Every project produces a unique product.* The outcome could be tangible, such as a building or a software product, or it could be intangible, such as new hiring guidelines. Part of the recent interest in project management stems from the realization that firms that deliver services have plenty of projects and can manage them with the same tools that have been used successfully in companies that produce tangible goods.

Projects abound in every industry. Here are a few examples, drawn from a variety of industries:

- Engineers redesign controls on an automobile dashboard.
- An advertising firm produces print and television ads to promote a new razor.
- Hospital administrators restructure responsibilities for nurses in their maternity ward.
- Manufacturing engineers document their processes to gain ISO certification.

Notice that each of these projects is plowing new ground, and each will be finished when it reaches the goal. Projects are unique and temporary.

Notice also that some of these projects produce tangible products, such as new ads or a redesigned dashboard, while others, such as the restructuring of responsibilities for nurses, are intangible. Project results may be tangible or intangible.

## Definition of Ongoing Operations

Ongoing operations have the opposite characteristics of projects in that they have no end and they produce similar, often identical, products. Ongoing operations are often the primary purpose of a firm or a department. Let's look at a few examples:

- An insurance company processes thousands of claims every day.
- A bank teller serves over 100 customers daily, providing a few dozen specific services.

- Power companies operate hydroelectric dams, controlling the water flowing through and the energy produced, day after day, for decades.

Ongoing operations produce similar products and have no defined end.

Traditional management theory has focused almost exclusively on ongoing operations like the ones in the preceding list. Experts in accounting practices, process improvement strategies, inventory management, staffing, and human relations have all viewed the organization as an ongoing set of activities. The focus on managing ongoing operations continues to be relevant in the twenty-first century, but now these experts must also master the techniques necessary to manage work that is temporary and unique.

## THE CHALLENGE OF MANAGING PROJECTS

Work that is unique and temporary requires different management disciplines. Because projects have different characteristics than ongoing operations, they pose a brand-new set of challenges. Here are some of the challenges that face project managers:

- *Personnel.* Every project has different personnel needs. The number of people needed and their different skill sets are different for each project. Where do these people come from? Where do they go, once they are no longer needed? These staffing problems may be compounded if several projects are running simultaneously. If all projects hit their resource peak at the same time, it could place an impossible burden on an organization. And if all the projects should end around the same time, the company may be forced into layoffs.

- *Estimating.* In order to evaluate potential projects, organizations need accurate estimates of costs and schedules. But because each project is different, estimates may contain more assumptions than facts.

- *Authority.* Organization charts define authority within a firm, but they usually represent the ongoing operations of the firm. When projects cross organizational boundaries, it is no longer clear who has authority for many decisions. This can lead to political maneuvering and a gridlock that blocks progress.

- *Controls.* Normal accounting practices match operational budgets to operational costs on a quarterly or an annual basis. But these time frames are not sufficient to keep a project on track. By the time quarterly accounting reports show a project to be over budget, it may be so far out of control that it's beyond recovery.

This list of difficulties and challenges could go on, but it should be clear by now that managing projects is not the same as managing ongoing operations. Notice that this does not mean project management is more difficult than managing ongoing operations—only that managing projects presents a different set of challenges.

The project management techniques within this book have evolved to meet these challenges. As you progress through this book, you can review this list of problems to see just how the tools and techniques you are learning address each one.

Clearly, projects and ongoing operations overlap and interact. Projects initiate or change ongoing operations. At times, projects exist within an ongoing operation, while at other times the reverse is true. Both may be funded out of the same budget process and use many of the same people. Both require a wide range of the same management skills: written and oral communication, conflict resolution, motivation, accounting, and negotiating, to name just a few.

But these similarities can obscure the real differences between projects and ongoing operations. Recognizing these differences leads to a better understanding of their different challenges. Projects, as we have seen in the preceding section, have unique problems that require different management disciplines. Project managers must learn these disciplines to become effective leaders.

## THE EVOLUTION OF A DISCIPLINE

> If one of you decides to build a tower, will he not
> first sit down and calculate the outlay to see if he
> has enough money to complete the project? He
> will do that for fear of laying the foundation and
> then not being able to complete the work.
> —Luke 14:28–29

From the time humans first worked together to build a shelter or cultivate a crop, there have been projects and project management. Yet it has been only since World War II that a formal project management discipline has emerged. During and immediately after the war, the U.S. government was engaged in enormous weapons development projects. The Manhattan Project, in which the first atomic bomb was designed and built, is generally recognized as the first project to use modern project management techniques.

Subsequent government initiatives to build nuclear-powered submarines and warships required so much innovation and invention and were so hugely expensive that they could not be governed by existing management techniques. The first modern project management methods were constructed to deal with these enormous projects. Their names—*program evaluation and review technique* (PERT) and *critical path method* (CPM)—are still well known today.

Understanding the development of project management as a discipline can lend insight into its role in the world today. Before World War II, project management was considered a subset of technical knowledge. For example, John Roebling, who conceived and led the building of the Brooklyn Bridge with his son, Washington, was a civil engineer who pioneered the building of suspension bridges with steel cables. But even though Roebling was known as a great civil engineer, his triumphs building this and other bridges were due at least as much to his management skills. Similarly, Michelangelo, the architect of Saint Peter's Basilica in Rome, also managed the project, which included tasks such as wrangling with the popes over finances. Even today, as project management gains recognition as an independent discipline, it is still common to view it as the rightful domain of the lead technician, whether this individual is an engineer, an accountant, or a physician.

The experience of the U.S. government with the aforementioned atomic and nuclear projects began to change this notion. Because there were so many facets to these giant projects, no one person could be responsible for all the technical decisions. Bottlenecks involving coordination and communication began to restrict progress. In addition, Congress demanded some accounting of the enormous amounts of money pouring into these programs. This crucible of change forged the first formal management procedures for planning and managing projects. Even though expert knowledge of nuclear physics or submarine warfare was still necessary, the managers of these projects were no longer required to be the leading experts in their field.

Since then, the U.S. government has been a leader in developing and promoting project management techniques, for the very good reason that these techniques continue to be necessary to manage its huge defense, space, and civil projects.

Despite its long history, project management has only enjoyed wide-spread recognition since the mid-1990s. At that time it became a central focus of improving information technology projects and was embraced by the telecommunications industry, which was convulsed by changes that included the explosion of cellular telephone technology. The focus on excellence in project management quickly evolved to include multi-project management, giving rise to the project management office (PMO).

Project management has rapidly evolved from an unacknowledged skill set into a recognized profession, complete with academic degrees and certifications. But one key question remains: Is project management a set of knowledge and techniques that can be understood and applied independent of a technical specialty? To what degree is technical knowledge required to effectively lead a project? Could John Roebling have designed the Brooklyn Bridge and then employed a project manager with no engineering skills to complete it?

## KEY CONCEPT — Project Management Is Industry-Independent—Project Managers Are Not

The popularity of project management in recent years owes much to its ability to transcend boundaries. The techniques put forth in this book can be applied to projects in any industry. From Silicon Valley to Broadway, projects of every size are becoming more efficient, and their products are improving in quality, thanks to the use of solid project management methods.

This industry independence has been a major factor in the development of project management as a discipline, but that independence doesn't extend to the people practicing the discipline. Project managers must not only know how to operate in business and project environments, they must also be well acquainted with the focus of the project. Specifically, project managers require skills in three different areas:

1. *Project management.* This is the pure discipline described in this book.

2. *Business management.* Negotiating, finance, customer recruitment, organizational development, communication, and motivation are skills that any good manager should have, whether managing projects or operations.

3. *Technical.* Nearly every company that has developed a career path for project managers begins the path with technical competence. Whether it's accounting, advertising, computer chips, or oil pipelines, the person leading the work needs to know it thoroughly. These same career paths, however, don't require candidates for project lead roles to be the best technicians in the group.

Project managers are more likely to be involved in technical decisions on small projects, but even on large programs, managers need to understand the work being performed. If they don't, they might be able to act as facilitator, catalyst, motivator, and cheerleader, but they won't be able to understand or participate in technical problem solving. "Good," you might be thinking. "I don't want to be involved in the detail work." But project managers who don't understand the technology they are managing can lose the confidence of their teams, particularly teams that are proud of their technical ability.

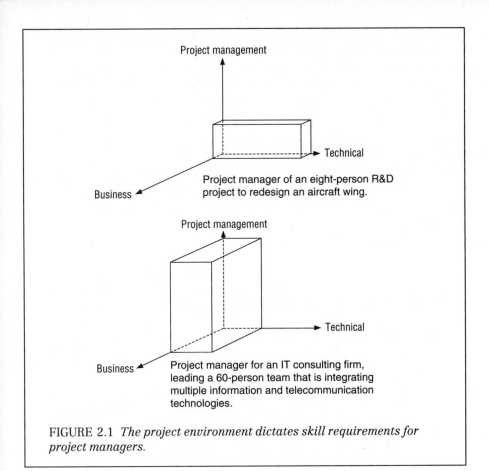

FIGURE 2.1 *The project environment dictates skill requirements for project managers.*

It makes sense that the best project managers bring a mix of skills to their job, and that the larger the project, the more project management skills are required. But even the leader of a one-person project needs to be able to organize work and communicate clearly with customers and management. (Figure 2.1 uses a three-axis graph to illustrate how the project environment dictates different skill requirements for project managers.)

Perhaps the best proof that management theory is portable comes from the companies that work with the discipline the most, that is, the project management consulting firms. These firms work effectively in all industries—not by having all the right answers, but by having all the right questions. Bring them in to kick off a project and they'll focus your team on the key issues, help you to perform risk assessments, and build project plans. Throughout this process, however, they will be acting as a catalyst and facilitator—not as a decision maker. The decisions will be made by the project manager with the help of his or her team, because they are the ones who possess the technical skills demanded by the specific project.

Project management is industry-independent—the theory works in all kinds of industries. But project managers are not industry-independent—they must have good technical skills in their field.

## THE DEFINITION OF SUCCESS

Each project is initiated in order to make an important change for the organization. Whether that change is actually valuable can be understood through the success criteria of time, budget, and quality.

*On time.* The product is delivered according to schedule. Some projects are essentially worthless if they aren't on time. For example, the information technology (IT) infrastructure required to operate the Olympic Games is no good if not ready until after the games are complete.

*On budget.* The project meets forecasted cost estimates. Projects are investments, and those that run over budget can end up costing the organization more than they bring in.

*High quality.* The outcome of the project must meet the customer's expectations for use. Quality is often difficult to define and is far more difficult to measure than *on time* or *on budget.* "Fitness for use" (Joseph Juran) and "conformance to requirements" (Philip Crosby) are two common definitions. For project managers, quality has two components:

1. *Product scope.* Scope is what the product is supposed to do. How many people will the airplane carry? How many operating rooms will be in the hospital wing? What features will the website have?

2. *Performance.* A measure of how well the functionality works. For example, compare the audio systems in a luxury sedan and an economy car. Both can connect wirelessly to your phone's music (a feature), but one probably sounds a lot better.

Product scope and performance can and should be specified early in the project. How they are specified will depend on what's being built. Process requirements for a hospital reengineering project, for instance, will be documented differently than requirements for a new model of a commercial aircraft. Chapter 19 provides advice on gaining agreement on requirements.

## The Cost-Schedule-Quality Equilibrium

Cost, schedule, and quality are the three primary variables of a project. Change one or more of these variables, and the ones remaining will also be changed. For example, if the amounts of time and money available for a project are reduced, this will almost certainly limit the quality of the product. Similarly, to deliver the same quality in a shorter period will cost more. This relationship also leads to the term *triple-constraint*. Your challenge, as a project manager, is to balance these variables to create the optimal cost-schedule-quality equilibrium.

## Meet Stakeholder Expectations of Value

Unfortunately, delivering a project on time, on budget, with high quality doesn't always mean you are successful. Why not? Because your definition of the cost-schedule-quality equilibrium may not have been the same as your customer's or manager's definition. Even if their expectations of cost and speed are unrealistic, nevertheless they are the final judges of your project, and in their eyes it may be late, over budget, or poor quality.

This may seem unfair, but it does happen. This kind of dis-agreement, however, is preventable. Recognizing that our project's success is defined by the perceptions of others is a powerful incentive to make sure that all parties involved in the project agree on how the cost-schedule-quality equilibrium relates to the original purpose of the project. This leads us to a new success formula for project managers:

1. Set realistic expectations about the cost-schedule-quality equilibrium with all the project's stakeholders and connect these constraints to the business case used to justify the project.

2. Manage expectations throughout the project. If the equilibrium changes, make sure everybody knows and accepts the new equilibrium.

3. If at any point it appears that delivering to the cost-schedule-quality target will fail to meet the original business objective, re-evaluate the target.

4. Deliver the promised product, on time and within budget.

## The Ultimate Challenge: No Damage

In an environment where the focus is delivering high quality on time and under budget, project managers can be tempted to meet impossible goals by sacrificing the people on the team. It happens in every industry, and always for the same reason: Meeting the project goals outweighs the needs of the individual team members. And this attitude isn't reserved just for the project team; vendors and even customers are often put through the wringer to satisfy the project goals. But asking people to give 120 percent, project after project, just doesn't work. They get worn out, demoralized, and just plain angry. The ultimate challenge for project managers is to meet the cost, schedule, and quality goals of the project without damage to the people. That means the project ends with high morale, great relationships with customers, and vendors that can't wait to work with you on the next project.

## PROJECT MANAGEMENT FUNCTIONS

Setting realistic expectations, fostering agreement among all parties, and then delivering the product is frequently challenging and always requires a wide array of techniques (see Figure 2.2). From a high level these techniques can be grouped into the three project management functions:

1. *Project definition* lays out the foundation for a project. There are two activities involved in this groundwork.

   - The project manager must determine the purpose, goals, and constraints of the project. He or she must answer questions like "Why are we doing this?" and "What does it mean to be successful?" The answers become the foundation for making all project decisions because they describe the cost-schedule-quality equilibrium and connect the project to the mission of the organization.

   - The manager must establish basic project management controls. He or she must get agreement on which people and organizations are involved in the project and what their roles will be. The manager also needs to clarify the chain of

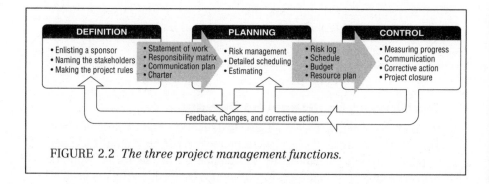

FIGURE 2.2 *The three project management functions.*

command, communication strategy, and change control process. The documented acceptance of these decisions and strategies communicates expectations about the way the project will be managed. It also becomes an agreement to which you can refer to keep everyone accountable to their responsibilities in the project.

The written document that comes out of this process of definition can be defined as the *project rules* because, like the rules to any game, they outline how to play and what it takes to win.

2. *Project planning* puts together the details of how to meet the project's goals, given the constraints. Common estimating and scheduling techniques will lay out just how much work the project entails, who will do the work, when it will be accomplished, and how much it will cost. Along the way, risk management activities will identify the areas of greatest uncertainty and create strategies to manage them. The detailed strategy laid out in the plan becomes a reality check for the cost-schedule-quality equilibrium developed during project definition.

3. *Project control* includes all the activities that keep the project moving toward the goal. These activities include:

- *Progress measurement.* Measuring progress frequently identifies any problems early, making them easier to solve. Progress measurement is also a feedback mechanism, validating the estimates in the plan and the cost-schedule-quality equilibrium.

- *Communication.* Communication is critical in controlling a project, because it keeps all the participants coordinated and aware of project progress and changes.

- *Corrective action.* This consists of the day-to-day responses to all the obstacles and problems a project may encounter.

These functions sum up the responsibilities of the project manager. The functions are sequential: A project must begin with definition, then proceed to planning, and finally to control. And the functions must be repeated time and again, because planning will inevitably lead to modifications in the definition, and controlling actions will require constant changes to the plan and, occasionally, changes to the definition. During an ongoing project, a manager may spend time every day defining, planning, and controlling the project.

Parts 2, 3, and 4 of this book correspond to these three functions of the project manager: project definition, project planning, and project control. Each part deals in detail with the techniques necessary to perform each of these functions.

## PROJECT LIFE CYCLE

A project life cycle represents the linear progression of a project, from defining the project through making a plan, executing the work, and closing out the project (see Figure 2.3). At first glance, it might seem that this life cycle is the same as the project management functions. Define, plan, and execute seem to map directly to definition, planning, and control. The difference is that the life cycle is linear and the phase boundaries represent decision points. Let's look more closely at these four decision points:

1. *Define.* The phase begins when a project and a project manager are named in a *project charter*, and it is completed when the project rules are approved. Approving this written document means that all interested parties agree on the project goals, approach, and cost-schedule-quality equilibrium.

2. *Plan.* After the rules are approved, the project manager begins building the project plan. Of course, as the details of how to execute the project are worked out, it's likely that some of the decisions in the project rules will change. At the end of the planning phase, all parties must approve not only the plan, but also any necessary changes to the project rules.

   Defining and planning can be short phases, particularly for short projects. Since planning often changes the project rules, it is possible there will be some iteration before definition and planning are complete. That tempts some companies to blend these activities into a single phase. The best argument for keeping the phases separate is that a number of questions need to be answered in the definition phase before a detailed plan can be produced. The basic assumptions and agreements worked out during definition make the planning activities more focused and productive.

3. *Execute.* We are now at the stage of performing the actual work as approved in the plan. This phase probably takes 90 percent or more of the project's effort. The execution phase is complete when the goal of the project is reached.

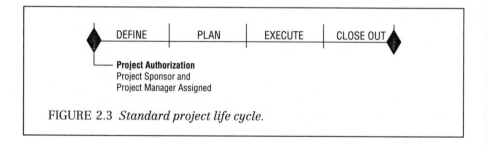

FIGURE 2.3 *Standard project life cycle.*

4. *Closeout.* This is the smallest phase of the project, but no less important than the others. Closeout activities perform three important functions: (1) making the transition to the next phase, whether that is operations or another product development phase; (2) establishing formal closure of the project in the eyes of the customer; and (3) reviewing project successes and failures with a view to improving future projects.

The importance of the first two phases in the project life cycle cannot be overemphasized. Even though these two phases—define and plan—usually represent 10 percent or less of the total effort, they are essential in preparing the team for efficient performance during the execution phase.

**KEY CONCEPT**

## A Product Development Life Cycle May Contain Many Projects

One of the reasons project management techniques are increasing in popularity is due to their role in new product development. Whether the effort is a new drug, a new software product, a new model car, or a new baseball stadium, it is done one time and produces a unique product. Since product development has the same characteristics as a project, creating these new products provides excellent opportunities for applying project management. The steps necessary to create a new product are known as the *product development life cycle*. Chapter 3 provides examples of how a product development life cycle will change depending upon what is being created. For purposes of discussion, this book will use a simple, four-phase process that highlights the most common activities in a development process:

1. *Requirements.* This step defines the function and performance requirements for the product. Whether you're building a house, an airplane, or an information system, requirements describe how the product will meet the needs of the customer.

2. *Design.* Design conceives a product that will meet the requirements and describes it in detail. For instance, a blueprint is a detailed description of a house.

3. *Construct.* Next, the product is built, and any documentation necessary for its operation is written. If a building is being constructed, this is where workers dig the holes and pound the nails. In the case of a new model of an aircraft, construction might encompass a wide range of activities, including the creation of new manufacturing processes. (In this case, the product isn't

| REQUIREMENTS | DESIGN | CONSTRUCT | OPERATE |

FIGURE 2.4 *Product development life cycle.*

exactly a new airplane, but rather a new process for building airplanes.)

4. *Operate.* After the product is developed, it has a life span in which it is actually used. Projects then turn into ongoing operations: A baseball stadium holds games, a manufacturing process turns out new automobiles, or a software product company supports its users. The operation phase can last for years and may contain many projects.

Chapter 3 elaborates on the role a consistent development process plays in creating useful products and services and the evolution of new development approaches that are suited to innovation.

Even though it is simplified, the product development life cycle model (as portrayed in Figure 2.4) can serve as a conceptual model to show the basic differences between product development life cycles and a project life cycle.

 **Product Life Cycle Versus Project Life Cycle**

CONCEPT    Although new product development, like a project, has a beginning and an end and produces a unique product, *it may consist of more than a single project* (see Figure 2.5). Anyone wishing to apply

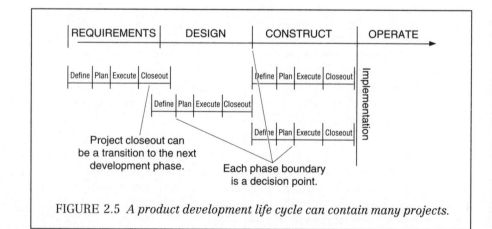

FIGURE 2.5 *A product development life cycle can contain many projects.*

project management to new product development must understand the differences between a product life cycle and a project life cycle:

- The product development life cycle describes the work required to create the product. The project life cycle focuses on managing the work.

- A product development life cycle may contain many projects, each of which must go through the full project life cycle.

*Understanding that any development effort can contain multiple projects and that each one needs to be managed as a complete project is one of the keys to success in project management.*

## ORGANIZING FOR PROJECTS

Certain firms perform nothing but project work; large construction companies fit this model. The majority of their organization is devoted to specific projects. On the other end of the spectrum, utilities are operations-oriented. The majority of companies, however, conduct ongoing operations *and* projects.

Creating an organizational structure that supports projects has never been easy. After all, if a project happens only one time, requires a unique mix of people, and has a unique reporting structure, how can any firm create an organization chart that will last beyond the end of the next project? While projects can play havoc with organization charts, over the years there have been some classic organizational responses to the project environment (see Figure 2.6). The following spectrum of organizational styles favors ongoing operations on the one end and projects on the other.

*Function-driven firms* are organized around primary functions such as advertising, engineering, information systems, manufacturing, and human resources (see Figure 2.7). Workers have one manager who

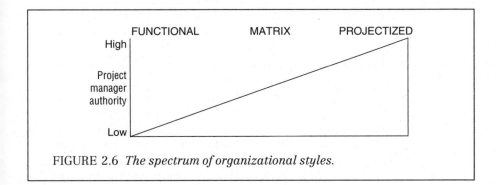

FIGURE 2.6 *The spectrum of organizational styles.*

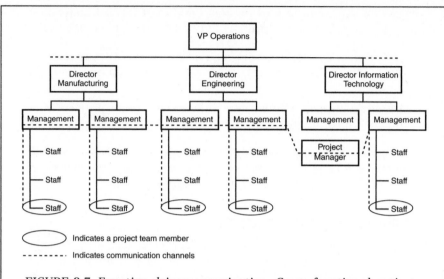

FIGURE 2.7 *Function-driven organization. Cross-functional projects are challenging to manage because the project manager has little authority and must win cooperation from functional managers in other departments.*

both assigns and monitors their work and handles administrative tasks, such as compensation. Projects *within* functional groups pose no organizational problems, but projects that *span* functional groups are arduous to manage because project managers have no functional authority and must work through the functional managers to assign, monitor, and coordinate work.

*Matrix organizations* are required when many projects span functional boundaries. This structure gives authority to both project managers and functional managers by having all of them report to the same executive (see Figure 2.8). Functional managers will be involved in deciding who will work on project teams and will maintain responsibility for long-term administration issues. Project managers assign, monitor, and coordinate work among members of the project team. The main problem with the matrix organization is that every person working on a project has two bosses—and if these people work on more than one project they will have even more.

*Project-oriented organization* is appropriate for firms that work on large, long-term projects. Rather than finding projects within and among functional departments, functional departments exist within the project (see Figure 2.9). Project-oriented firms (also called *projectized firms*) may have redundant operations among multiple

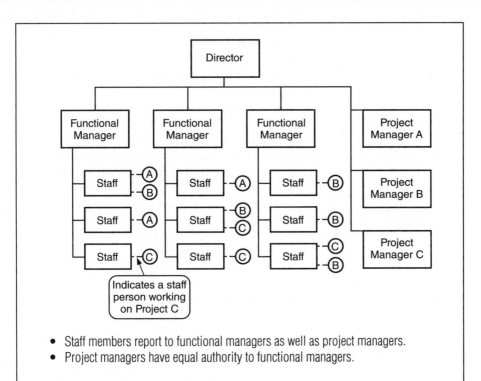

- Staff members report to functional managers as well as project managers.
- Project managers have equal authority to functional managers.

FIGURE 2.8 *Matrix organization.*

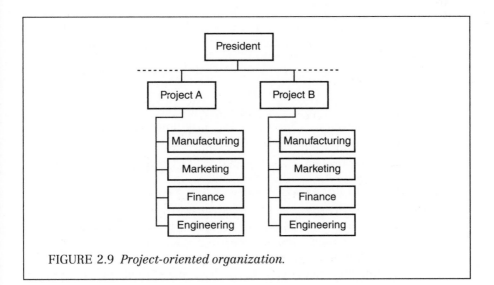

FIGURE 2.9 *Project-oriented organization.*

projects, but they're willing to put up with that organizational inefficiency in order to maximize management effectiveness on each project. For example, in the heavy construction industry, such firms set up an entire organization for managing every aspect of each of their enormous projects.

Another style of project-oriented organization is the *program*. Programs consist of many related projects, but unlike a single project, they have no specific completion date expected. For example, when Boeing develops a new model aircraft, the company establishes a program that is responsible for everything from selling the aircraft to developing customer service processes—a wide variety of separate but related projects. A variation of the program is a *product-oriented structure*, which uses the firm's products as the driving organizational factor. Product-oriented organizations replicate functional disciplines such as marketing and product development for each product organization. An example is a software company that has marketing, development, and testing personnel assigned to specific product groups, such as word processing and spreadsheet groups.

## Surviving Your Organizational Structure

CONCEPT    Understanding organizational styles is more than an academic exercise because choosing the right structure could provide a competitive advantage for a firm. But how does the structure affect you as a project manager? Consider the following five issues:

1. *Authority.* Clearly, the difference between the organizational styles is that some favor projects while others favor ongoing operations. In the function-driven organization, the project manager has almost no authority; in the project-oriented firm, the project manager has total authority (see Figure 2.6). Less authority requires more effort to make and implement decisions.

2. *Communication.* Communication is a primary project success factor no matter what the organizational style. Most organizational structures facilitate vertical (top-down and bottom-up) communication patterns, but your communication requirements may run counter to the prevailing patterns. Crossing organizational boundaries always takes more effort, but you must do whatever is necessary to keep all the stakeholders informed and coordinated.

3. *Priority.* Multiple projects often compete for limited quantities of people, equipment, and funding, especially in firms with the traditional, function-driven management style. Project managers in a function-driven structure often have their teams and

resources raided to handle a problem with ongoing operations or to work on a new project.

4. *Focus.* If a firm is project-oriented, you can be certain that projects are the center of its attention and the reason for its existence. Everyone has a unifying purpose that drives all decisions and helps to increase productivity. This compares favorably with matrix and function-driven organizations, where project team members are often working on projects less than half their time. In these companies, the diffused focus and increased span of responsibilities tend to lower emotional commitment and productivity.

5. *Chain of command.* If the chain of command for a project runs counter to the organizational structure, it takes more effort to bring a problem to the attention of the proper manager. As the project breaks through functional boundaries, more and more functional managers are required to approve decisions. And if certain functional groups have competing interests, clashes over authority can bring progress to a standstill.

Project-oriented firms make it easy to run projects because their entire structure is set up for that purpose. In most organizations, however, project managers may have difficulties in dealing with the authority structure. In these cases, they will have to rely more on the authority of their own expertise—and on the project management tools presented in this book.

## PROJECT MANAGERS ARE LEADERS

**KEY CONCEPT** The discipline of project management can be compared to a set of woodworking tools. Both are designed for specific purposes, and both are capable of amazing results in the hands of a master.

Every project needs someone who, regardless of his or her title, performs the functions of project management. It is a role that can be fulfilled in a few hours a week on small projects or spread among many people on very large projects. But this role cannot be defined purely in terms of the functions of project management or the project management tool set. It must also be understood that the primary responsibility of a project manager is to lead all the stakeholders—the customers, management, vendors, and project team—and encourage them to work together during the course of the project.

Bringing a project to a successful conclusion may require every technique in this book, but none of these techniques will be enough unless the manager wants to lead. The project manager is the catalyst—the initiator who lifts the entire project and puts it into motion. As you learn the techniques presented here, never forget that your energy and attitude are what give them power!

### END POINT

Projects differ from the ongoing operations of a firm in that they are temporary and unique. These qualities mean that factors like personnel management, lines of authority, budgeting, accounting controls, and communication need to be handled differently in the project environment. The project management techniques discussed in this book have evolved to meet these challenges.

Modern project management evolved from the giant defense projects during and after World War II. These endeavors were so enormous that normal management techniques proved inadequate. In addition to technical knowledge, managers of projects came to need business skills and the new skills related to managing temporary and unique projects. Project management techniques have now become industry-independent, even though each project manager must have skills specific to his or her industry.

Successful projects deliver a high-quality product on time and on budget. Project managers, however, need to be aware that everyone involved in a project—all the stakeholders—must agree on what success means. Managing expectations is one of the main jobs of a project manager. Success depends on the manager guiding the project through four stages in its life cycle: definition, planning, execution, and closeout.

One of the reasons for the present popularity of projects is the growing number of new products. Product development employs a process roughly similar to that of projects; the differences are that a *product development life cycle* describes the work required to create the product, while a *project life cycle* focuses on managing the work. This need for new projects has brought about the creation of companies organized around doing projects—project-oriented organizations.

# Stellar Performer: Seattle Children's Hospital and Regional Medical Center
## Hospitalwide Process Redesign

### VIRGINIA KLAMON

The growth in project management is powered by the speed of change in every sector of the American economy. The techniques traditionally applied to the manufacturing or aerospace industries are proving equally valuable in the services sector, particularly when applied to process redesign or improvement efforts.

Children's Hospital of Seattle, Washington, a regional leader in pediatric medical services, initiated a large-scale redesign of its patient management process due to mounting customer complaints and signs of deteriorating employee morale.

The hospital organized a team to undertake the effort of redesigning patient management systems and named the project "Encounters." The new system would streamline and standardize processes such as admitting, registration, scheduling, and insurance verification. The goal was to make things easier and more efficient at Children's, from the initial call from a family or doctor to the visit or stay, and following discharge.

### STAGE ONE: DIAGNOSTIC ASSESSMENT

From August to November the project team performed a diagnostic assessment as stage one of the effort. The team gathered customer feedback data, interviewed key organization stakeholders, created a process map of the current system, and identified external business needs driving current industry changes. The primary deliverable from this stage was the project charter. This document included a scope definition, process goals and objectives, project approach, resource requirements, cost-benefit assessment, and risk matrix. The project scope definition included the boundaries of the organizational change and the work required to accomplish it.

### STAGE TWO: PRELIMINARY DESIGN

The project team quickly moved to the second stage—preliminary design—once the project charter was drafted and approved.

Using creative thinking and proven process modeling tools, the team was ready to move forward to design a new patient management system. During this stage each new process link was painstakingly identified and documented. An iterative approach allowed successive design ideas to be layered in on top of the ever-developing process model. Patient scenarios were used to test the evolving design, allowing the team to walk through each step patients would encounter as they were admitted or treated.

Stakeholder involvement is critical to organizational redesign, particularly during the development of the preliminary design, the new conceptual process model. To promote involvement and stakeholder input, a display room was open 24 hours a day, seven days a week. From March through July, employees, patients, and physicians were invited to view the new preliminary design. Feedback was encouraged and received, creating repeated design adjustments throughout the phase.

### STAGE THREE: DETAILED DESIGN

From July through December the team drilled the new processes down to the lowest level of detail as part of the third stage, detailed design. The new designs were rigorously tested through hours of computer-based process simulation. Using simulation, the project team was able to model system performance, running what-if scenarios to determine how long patients would have to wait to check in for a clinic visit and what it would cost if they added additional staff during specified shifts.

It's important to realize that redesigning the process meant redesigning all aspects of the patient management system, including work flows, process performance measures, information systems, facilities and space, roles and job descriptions, and organizational culture. Computers don't simulate the social system components, so stakeholder involvement was designed into the process every step of the way. The communication plan consciously chose a variety of mediums to keep the information flowing, including a newsletter, all-hospital forums, and presentations to the hospital steering committee (HSC).

### STAGE FOUR: IMPLEMENTATION

Eighteen months after the re-engineering effort had launched, the team began to prepare for stage four of the project: implementation. Significant changes were required for the hospital computer systems. New software was selected to meet the requirements of the new system design. New services were planned for rollout. Detailed comparisons of the current process were made against the new design so that changes would be identified and documented. Sequencing of dependent activities was determined and tracked on a master project plan.

With implementation under way, the hospital has already begun to reap the benefits of its new Encounters patient management system. A more streamlined admissions process, including patient/family valet parking, is producing increased customer satisfaction. The segments of referral processing installed so far are already producing enhanced efficiencies during the patient check-in process.

### STAGE FIVE: CONTINUOUS IMPROVEMENT

Seattle Children's Hospital, like many organizations today, faced the formidable challenge of redefining the organizational culture. It endeavored to develop new norms for promoting continuous learning and continuous improvement. While continuous improvement is defined as the final stage of the redesign life cycle, it represents much more than the completion of the hospital's redesign project. It represents the cyclical nature of an improvement process.

Encounters is changing both the processes and the culture of Children's Hospital. The team attributes its successes to many factors, including some of the universal best practices of project management.

## Sponsorship

The Hospital Steering Committee (HSC), led by the hospital's chief operating officer (COO) and medical director, was visibly involved in the project. The members publicly supported the project by attending project functions, feedback sessions, and design review sessions and by representing Encounters to the greater hospital organization, including the board of trustees. The COO acted as the primary contact point and was the most visible member of the HSC to the project and the hospital staff.

## Early Stakeholder Identification and Involvement

During stage one, the team developed a comprehensive system map defining all process areas impacted and the extent of the interrelationships. Most areas of the hospital were impacted in some way. While the Hospital Steering Committee acted as the representative body for all stakeholders, other stakeholders were clearly recognized and represented, including patients and families, physicians, insurers, and employees.

## Communication Plan

A communication plan supported the project from start to finish, identifying the different stakeholder groups, their information needs, and the channels for reaching them. The channels ended up covering the spectrum: visibility rooms, all-hospital forums, project e-mail, intranet updates, a newsletter, and a 24-hour voice mail hotline open for project-related questions and comments.

## Team Building

The project team was carefully selected based on members' functional or technical knowledge and prior experience working on similar projects. Initially, just a handful of individuals were working together, but during the preliminary design and detailed design phases the team eventually grew to more than 50 to 60 and edged up close to 100 at times. Experiential team-building exercises and creative problem-solving training prepared them to think beyond the status quo and endure the challenges of organizational and cultural change.

## Risk Management

A consistent obstacle to organizational change is the fear and resistance people have to leaving old ways behind. Encounters consciously addressed this risk by bringing in resources to assist the team in defining behavioral and cultural change requirements that would support the new processes going forward. Workshop sessions had also been held prior to this effort, which provided information and practical tips for understanding the human side of change. These activities helped to make employees aware of the dynamics of dealing with change and to understand how people move through the change curve, thus helping them respond constructively.

## Detailed Planning

Each stage of Encounters was progressively more complex and forced the team into areas beyond its experience. To keep the project controlled and to support the team members who were learning while performing, the project plans were broken into great detail, often listing task assignments day by day. At times the amount of planning and oversight activity and project work grew so much that several outside project management specialists were temporarily brought onto the project.

### Scope Management

Organizational change projects are particularly susceptible to scope creep because they have so many dimensions and touch so many parts of the firm. To fight this tendency, all the process design deliverables were subject to rigorous change control, beginning with the project charter in stage one. All requests for changes were logged and addressed weekly by a project oversight team consisting of two process managers, the information systems director, members of the project team, and the project manager.

### SUMMARY

Health care is changing more rapidly than nearly any other industry. Seattle Children's Hospital and Regional Medical Center shows that dramatic change can take place and improve the service provided to its young patients. Its success is testimony to the potential for the industry, the commitment required from every level of the hospital's staff, and the need for a structured and disciplined approach to organizational change.

Virginia Klamon is a process engineering consultant.

## PMP Exam Prep Questions

1. Of the following, which is not an example of a project interacting with operations?

   a. Retooling a factory to increase production efficiency.

   b. Opening a new call center.

   c. Increasing rose bouquet production in anticipation of Mother's Day demand.

   d. Preparing the document center to utilize new imaging hardware and software.

2. The Inter-State bank has approved the project to replace its legacy system with a web-based interface and SQL database. It will use cross-functional work teams to accomplish the planning and testing. Which of the following is the most accurate description of a cross-functional work team?

   a. A team comprised of participants that have been trained to work in more than one department.

   b. A team comprised of participants that understand computer concepts and are experts in their fields.

   c. A team comprised of participants from all groups across the company.

   d. A team comprised of participants that are adept in the performance of multiple functions.

3. Of the following, which is the most comprehensive definition of a project?

   a. An environment created to deliver a product, service, or result.

   b. A collaborative enterprise that delivers a product, service, or result.

   c. An initiative that has a specific purpose, creates specific results, has a definite start and end date, and is temporary.

   d. An initiative that has a specific purpose, creates specific results, and is temporary in nature.

Answers to these questions can be found at www.VersatileCompany .com/FFMBAinPM.

**3**

# Build Great Products: Lessons from Agile, Lean Start-Up, and Stage-Gate

## INTRODUCTION

"I love my phone!" "This report is useless!" "It's so easy to pay my bills online." "What a hassle to take time off my job to go the clinic—the hours are so inconvenient." "The building is beautiful!"

These are stakeholders talking. To be specific, these are customers and end-users. Here's another stakeholder's point of view. "There will never be enough traffic to generate the revenue we need."

After all the effort that goes into a project, have we actually produced something that is desirable? Do the benefits of the outcome outweigh the cost of the development? Did we realize the expected value?

As we create products and services, hitting the value target is always a challenge. The project teams need to figure out exactly what should be built, and then build it correctly. That is true whether we are working on a residential remodel, bringing a new drug to market, or expanding online banking services. We call this journey from requirements discovery through construction and turnover a *product development life cycle* or *product development process*.

By creating a standard development life cycle, firms make product development repeatable, and thus set the foundation for improving quality and reducing cost.

Unlike project management, which is practiced essentially the same in every industry, the steps of your development process will be unique to your industry. And as the demand for innovation increases, there is also a demand for new and better product development processes.

This chapter will:

- Revisit the definition of project success, adding a new perspective on what it means for a project to deliver value.
- Demonstrate how companies can create a repeatable process that builds in the key activities that lead to products that resonate with customers.
- Establish the role of a consistent development process in improving quality, reducing risk, and improving estimates.
- Explore how agile software development, Lean Startup, and Stage-Gate address the challenges of building innovative products.

Product development processes are separate from and complementary to project management. Project managers that understand this relationship are better equipped to lead projects that deliver outcomes worthy of the investment of time and money.

 **DEFINING VALUE: A NEW LENS FOR JUDGING PROJECTS INFORMS THE DEVELOPMENT PROCESS**

The most traditional definition of a successful project is one that meets the budget, the schedule, and delivers the product to specification. However, if the specification isn't right or the business context changes during the project, it is possible that the result won't really be valuable to the stakeholders who paid for it or have to use the result. If a project manager takes responsibility for delivering business value, then it is worthwhile to view our projects through other perspectives.

### IDEO Framework: Viable, Feasible, and Desirable

IDEO is a design firm that has become famous for its contribution to innovation. IDEO consultants work with firms in every field to promote organizational cultures and practices that foster creativity and innovation. A signature concept is their triad of factors for evaluating potential solutions.[1]

- *Feasibility.* The solution is technically feasible.
- *Desirability.* There is a market for this solution. People want it.
- *Viability.* The solution can be delivered within a sustainable business model.

This framework is startlingly easy to understand and can be applied to any project—even those that don't claim to be innovative. The IDEO variables don't conflict with traditional cost-schedule-quality metrics, they just look at them from a different perspective.

These three variables are particularly useful for evaluating potential projects. In fact, a project proposal, as described in Chapter 4, should address each variable. We will reference these IDEO variables throughout this chapter.

## KEY CONCEPT — LEVERAGE A CONSISTENT PRODUCT DEVELOPMENT PROCESS

The project management toolset is full and varied, rich with techniques and processes. Yet this toolset still lacks the ability to guarantee that we are *building the right product* and *building it correctly.* That is the job of a *product development process*, also known as a methodology or as a framework for product development.

### What Is a Product Development Process?

A product development process describes the work to be performed at both a macro and micro level, laying out the overall flow as well as detailed activities. It is explicit in its techniques for determining the right product or service to build and the methods for ensuring it is developed correctly and efficiently. It also serves as the repository for institutional knowledge, because lessons learned from each project can be incorporated into the details of the process.

It should be no surprise that a development process is specific to the nature of the work and the product or service being created. Table 3.1 contains an example of the process for development and commercialization of a new pharmaceutical drug. Table 3.2 is an example of a prouduct development process for capital projects that could apply to any college or corporate campus.

Comparing these two linear processes, we see some similarities:

- At each new phase there is a progression from uncertainty to certainty.

---

### *TABLE 3.1* **Pharmaceutical Development Process**

---

*The following major phases are representative of a typical development process to bring a new drug to market.*

**Research and Preclinical**
Discovery of possible treatments and testing to ensure a potential drug is safe for humans.

**Phase I Clinical Trials**
The drug is tested in healthy volunteers to test for safety.

**Phase II Clinical Trials**
The drug is tested on a small population of people with the target disease to evaluate efficacy, safety, and side-effects.

**Phase III Clinical Trials**
A test population of 1000 or more patients is used to confirm the results of previous testing on safety, side-effects, and efficacy.

**New Drug Application**
The company applies to regulatory agencies in different countries for approval to release the drug to the market.

**Launch and Production**
The new drug is used. This phase often contains additional clinical testing as well as collecting data on the performance of the drug.

---

- Each step of the process is devoted to a particular aspect of development. In fact, the nature of the work within each phase can be substantially different and is typically devoted to solving a specific set of problems, isolating or removing some unknowns, making key decisions, and creating deliverables that may be used as inputs in later stages.

- A development process frequently includes phases and clear Go/No-Go decision points between phases. These decision points serve two purposes: to evaluate the quality of the work completed in the phase and to reevaluate the business case, or value equation, based on the new information that was added during the phase. Dr. Robert Cooper pioneered this concept under the name of Stage-Gate$^{TM}$ and introduces it in a Stellar Performer profile at the end of this chapter.

There are also clear differences between the drug development and capital construction life cycles, because a development process reflects the unique challenges associated with the product.

- The new pharmaceutical product shows the enormous cost of research and development, as well as the high cost of ensuring

### TABLE 3.2  Capital Project Development Process

*The following major phases are representative of a typical development process for new construction or major remodeling on a corporate or college campus.*

**Scoping**
Gather the goals for a potential building project from the people who will use the new space.

**Feasibility**
Explore multiple options for meeting the user goals, including financial feasibility. Select the best option.

**Programming**
Refine the user's goals and develop more details of the selected option, including design concepts, operational impact to other buildings, schedule, and budget.

**Schematic Design**
Overall design is established, including environmental impact, contract type, constructability review, and updated budget and schedule.

**Design Development**
Architectural drawings present a total view of the building including architectural, mechanical, electrical, structural, landscaping, etc.

**Construction Documents**
Produce a final set of specifications and drawings to obtain permits and enable a contractor to perform construction.

**Construction**
Construction of the facility according to specifications, schedule, and budget.

**Closeout**
Turnover of the project to the tenants and to the facilities team for management.

---

the product is safe and effective. The three stages of trials that are dictated by the U.S. Food and Drug Administration also demonstrate how a development process can be standardized within an industry.

- In the capital construction life cycle, actual construction is only one phase, even though that phase contains the majority of the expense. Capital construction invests heavily in design. The cost of revising a design during the design phase is minimal compared to the cost of rework once actual construction has begun. (For more on the cost of rework, read how fast-tracking a Major League Baseball stadium increased costs by 25 percent in the Safeco Field Stellar Performer at the end of Chapter 12). Notice, too, that this development process focuses on the *owner's perspective*. Architects and contractors each have their own phases and deliverables that focus on reducing their risk or improving their own performance.

## A Development Process Reduces Risk and Increases Repeatability

A defined development process results in repeatability and focuses on the right work being performed in a particular sequence. Every phase can have a completion checklist, which is a way to integrate lessons learned from past projects. Standard work guidelines and deliverable examples can be developed so that every project team does the work at least as well as the previous team.

In Chapter 8 we'll introduce the term "work breakdown structure (WBS)," which is the complete list of tasks for a project. It is common for a development process to contain a standard WBS for each phase of a project. This common list of tasks speeds up planning and ensures that all the bases are covered during every project, particularly those that address quality assurance.

A consistent development approach is the foundation of accurate estimating. Collecting actual cost and schedule performance information by phase and by task is easier and more meaningful when every project has the same phases and tasks. Actual performance data from past projects make it easier and more accurate to estimate future projects. (Read more about estimating in Chapter 9.)

## A Development Process Addresses Feasibility, Viability, and Desirability

The three IDEO solution evaluation criteria provide a new insight into a development process. The drug development process focuses on feasibility during the early research phase, because that is the greatest unknown. Many experiments take place to identify the chemical compounds that might eventually become a drug. Feasibility is really the number one question for a new drug, just as it is with other new product development efforts where invention and discovery are the critical components.

Contrast that to the capital projects development process, where technical feasibility isn't really in question. Most buildings on corporate and college campuses don't push the envelope on constructability. Instead, the capital project phases focus on balancing desirability—what the users want—with viability—what the organization can afford. Each phase progressively refines this balance. The multiple phases of design highlight how important it is to get the design correct when it's on paper and revisions are still inexpensive.

 **BEST PRACTICES FOR CAPTURING REQUIREMENTS ARE INTEGRATED INTO A PRODUCT DEVELOPMENT PROCESS**

Successful projects meet stakeholder expectations about desirability and viability. That's easy to say, but it is often difficult for stakeholders to clearly envision what they want, leading to requirements and specifications that produce useless outcomes. This difficult task is well served by standardized tasks and quality reviews.

The Capital Projects example in Table 3.2 is focused early and often on understanding how the tenants want to use the new facility. The right questions and standard methods for capturing user requirements are found in the early phases of the product development process. In every industry where products are built for specific clients, the methods for capturing requirements are a key element of the development process.

As the number of customers grow for a product, discerning requirements becomes a very big challenge. For example, how does an automobile manufacturer really know what will sell? Delivering an innovative design becomes extremely risky without a process to capture the "voice of the customer," also known as VoC.

Capturing and managing requirements is known as "requirements engineering," a topic that is introduced in Chapter 19. These activities prevent delivering products or services that don't meet the real needs of the people who use the outcome of the project. The better a project team performs requirements engineering, the more likely the result of the product will actually provide the value originally envisioned by the users and other stakeholders who initiated the project.

## A DEVELOPMENT PROCESS IS *NOT* PROJECT MANAGEMENT

There is a strong relationship between a development process and project management, but we must be clear that they are two different, complementary processes. The development process explains what the work is, and how to do it correctly. Project management emphasizes communication and coordination so the work is performed efficiently.

A single development life cycle can consist of one or more projects. This is particularly evident when viewing the new drug development process in Table 3.1. This process, which could require ten to fifteen years, can contain hundreds of discrete projects, each of which follows the project management life cycle of Define, Plan, Execute, Close that was introduced in Chapter 2. The same is true for managing the phases of the Capital Projects life cycle in Table 3.2. It is not uncommon in large development life cycles to manage every phase as at least one project.

For firms that have neither a standardized development process nor consistent project management, it may be easier to start with project management. That was the conclusion of the Software Engineering Institute (SEI) at Carnegie Mellon University over 25 years ago when it released its first Capability Maturity Model (CMM) for software projects.[2]

In that model, SEI advised software development shops to focus first on being able to plan and manage their work consistently. Once that capability was in place, the next step was building a development process. Although SEI has subsequently released updates to the CMM and additional models, they've retained this insistence that consistent project management is a foundation for building a development process.

## INNOVATION PROJECTS EXPERIMENT TO DISCOVER DESIRABILITY AND VIABILITY

Innovation, as introduced in Chapter 1, is forcing itself into strategies in every kind of organization. In this book innovation is considered a fresh, new way of solving a problem that many people want solved. In the past, innovation tended to be associated with inventions—making something feasible that was previously not technically possible. While invention continues to be a factor, many of the innovative products and services that are transforming the way we live and work in the early twenty-first century are really not about inventing technology. Instead, they are about uncovering problems to solve and bringing a fresh insight to solving the problem.

A simple example comes from Procter & Gamble, the makers of Tide laundry detergent. In an effort to rejuvenate the growth of Tide, P&G re-examined their target markets. In one case they realized that the vast majority of people in India wash clothes by hand, something poorly suited to detergent designed for a washing machine. In response, P&G produced Tide Naturals, a detergent that is easy on the skin, and the product quickly found a large Indian market.[3]

Innovation of this kind is rampant on the Internet. Companies offer a continually evolving range of services through websites and Internet-based technology. These companies do have excellent software developers, and these developers do create original products. However, of IDEO's three variables, feasibility seems to be the least of the barriers to releasing new products. Instead, these entrepreneurial companies focus on the art of finding an idea that is both appealing to the public and that has a profitable business model. In other words, an idea that is desirable and viable. To do this, they have abandoned the traditional linear development process, as illustrated by the life cycles in Tables 3.1 and 3.2. What has emerged over the past 20 years are incremental delivery life cycles that allow the project teams to *experiment* with both features and business models in order to find the perfect combination that delivers the greatest value to all stakeholders.

## Incremental Delivery Is Less Expensive Than Requirements Failure

What do we mean by incremental delivery? It means focusing on producing some small piece of the product as quickly as possible, so that customers and users can actually try it out and tell us what they think. Then, based on that feedback, the project team quickly delivers another piece of the product. This is also called iterative development, with each iteration delivering an additional, user-ready increment of the product. Eventually, the entire product is delivered.

Iterative, or incremental, development has been embraced by many software developers for several reasons. First, software products can be delivered in this incremental fashion. More importantly, too many software projects in the past delivered the specified product only to find out the system didn't actually meet the needs of the users.

The history of software and information technology projects is heavy with requirements failure. The linear life cycle that is embraced for constructing buildings fails for projects where it is too difficult to discern requirements. After years of working harder and harder at eliciting and documenting requirements and still producing systems that didn't provide value, many in the software community decided it would actually be less expensive to just let users experiment. This approach has become known as *agile* software development, and it is introduced in more detail at the end of this chapter in a Stellar Performer profile written by Alan Shalloway, the author of many books on the subject. Chapter 10 describes a particular technique called Scrum, which is used to manage teams using an incremental delivery process.

### Entrepreneurs Release Minimum Viable Products to Discover Requirements

Incremental development works very well for Internet-based products. An entrepreneur with a new business idea can construct a basic website for e-commerce in a matter of days. Rather than go through a lengthy business analysis process and attempt to launch a fully functioning product and business, the entrepreneur offers the simplest version of the product that actually works as an experiment to learn how customers really react. This simple product is sometimes called a *minimum viable product*. This is an experiment in both desirability and viability, because the entrepreneur learns both about the features that customers like and how much people are willing to pay for the product. This method of rapid experimentation has been labeled The Lean Startup by Eric Ries,[4] who authored a book by that name. Read more about the Lean Startup concept at the end of this chapter.

## When Is Incremental Delivery Most Appropriate?

Incremental delivery is appropriate when requirements are difficult to identify; when customers seem to say, "I can't tell you what I want exactly, but I'll know it when I see it." It is also a useful life cycle for innovation projects, where the goal is to introduce something that nobody is asking for, but might really want if they saw it.

For people familiar with software development, it is pretty easy to understand the concept of incremental product delivery. But try to imagine applying this to constructing a building or highway, and it seems impossibly inefficient and expensive. In other words, for some types of products and services it is prohibitively expensive to experiment using incremental delivery, so these products stick with the linear life cycles introduced in Tables 3.1 and 3.2.

There are also times when it is appropriate to combine linear and incremental development approaches. Dr. Robert Cooper pioneered a new product development process over thirty years ago. His Stage-Gate™ process has become an industry standard. It incorporates both experimentation to understand the voice of the customer and a linear process with strict gates to control product development decisions. Read Cooper's detailed introduction to Stage-Gate™ at the end of this chapter.

**END POINT**

Successful projects deliver to a goal that balances a timely delivery of a useful product within a budget that is affordable. The process for discerning the right product to build and then building it correctly is known as a product development process or development life cycle.

When a firm establishes a consistent development process they experience several benefits:

- They institutionalize the best practices for discerning product requirements and efficient methods of creating their products and services.

- Quality increases and costs decrease, because lessons learned from the past are integrated into their development activities.

- Estimating becomes more accurate, as actual performance costs from past projects is easier to correlate to future projects.

It is important to understand that the product development process is *not* project management. Instead, these are separate and complementary processes.

An effective product development process reflects the nature of the risks associated with delivering value. Traditional development methods have been linear, with the work of each phase built on the output of the previous phase. New development processes have been created to address the risks associated with innovation. Incremental delivery has been adopted by software developers under the name of agile, and entrepreneurs can also use incremental delivery to experiment with what users and customers really want, as described by the Lean Startup movement.

When firms understand the principles and benefits of different forms of development processes they are able to build a development process that is best suited to their own kinds of projects.

Agile, Lean Startup and Stage-Gate all contribute different insights to the challenges of creating a valuable product. Each is examined in greater detail in separate Stellar Performer profiles at the end of this chapter.

# Stellar Performer: The Lean Startup Innovation Movement

Project managers like clear goals and controlled scope. They can build detailed, rigorous plans to construct nearly anything when the requirements are firm. But that's not always the way innovation works. Innovation means doing something that hasn't been done before, where the pathway isn't exactly clear. When the challenge is to create a revolutionary product or service for a new market, project managers, sponsors, and project teams can learn from a new set of principles gaining traction among entrepreneurs, the principles of Lean Startup.

Entrepreneurs, according to Eric Ries, an early evangelist of the Lean Startup movement, face the daunting challenge of both discovering what the customer wants and delivering that within a business model that is sustainable. That's a challenge that faces an increasing number of organizations, not just the classic 'garage startup.' Ries defines the problem this way: "A startup is a human institution designed to create a new product or service under conditions of extreme uncertainty".[1] Using his work with governments, Fortune 100 firms, non-profits, and, yes, garage startups, Ries makes it clear that any kind of institution can find itself facing extreme uncertainty.

To be clear, not every entrepreneur faces the extreme uncertainty characterizing a startup. An established franchise restaurant owner moving into a new state has a proven product, business model, and supply chain. Their challenge is good planning and efficient execution.

Through his blog and 2011 book, *The Lean Startup*, Ries has established a vocabulary and principles that help anyone faced with extreme uncertainty to navigate through the ambiguity. Ries builds on the work of others who have studied the successes and failures of Silicon Valley, and now new authors are building upon the work of Ries, creating a network of books, blogs, conferences, and training and consulting firms, all offering advice on applying the techniques and guidelines known as Lean Startup.

## ROOTS IN AGILE SOFTWARE DEVELOPMENT AND LEAN MANUFACTURING

The extreme uncertainty described by Ries goes beyond discovering what the customer desires. It also includes uncertainty about whether that product can be created, the right kind of business model to fulfill the need, and the right organization to deliver it; essentially the entire business plan. Given so many questions, Lean Startup emphasizes learning quickly and a willingness to change direction over traditional planning and execution.

Lean Startup's preference for rapid learning comes from the agile software movement, where they've learned that giving users something real to look at is the best way to get accurate feedback on what the user really wants, and the sooner the better. (Read more about agile software development later in this chapter.) The *lean* in Lean Startup refers to the principles of Lean Manufacturing that emphasize reducing waste and focusing on activities that create value. Lean applies to startups because developing complicated products and marketing plans when facing extreme uncertainty is very high-risk and has the potential to waste a lot of time, effort, and money.

Blending principles from lean and agile, Ries articulates how a focus on rapid, incremental delivery produces faster learning, allows for frequent course corrections—what he calls pivots—and produces more meaningful metrics, all of which guide the startup to produce something of value as quickly as possible.

## USE MINIMUM VIABLE PRODUCTS TO ACCELERATE LEARNING

Innovation often springs from inspiration. Startups—whether at a government agency or a Silicon Valley incubator—envision a new way to solve a problem, perhaps a problem most people aren't even aware of. Remember that really new ideas aren't a response to stated needs. iPods and Facebook were created by people who saw a problem or opportunity that others weren't seeing. But inspiration of this type is based on a lot of assumptions, particularly assumptions about whether the potential customers will really embrace the solution. Lean Startup advocates experimenting to confirm your assumptions.

We can experiment with any part of the business plan, but some of the most popular examples experiment with customer desire and rely on a *minimum viable product*, or MVP. The MVP concept is also found in agile software development. An MVP represents a feature or set of features that we are trying out on real customers to capture the most authentic feedback possible. In *The Lean Startup*, Ries gives the example of Food on the Table, a successful company whose website technology helps families compose a shopping list every week based on their favorite recipes and the best prices available at the local grocers where these people shop.[2] You can imagine that this requires a pretty complex combination of systems and grocery store partners. Long before the technology was built, the concept was tested with a no-tech minimum viable product: the founder and VP of Products personally provided the service to the first customers, performing all the work themselves. The first customer and each additional customer provided feedback on the service, educating these entrepreneurs on what mattered to their target market.

The journey from these early, hand-built shopping lists to a company with a national audience wasn't built on a single MVP experiment, but on a chain of experiments that provided constant feedback and course correction.

## STARTUP METRICS MEASURE OUR ASSUMPTIONS

Measuring progress is critical to a startup, but the way the progress is measured must reflect the core assumptions driving the business plan. For example, an online gaming product wants the number of users to grow, so they'll closely measure how many new users they have each month, and they'll experiment with various ways to drive new users to the site. But the number of new users isn't the only important metric. They also want to know how long a new user engaged with the game and how many times the user came back to the site within 30 days. Each of these variables is important, so all of them are on the startup's dashboard.

Within the vernacular of Lean Startup, these are known as *actionable metrics*, because each of these metrics represents a variable that can be the basis of an experiment. As our experiments teach us how to drive these metrics higher, we know that we are making true progress toward our goal of a sustainable business.[3]

Contrast these startup measurements with the classic project progress measurements of schedule progress and actual versus planned cost. These traditional measures may be more familiar to our chief financial officer, but they don't offer a truly useful tool for assessing progress when the destination is beyond the horizon.

## PIVOT: EXPERIMENTS INFORM STRATEGY

Ash Maurya summarizes a key principle of Lean Startup in the subtitle of his book, *Running Lean: Iterate from Plan A to a Plan That Works*. Maurya's book is designed as a 'how to' manual for entrepreneurs who want to follow the Lean Startup process. His point: Plan A is built on a lot of assumptions, and every assumption is a risk. So pick your biggest risks and start to validate your assumptions through experiments. Every experiment is an iteration that will take you closer to a sustainable business if you are willing to change direction based upon the results of your experiment. He underlines this point by emphasizing to startup leaders that "your product is NOT 'the product.'"[4] Instead, your product is a sustainable business.

When experiments tell you that customers love your product but won't buy it, then the question becomes, "How do we package this in a new way that does make money?" In other words, we make a fundamental change in the business model—a pivot, in the language of Lean Startup. The pivot isn't just an adjustment in product features; it is a change in strategy. The necessity of pivoting to a new strategy reminds us of the enormity of the startup challenge and the tenacity required from startup leaders and teams.

A change in strategy can bring on a whole new set of assumptions and risks, so it is important to understand the difference between a pivot and a leap. A pivot builds on the learning from the past to inform a potential new path, which will be explored with new experiments—unlike a leap, which abandons the old, and starts afresh with new inspiration.

## PRODUCT/MARKET FIT PRECEDES SCALING

Experiments, MVPs, and pivots all work together to discover a *product/market fit*, the business model that matches the right product with a sufficiently attractive market. When this elusive combination is revealed, the next stage is to scale, or grow, the business. Scaling is less about discovery and more about implementation. We have eliminated much of our uncertainty, we know what works and what we want to multiply. In short, it is time to engage the traditional business management tools for setting goals, planning, and rigorous execution.

This isn't a time to forget about lean, iteration, or learning, because there are still plenty of opportunities for improvement. But it is important to understand that the key principles of Lean Startup are designed to move us through the extreme uncertainty phase so that we actually find something worth building up.

## THE LEAN STARTUP MINDSET

A fundamental attitude soon becomes apparent when reading the blogs and books that are blossoming around Lean Startup: accept that when faced with extreme uncertainty you have to abandon a traditional linear approach that requires huge upfront product development, large-scale launch, and massive roll-outs. Even a product development lifecycle with established stages and gates can be too restrictive. Every member of a Lean Startup organization, from top management to product development teams, needs to be comfortable with measuring progress by demonstrating learning, designing experiments to validate assumptions, and pivoting away from strategies that aren't working until you find the plan that does.

Perhaps the most important lessons for project managers are about risk and waste. Experimenting and pivoting from your original assumptions to a working business plan may not be quick, but it is the lowest risk, most cost-effective approach for navigating through the extreme uncertainty that can accompany our attempts to innovate.

The Lean Startup gives us a model for running projects that have set their sights on discovering new markets and new products. And remember Ash Maurya's advice: your *deliverable* is a sustainable business.

## SOURCES

1. Eric Ries, *The Lean Startup: How Today's Entrepreneurs Use Continuous Innovation to Create Radically Successful Businesses.* New York: Crown Business, 2011, page 27.

2. Ibid, page 99.

3. The How, http://how.com/lean-startup-101/

4. Ash Maurya, *Running Lean: Iterate from Plan ! to a Plan That Works.* Sebastopol, CA: O'Reilly Media, 2012, page 6.

# Stellar Performer: The Agile Approach to Software Development

Alan Shalloway

## INTRODUCTION

There is much buzz in the project management and software development communities about agile. It is a significant new development in the way software is designed, built, and delivered, and has implications for how software development projects are managed.

What is agile and what is really different about it? There is a lot of confusion about the answer. One source of the confusion is that a movement was created around the term *agile* but the movement is not governed by a single body and agile methods continue to evolve.

The agile movement developed in response to the many failures of the waterfall approach to software development and to poor, overbearing management. The major failings of the waterfall approach include:

- It takes a long time to deliver business value.

- Many of the features that are delivered either do not meet the need as originally understood or are not as important as originally thought.

- Feedback about features being implemented comes very late in the waterfall process. This can result in delivering a less than optimal mix of features.

- It is unclear how far the project actually is to completion.

- Code quality is often poor due to overbuilding frameworks that still do not cover what is needed.

The purpose of this article is to summarize the essence of agile thinking. It describes the essence of agile, its relation to delivering value, agile construction methods, agile management methods, the characteristics of an agile organization, and the misperceptions of agility. "Agile" is not an absolute. Instead of asking the question "Do you practice agile?" the better question is: "How agile are you?"

## THE ESSENCE OF AGILE

Agile answers the following questions:

- How do we deliver value quickly to our customers?

- How do we discover as early as possible what is needed?

- How do we accurately gauge the progress we're making in our project?

- How can we accelerate the learning of the development team?

- How can we ensure that the software written will be able to grow and be extended effectively when new requirements are introduced?

This section discusses each of these questions.

## Delivering Value Quickly

Imagine you have 10 months to complete a project with 100 features. How would you define the goal? In a typical project, the goal would be stated in terms of on-time, on-cost, on-scope completion of the 100 features. Another approach is to define the goal as *delivering the most value as quickly as possible*. This requires delivering the software in stages. For example, suppose that if the business got half of the features, it could start putting them to use, and that having that set of functionality would allow for greater market penetration by getting it out into the field earlier and forcing the competition to play a game of continual catch-up. Wouldn't it be worthwhile to deliver this set of 50 features earlier? This is the notion behind incremental delivery of value.

Of course, partial, incremental delivery is not always possible. It is not acceptable to deliver a flight control system that can only turn left with the promise that, in another five months, it will also turn right! But more often than not, delivering features in stages provides significant value. This is a judgment call based on both business and technical considerations. Having this conversation and exploring ways to deliver business value more quickly comprise a key element of agility.

Here are a few factors to consider:

*Extra costs.* More frequent releases do involve extra costs, either for developers or for customers. Are these costs mitigated by getting features early? Would it work to have early, partial releases?

*Release size.* What is the right size to release? What are the features that are required for a release? In *Software by Numbers: Low-Risk, High-Return Development,* Mark Denne and Jane Cleland-Huang introduce the notion of a minimal, marketable feature (MMF), or minimum business increment (MBI). An MBI is a feature that is as small as possible while still providing value and being worth the transaction cost of delivery. That is, an MBI is the smallest feature that is marketable from a value proposition point of view. Thinking in terms of MBIs is what makes incremental delivery possible. It does require the business to think in a new way: how to split up the overall functionality so as to deliver the greatest value over time.

*Enough.* Building core functionality and then expanding it offers the business the opportunity to ask, "Has enough value been delivered?" That is, now that some set of functionality has been released, are there more important things to do? Very often, the tail end of one project is not nearly as important as the front end of another. This is a very different way of thinking. The possibility for doing so can help the business continually prioritize based on greatest value and keep developers focused on what is most important.

## Discovering What Is Needed Early

Ask developers when their customers know what they want, and the reply you will get is: "After I've shown them what they *don't* want." So when should you show them what it is they don't want? As soon as possible!

Delivering business value quickly is the goal. Before you can deliver it, you have to discover what it is. The agile approach is to discover it as early as possible. Build a little bit of the system, show it to a customer who can give feedback about it, and then build the next piece. With this approach, it is often possible to build exactly what customers need without building features they really don't need.

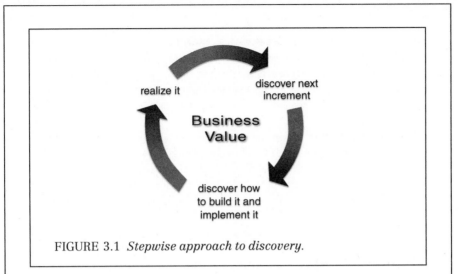

FIGURE 3.1 *Stepwise approach to discovery.*

This stepwise approach to discovery is shown in Figure 3.1. It is based on the notion that people learn best by doing. They discover what they need from a system by using it rather than trying to guess what they need. This works even if what you are showing them cannot yet be delivered for use in the field. Just seeing the product so they can learn how it works will create insight.

Reflect for a moment about how much customers actually know about the functions they are requesting. How much of what they request at the beginning of a project will still hold true at the end of the project? Once they see the results of their request, how likely are they to say, "That is exactly what I asked for," and how likely are they to say, "Now that I see this, I know what I really meant was something else"? The former is what they know that they know and the latter is more like anticipation and guessing. Experience and anecdotal evidence suggest that the "known" amount is about 20 to 30 percent of the initial request.

Customers have certainty about only some small portion of a system. It is likely that this is also what is most important to them. We should focus on developing the *known* part of the system first. This is what the stepwise approach to discovery does.

Focusing on the most important features and getting early feedback helps development teams zero in on the most important functions that are needed. It results in smaller and, therefore, less complex systems. It lowers maintenance costs and increases code quality.

### Accurate Project Status

Waterfall methods are notorious for leading one to believe projects are on schedule when, in fact, they are not. It is all too common to supposedly be on schedule at six months, only to be behind two months at seven! The truth is you were not on schedule at six months; you just didn't know yet that you were behind. Isn't this why so many projects follow the pattern: 40 percent done, 80 percent done, *canceled*?

The reason is that waterfall methods make a number of wrong assumptions: completing requirements on time implies completing design on time; timely completion of code implies timely completion of test; when software is completed, its quality is sufficient. This latter assumption is especially bad because the quality of each stage of work cannot be determined until later stages have been completed—sometimes as late as completion of the entire project. It means errors are hidden. And when they are discovered, it is hard to see where they came from. And trying to find errors causes significant delay. Detecting and fixing errors later in the game takes more effort than if they are detected early.

Agile methods track status in a different way. Working code is the measure. The project's status is directly related to the amount of code actually working. Having 20 percent of your code done and working means your project is 20 percent done. While it may not be perfect, this approach offers a much better indicator of true project status. And if you take steps to ensure that your project is not blindsided by architectural changes, this works reasonably well. Approaches to do this are mentioned later in this article.

The key to the agile approach is understanding what is meant by code that is "working." To be working, the team must be able to demonstrate the software feature to customers. The feature must have gone through a complete cycle of development, including meeting quality requirements. The feature is done when the customer accepts it. This is also how agile projects mitigate the biggest risk to software, that customers will reject software that has been created.

Compare the waterfall and agile approaches to working code.

Figure 3.2 shows a typical waterfall approach. As work progresses over time (left to right), work for a stage is finished before the next stage starts: analysis, then design, construction, test, deployment. Notice how no feature will be completed until the end of the project because true validation is deferred until then.

Figure 3.3 shows the agile approach. Again, progressing over time (left to right), features are built one at a time. All stages of work (analysis, design, construction, test, and possibly deployment) are done on a feature and then the team moves on to the next feature. Validation of the requirements is done much more quickly and frequently. This greatly reduces the risk of having made an error and failing to detect it until late in the project.

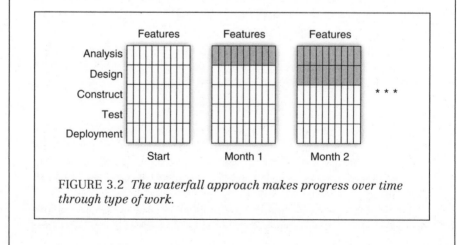

FIGURE 3.2 *The waterfall approach makes progress over time through type of work.*

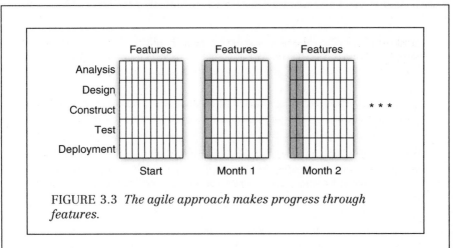

FIGURE 3.3 *The agile approach makes progress through features.*

### Learning Early

The agile approach emphasizes learning early. Building in stages causes problems to manifest themselves quickly. That is, by requiring teams to create potentially deliverable code every one to four weeks, problems are highlighted early—and teams are forced to solve them early—while there is still time to do something about them. Contrast this with the waterfall approach, which is a late learning method: Problems in one stage of work may not surface until much later in the cycle. A problem in design might not get noticed until late in the test stage.

### Agile Construction and Quality

There is a cost to this incremental delivery, of course. But the methods required for incremental delivery can also be turned to our advantage.

Agile methods take an approach called "emergent design." Emergent design demands high code quality that can be extended as needed. It is guided by a variety of technical skills, including design patterns, refactoring, and test-driven development.

- Design patterns focus on code quality and extensibility.

- Refactoring is a way of improving the quality of code without extending its functionality. Now, refactoring has been tarnished by developers who use it as an excuse to write poor quality code ("Just write it poorly now and we'll re-factor it later"). This should never be! Refactoring is both about extending the design of high-quality code and improving the quality of poor code.

- Test-driven development is a method by which tests are written first and then code is written to implement them. These tests are also automated, making refactoring code safe while ensuring that new changes to code do not break old code.

Emergent design is different from other approaches that focus on building full frameworks for the system and then filling them in. This does not work. It requires understanding the needs of the full system. And having to do full analysis defeats much of the power of the agile approach. Even if you could build a full framework, there is a trap waiting for you. If the framework meets the needs of release 1.0, what happens for release 2.0? Release 3.0? Release 10.0? No matter how well they are researched, frameworks that are built to handle a specific set of needs will eventually need to handle new requirements for which they were not designed. How much delay and wasted time did this involve?

In waterfall methods, testing the quality of the system is done at the end of construction. This means a lot of time is going to be spent finding and fixing errors, which is a poor approach to quality assurance. A better approach is to avoid errors in the first place. This is particularly important in avoiding the most common error in software: writing code that isn't particularly useful. By some estimates, this accounts for as much as 64 percent of the features that are built. This not only wastes effort but also causes the system to be much more complex than is needed. And that slows down the implementation of future requirements.

A relatively recent method that most agile methods embrace is acceptance test-driven development (ATDD). In ATDD, actual test specifications for requirements are created prior to design or construction. This is similar to creating test plans in the waterfall method; the difference is in scope and depth. By constructing software at the feature (functional) level, the team can write test cases for smaller pieces of the system. Furthermore, these are actual examples, not merely statements of the concept to test. A description of ATDD goes beyond the scope of this chapter; however, many good books on ATDD are available.

### Putting It All Together

When you put these all together—a focus on delivering value quickly, discovering early, focusing on working code, learning early, emergent design and quality—you have a software development approach that can deliver the most important business capabilities to customers as quickly as possible and in a way that is extensible for the future. Agile is an approach that delivers smaller, more important pieces through the software development pipeline, and that is always more efficient than trying to cram big pieces through. You are assured that the quality is what the customer requires and that the design can handle future needs.

### MISPERCEPTIONS ABOUT AGILITY

As you might expect, there are some misperceptions about agile methods. Some of these are:

- Agile teams do not document anything.
- With agile, you cannot predict when software will be done.
- Developers don't need to do any design; they just jump in and start coding.
- Agile and Scrum are the same thing.

  There are many others, but let's deal with these.

- *Agile teams do not document anything.* Agile does not say not to do documentation. It does say that much documentation is worthless. Winston Churchill once described a requirements document for a tank by saying, "This report, by its very length, defends itself against the risk of being read." Requirements documents that are so big as to not be understandable are a waste of effort. An additional tragedy is that when people are spending time writing such documentation, they are not available to do more valuable work. And that creates a ripple effect of blockage. Agile does say not to do *this* sort of documentation!

- *With agile, you cannot predict when software will be done.* This is mixed. Some agile approaches—especially team-based agile methods such as Scrum—do tend to have this challenge. Other methods, such as Lean-Kanban, tend not to.

- *Developers don't need to do any design; they just jump in and start coding.* Early in the agile movement, this was a widespread belief. However, this has pretty much been recanted. You don't do a large, up-front design, because that is typically more than you need. What is essential in agile is to design so as to ensure the ability of your code to grow and the proper architecture to emerge.

- *Agile and Scrum are the same thing.* Scrum is currently the most popular method in agile. However, it is not necessarily the best. Its popularity came about for a variety of reasons:

  - It is an easy place to start, although it can be difficult to spread throughout the organization.

  - Its certification program attracted many individuals who, upon becoming certified, went on to evangelize it throughout their organizations.

  - It is based on prescribed practices, which is an approach many people like.

  - There are currently many other methods prevalent in the agile community. Where to look for more information is given at the end of this article.

## TROUBLE IN PARADISE

Agile methods have been around for at least 15 years. While agile is growing in popularity, there are growing differences in the agile community. The main camps, so to speak, are Crystal, eXtreme Programming (XP), Kanban, Lean Software Development, and Scrum. XP and Scrum are somewhat limited to team projects, while Kanban and Lean can be useful in both team and organization-wide agile transitions.

It is beyond the scope of this article to go into these different approaches. Suffice it to say that, although all of these camps believe in incremental construction and delivery of software, there are as many differences as there are similarities. In the agile world, most popular does not necessarily imply best. It is anticipated that many readers will have serious doubts about the efficacy of some of these methods to their organizations. Be clear that only basic agile methods are described here, and more advanced methods are, in fact, available and have succeeded in organizations with tens of thousands of developers. The end of this article contains resources for interested readers to follow to pursue their education in and transition to agile methods.

## SUMMARY

Agile is an approach to software development with specific implications to project management. Agile is concerned with:

- Delivering value quickly.
- Discovering what is needed before building it.

- Doing work in stages so as to minimize the time between getting requirements and using them and between writing code and testing it.

- Avoiding creating additional work for the team.

- Having an accurate measure of where a project really is by using working (actually constructed and deployable) code as a basis of progress.

- Learning fast—both the good and the bad.

- Emerging designs and construction so less useful code is never built.

There are many agile methods out in the world today. If you are starting to explore agile methods, you should consider at least the four most popular methods: Scrum, eXtreme Programming (XP), Lean, and Kanban. They are not all equal.

### RESOURCES FOR FURTHER LEARNING

There are numerous resources for learning more about agile. Start with www.AgileAlliance.org and www.NetObjectives.com, which offers numerous webinars and articles.

Alan Shalloway is the CEO of Net Objectives and the author of several books, including *Lean-Agile Software Development, Design Patterns Explained,* and *Lean-Agile Pocket Guide for Scrum Teams.* He has been a leader in the agile movement for over a decade.

# Stellar Performer: The Stage-Gate System for New-Product Development

Robert G. Cooper

## INTRODUCTION

New products fail at an alarming rate. Only one new-product concept in seven is a commercial success, and an estimated 44 percent of developed products fail to achieve their sales targets. Many of the *critical success drivers* in product development have been uncovered by investigating large samples of successful new products versus unsuccessful ventures.[1] Observing what highly successful project leaders and teams do during their projects, together with a knowledge of the critical success drivers, ultimately led to the *creation of a model for successful development,* namely the original *Stage-Gate*® system.* Many leading firms then adopted the system. And significant improvements have been made over the years, so today's *Stage-Gate* is very different than models envisioned just a decade ago. This article outlines what a *Stage-Gate* system is and how it works; how the system builds in critical success drivers; and how the newer generation *Stage-Gate* is more agile, adaptive, and accelerated.

## THE STRUCTURE OF STAGE-GATE[2]

A *Stage-Gate* system is designed to drive new-product projects to market, quickly and effectively. *Stage-Gate* breaks the product innovation process into a predetermined set of stages, each stage consisting of a set of prescribed, cross-functional, and parallel activities (a typical 5-stage, 5-gate process for major projects is shown in Figure 3.4). Gates are the entrance to each stage, and serve as quality-control check-points and Go/Kill investment decision-points. This stage-and-gate format leads to the name "*Stage-Gate*" process.

**Stages are cross-functional.** There is no R&D or Marketing stage, and handoffs from one department to another are not permitted. Rather, *Stage-Gate* is an *integrated business process*, with each stage consisting of a set of parallel tasks undertaken by *people from different functional areas* within the firm, working together as a team and led by a project team leader.

**Stage-Gate manages risk.** Tasks in each stage are designed to gather the technical, market, financial, and operations information needed to validate assumptions and thereby reduce *both* the *technical* and *business risks* of the project. Each stage is more expensive (more resources required) than the previous one, and thus there is an incremental commitment to the new product: with more and better information at each stage, resource commitments increase.

## EACH STAGE HAS A FOCUSED PURPOSE

There is a *fairly standard* or *prescribed list of actions* for each stage, based on research into best practices and also insights into how winning project teams do so well. The flow of the typical *Stage-Gate* model is shown in Figure 3.4.

0. *Discovery*: pre-work designed to discover opportunities and to generate new-product ideas.

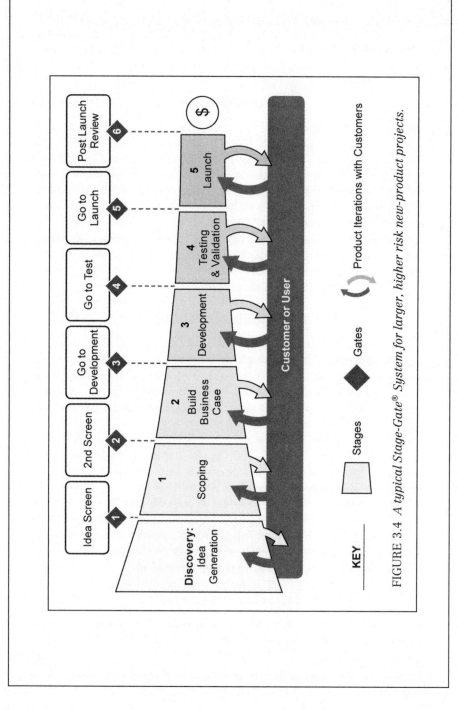

FIGURE 3.4  *A typical Stage-Gate® System for larger, higher risk new-product projects.*

1. *Scoping*: a quick, preliminary investigation, and scoping of the project. This stage provides inexpensive information — based largely on desk research — to enable the list of projects to be narrowed before Stage 2.

2. *Build the business case*: a much more detailed investigation involving primary research — both market and technical — leading to a *business case*. This is where the bulk of the vital homework is done, which results in a business case that includes the product definition, the project justification, and a project plan.

3. *Development*: the detailed design and development of the new product, along with some product testing work. The deliverable at the end of Stage 3 is an alpha-tested or lab-tested product. Full production and market launch plans are also developed in this potentially lengthy stage.

4. *Testing and validation*: tests or trials in the marketplace, lab, and plant to validate the proposed new product, and its marketing and production or operations. Tasks include field trials or beta tests; test market or trial sell; and operations trials.

5. *Launch*: commercialization — beginning of full operations or production, marketing, and selling. Here the market launch, operations, distribution, and post-launch plans are executed.

## GATES PRECEDE EACH STAGE

Effective gates are central to the success of a fast-paced, new-product process:

- Gates serve as quality-control check-points, ensuring that the project is executed properly.

- Gates also serve as Go/Kill and prioritization decisions points: mediocre projects are culled out at each successive gate.

- Finally, gates are where the action plan for the next stage is agreed upon, and the resources needed to execute the plan are committed.

Gate meetings are usually staffed by senior management from different functions — the gatekeepers — who own the resources required by the project team for the next stage.

Gates have a common format:

- *A set of required deliverables*: what the project team must bring to the gate decision point. These deliverables are visible, and based on a standard menu for each gate, and are decided at the output of the previous gate. Management's expectations for project teams are thus made very clear. Deliverables are both *hard* (such as a "field-tested prototype" or "set of CAD design drawings") and *soft* (such as a "full business case" or "launch plan").

- *Go/Kill Criteria*: the project is judged against these to make the Go/Kill and prioritization decisions.

- *Defined outputs*: for example, a decision (*Go, Kill, Hold, or Recycle*), an approved action plan for the next stage, the resources committed to execute the next stage, and the agreed-to deliverables for the next gate.

## THE SUCCESS DRIVERS BUILT IN

*Stage-Gate* was based on research into why some projects and project teams do so well. Here are some of the research-based best-practices that are built into *Stage-Gate*:[3]

### 1. Striving for Unique Superior Products

Delivering products with *unique benefits and a compelling value proposition* to customers and/or users distinguishes winners more often than any other single factor! Such superior and differentiated products have five times the success rate, over four times the market share, and four times the profitability than me too, copy-cat, reactive and ho-hum products. Achieving a unique superior product is the goal of every stage in the *Stage-Gate* process: numerous actions are built into stages that ensure customer input and feedback is available to the product designers and developers; and gate Go/Kill scorecards emphasize product superiority as a criterion for moving forward.

### 2. Market Driven and Building In the Voice of Customer (VoC)

A thorough understanding of customers' needs and wants, the competitive situation and the nature of the market is an essential component of new product success. This tenet is supported by virtually every study of new-product success factors. Thus a *market focus, VoC and constant interaction (iterations)* with customers are integral facets of Stage-Gate: New generation Stage-Gate systems have integrated iterative and spiral development methods into individual stages (the circular arrows across the bottom of Figure 3.5), from idea generation right through to launch. This means getting something in front of customers or users *early, cheaply and often* via a series of "build-test-feedback-and-revise" iterations.

### 3. Pre-Development Work — The Homework

Solid front-end homework is critical. Countless studies reveal that the steps that precede the actual design and development of the product make all the difference between winning and losing. The message is to *front-end load the project* — to undertake a higher proportion of the project's work in the early stages. Thus, *Stage-Gate* builds in two vital homework phases (Stages 1 and 2), with extensive actions required in Stage 2 in particular: VoC research, concept testing, market and competitive analyses, technical and source of supply assessments, financial and risk assessment, etc.

### 4. Sharp, Early and Stable Project and Product Definition

Two of the worst time-wasters in a new-product project are "project scope creep" and "unstable product specs". Securing *sharp, early, stable and fact-based product definition* during the homework phase is a solution. How well the project and product are defined prior to entering the development stage is a major success factor, impacting positively on both profitability and reduced time-to-market. Thus, crafting a fact-based product definition is a key action in Stage 2, Build Business Case in Figure 3.4; and this definition is confirmed throughout the rest of the project via spirals or iterations with customers.

### 5. Effective Cross-Functional Teams

Product innovation is very much a team effort! Do a post mortem on any bungled new product project and invariably you'll find: each functional area doing its own piece of the project, with very little communication between players and functions—a fiefdom mentality, and no real commitment of players to the project. Key best practices here, built into *Stage-Gate*, include: a clearly assigned team of players for each significant new-product project, complete with time commitments; cross-functional project teams, with team members from Technical, Sales, Marketing, Operations, etc.; a clearly identified team leader; the project team and leader remaining on the project from beginning to end of project; and project teams accountable for their project's end result.

### 6. The Resources in Place

Too many development projects simply suffer from a lack of time, people and money! The results are predictable: When people and resources are spread too thinly over too many projects and other tasks, short-cuts are taken, quality of execution suffers, some key tasks don't get done at all, and timelines stretch. The end-result is much longer times-to-market and lower success rates. A key feature of Stage-Gate is cross-functional teams, one team per project, and also gates: note that *gates are not just project approval points; gates are resource commitment decisions* made by senior people. A vital Stage-Gate improvement in recent years is that projects are *properly resourced* and important projects are fully staffed by a *dedicated* cross-functional team for maximum speed to market. This requires integrating *Stage-Gate* with *portfolio management* and resource management, ensuring that the number of projects in the pipeline is consistent with the resources available.

### 7. Sharper Focus, Better Prioritization

Most companies' new-product efforts suffer from a lack of focus: too many projects, and not enough resources... and often the wrong projects. The need is for a *new-product funnel*, rather than a *tunnel*. A "new-product funnel" builds in tough Go/Kill decision points throughout the process; mediocre projects are weeded out; scarce resources are redirected towards the truly deserving projects (the high value ones); and more focus is the result. Note that *Stage-Gate* is *built around a set of gates* or Go/Kill decision points. Gates pose two fundamental questions:

* Are you doing the project right?
* Are you doing the right project?

The gates in Stage-Gate are thus a critical component of overall portfolio management—making the right R&D investment decisions.

### GETTING THE RIGHT SYSTEM FOR YOUR BUSINESS

As with any good concept, there are issues. Most of the challenges have to do with getting the right system for your business and also problems regarding ineffective implementation.

For example, newer systems are flexible, with actions for each stage and deliverables to each gate being unique to each product, and *based on the project's context*: the nature of the market and the needs of the specific development project. Figure 3.5 shows three different versions of *Stage-Gate* for high risk, moderate risk, and low risk projects; there is also a version of *Stage-Gate* for technology platform projects. And newer systems also build in elements of Agile development, such as sprints and scrums within the Development and Testing stages.

The *Stage-Gate* system has been widely adopted, partly because the results achieved are positive. According to various independent studies, new-product success rates increase by 37 percent, projects hitting profit targets increase by 72 percent, and percentage of sales from new products more than triple with an effective gating system installed.

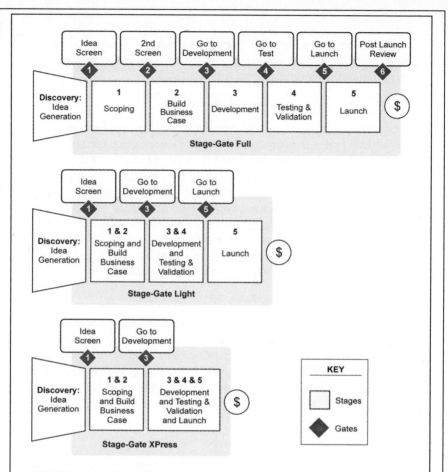

FIGURE 3.5 *Three different versions of Stage-Gate® for high risk, moderate risk, and low risk projects.*

If you already have *Stage-Gate*, but it's more than five years old, it's probably a little slow, cumbersome and dated, so time for a good overhaul.[4] Do consider getting help from firms that specialize in implementing *Stage-Gate*.

This introduction has scratched the surface of the Stage-Gate principles and guidelines that have been proven over decades of use. Every project manager who is responsible for new product development will benefit from further exploration of this topic.

Dr. Robert G. Cooper is President of Product Development Institute Inc., Professor Emeritus, McMaster University, Canada, and ISBM Distinguished Research Fellow, Penn State University. Cooper is a world expert in the field of new product management, having published eleven books and more than 120 articles on the topic. www.bobcooper.ca

*Stage-Gate® is a registered trademark in different countries of Robert G. Cooper, R.G. Cooper & Associates Consultants Inc., and Stage-Gate International Inc.

## SOURCES

1. For an outline of all 14 critical success drivers in new-product development, see: R.G. Cooper, "New Products—What Separates the Winners from the Losers and What Drives Success," in Kenneth B. Kahn (ed.), the *PDMA Handbook of New Product Development* (3rd ed.). Hoboken, NJ: John Wiley & Sons, 2013, Chapter 1.

2. Stage-Gate is described in R.G. Cooper, *Winning at New Products: Creating Value Through Innovation* (4th ed.). New York, NY: Basic Books, 2011.

3. See success drivers, note (1); and Chapters& 3 in note (2).

4. Key improvements (next generation *Stage-Gate*) are outlined in R.G. Cooper, "What's Next? After Stage-Gate," *Research-Technology Management*, 157(1), January-February 2014, pp 20–31 and also in R. G. Cooper, "The Next Stage for Stage-Gate," *Pragmatic Marketer*, Winter 2014, pp. 20–24. Also see note (2) in Chapter 5.

## PMP Exam Prep Questions

1. How do project management and quality management complement each other?

   a. Both focus on continuous improvement, management responsibility, customer satisfaction, and prevention over inspection.

   b. Both focus on prevention over inspection, continuous improvement, management responsibility, and product excellence.

   c. Both focus on management responsibility, fulfillment of requirements, continuous improvement, product excellence, and prevention over inspection.

   d. Both focus on fulfillment of requirements, management responsibility, prevention over inspection, continuous improvement, and customer satisfaction.

2. The project manager and the functional manager at the pharmaceutical company are having a discussion about the project to create a system to produce antibiotic and intravenous injection vials. The functional manager continually brings the discussion back to the costs of running the system and the length of time the system will be viable. Of the following, what best describes the functional manager's primary focus?

   a. Project management life cycle

   b. Product life cycle

   c. Program management life cycle

   d. Project life cycle

## PART 2

# Defining the Project

Why is this project important? What benefit does it promise, and to whom?

Who is responsible for what? Who has authority? What are our goals? How do we communicate? How will we judge success?

The questions are the same every time we undertake a new project. How they are answered will constitute the rules of the game, and all those involved in the project—the stakeholders—have to agree on these project rules.

The rules define the project, and this structure of rules then provides the foundation for the next two stages of the project: planning and control. Chapters 4, 5, and 6 show us how a project begins and the critical actions that bring the necessary stakeholder to agreement on the definition and direction of the project.

# Project Initiation: Turning a Problem or Opportunity into a Project

## INTRODUCTION

Of all the decisions made in the life of a project, which one will have the greatest impact?

The answer is the first decision, the decision to pursue the project. That decision puts all the wheels of execution into motion and leads to a chain of events that could potentially go on for years, depending on the nature of the project.

With that in mind, it would make sense that any and every decision to launch a project is preceded by careful analysis of the potential benefits, costs, resource requirements, strategic alignment, and many other factors associated with the project. The key deliverable of project initiation is a project proposal, which is variously referred to as a project justification, business case, or a similar term.

This chapter emphasizes the importance of the project initiation process: that launching a new project should rely on disciplined, thorough analysis, and that any project, no matter how valuable, must be considered in the context of the organization's other projects and strategies. We will place project initiation into the context of the entire project life cycle, examine the skills and techniques required during initiation, and recommend guidelines for turning a problem or an opportunity into a project proposal. This chapter also introduces a powerful technique, the *logical framework approach*, which has been proven on major projects around the world, yet has only recently found its way into corporate decision-making processes.

Project initiation is deeply connected to the topics in Chapter 20, "Project Portfolio Management," as well as other topics in this book. That connection will be reinforced throughout this chapter.

## KEY CONCEPT — PROJECT INITIATION'S PLACE IN THE PROJECT LIFE CYCLE

Even though the decision to pursue a project is enormously important, the steps and processes leading up to that decision are outside the traditional scope of project management.

The reason for this is apparent when we consider who really conducts the initiation work. Throughout this chapter we view project initiation from the perspective of the owner, or sponsoring organization, the entity that will fund the project and enjoy the benefits. The project owner may not be responsible for project execution, which is another reason that initiation is separated from project management. Two classic examples include a real estate development company that hires a general contractor to build an apartment building or a marketing department that relies on its information technology department to implement a customer relationship management (CRM) solution. Both the real estate development company and the marketing department are responsible for the feasibility study that precedes project authorization and execution. How will the project deliver value? The answer is found during the project initiation activities.

### A Mini-Analysis Phase or a Complete Project

Project initiation consists of the work required to study a problem or opportunity. The result can be a recommendation to launch a project. It can also be a decision that the problem or opportunity being studied just doesn't merit further action.

This analysis work often begins informally. It could be a recurring problem that sparks a manager to assign someone to "see what we can do about that." Or it could be an idea for a new product that will create or expand a market or reduce operational costs. These new ideas can come from anywhere, including attending trade shows, reading articles, suggestions from employees, and listening to customers. Once we see that initiation starts informally, it is easy to see why the rigor that should be applied is sometimes missed. That's why it is important to have clear criteria for approving a project. No matter how misty or ambiguous the project's beginning, it will eventually undergo a formal analysis.

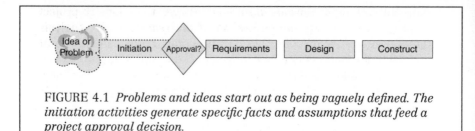

FIGURE 4.1 *Problems and ideas start out as being vaguely defined. The initiation activities generate specific facts and assumptions that feed a project approval decision.*

Figure 4.1 shows where project initiation connects to the product development life cycle discussed in Chapter 3. To see project initiation through the lens of requirements evolution, view Figure 4.2. The work to develop a project proposal could be thought of as a mini-analysis phase. It is sometimes called a feasibility study. If the effort is significant enough, it becomes a project in its own right.

## The Role of a Project Manager in Project Initiation

If initiation activities happen before a project is formally authorized, what is the role of a project manager during initiation? There are three possibilities: manage the initiation phase, perform the analysis work, or merely review the resulting proposal after the project is approved.

The effort to accomplish the analysis could be large and complex, and therefore require the skills of a project manager to coordinate the people and work as in any project.

People who have project management skills may also have the ability to perform the work of initiation. As we'll see in this chapter, that work consists of stakeholder analysis, problem solving, root cause analysis, creative design of potential solutions, and cost-benefit analysis. The skills and techniques required for this work fall outside the normal boundaries of project management. However, these capabilities are extremely complementary to project management, so it is realistic for one person to have the ability to both *manage* the initiation work and also to *perform* that work.

It is also possible that the project manager who is ultimately responsible for managing an approved project has no involvement at all in project initiation. In fact, this is probably the norm. Whoever will pay for the project may assign a person or team to generate requirements and produce a proposal. For example, within an information technology organization, the work is usually done by business analysts. This hand-off, however, has a potential risk. Will the project manager really understand the *business value* that the project is intended to deliver?

In any of the scenarios described above, the more a project manager can at least *understand* all of the *results* of the analysis that is performed during initiation, the better he or she will be at managing the project to deliver on the business case. The topics in this chapter may be outside of your direct responsibility as a project manager, but they will increase your overall contribution to your projects and your organization.

## Initiation Is Linked to Project Portfolio Management

Project initiation produces a proposal that is the basis for evaluating the project. If an organization has a portfolio management process in place, each proposal provides consistent information and all potential projects are ranked against each other. Project portfolio management, described in Chapter 20, ensures that the limited resources of an organization are assigned to the projects that provide the best results, whether those results are measured in purely financial terms or in other, more intangible ways. As we examine the standard content of a project proposal later in this chapter, we'll see how proposal content reflects portfolio selection criteria.

## KEY CONCEPT — A PROPOSAL DEFINES THE FUTURE BUSINESS VALUE

Projects are approved in order to achieve benefits. The proposal articulates these benefits in contrast to the expenses that will be incurred. A useful proposal, therefore, explains the core reason for the potential project, the balance of expected costs and expenses, and begins to articulate the future state that will be achieved if the project is performed.

To consider whether a project is worthwhile, it is useful to reflect on the three dimensions which the design firm IDEO promotes and that were introduced in Chapter 3: viability, feasibility, desirability.[1] These are directly relevant for evaluating a commercial product, but in general they form the lens through which any future project can be judged.

- *Desirability.* Will the functionality that we intend to deliver be compelling to potential users? If we expect to generate revenue from these users, how much can we realistically expect they'll pay? Public agencies must consider this factor if they are contemplating projects from bike lanes to tolled highways.
- *Viability.* What is the needed return on investment? Viability looks beyond the implementation cost; it balances the lifetime

cost against the lifetime benefit. Lifetime costs and benefits span development on the front end, operating costs and revenues, and the costs of decommissioning when it reaches the end of its life.

- *Feasibility.* Is this technically possible? What technical risks will exist over a solution's lifetime?

The process of initiation explores these questions, and the proposal found at the end of this chapter summarizes these answers.

## Business Risk and Project Risk

Building a proposal demands that we make assumptions and forecasts—all of which could be wrong. A real estate developer invests in a new apartment complex, breaking ground twelve months before the first tenant will move in. And it will take years of rental income before the project breaks even. Will the demand for these apartments be sufficient over the years to maintain high occupancy? Will the overall rental market produce the anticipated rental rates? These questions address business risk, the risk an owner bears when investing in a business venture.

Business risk is separate from project risk. Project risk is primarily concerned with delivering the promised deliverables for expected cost and schedule. If the apartment complex is built correctly, delivered on time and budget due to effective project management, then the project risk was successfully managed. The business risk remains, throughout the life of the apartment complex. Business risk is outside of the project manager's responsibility.

## MANAGING REQUIREMENTS IS TIGHTLY LINKED TO PROJECT INITIATION

Judging the success of a project at completion is tied to setting the purpose and goals as the project is initially conceived. Setting this target relies on eliciting and managing requirements, which falls within the domain of Requirements Engineering, a topic that is explained in greater detail in Chapter 19.

For the purposes of creating a project proposal, the most important requirements concept is that there are different types of requirements, as shown in Figure 4.2. The earliest requirements are called enterprise requirements, because they describe the needs of the enterprise that is contemplating the project. Another term for these initial, high-level requirements is business requirements. Enterprise requirements describe what various stakeholders will *be able to do* in the future as they use the project's deliverables.

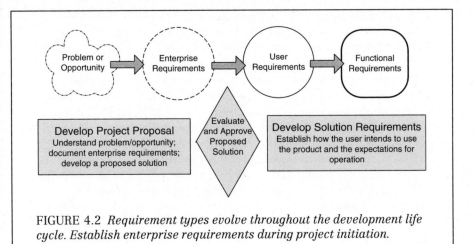

FIGURE 4.2 *Requirement types evolve throughout the development life cycle. Establish enterprise requirements during project initiation.*

Business requirements are tightly linked to the benefits the project will deliver, because if we can deliver the capability described in the requirement, the stakeholder will enjoy a benefit.

The proposal template described in this chapter includes a section for business requirements.

## Monitoring Benefits Realization Begins with the Proposal

For most projects, the benefits they produce won't be experienced until the project is completed and the change has become operationalized. The project may be closed down and the project team dispersed long before the value of the project investment is realized. That causes a common problem, which is that no matter how thoroughly we study a project before it is launched, the result is not measured. When that happens, we don't really know whether the desired cost savings materialize or the market share increases, which reduces the validity of the project approval process.

One source of failure for benefits monitoring was expressed by a PMO (project management office) leader at a hospital: "We have a hard time seeing the impact of an individual project. There are so many variables that affect our environment that we can't always draw a line to the project." She said that the hospital tracked many important metrics and that projects were initiated and aligned to these governing metrics. But strategic metrics are often lagging indicators, meaning they are the result of many factors.

The initiation stage is the time to drill down to the root cause to see the driving metrics. The goal of the project will be to address the root cause. That means monitoring benefits realization should be focused on watching the change that occurs to the root cause. A metric related to a root cause is sometimes referred to as a *leading metric*, because changes here lead to changes in the strategic metric.

Companies are placing an increasing importance on monitoring the actual benefits of their projects. *The content of a proposal should clearly identify what will be measured, when, and how*. That doesn't ensure that benefits will be measured, but it provides the foundation of the rigor we desire. Disciplined monitoring of benefits is part of project portfolio management, which is described in Chapter 20.

The ability to drill down on a process to create measurable benefit metrics also falls into the domain of requirements engineering.

It is worth noting that it takes skill to articulate enterprise requirements. The stakeholders who want to see a change often have a vision of what they want, but they can't describe it in a way that fosters the best problem-solving approach. Business analysts contribute this skill on information technology projects. Through their facilitation skills, they help stakeholders identify what they really want to accomplish, which expands the realm of possible solutions. This skill is directly related to a recommended practice described later in this chapter: Clarify the problem before proposing a solution.

### The Logical Framework Approach Connects Requirements with Metrics

It should be clear that connecting the strategic goals of a project with a specific measurable outcome increases the rigor of the proposal. A method for doing this is called the Logical Framework Approach. At the end of this chapter you'll find an introduction to this technique, written by Terry Schmidt, who was part of the team that pioneered it more than 30 years ago. Make a Logical Framework a part of any proposal.

### KEY CONCEPT — COMMON PRINCIPLES FOR PROJECT INITIATION

Will the U.S. Army consider replacing the Humvee personnel carrier using the same process that a marketing department uses to analyze the addition of a CRM system? Does a real estate developer research the feasibility of a new shopping mall the same way a university evaluates the addition of a purely online degree program? Clearly, these are all quite different types of potential projects, and the proper analysis for each one varies. The most complex products require the most sophisticated and time-consuming evaluation. The U.S. Army and major real estate developers have sophisticated procedures and legions of professionals trained to perform rigorous analysis. That just

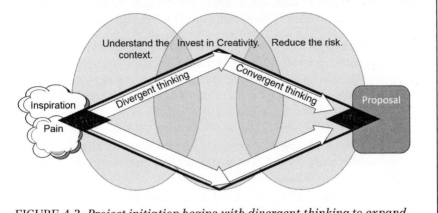

FIGURE 4.3 *Project initiation begins with divergent thinking to expand our understanding of the project before attempting to choose a solution.*

isn't possible or appropriate in many organizations. But that doesn't mean every project can't apply some commonly accepted best practices before plunging into a project.

Figure 4.3 illustrates the principles that transcend industries during project initiation:

- Understand the context of the issue through the eyes of all stakeholders.
- Invest in creativity. Initiation presents the greatest opportunity to approach the issue with fresh, original ideas.
- Be methodical in evaluating the options and testing assumptions. Risk identification in this phase pays huge dividends.

The wise organization is able to extrapolate from the guidelines that follow and match them to their projects.

## Involve a Wide Variety of Stakeholders

Stakeholders are all of the people who will engage in the project or be affected by it. As we'll see in Chapter 5, good project managers invest in early identification of stakeholders as the first step in understanding a new project.

Stakeholder involvement is even more important and more difficult during project initiation—more important because this is the time we set the goals and direction of the project, and more difficult because there will be a much broader group of potential stakeholders during this early analysis. Use the following perspectives as a guide for your own efforts to include and engage the right stakeholders:

- Understand the problem or opportunity from the perspective of everyone it will affect. Using the example of the U.S. Army's new vehicle, stakeholders include the people who maintain and manufacture the vehicle as well as the soldiers using it in the field. Imagine all the people who will touch the product during the full product life cycle. What are their concerns or desires related to the problem or opportunity?

- There may be advocates for change and advocates for maintaining the current state. Why? What stake does each have in making (or not making) a change?

- Federal, state, and local government agencies are full of stakeholders. Laws and regulations form constraints to the situation. Zoning laws, for example, restrict the use of real estate, governing what types of buildings and activities are allowed.

- Integration with existing systems is an issue on all kinds of projects. An e-commerce website will integrate with a secured payment processor. A military fighter jet that needs to refuel in flight must consider the tanker aircraft that provides the fuel. A new mobile phone app must work with the phone's operating system.

Viewed from this perspective, it might seem that there is a never-ending list of stakeholders and that seeking them all out will take an eternity. That is not the intention. However, it reinforces that the analysis performed to build a project proposal is not trivial and often requires specialized skills and knowledge. The bottom line is that listening to stakeholders will expose requirements and constraints. The earlier these are exposed, the cheaper they are to manage.

Chapter 5 is devoted to stakeholder identification. We'll see that casting a wide net for stakeholders during initiation is just the beginning of delivering value to stakeholders.

## Clarify the Problem Before Proposing a Solution

It seems pretty obvious that we should agree on what problem is being solved before coming up with great ideas to solve it, but not doing this is a classic mistake. Failure to clarify the problem is a common source of disappointment, particularly because it is routinely discovered after the project is complete. Call it human nature. Reinforce it by applauding it as being decisive and action-oriented. Do it because "that's what the customer asked for." But taking action without clarifying the problem will always be a mistake.

Every sound product-development or problem-solving approach shares this principle. Define the problem as the gap between the current state and the ideal state, often literally referred to as *gap analysis*. The ideal state should not include a specific solution, but rather the capability we want but don't have. This is the tie to enterprise requirements, as described earlier in this chapter. The enterprise requirements are the ideal future state. The downloadable Project Proposal template specifically calls for this in the requirements section.

Describe the primary success criteria in terms of what the organization or customer will be able to do as a result of the project's successful completion. Many completed projects are a disappointment to the customer because they don't really address the core business or functional need that the customer had. It takes skill to uncover and document enterprise requirements, because they usually lurk beneath the surface—below the symptoms of the problem or the customer's perception of what solution should be implemented. Remember that these requirements will be elaborated on during subsequent phases of the project.

Wherever the need for innovation is high, this factor becomes even more important. By disciplining ourselves to focus on defining the problem, we expand the range of possible solutions. We are able to go beyond the initial solution that seems so obvious and explore all the possible ways to achieve our goal. Further, the "ideal state" requirements provide the framework for evaluating the possible alternatives.

## Invest In Creativity

Maybe it goes without saying that when we analyze a problem or opportunity we need to generate several options, rather than just pursue the first one that bubbles up. That is certainly the only way that truly new ideas are created.

The initiation stage is perhaps the greatest opportunity for adding value through creativity in the life of the project. It is the stage where the least amount of money has been spent, and the greatest number of options exist. The cost of exploring a new idea can be small, perhaps a few days or weeks. Learning and insights at this early stage create other possibilities. Conversely, once the project is approved with a solution, budget, and deadline, the appetite for innovation and original approaches is lost in the focus on efficiency.

According to Peter Drucker, the famed management consultant and writer: "Efficiency is doing things right; effectiveness is doing the right things." Here, before we put the project team in motion, is the time to ensure we are doing the right thing.

Investing in creativity takes courage. Everyone wants the fresh, insightful solution, but nobody wants to pay for the twenty ideas that came before it that just wouldn't work. Testing assumptions, experimenting with new approaches, and a general willingness to "get outside the box" do take time and effort, yet that is the only way to break away from the usual solutions.

Of all the guidelines for investing in creativity, here is the most relevant for project initiation:

*Creativity in the workplace is anchored by our understanding of the problem or opportunity. Creativity for innovation finds its inspiration in understanding the stakeholders and their needs.*

Creativity is no accident. It requires time and intention. Building creative activity into your project initiation activities will require its own act of creativity. Yet, now more than ever, creativity pays enormous dividends.

## KEY CONCEPT — Quantify the Benefits and Costs of the Alternatives

For each of the many possible approaches that have been proposed, rank them against the enterprise requirements and quantify their benefits and costs as much as possible. Quantifying the benefits will demonstrate how the alternatives vary in their results. Quantifying the costs will provide a foundation for a financial analysis, such as return on investment (ROI). Since most alternatives analysis requires us to compare apples and oranges (options that have different advantages and disadvantages), finding ways to quantify the costs and benefits will allow us to see why we might want to pursue a lower-cost option that produces a lesser result. Or it could justify making the big investment with the big payoff.

As this analysis is performed, keep in mind that a similar comparison will be made for the proposed project and other potential or active projects during final project selection. This project must not only produce benefits that outweigh its costs, but the project must be a better use of the firm's limited resources than other projects.

### Use Risk Management to Improve the Solution

It takes a lot of courage to develop an innovative idea. It takes even more courage to expose the idea and invite criticism. But doing that will make your best solution even better.

The risk management process described in Chapter 7 can be used to uncover weaknesses to examine both the solution itself and the planned implementation.

Invite others to play the role of "devil's advocate," to critically challenge every assumption about your best idea. Ask questions about the three IDEO variables: viability, desirability, and feasibility.

Go beyond documenting assumptions: actually test them as much as possible. The expense of testing assumptions in this phase will be far smaller than the cost of finding out your assumption isn't true during implementation or after the project is over. (Recall the introduction to Lean Startup in Chapter 3, which emphasized constant experimentation.)

Risk management is an excellent counterpoint to creativity. It subjects all of our crazy, out-of-the-box ideas to rigorous evaluation. When we do find problems or weaknesses, that doesn't mean our fresh idea isn't any good, it just means it can be made better.

## Follow an Industry Best Practice

The principles just described are found in greater detail within your industry's best practices. Architects, for example, call it "programming" or "establishing the program." Just as design techniques are different for software, bridges, and television programs, the techniques for starting with an idea or a problem and turning it into a project proposal are specific to the industry.

## BASIC PROJECT PROPOSAL CONTENT

The outcome of project initiation should be a proposal that is suitable for a selection process. Selection may be a part of a total project portfolio management process, or it could be reviewed by a single manager or executive who has the authority to commit the resources.

The basic content of the project proposal overlaps the content found in the statement of work described in Chapter 6. That makes sense because both are used to move a project from an inspiration to a tangible, achievable goal. Since the proposal is written first, any overlap with the statement of work represents an opportunity either to verify an earlier assumption or to develop that topic in greater detail. The proposal that follows will become much more powerful when accompanied by the Logical Framework Approach described at the end of this chapter.

As previously emphasized, the information and analysis required to select a project will vary dramatically depending on your industry and the size of your projects. The content described here addresses the minimum topics most project selection boards require. You may find it useful to reference the online Project Proposal form as we explore each section of the proposal.

## 1. Project Goal

State the specific desired results from the project over a specified time period. Remember, this is the business value that we begin to experience after the project completes. For example, the goal of a training project could be: "This project will improve our ability to plan projects with accuracy and manage them to meet cost, schedule, and quality goals."

## 2. Problem/Opportunity Definition

Describe the problem/opportunity without suggesting a solution. The people approving the project must understand the fundamental reason the project is being undertaken. This problem/opportunity statement should address these elements:

- Describe the problem/opportunity. If possible, supply factual evidence of the problem, taking care to avoid assumptions.
- Describe the problem/opportunity in the context of where it appears in the organization and what operations or functions it affects.
- List one or more ways to measure the size of the problem. Qualitative as well as quantitative measures can be applied.

## 3. Proposed Solution

Describe what the project will do to address the problem/opportunity. Be as specific as possible about the boundaries of the solution, such as what organizations, business processes, information systems, and so on will be affected. If necessary, also describe the boundaries in terms of related problems, systems, or operations that are beyond the scope of this initiative.

## 4. Project Selection and Ranking Criteria

Ideally, your firm has specific selection or ranking criteria that are addressed here. If a formal project portfolio management process exists, this section will match the categories that assist a selection board in ranking one project against another.

**Project benefit** *category*. Projects typically fall into one of the following categories:

- *Compliance/regulatory.* Laws or regulations dictate the requirements for the project.
- *Efficiency/cost reduction.* The result of the project will be lower operating costs.
- *Increased revenue.* For example, increased market share, increased customer loyalty, or a new product could all produce increased revenue.

**Portfolio fit and interdependencies.** How does this project align with other projects the organization is pursuing and with the overall organization strategy?

Project *urgency.* How quickly must the organization attempt this project? Why?

## 5. Cost-Benefit Analysis

This section summarizes the financial reasons for taking on the project. It consists of an analysis of the expected benefits in comparison to the costs and attempts to quantify the return on investment.

**Tangible benefits.** Tangible benefits are measurable and will correspond to the problem/opportunity described. For each benefit, describe it and quantify it, including a translation of the benefit into financial terms such as dollars saved or gained. Include any assumptions you used in calculating this benefit. Forecast benefits are usually not certain, so describe the probability of achieving the result. This is the place to establish the benefit-realization metrics that will be monitored after implementation.

**Intangible benefits.** Intangible benefits are difficult to measure, but are still important. For example, reducing complexity in a task may increase employee job satisfaction, a worthwhile benefit but a difficult one to measure. Again, describe the benefit, the assumptions used to predict the magnitude of this benefit, and the probability the benefit will be realized.

**Required resources (cost).** What labor and other resources will be required? Include a comment about the accuracy of these figures. Typical cost categories include internal (employee) labor hours, external labor, and capital investment. New ongoing costs to support the result of the project should be recognized but separated from the project costs.

**Financial return.** There are many financial methods that compare the tangible up-front cost of the project with the expected tangible benefits achieved over time. These are beyond the scope of this book, but your project selection committee should describe which of these financial measures to use.

## 6. Business Requirements

These are the enterprise requirements we've emphasized earlier in this chapter. Describe the requirements from the owner/customer perspective. If you describe a requirement using one of the following phrases, you are more likely to be accurately describing the true end state desired by the customer.

The project will be judged successful when . . .

We know   _____ .

We have   _____ .

We can    _____ .

We are    _____ .

You can substitute the names of specific users or customers in these statements, such as "Project sponsors know the cost and schedule status of all projects for which they have responsibility."

### 7. Scope

List and describe the major accomplishments required to meet the project goal. These may include process or policy changes, training, information system upgrades, facility changes, and so forth. Clearly an overlap to the statement of work, the scope description in the proposal is likely to be less detailed than the one developed for that document.

### 8. Obstacles and Risks

Describe the primary obstacles to success and the known risks (threats) that could cause disruption or failure. The difference between obstacles and risks is that risks might occur, but obstacles are certain to occur. Chapter 7 describes how the risk management process works continuously throughout the project to help identify potential threats and either avoid them or reduce their negative impact.

### 9. Schedule Overview

At a high level, describe the expected duration of the project (planned start and finish), significant milestones, and the major phases. This is an initial schedule estimate that will be refined during project definition and planning, but it is always useful to manage expectations by commenting on the accuracy of this schedule prediction.

 **DESIGNING A REALISTIC INITIATION PROCESS**
Initiation can be a project. The research and analysis just described demand skill and effort. For some projects initiation could take months or years. For smaller projects it will take hours. Clearly, a balance must be found between irresponsibly plunging into new projects and being stuck with "analysis paralysis."

There are two key factors to consider when designing the initiation process: risk and estimating; and both are related to the inherent unknowns that exist at the time a project is approved.

1. *Risk.* Risk management, as described in Chapter 7, is our process of identifying threats and opportunities and actively working to reduce the threats and optimize the opportunities. No matter how thorough the work during project initiation, our proposal still contains many assumptions. Any forecasted costs or benefits are subject to change. So the question for our initiation process is: Have we studied the problem *enough* that we can accept the amount of uncertainty that remains in the proposal? Or do we commit more resources and time to study it further?

2. *Estimating.* We know that estimates are a reflection of the known and unknown remaining in the life of the project. The earlier the estimate, the less accurate it is. The only completely accurate estimate is for a project that is complete, because it has no surprises left. What amount of accuracy do we require to approve a project, and how will we update that estimate as the project is being executed?

A realistic project initiation process accepts that projects are approved based on many assumptions that won't be proved true or false until the project is under way or even completed. The phased estimating technique described in Chapter 11 is the best approach to striking the balance. In addition, the phase gate approach provides the best framework for the monitoring activities within project portfolio management, as discussed in Chapter 20.

## END POINT

The project management discipline has long focused on excellent delivery of projects. However, that ignores the most important question we can ask about the project: Why do it?

Project initiation starts with an idea or problem and performs just enough study and analysis to produce a project proposal. It is a difficult task because it is a combination of discovery, stakeholder negotiation, problem solving, and financial analysis, and it may require considerable technical expertise. Because of the specialized skills and knowledge that are necessary, this work is often not performed by project managers.

The final pages of this chapter contain a description of the Logical Framework Approach and a template for a project proposal. Together, these form a sound basis for evaluating a potential project and setting the target that will be monitored after the project is completed.

# Stellar Performer: The Logical Framework Approach
## A Practical Methodology for Project Initiation and Planning

Terry Schmidt

### INTRODUCTION

*Agreement among the project team, customers, and management on the goals of the project* is one of the five project success factors repeated throughout this book, and it is easy to acknowledge its importance. It is also clear that the goals of a project should be aligned with higher-level program or strategic goals—this is a critical factor of project selection. Therefore, goal alignment is easily the *most important discussion* that takes place on a project.

The Logical Framework Approach (LFA) is designed to ensure a systematic methodology to turn strategic intent into executable project plans. It uses a clear, simple graphic to illustrate that objectives are fully understood, success measures are identified, and the cause-and-effect linkages between the project and larger program are made explicit.

The Logical Framework offers a systems thinking perspective proven especially useful during the so-called fuzzy front end of project initiation and planning. The Logical Framework offers a common management vocabulary and robust concepts that logically connect project deliverables with strategic intent. Using the Logical Framework helps shape agreement on higher-level objectives and aligns the project with the overall program or corporate strategy.

It is useful to distinguish between the two terms that are sometimes confused: the Logical Framework Approach (LFA) and the Logical Framework. The Logical Framework *Approach* is a project design methodology, while the Logical Framework or "LogFrame" is a document that results from using the methodology.

The Logical Framework appears as a 4×4 matrix that organizes project information in a specific way (Figure 4.4). Each cell in the matrix is related to the others by interlocking principles of good management and common sense. The completed matrix can communicate a complicated project clearly and understandably on a single sheet of paper.

### Origin of the LogFrame

The Logical Framework Approach was originally created in 1969 by Leon Rosenberg of the management consulting firm Practical Concepts Incorporated (PCI) to help the United States Agency for International Development (USAID) more effectively plan, implement, and evaluate the thousands of development projects in its global multibillion-dollar foreign aid program.

Projects in developing countries are particularly challenging because many involve difficult-to-measure intangibles such as shifting a culture, building institutional capacity, or changing behavior of the rural poor. The ability to bring rigor to complex projects involving intangibles and processes makes the LogFrame well suited to tackle today's challenging projects.

| Objectives | Success Measures | Verification | Assumptions |
|---|---|---|---|
| **Goal** **Why?** | | | |
| **Purpose** **Why?** | | | |
| **Outcomes** **What?** | | | |

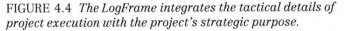

| *Inputs* How? Who? | When? |
|---|---|

FIGURE 4.4 *The LogFrame integrates the tactical details of project execution with the project's strategic purpose.*

The LogFrame Approach brings clarity to diverse projects, such as improving internal procedures, developing new systems, streamlining operations, leveraging quality improvement, implementing change initiatives, and other important topics that require a systematic approach. The concepts scale and flex to accommodate one-person projects, team efforts, or larger programs or functions.

## FOUR CRITICAL QUESTIONS FOCUS OUR THINKING

Since inception, the LogFrame concept has been adapted and revised by many organizations, including international NGOs and government agencies. The author of this article worked with the original LogFrame team and made it easier to use by identifying four strategic questions, the answers to which flesh out a solid design.

The Logical Framework recognizes that every project is part of a larger system, and we must understand how that larger system affects our effort. At the heart of the methodology is the simple concept of causal thinking, allowing a project to be described as a series of linked hypotheses of the form *if-then*. The LogFrame offers a step-by-step design process based on answering these four critical strategic project questions:

1. What are we trying to accomplish and why?
2. How will we measure success?
3. What other conditions must exist?
4. How do we get there?

Answers to these questions populate the cells of the Logical Framework, an interactive matrix that helps teams design projects in a way that covers all the issues. The questions guide project team conversations. Each question is important, but the first three are often glossed over in the pressure to develop a detailed action plan and begin execution.

### CRITICAL QUESTION 1: WHAT ARE YOU TRYING TO ACCOMPLISH AND WHY? (OBJECTIVES)

Think of project strategy as a set of linked *objectives* of the form *if-then*. Project design establishes a series of linked *if-then* hypotheses or educated guesses believed to be true.

The LogFrame's first column summarizes project objectives and the logic linking them by recognizing that projects involve four distinct levels of objectives, defined as follows:

**Goal** = big-picture strategic intent.

**Purpose** = change or benefit expected from project.

**Outcomes** = project deliverables.

**Inputs** = tasks and resources needed to produce outcomes.

Reading this from the bottom up, the underlying project logic becomes:

- "*If* we manage inputs, *then* we can produce or deliver outcomes.
- *If* we produce or deliver outcomes, *then* we will achieve a purpose.
- *If* we achieve a purpose, *then* we contribute to an important goal."

Or, expressed more succinctly:

- "*If* inputs, *then* outcomes.
- *If* outcomes, *then* purpose.
- *If* purpose, *then* goal."

The level at which each objective sits in the project's causal hierarchy has a particular and precise meaning. While the choice of words used to define these levels (goal, purpose, outcomes, and inputs) may seem arbitrary, the meaning each term expresses is not. Together, the logic between levels establishes the critical linkage between project tasks and strategic goals.

As previously stated, goal alignment is easily the *most important discussion* that takes place on a project. Every project *implicitly* centers on a set of linked hypotheses, but these are seldom put out on the table for discussion, review, and improvement. Clearly identifying your underlying hypotheses — the chain of *if-then* connections — forces the rigorous thought that leads to shared understanding of how the project deliverables ripple out and up to impact business goals.

### CRITICAL QUESTION 2: HOW WILL YOU KNOW YOU ARE SUCCESSFUL? (SUCCESS MEASURES AND VERIFICATION)

Vague or immeasurable objectives are a threat to the logic and rigor necessary for initiating and evaluating projects. This second question helps select appropriate measures of quantity, quality, time, cost, and customer measures to pin down what each objective means. Therefore, for each objective we must state *what* we will measure and *how* we will measure it. The LogFrame captures the *what* in the second column, "Success Measures," and the *how* in the third column, "Verification."

Purpose-level measures are especially important because they define the conditions that will exist when the project team will consider the project to be a success. Project *completion* (outcomes delivered) is not the same as project *success* (purpose achieved).

## CRITICAL QUESTION 3: WHAT OTHER CONDITIONS MUST EXIST? (ASSUMPTIONS)

Every project involves risk, which can be managed if recognized early enough. The fourth column pinpoints *assumptions*—those ever-present but often neglected conditions required for success that may lie outside project scope. (Murphy and his infamous law dwell here.) Identifying and analyzing internal and external assumptions lets you eliminate potential problems in advance. Assumptions become an entry point to more rigorous risk analysis.

Assumptions force us to consider how project interfaces, external events, and other important conditions in the larger project environment affect the project. The concept of assumptions allows us to expand our hypothesis to accommodate these ever-changing conditions. Figure 4.5 illustrates how assumptions reinforce the logical connections between levels.

We can incorporate ever-changing assumptions into the strategic hypotheses to gain a broader and dynamic view of the project environment.

"*If* inputs and assumptions, *then* outcomes.

*If* outcomes and assumptions, *then* purpose.

*If* purpose and assumptions, *then* goal."

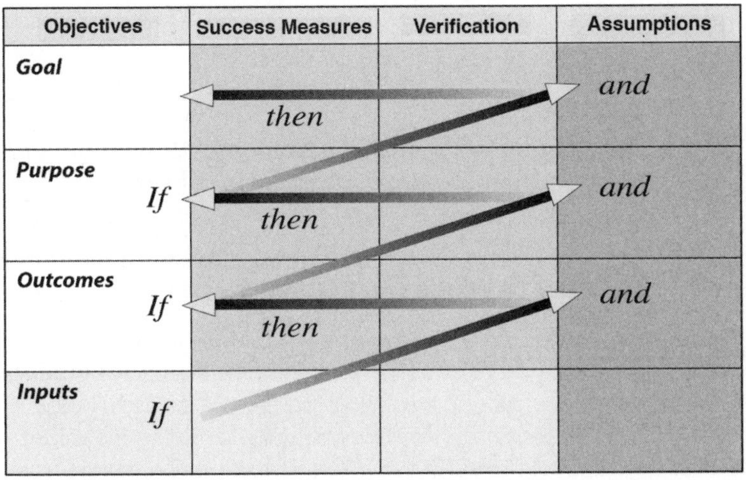

FIGURE 4.5 *Reading the LogFrame from the bottom up establishes the critical linkage between project tasks and strategic goals.*

The Implementation Equation$^{TM}$ elevates managerial focus to the larger context and prevents project leaders from myopically focusing their attention primarily on input tasks and outcome deliverables.

## CRITICAL QUESTION 4: HOW DO WE GET THERE? (INPUTS)

With objectives, measures, and assumptions in place, we can confidently turn to the input level—the tasks to produce outcomes, and their associated resources. This is the realm of project planning that is addressed in Chapters 8 and 9. Once the higher-level objectives and assumptions are defined, the inputs correlate to the first tier of a work breakdown structure and form a strong link to the detailed project plan.

## A TOOL TO COMMUNICATE AND COLLABORATE

The LogFrame readily scales and adapts to programs, projects, and tasks of all types. The matrix structure clearly captures answers to the standard interrogative questions—Why, What, Who, When, and How.

The LogFrame's common logic and standard vocabulary help teams to communicate and collaborate across functions and disciplines. This shared understanding facilitates teamwork and gets projects moving faster, which produces superior solutions. When applied during initiation and planning, the Logical Framework Approach will help to:

- Turn fuzzy strategy into shared and measurable objectives.
- Design practical action plans for any problem, idea, or opportunity.
- Align projects with the big-picture goals and vision.
- Clearly communicate project strategy among stakeholders.
- Discover and eliminate potential pitfalls in advance.
- Get teams aligned and moving faster.

The experience of managers around the world demonstrates that this thinking approach simplifies and accelerates the process of developing and communicating sound plans for projects of all types and sizes.

## EXAMPLE OF THE LOGICAL FRAMEWORK APPROACH

Let's take a look at a specific example to see how powerful the LogFrame can be. This is a true story that comes from a consumer electronics company. The company had three separate business units: one manufactured television sets, one manufactured monitors, and the third produced laptop computers. These separate business units shared the same facility, but their business processes were different and redundant. Each business unit spent millions purchasing many of the same component parts, but purchases were not coordinated across business boundaries for maximum discount. Inventory management was a problem, purchasing paperwork was cumbersome, and payments were late. Their inefficient, cumbersome, and costly processes begged for improvement.

Following an on-site Logical Framework workshop for managers from all three business units, a small team from Purchasing, Receiving, and Accounts Payable worked across business unit and functional silos to solve this costly problem. Guided by *if-then* logic, they hypothesized that if they completed a system redesign (the set of outcomes), then they would improve the Purchasing/Receiving/Payment cycle (purpose), which would result in better management of financial resources (the goal). Figure 4.6. shows the resulting LogFrame.

At this early planning stage they could not know what the improved process would look like, but the set of outcomes provided a clear road map that would get them there. Input task details would be fleshed out using other tools from the project manager's tool kit.

In this example, the LogFrame was created to initiate the project. The first phase of this project develops a solution. The next phase will be implementation. To tie phases together for continuity, note that the eighth outcome is a LogFrame for the implementation phase.

The team presented this strategic project management plan to senior management, and got strong support because the approach was sound and benefits were crisply communicated in a brief Logical Framework.

## MORE RESOURCES

You can get examples of LogFrame applications at www.ManagementPro.com, or by contacting Terry@ManagementPro.com.

Adapted from *Strategic Project Management Made Simple: Practical Tools for Leaders and Teams* (John Wiley & Sons, 2009), by Terry Schmidt.

Terry Schmidt, PMP, is the author of seven books and has assisted hundreds of teams in 34 countries to apply the Logical Framework Approach to their needs. He teaches in executive programs at UCLA, MIT, and corporate universities worldwide, and conducts practical programs and seminars.

| Objectives | Success Measures | How to Verify | Assumptions |
|---|---|---|---|
| *Logical Hierarchy of If-Then Objectives* | *Conditions When Objectives Are Achieved* | *Source of Evidence to Verify Measures* | *Additional Factors Necessary for Success* |
| **Goal:**<br>ABC Company better manages its financial resources. | **Goal Measures:**<br>1. ABC can safely reduce on-hand inventory from 7-day to 2-day supply by 5/1.<br>2. No production lines down for inventory errors after 5/1. | 1a. Month-end financial reports.<br>1b. On-hand inventory reports.<br>2. Production downtime report. | **Assumptions to Reach Goal:**<br>1. Market changes do not alter and impact ABC's management of financial resources. |
| **Purpose:**<br>Improve the Purchasing/Receiving/Payment cycle. | **Purpose Measures:**<br>1. Reduction in Receiving errors by 15% by 8/1.<br>2. Reduction in past-due invoices by 20% by 8/1.<br>3. Reduction in raw material inventory adjustments to less than $10 per month by 8/1. | 1. Compare date rec'd in Receiving vs. date delivered to warehouse.<br>2. Unpaid invoices aging report.<br>3a. Inventory value report.<br>3b. Material transaction report. | **Assumptions to Achieve Purpose:**<br>1. ABC suppliers providing invoices to be paid (on time).<br>2. ABC suppliers providing shipping documents with deliveries.<br>3. New process will be approved and implemented. |
| **Outcomes:**<br>1. Solution Task Force selected.<br>2. Current process (as is documented).<br>3. Causes of problems clearly identified.<br>4. Best practices identified and shared.<br>5. Solution parameters and system constraints defined.<br>6. Alternate solutions identified.<br>7. "To Be" process designed.<br>8. Implementation plan developed. | **Outcome Measures:**<br>1. By 2/1, recruit two Task Force members each from Procurement, Receiving, and Accounts Payable.<br>2. Current process documented by 2/8 for each department and consolidated by 2/15.<br>3. Root causes of problems identified by 2/21.<br>4. Listing of three best practices by discipline by 3/1 (Procurement, Receiving, and Accounting).<br>5. Solution parameters and system constraints (e.g., resources and scope) defined.<br>6. List of alternate solutions — three best based on price, functionality, and system support — by 4/1.<br>7. Draft design of "to be" process completed by 5/11.<br>8. Implementation plan developed for next project phase following approval of "to be" process. | 1. Two members attend kickoff meeting on 2/1 from each group.<br>2. Presentation using flowcharts and Word docs given to the Task Force.<br>3. T-chart analysis distributed.<br>4. Presentation of three best practices given to the Task Force.<br>5. Presentation of solution parameters and constraints given to the Task Force.<br>6. Alternative solutions presented to the Task Force.<br>7. Draft design signed off by all Task Force members and approved by management.<br>8. Completed Logical Framework approved by management. | **Assumptions to Achieve Outcomes:**<br>1. Team members willing to participate and devote necessary effort to project.<br>2. Management provides support.<br>3. Data available that captures problems and root causes.<br>4. Related systems/processes remain constant.<br>5. Other accounting sites provided correct information. |

| Inputs: How Team Will Produce Outcomes | | | Schedule | | | | | | | | | | Assumptions for Activities |
|---|---|---|---|---|---|---|---|---|---|---|---|---|---|
| **KEY TASKS** | **WHO** | **RESOURCES** | MAY | JUN | JUL | AUG | SEP | OCT | NOV | DEC | JAN | |
| 1. Select Task Force | | | | | | | | | | | | 1. Team members volunteer and are not pulled from project. |
| 2. Document Current "As Is" Process — Word or Flowcharts | | | | | | | | | | | | 2. Current process flow is documentable. |
| 3. Identify Causes of Problems | | | | | | | | | | | | 3. Problems and root causes are clearly identifiable. |
| 4. Identify Best Practices | | | | | | | | | | | | 4. Access to other people using Oracle. |
| 5. Define Solution Parameters and System Constraints | | | | | | | | | | | | 5. Management approves budget needs. |
| 6. Identify Alternate Solutions | | | | | | | | | | | | 6. Access to information. |
| 7. Design "To Be" Process | | | | | | | | | | | | 7. Team understands what needs to be included in process design. |
| 8. Develop Implementation Plan | | | | | | | | | | | | 8. "To be" process is designed. |

FIGURE 4.6 *Logical Framework project plan to improve the purchasing/receiving/payment cycle.*

# Know Your Key Stakeholders and Win Their Cooperation

## INTRODUCTION

At times, it seems as though technology does all the heavy lifting in our economy. A closer look, however, reveals that it is always *people* who make the technology produce. On projects, we call these movers and shakers *stakeholders*, because they have a stake in the project. The first task of a project manager is to identify these stakeholders.

Customers, decision-makers, vendors, and employees obviously belong in this group, but, in a larger sense, anyone who contributes to the project or who is impacted by its result is a stakeholder.

Identifying stakeholders is a primary task because all the important decisions during the definition and planning stages of the project are made by these stakeholders. These are the people who, under the guidance of the project manager, establish agreements on the goals and constraints of the project, construct the strategies and schedules, and approve the budget. In addition, the people and organizations that ultimately judge the success of the project are considered stakeholders.

It's clear that we need to know who our stakeholders are. It is also true that many projects fail to involve one or more critically important stakeholders during project definition and planning. The resulting problems are easily predictable: requirements conflicts and rework, at a minimum, and sometimes more dire consequences, including lawsuits or hefty fines.

This chapter is designed to guide the stakeholder identification process. We recognize the most common stakeholders and introduce a checklist tool for making stakeholder identification more methodical.

## STAKEHOLDER FOCUS THROUGHOUT THE LIFE OF THE PROJECT

Defining our stakeholders as the people and organizations involved in project performance or affected by the project casts a wide net. How can we possibly find or manage such a large and diverse group?

Start by putting them into two large categories: those who are *engaged* in the work of the project and those who are *only affected* by the project. Engaged stakeholders are also affected by the project, so guidelines that apply to affected stakeholder may also apply to engaged stakeholders. Figure 5.1 illustrates engaged stakeholders as a sub-set of all stakeholders.

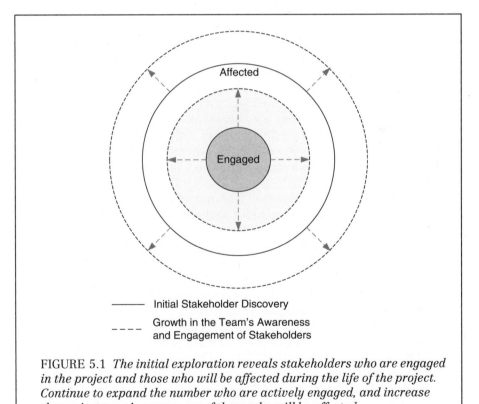

——— Initial Stakeholder Discovery

‒ ‒ ‒ Growth in the Team's Awareness and Engagement of Stakeholders

FIGURE 5.1 *The initial exploration reveals stakeholders who are engaged in the project and those who will be affected during the life of the project. Continue to expand the number who are actively engaged, and increase the project team's awareness of those who will be affected.*

Engaged stakeholders are typically easier to identify. They play a predictable set of roles that are required to accomplish most projects. Recognizing these classic roles makes it easier to seek out these critical people and understand their stake in the project. Since these are common stakeholder *roles*, it follows that some people will play more than one role and some roles will be filled by more than one person. This chapter explains four major roles: project manager, project team, management, and customer.

Affected stakeholders present a different challenge. We may not need them to accomplish the work of the project, but we may find that their cooperation is essential to realizing the actual value of the project. In other cases, when we understand their stake we can avoid creating opponents. The latter half of this chapter suggests key questions to ask that will help to expose affected stakeholders and their interest in the project.

### Early Awareness and Growing Engagement

When does stakeholder identification and engagement begin, and how does it change over the life of the project?

Chapter 4 described the importance of stakeholder awareness as the business case is developed. At this stage, our stakeholder identification awareness may be at its broadest. It isn't necessary to actively communicate with all potential stakeholders at this point, but the more stakeholders we recognize, the better our assumptions will be about how the project will be perceived by all those it affects. This early awareness could change assumptions about costs and risks as we identify other departments, systems and processes that interface with the changes our project is contemplating.

After the project is authorized and the project manager and team begin their work, the number of stakeholders that are actively engaged in the project will grow until the project is completed as shown in Figure 5.1. As the project gathers momentum and stakeholders, it will be easy to lose sight of the "affected but not actively engaged" group. That is always a mistake. If forgotten, these stakeholders will emerge as obstacles and even adversaries as they become aware of the changes being made.

A new and important trend in project management is to actively engage the people who will have to change their behaviors as a result of the project. Rather than assume their cooperation at deployment, the project team begins early to alert these affected people to the coming change and to win their cooperation. These strategies and techniques fall into the discipline of *change management*, which is introduced later in this chapter and expanded upon in Chapter 14.

## KEY CONCEPT — STAKEHOLDER MANAGEMENT IS RISK MANAGEMENT FOR PEOPLE

The more systematic we can be in our attempts to identify and engage stakeholders, the greater the value our project will deliver. The process for stakeholder management can easily be compared to the risk management process that is described in Chapter 7. Both begin with identification, then progress to prioritization and analysis. Risk analysis produces strategies for optimizing opportunities and reducing threats. Stakeholder analysis produces strategies to improve communication and to involve the right people at the right time. It also identifies potential opponents and creates strategies for reducing their impact. As the project progresses, the project team monitors existing stakeholders and seeks to identify new ones; the same activities that occur for risks.

This chapter will focus on the critical first step of finding stakeholders. It describes four stakeholder roles that are necessary to most projects and their typical stake in the project. Then it goes on to offer suggestions for finding other, less obvious but affected players.

Chapter 14 describes methods of understanding stakeholder interests and planning for engagement.

### Make Stakeholder Identification a Repeatable Process

Sometimes identifying stakeholders is easy; other times you have to go out and find them. When searching for stakeholders, rather than asking, "Who is the customer?" or "Who is the project team?" ask, "Who will make a contribution?" and "Who will be affected by this project?"

These first two questions will generate an unexpectedly large list, but it is seldom a complete list. After this initial brainstorming on stakeholders, consult a checklist of potential stakeholders derived from past projects.

The Fast Foundation Stakeholder Analysis form included at the end of this chapter is an example of this checklist. It is more than just a list of roles; it is a list of questions that will prompt us to consider additional people and organizations.

The form is intended to be a standard checklist your organization can use to methodically find project stakeholders. Over time, the questions can be modified or new ones added to make the tool more specific to your projects.

## STAKEHOLDER ROLES: PROJECT MANAGER

What does a project manager contribute to the project? Magic, or, more precisely, practical magic. Just as a symphony conductor directs the orchestra to bring out the magic in the music, the project manager must keep all the disparate groups in a project moving in harmony. Whether he or she is planning the project, identifying the stakeholders, watching for cost overruns, or refereeing disputes, the project manager has the primary role in any project. And, while balancing all the various tasks can make project managers appear to be magicians, the skills that form the basis of this magic can be learned.

Because this book is mostly about the contribution project managers make to projects, the description here is brief; however, one point needs to be made. Once selected, the project manager should clearly identify the stakeholder roles on the project, *including his or her own*. The project manager must ask questions like: "What is my authority?" "To whom do I report?" "Does this mean I'll be relieved of other responsibilities?" "What are my expectations?" If you are a project manager, you are an important stakeholder, too. Don't forget to satisfy yourself!

### Find All the Project Managers!

As projects grow in size and cross organizational boundaries, the role of project manager can be spread among multiple people. Titles such as *technical lead* and *team leader* recognize an attempt to spread project management duties around. That's okay, but be clear about everyone's responsibilities and authority.

## STAKEHOLDER ROLES: PROJECT TEAM

Who will do the work? The answer is the project team, in tandem with the project manager. All groups and individuals who contribute time, skills, and effort to the project are considered team members. In addition to the people from the company assigned to the project, these can include contractors, vendors, and even customers.

The concept of customers as team members might seem confusing, because they are the ones being served by the project. But it is not unusual for customers to have specific project tasks to perform. For example, on information systems projects, customers are often active participants in the system definition and design phases. Or, when the project involves switching to a new office complex, the customer might take responsibility for organizing the training associated with operating the new facility.

Determining who will be a part of the team happens at the start of the project, during definition and planning. This process is complete when the team members have agreed to their responsibilities and roles on the project. Let's look at the steps of this process, from start to finish:

- Tasks are broken down until the different skill requirements emerge.
- The project manager and sponsor then begin recruiting people and organizations with the necessary skills.
- The project manager negotiates the involvement of these new team members.
- The project manager clarifies the plan and ensures that all members understand it.
- Team member responsibilities are documented in both the statement of work (SOW) and the project plan.

It's often easy to identify the essential players on small projects, but much more difficult and time-consuming on large projects. However, this time is well spent because the makeup of the project team is critical to project success.

## STAKEHOLDER ROLES: MANAGEMENT

**KEY CONCEPT** Working productively with company management is important to the success of any project. *Management*, in this case, refers to *functional management*, also known as *line management*. These can be department managers, first-level supervisors, or executive vice presidents. With the exception of a project-oriented organization, functional managers are responsible for an organizational unit, such as "Engineering" or "Internal Audit," rather than for a specific project. These are the people with long-term control over employees and other resources in the firm. They are also involved in setting company policies—policies that may impact the project. In Chapter 2, Figure 2.8 shows a typical matrix organization.

Chapter 1 identified "management support" as one of the commonly stated characteristics of successful projects. When asked to expand on what kind of management support is most helpful, most project managers describe help in "getting the right people at the right time" and "timely decisions based on the facts presented by the project team." These perceptions highlight the contributions that functional management makes to the project team. They can also guide the project manager in identifying which functional managers might be stakeholders on a specific project.

There are two essential contributions managers make to every project:

- *Sponsorship.* A specific executive accountable for project success.
- *Resources.* Functional managers who assign specific people and resources to a project.

Each of these contributions corresponds to a classic management role described in the next sections.

## Project Sponsor

Many projects are organizational anomalies. They cross department and corporate boundaries; they staff up for short periods, then disband; they may span a portion of a budget cycle while drawing funding from multiple groups within a company. The temporary, ad hoc nature of projects can create major problems for project managers because their authority is typically insufficient to cope with these organizational challenges. The sponsor is the solution to these problems.

The sponsor is the person with formal authority who is ultimately responsible for the project. A sponsor may be a senior executive or a junior manager. The sponsor's position and authority in the organization are independent of any project, which enables the sponsor to act as a connection between a project and the normal decision-making process. The sponsor might use his or her power on behalf of the project manager, provide advice, or influence project priority. The sponsor provides the authority that the project manager often lacks.

There are two basic concepts in understanding the importance of sponsors to the project. First, sponsors are ultimately responsible for the success of the project. The real, formal authority that comes from their title and position in the organization endows them with this responsibility. Second, the sponsor's primary task is to help the project team be successful. The best sponsors know they aren't sponsoring a project; they are sponsoring the *project manager* and the *project team.* The sponsor's job is to help these people be successful. That's why another term for sponsor is *champion,* as in "I am championing this project team and I will not let anything stand in their way!"

### Duties of a Sponsor

A sponsor's primary contribution to a project is his or her authority. There are many tangible ways sponsors lend their authority to projects. A sponsor may:

- Prominently support the project manager by issuing a *project charter.* The charter is an announcement that names a new project, the purpose of the project, and the project manager. (For more on charters, see Chapter 6.)

- Assist in developing a *responsibility matrix*. The responsibility matrix shows how different stakeholder groups will be involved in the project.

- Review and approve the *statement of work* (SOW). The SOW describes the goals, constraints, and project management guidelines of a project.

- Review and approve the *project plan*. The sponsor must endorse the cost-schedule-quality equilibrium represented in the plan.

- Advise the project manager, and discuss the status of the project with this manager on a regular basis. Sponsors must involve themselves in a project before problems arise so that they're able to join in the problem solving. Uninformed sponsors—sponsors in name only—are of little help to a project manager when obstacles arise.

- Monitor and maintain the priority of the project relative to other projects. Because an organization has limited resources, there are always more valid projects proposed than time, money, and people can deliver. To execute projects efficiently, an organization must be clear about the priorities of its various projects, including the amount of funding and other resources assigned to each. In spite of stated intentions to prioritize, however, the reality is that people are often pulled from one project to fight fires on another. This robbery may continue until the original project falls so far behind that people are thrown back at that one. The sponsor's job is to keep this unproductive staffing practice from affecting the project. He or she must keep the size of the project team and the size of the budget as constant as possible.

- Assist the project manager in overcoming organizational obstacles. When the project manager lacks the authority to overcome bureaucracy, the sponsor will have to step in on behalf of the project. Proof of the value of this type of intervention comes from a study by an information systems department in a Fortune 500 firm. This study determined that having a known and active sponsor was the *number one reason* for a project's success, because problems were given timely attention by a manager who had authority to effect a solution.

In most corporate environments, enlisting a powerful, interested sponsor is critical to the success of a project. This manager will promote and protect the project and provide the formal authority in the organization that a project manager often lacks. We have discussed the qualities to look for in a sponsor. Now we turn to the second type of management stakeholder.

### Resource Manager

The project manager must work closely with functional managers in assigning the best people for the job. After management has initiated a project and described its scope, the project manager designs a work plan that details the skills required for the project and which departments the workers possessing these skills will come from. Armed with this information, the project manager is now ready to identify the managers of those departments; these are the managers who will have control over the workers assigned to the project team and who will decide when they are available. These managers must approve the statement of work (as described in Chapter 6) and the project plan, because the potential team members identified in these documents will come from their department. Throughout the life of the project, these functional managers can be extremely helpful in solving personnel or performance problems.

### STAKEHOLDER ROLES: THE CUSTOMER

Whenever a project exists, somebody will be paying for it. And whoever pays usually gets the first and last word on product description, budget, and the criteria by which success will be measured. Although other stakeholders may try to squeeze in extra requirements, the final say on the product will come from the customer, because the customer is paying the bills.

This sounds simple enough—the customer is the one who pays the bills—but in reality, identifying the customer is not always that simple. Consider a project manager who is given the task of installing the latest Microsoft operating system on all the desktop computers in her company. Since there are a number of possible options when installing this operating system, the question arises: Who should decide which options will be installed? Should this decision come from the 335 employees using the computers? Is this group the customer? Or is the president of the company, who is funding the project, the logical choice? In this case, the project manager must go beyond the question, "Who is the customer?" and instead ask, "What process should I use in determining the installation requirements, and who should be involved in making the cost-benefit trade-off decisions?"

As this example demonstrates, accurately identifying the customer on a project can be difficult. In a large and diverse customer group, it can be unclear exactly who has the authority to represent the group.

Therefore, in our search for stakeholders, it is useful to break the customer role into two primary contributors: those who supply requirements and those who provide funding.

## Customers Establish Requirements

Requirements are essential to defining the quality dimension of the cost-schedule-quality equilibrium. That means answering questions that include: "Who can approve the product requirements (or changes to the requirements)?" "Who will judge the success of the product?" "How will the product's users be represented to the project?" Those answers will unearth a variety of customers. Here are some guidelines for dealing with different customer groups:

- The project manager must distinguish between the people with final authority over product requirements, those who must be consulted as the requirements are developed, and those who simply need to be informed what the requirements are. Where there is a known customer, such as on defense, construction, professional service, or information system projects, it might seem easy to identify this stakeholder. But problems arise from the fact that so many people in the customer organization are anxious to offer product requirements, while so few of them will actually be paying the bills. (The responsibility matrix, described in Chapter 6, is a good tool for managing this challenge.)

- In the case of industries whose products have many customers (automobiles, software, appliances, etc.), the project manager must ascertain which departments should be included as stakeholders. In companies like these, there are so many ultimate customers that the project must develop alternate *customer representatives*. Marketing departments often fill this role by performing market research on what the next product should be, but problems may arise when other departments also want to be included.

Identifying the people and organizations with a stake in the product's features and performance is the first step toward managing the cost-schedule-quality equilibrium.

## Customers Provide Funding

The resources for any project are paid for by someone. It doesn't matter whether the resources are external vendors, purchased equipment and materials, or internal salaried staff. All of these resources cost money. Who approves this expenditure?

Funding for internal projects may seem to cloud this role, particularly when the same manager who is a project sponsor is also paying for a project. Simplify the discussion by staying focused on who approves the expenditure and who judges whether the money was effectively spent. These people will be key stakeholders.

## AFFECTED STAKEHOLDERS CAN MAKE CRUCIAL CONTRIBUTIONS

The effects of a project can be like the ripples caused by a stone hitting the water. Thinking past the first few ripples helps identify people and organizations that are necessary to complete the project or that will evaluate the project's success. The following examples of potential stakeholders should serve to stimulate the imagination of any project manager.

### Managers with Decision Authority

The project sponsor and customer make a lot of big decisions. But they don't make all the decisions. That's important to recognize early in the project, because waiting for a decision from a previously uninvolved person or organization can idle an entire project team.

Identifying the managers who will make decisions can be tricky. Start with the obvious ones:

- Managers whose operations will be affected by the outcome of the project.
- Managers representing other stakeholders, such as the customer.
- The manager to whom the project manager reports.

For each of these managers, keep in mind why they will be interested in your project and which decisions they will influence.

One less obvious decision-maker is the one with veto authority. As an example of the importance of this task, consider the story of a training department in a large company that decided to create a project management curriculum. The training specialist responsible for the curriculum proposed a progression of courses, from basic topics, such as scheduling through advanced topics, such as negotiating and program management. It was a very thorough curriculum, based on requirements gathered from organizations throughout the company and available courses from respected vendors. But the proposal wasn't implemented. The manager responsible for purchasing and administering this curriculum looked at the number of students projected annually for the intermediate and advanced topics and decided there was not enough demand to warrant the overhead associated with these courses. It was difficult to dispute the decision because this manager was applying sound, stated company policy.

The training specialist had not considered this stakeholder or his veto power, and the result was a dramatically scaled-down curriculum with a far smaller scope. The question that wasn't asked soon enough was: "Who will be involved in approving this curriculum?"[1]

## Ask the Right Questions About Managers

Which managers will make decisions? Who has veto power? Who is indirectly affected by these decisions? These are the kinds of questions a project manager needs to ask when searching for stakeholders in the ranks of management. The responsibility matrix described in Chapter 6 is an excellent tool for distinguishing between the different types of stakeholder involvement.

## No Project Is an Island

Every project happens within the context of a larger community. The ripples of a project may include compliance with specific regulations regarding stakeholder engagement.

At public-sector agencies, project managers need to follow the customs and laws governing public works projects. These municipal projects present special challenges, because the customer group is composed of all the citizens who will use the utility, road, or other service built by the project. Citizens also fund the project.

Federal, state, and local government agencies have laws and regulations affecting all facets of our lives, and their representatives are frequently stakeholders on all kinds of projects. Do you need a permit? An inspection? Approval from the Federal Energy and Regulatory Commission or the Food and Drug Administration?

Are you borrowing money to fund a project? The bank may require more insurance than you consider necessary. Will your computer system communicate with other systems? That interface represents an external constraint.

These stakeholders are neither for nor against your project, but they all impose their own requirements that your team must understand.

The list of stakeholders that represent external constraints goes on and on. To find these stakeholders, ask these kinds of questions:

- Are there laws and regulations directly affecting my project? If yes, who represents these rules and laws?
- Does the project require approvals from outside people or organizations?

- How does my project or product connect to existing systems, infra-structure, and processes, and who represents these interfaces?

Continuing to follow the ripples caused by the project leads to the innocent bystanders who could become opponents if you don't under-stand their stake. Here are a few more questions: Whose daily routine, whose property, and whose products or profits will you affect either during the project or as a result of it? Who will be worse off because of your project?

By considering more than the obvious stakeholders, we encounter a much wider audience. These people and organizations may become advocates or opponents, but you can't influence them if you don't understand their stake.

### Small Projects Can Have a Big Impact

Some small project teams can have a disproportionately large number of stakeholders. A cross-functional team formed to redesign a busi-ness process that cuts across the enterprise will find that stakeholder identification and management consumes a large amount of the team's effort. While a small team might feel justified in a few project management shortcuts, thorough stakeholder analysis is never the place to scrimp. A strategy for effective stakeholder engagement applies equally to large and small projects.

### ENGAGE AFFECTED STAKEHOLDERS

It should be clear by now that the obvious stakeholders are often just the tip of the iceberg. As illustrated in Figure 5.1, stake-holder identification extends our circle of engagement as we recognize those who will make a key contribution or will evaluate the success of the project.

Table 5.1 shows an initial stakeholder analysis tool. Use it to capture assumptions about stakeholders. The most important stake-holders will become clear. Others will safely be ignored because of their low contribution to or impact from the project. From here, the analysis of how to engage stakeholders begins.

This initial analysis reveals a particularly critical group of stake-holders: those who will have to change their behaviors in order for the project to deliver results. Much experience has demonstrated that it isn't enough to *tell* these people to change; they must be actively engaged to win their cooperation. These strategies and techniques fall into the practice of *change management*, which is introduced in the following box.

**TABLE 5.1    Initial Stakeholder Inventory**

Each stakeholder either contributes to the project, expects something from the project, or both. Some stakeholders are much more important to the project than others, so rank them using the second column.

| Name, Title, Organization | Importance to Satisfy 1-2-3 | Contribution (Input) | Expectation (Output Received) |
|---|---|---|---|
|  |  |  |  |
|  |  |  |  |
|  |  |  |  |

*Used by Permission of Mandy Dietz*

## CHANGE MANAGEMENT: ENGAGING THE OFT-FORGOTTEN STAKEHOLDERS: IMPACTED EMPLOYEES

### Tim Creasey

An excellently managed project, a perfectly optimized process, a perfectly designed technology — none deliver the expected value if they aren't adopted by the employees who must change the way they do their jobs as a result of your project — a group of stakeholder who are often forgotten. *Change management* has emerged over the past two decades as a complementary discipline to project management. The practice is backed by research and focuses on the individual transitions that impacted employees experience during a project. It applies rigor, processes, and tools to drive the people-dependent portion of project ROI.

Motivating individual employees to adopt and use new solutions is important because new systems and tools do not create expected results unless people use them. Some portion of the project's benefits comes from installation of the solution, but much of the benefits depend upon the solution actually being adopted and used. Change management assists the people who adopt the new solution to understand why and how to make that transition. Research shows a direct correlation between effective change management — catalyzing employee adoption and usage — and project success. Additionally, research shows that by investing up-front in supporting employee transitions, projects are more likely to finish on time and on budget as well.

### A Model for Change Management

The Prosci ADKAR Model identifies the five building blocks of successful individual change: Awareness, Desire, Knowledge, Ability and Reinforcement®. The elements of ADKAR are the individual milestones of successful change.

**The first step** in applying effective change management is to understand who will have to do their jobs differently as a result of the project. Prosci has identified 10 aspects of an employee's job your project might impact: processes, systems, tools, job roles, critical behaviors, mindsets/attitudes/beliefs, reporting structures, performance management, compensation, or location. Given each of these ten areas, ask, "Which groups of employees will your project impact?" And "How much of each aspect are you impacting for each group?" This inventory of impacted groups forms the foundation of planning for effective change management, including: creating the change scorecard, segmenting communication audiences, evaluating sponsor support requirements, and developing training.

**The second step** is to leverage the activities that research has established for driving employee adoption and usage. Prosci's eighth benchmarking study (2014) identified seven top contributors to change management success: sponsorship, communication, manager engagement, employee engagement, use of a structured approach, use of a dedicated change management leader, and integration with project management. The first four directly drive adoption and usage while the three govern how change management is applied. Since all changes are unique, a customized strategy provides direction. And the resulting plan of scaled and targeted activities for supporting individual transitions become the project team's change management deliverables that can be integrated as a project work stream.

### Add Change Management to Your Project Plan

When launching a new project, consider how much of your expected results and outcomes depend on employee adoption and usage. Then integrate activities focused on supporting individual transitions into your existing project management activities. Incorporating individual transition milestones and change management deliverables enables project teams to deliver more than just an installed technical solution; the organization realizes the actual promised value of the project.

Tim Creasey, Prosci chief development officer, is a dynamic thought leader and speaker whose focus is enabling change teams to deliver results by catalyzing employee adoption and usage. Prosci has researched change management for 20 years and provides holistic solutions to build organizational change competency.

## LEAD THE STAKEHOLDERS

This chapter has emphasized the importance of stakeholders, the people who will judge the success of the project and those who make essential contributions. As the project manager, you not only need to know who your stakeholders are, you also need to exercise leadership with this diverse group. Since no one knows more about your project than you do, it is up to you to lead the project in the right direction. Here are a couple of ways to exercise this leadership:

- *Control who becomes a stakeholder.* As noted, among functional managers and customers there are always plenty of people anxious to influence your project. However, if you feel that certain people don't have the right to this influence, you need to push back. You can obtain the support of your sponsor or other stakeholders in this endeavor, but you have to use whatever persuasive skills you possess to control who is allowed to influence the project.

- *Manage upward.* Many of the stakeholders, including your sponsor, functional managers, and some of your customers, will have more formal authority than you do as the project manager. But they need you to lead them. They need you to ask the hard questions, provide reasonable alternatives, confront them with facts, and continually motivate them toward action by your own persistence and enthusiasm.

## END POINT

Because they include everyone with a vital interest in a project, stakeholders are the heart of a successful project—and the heart of successful project management involves satisfying the expectations of these stakeholders. Finding the key stakeholders is easier said than done. The project manager and team must make a focused effort, asking over and over in different ways the two basic questions:

1. Who will contribute to accomplishing the project?
2. Who will be affected—either during or as a result of the project?

### FAST FOUNDATION IN PROJECT MANAGEMENT

At first, stakeholder identification sounds pretty straightforward—name the people who will affect the project or be affected. In fact, all too frequently some very important stakeholders are forgotten. The online Stakeholder Analysis form is a starting point for solving this problem. It is a checklist of possible stakeholders. The 20 questions on the form will prod the team to think about all possible stakeholders, rather than just the obvious ones they already know. The real value will come as new questions are added to this list that are specific to your projects or industry.

Revisit this form at the end of your projects. Did you miss any important stakeholders during your initial stakeholder identification process? Could you add a question to the list that would have uncovered this stakeholder? As your list grows, so will the probability that you've found all the important stakeholders.

Turn to page 491 to see an example of this form.

### PMP Exam Prep Questions

1. You are assigned to a new data warehouse project and notice in the charter that there are four business units listed as sponsors. The data warehouse system has been discussed at your organization for some time, but it's everyone's first exposure to implementing one. Which of the following could present the biggest challenge on the project?

   a. Conflicting goals of the sponsors

   b. The implementation team

   c. The work breakdown structure (WBS)

   d. Integrated change control

2. The project manager is in the process of meeting with various people who are impacted by his new project. He is attempting to find out what their needs are for the project as well as any constraints and assumptions that they might be aware of. At the same time, the project manager is beginning to set expectations for the project. Which of the following is the best description of this?

   a. Stakeholder management

   b. Change control board

   c. Team member analysis

   d. Stakeholder identification

3. When creating a project management plan, which of the following is the best choice to create it?

   a. Project manager

   b. Project manager and team

   c. Team

   d. Sponsor

4. An Internet project is about 65 percent complete and has had its challenges. As of the last status report, it appears to be on track regarding cost, schedule, and scope. Senior management tells you that the sponsor has some serious concerns about the project. You don't understand why, based on the last status report. What would be the best thing to do first?

   a. Evaluate the schedule and budget to verify the triple constraint health of the project.

b. Ignore senior management, as the project is in good shape.

c. Tell senior management that the project is in good shape.

d. Meet with the sponsor and find out what the sponsor's concerns are.

5. The customer has just attended the weekly staff meeting for the infrastructure project and has stated that the market is changing for the product being created. As a result of this, the customer has requested a significant change to the project. The project is 85 percent complete. What does the project manager do?

a. Tell the customer the project is too close to being complete to integrate the change.

b. Evaluate the impact to the project and let the customer know the options and impact of the change.

c. Ignore the customer, hoping the change will disappear.

d. Make the new work a new project and release the project as is to the market.

Answers to these questions can be found at www.VersatileCompany .com/FFMBAinPM.

# Write the Rules: Key Documents to Manage Expectations and Define Success

## INTRODUCTION

Every project is different. Different schedules, different products, and different people are involved. And, on any given project, the various stakeholders may have differing ideas about what the project is about. Your job, as project manager, is to make sure that everyone involved understands the project and agrees on what success will look like. The term *project rules* is not in any project management text or glossary. But clarifying the rules of the game for a new project is exactly what skilled managers need to do. And before they can communicate these rules to the players, they must be absolutely sure of them themselves. As in any new game, a project manager might ask: Who is on my side? How will we keep score? What is the reward? Seasoned project managers know that a new project can be as different from its predecessor as ice hockey is from gymnastics.

The need for project rules is part of the challenge of each new project. Since each one is different, you have to re-create the basic roles and processes of management every time a project begins. A close parallel is what happens in a reorganization of a company.

After a reorg, the typical questions are: Who is responsible for what? How will we communicate? Who has authority? If these questions are not answered, the organization will fall apart; the same holds true for projects.

## PROJECT RULES ARE THE FOUNDATION

**KEY CONCEPT** Remember the five project success factors? These were defined in Chapter 1 and include agreement on goals, a plan, good communication, scope control, and management support. No less than three of these crucial factors are dependent on a careful writing of the project rules:

1. *Agreement on the goals of the project among all parties involved.*
2. *Control over the scope of the project.*
3. *Management support.*

This chapter looks at how to create project rules that will address these three factors. All project management activities flow from and depend on these rules, which is why there must be general acceptance of the project rules before the project begins. All the stakeholders—project team, management, and customer—must agree on the goals and guidelines of the project. Without these documented agreements, project goals and constraints might change every day. They are the guidelines that orchestrate all aspects of the project. Let's take a closer look at how a careful writing of the project rules can influence our three success factors:

1. *Agreement on the goals.* Getting agreement on project rules is rarely easy. This is because the views of all the stakeholders must be heard and considered. This give-and-take may be so time-consuming that some may push for moving on and "getting to the real work." This haste would be counterproductive, however. If the stakeholders can't come to agreement on the basic parameters of the project before the work begins, there is even less chance they will agree after the money begins to be spent. The time to resolve different assumptions and expectations is during this initial period before the pressure is turned up. One of the definitions of a successful project is that it meets stakeholder expectations. It's the job of the project manager to manage these expectations, and this job begins by writing them down and getting agreement. Project rules document stakeholders' expectations.

    Project rules also set up a means by which the project may be changed in midstream, if necessary. This *change control* stipulates that the same stakeholders who agreed to the original rules must approve any change in the rules. (For more on change control, see Chapter 15.) The possibility of changes emphasizes once again the necessity of having everything down on paper before the project begins. With this material in hand, the project manager will be well equipped to detail any effects that the changes might have on cost, quality, or schedule in an ongoing project.

2. *Controlled scope.* Because each project is different, each is an unknown quantity when it is started. This uniqueness adds to the challenge and fun of projects, but it can also lead to dramatic overruns in budgets and schedules. Later in the chapter, we'll look at several ways of avoiding these overruns by keeping the scope of a project clearly defined. A careful writing of the project rules is key in keeping the project team focused and productive.

3. *Management support.* It is a rare project manager who has sufficient authority to impose his or her will on other stake-holders. This is why a sponsor from senior management (as defined in Chapter 5) is a crucial factor in the success of a project. We will discuss how this management support may be written into the project rules. There are three methods to ensure that everyone understands, and agrees to, the project rules. The first, the *project charter*, is an announcement that the project exists. The other two, the *statement of work* (SOW) and the *responsibility matrix*, are developed concurrently and constitute the actual written documents containing the project rules.

*Note:* As you read this chapter it will be helpful to refer to the following online forms: Project Charter, Statement of Work, Small Project Statement of Work, and Definition Checklist.

## Stakeholders, Rules, and Project Communication

Putting together the lessons from the previous chapter on stakeholder identification with this chapter on setting expectations can feel a little bit like the old saying, "Which comes first, the chicken or the egg?" In reality, there are several things going on at the same time as a project starts up.

As you read this chapter, realize that you will probably be discovering stakeholders in order to write the statement of work and responsibility matrix. Another related project management deliverable that is often produced early in the life of a project is the *communication plan*. It will describe your expectations for who must be kept informed and how you'll do that. Read more about what that plan contains and related tips for creating it in Chapter 14.

## Embrace Your Opportunity for Leadership

Project definition is your first opportunity to step into a vacuum and fill it with momentum and direction. If you are lucky, the project was approved based on a solid proposal; however, it is not uncommon to start with a lot less. In many ways, you are creating something from nothing (or nearly nothing). Producing the documents described in this chapter is no small feat. This is not a technical writing task; it is a leadership challenge. Embrace the ambiguity as an opportunity to show you can bring people together. Recognize that others need you to step forward and take the reins. Envision the leader who can win cooperation from a disparate group of stakeholders, then be that leader!

## **KEY CONCEPT** PUBLISH A PROJECT CHARTER

In the early 1970s a television show began each episode with Jim Phelps, ably played by Peter Graves, accepting a dangerous, secret assignment for his team of espionage agents. Sometimes on an airplane, other times in a restaurant or at a newspaper stand, Phelps received a plain manila envelope containing photographs and a cassette tape. After describing the mission, the voice on the cassette always ended with the famous line, "This tape will self-destruct in five seconds." We knew the extent of their risk because week after week the message was consistent: Phelps and his agents were working alone and, if caught, would not be assisted or recognized by the government of the United States. Dangerous, mysterious, and always successful, *Mission: Impossible* brought a new cold war victory every week.

With his committed team and detailed plans, Jim Phelps is a study in successful project management, with one exception—the *Mission: Impossible* team required complete secrecy and anonymity. No one could know who they were or what they were doing. Most corporate and government projects are exactly the opposite. Project managers don't need secrecy; they need recognition.

Because projects are unique and temporary, a project manager's position and authority are temporary. When a project begins, most of the people and organizations necessary for its success don't even know it exists. Without formal recognition, the project manager operates much like Jim Phelps, mysteriously and without supervision, but with far less spectacular results. That's why a project charter is so important; it brings the key players out into the open where everyone can see them.

A project charter announces that a new project has begun. The purpose of the charter is to demonstrate management support for the project and the project manager. It is a simple, powerful tool. Consider the following example.

During a major software product release, Sam, the project manager responsible for training over 1,000 help desk workers, selected a printer to produce the custom training materials required for the project. This large printing order was worth more than $500,000. After authorizing the printing, he was challenged by a functional manager who asked, "Who are you to authorize these kinds of expenditures?" (Sam is not a functional manager.) Sam responded by simply producing a charter and the statement of work for his project, signed by the program manager responsible for the entire release of the new product. "Any other questions?" he asked. "No. Sorry to have bothered you, Sam."

The charter clearly establishes the project manager's right to make decisions and lead the project.

## The Content and Audience of a Project Charter

**CONCEPT**  A charter is powerful, but it is not necessarily complex. As an announcement, it can take the form of an e-mail or a physical, signed document. It contains the name and purpose of the project, the project manager's name, and a statement of support from the issuer. The charter is sent to everyone who may be associated with the project, reaching as wide an audience as practical because its intent is to give notice of the new project and new project manager. The simplicity of the charter can be seen in Project Charter form available online.

### Establishing Authority

From their positions of temporary authority, project managers rely on both expert authority and legitimate authority. *Expert authority* stems from their performance on the job; the better they perform their job and the more knowledge and ability they display, the greater authority they will be granted by the other stakeholders. *Legitimate authority* is the authority conferred by the organization. The project charter establishes legitimate authority for the project manager by referencing the legitimate authority of the sponsor. In the preceding example, Sam received authority from the program manager for his specific project. The charter said, in effect, "If you challenge Sam within the scope of this project, you are also challenging a powerful program manager."

### Project Managers Need Expert Authority

Don't be misled by the power of the charter. Legitimate authority is important, but it is not sufficient. Project managers, like all leaders, lead best when they have established expert authority.

## Getting the Right People to Sign the Charter

The charter establishes legitimate authority, so the more authority the signature has, the better, right? Not necessarily. If every project charter had the signature of the company president, it would soon become meaningless. The sponsor is the best person to sign the charter, because he or she is the one who will be actively supporting the project. For internal projects, the customer is another good choice for signing the charter. Every project manager would benefit greatly by a show of confidence from the sponsor and the customer.

### *Project Charter* Can Have Two Meanings

There are two ways most firms use the term *project charter*. One is the way it is described here: as a formal recognition of authority. This is the way the Project Management Institute recognizes the term.[1] The other refers to the project definition document described in this chapter as a statement of work. Both uses will probably continue to be widespread.

### The Charter Comes First

This chapter describes techniques that document the project rules: the statement of work and the responsibility matrix. Both of these are agreements among the stakeholders. The charter, on the other hand, is an announcement, which makes it different in two ways. First, it should precede the other documents, because formal recognition of the project manager is necessary to get the agreements written. Second, it is not meant to control changes that occur later in the project. The charter is a one-time announcement. If a change occurs that is significant enough to make the charter out of date, a new charter should be issued rather than amending the original.

## WRITE A STATEMENT OF WORK

Clearly documented and accepted expectations begin with the statement of work (SOW). It lists the goals, constraints, and success criteria for the project—the rules of the game. The statement of work, once written, is then subject to negotiation and modification by the various stakeholders. Once they formally agree to its content, it becomes the rules for the project.

### The Statement of Work May Be Called by Different Names

This is one project management technique that, though widely used, is called by many names. At least half the firms using the term *statement of work* use it as it is defined in this book. However, watch for these different terminologies and uses:

- The Project Management Institute favors *project scope statement*.
- Contracts between separate legal entities will contain a separate *statement of work* for each project or subproject.
- Some firms use the term *charter* instead of *statement of work*. This can be confusing because, as we have seen, the term *charter* has another common use in the project management vocabulary.

The term that an organization may use to describe the statement of work is ultimately unimportant. It is the content that matters, and this content must establish clear expectations among all stakeholders.

## ◇ DANGER! The Statement of Work Is Not a Contract

The statement of work content described next is used to manage expectations and establish agreements. However, the minimum content described cannot substitute for an actual contract between two legal entities. Rather, this format is best suited to initiating projects that are internal to an organization. You'll want to consult attorneys to add the additional content that a contracting document requires.

## STATEMENT OF WORK: MINIMUM CONTENT

Many different topics may be included in a statement of work, but certain types of content *must* be included. The Statement of Work form found online will help you create your own SOW.

### 1. Purpose Statement

*What* will we do on this project and *why* are we doing it? The purpose statement succinctly sets out the goal and justification for the project. Knowing the answers to what and why allows the project team to make more informed decisions throughout the project. In fact, nearly every decision on the project demands an understanding of why the project exists. This purpose describes the end result that justifies the effort and expense of the project.

Initiating a project actually requires answering *why* at many levels. The purpose statement does not attempt to provide all the answers. Neither the purpose statement nor the statement of work builds a complete justification for a project. That should be contained in a different document, typically called a *proposal*, a *business case*, or a *cost-benefit analysis*. If a project proposal exists, then reference it or even copy its summary into the SOW. Chapter 4 covers development of a project proposal in more detail.

### Purpose Statements Need to Be Clear

*TIP*

Avoid purpose statements like the following: "The purpose is to build the product as described in the specification document XYZ." "The purpose is to deliver the product that the client has requested." Neither of these statements explains why the project is being done, so they are useless as guides for decision making.

Here is an example of a good purpose statement from an information systems project:

> *The purpose of this project is to gather revenue data about our subsidiary. During the spin-off of the subsidiary, the finance group needs this information about the subsidiary's business in order to make projections about its future revenue. This data will come from the four months beginning June 1 and ending September 30. The finance group will be finished analyzing the data October 31, and won't need it afterward.*

Notice that this purpose statement doesn't describe in detail what data is needed. That belongs in another document called the *analysis document*. Because the purpose statement is so clear, the team is able to make other decisions, such as producing minimal system documentation. The project team knows that the life of the product is so limited that it -won't require lengthy documentation meant for future maintenance programmers.

The purpose can also include the measurable goal for the project's result. The success of an advertising campaign, for example, is the impact it makes on the target market. Therefore the purpose could include:

> *Retail sales of our product will increase by 5 percent among 25- to 40-year-old females living in the San Francisco Bay area within three months of the beginning of the campaign, and by 10 percent after one year.*

### 2. Scope Statement

*Project scope* is all of the work required to meet project objectives. *Scope creep* is one of the most common project afflictions. It means adding work, little by little, until all original cost and schedule estimates are completely unachievable. The scope statement should describe the major activities of the project in such a way that it will

**TABLE 6.1   Sample Scope Statement**

**Project Management Training Rollout**

This project is responsible for all training development and delivery. Specifically, this project will:

- Provide a detailed statement of training objectives for approval by the project office, VP of operations, and director of human resources.
- Purchase the necessary equipment and outfit training rooms at each division office.
- Acquire the rights to use and modify training materials previously developed by training suppliers.
- Modify or oversee modification of the training materials to be consistent with company standards for project management.
- Produce or contract out the production of training materials.
- Train and certify instructors.
- Promote the training to the management team at all divisions.
- Oversee the scheduling of classes, instructors, and shipments of course materials.
- Oversee and authorize travel requirements. Produce or contract out the production of training materials.

The following activities are critical to the success of the project, but beyond the scope of the project:

- Standardize the company's project management practices across divisions.
- Recruit trainers with subject-matter expertise.
- Identify the people who will attend the training.
- Schedule the classes at the individual sites at times that accommodate the people who will be attending.
- Administer training logistics for each site.

*This scope statement is only one section within the project's statement of work.*

be absolutely clear if extra work is added later on. Consider the scope statement for a training project in Table 6.1. It's not as detailed as a project plan, but the major activities are named clearly enough to define what the project will and won't do.

Clarifying scope is more than just a fancy way of saying, "It isn't my job." All the cost, schedule, and resource projections are based on assumptions about scope. In fact, defining the limits of a project is so important that you will find boundaries being set in several different places besides the scope statement. The deliverables section of the statement of work and the work breakdown structure also set boundaries that can be used later to determine if more work is being added to the project. Even a product description such as a blueprint can be a source for defining scope and setting limits on scope creep.

Use the scope statement to define a project's place in a larger scenario. For instance, a project to design a new part for an aircraft will be a subset of the life cycle of the total product (that is, the entire aircraft; see the discussion of projects versus products in Chapter 3). The scope statement is the correct place to emphasize the relationship of this project to other projects and to the total product development effort.

### Specify What Is Beyond the Project's Scope

Be sure to specify what the project will *not* deliver, particularly when it is something that might be assumed into the project. Some activities may be out of the scope of the project but nonetheless important to successful completion. For example, in Table 6.1, "Recruit trainers with subject-matter expertise" is obviously a necessary part of training development and delivery, but it is specifically excluded from the project by placing it in the list of activities "beyond the scope of the project."

### Product Scope Versus Project Scope

Product scope can remain constant at the same time that project scope expands. If that sounds confusing, remember that *product scope* consists of the features and performance specifications described in product design specifications. Project scope is *all the work* necessary to meet project objectives. For example, if an electrical contractor estimates the work on a job with the assumption that he or she will be installing a special type of wiring, the contractor would do well to clarify who is responsible for ordering and delivering the materials. Taking on that responsibility doesn't change the *product* scope, but it adds work for the contractor, so the *project* scope is expanded.

## 3. Deliverables

What is the project supposed to produce? A new service? A new design? Will it fix a product defect? Tell a team what it's supposed to produce. This helps to define the boundaries of the project and focuses the team's efforts on producing an outcome. *Deliverable* is a frequently used term in project management because it focuses on output. When naming deliverables, refer to any product descriptions that apply—a blueprint, for instance. Once again, don't try to put the product description in the statement of work; just reference it.

Realize that there can be both intermediate and end deliverables. Most homeowners don't have a blueprint for their houses, but they get along fine without it. At the same time, no home buyers would want their contractor to build without a blueprint. The distinction lies in whether the deliverable is the final product that fulfills the purpose of the project—in this case, the house—or whether it is used to manage the project or development process, like a blueprint. Here are some other examples:

- A document specifying the requirements of a new piece of software is an intermediate deliverable, while the finished software product is an end deliverable.

- A description of a target market is an intermediate deliverable, while an advertising campaign using magazine ads and television commercials is an end deliverable.

- A study of a new emergency room admissions policy is an intermediate deliverable. The actual new emergency room admissions process is an end deliverable.

It's important to note that project management itself has deliverables (as in the deliverables associated with each phase of a project life cycle, as discussed in Chapter 3). The statement of work can call for deliverables such as status reports and change logs, specifying frequency and audience.

### Always Start with a Detailed Product Description

If there is no detailed product description, then creating one should be the *only* deliverable for a project. Trying to nail down all the important parameters, such as cost, schedule, resource projections, and material requirements, is futile if the product specification isn't complete, because the project team doesn't really know what they are building. Software product and information system projects are famous for committing this crime against common sense. It is premature to give an estimate for building a house before the design is complete, and it doesn't work any better in other disciplines. (For more on this problem, see "Phased Estimating" in Chapter 11, and the discussion on development life cycles and phases in Chapter 3.)

### 4. Cost and Schedule Estimates

Every project has a budget and a deadline. But the rules should state more than just a dollar amount and a date. They should also answer questions like: How fixed is the budget? How was the deadline arrived at? How far over budget or how late can we be and still be successful? Do we really know enough to produce reliable estimates? In addition, because cost and schedule goals have to be practical, it makes sense to ask other questions, such as: Why is the budget set at $2.5 million? Why does the project need to be finished December 31? Since one of the goals of making the rules is to set realistic expectations for project stakeholders, these figures must be realistic and accurate. (Any reasonable cost or schedule estimate requires using the techniques laid out in Part 3, "The Planning Process.")

### Write It All Down!

**DANGER!** Someone once observed that, when given a range of possible dates and costs, the customer remembers only the lowest cost and the earliest date. (How nice that the customer is such an optimist and has such great confidence in the project manager and his or her team!) That is exactly why it is so important to get all assumptions and agreements written down and formally accepted. The written statement of work is a much better tool for managing stakeholders than is memory.

### 5. Measures of Success

How will we decide whether the project is complete and successful? If we produce the deliverables on time and on budget, what else does it take to be judged successful? This is an opportunity to shape the way the project is performed and to clarify the finish line. It may not be enough just to complete the deliverables. For example, on a project to replace a section of an oil pipeline, a measure of success was "No measurable oil spills," because the pipeline was in an environmentally sensitive area. When a department store chain installed a major upgrade to its nationwide inventory system, it was made clear that "Installation will not interrupt any customer interactions at the retail stores."

Specific and measurable goals provide the basis for agreement on the project. If the oil pipeline project had simply stated that "The project will be executed in an environmentally sensitive manner," a project team would have had to interpret what that meant. "No measurable oil spills" was a clear standard that would influence decisions on the project.

Measures of success also establish the exit criteria for the project, also known as customer acceptance criteria. "The project shall be judged complete when . . ." provides an opportunity to describe the target state and customer acceptance process. It is another perspective on managing scope.

### 6. Stakeholders

In any statement of work, the project manager should identify anyone who will influence the project—that is, all the stakeholders.

Stakeholders are described in Chapter 5. List the major stakeholders, what role they'll play, and how they'll contribute to the project.

### 7. Chain of Command

Who reports to whom on this project? A statement of work must make this clear. A common way to illustrate the chain of command is with an organization chart. The need for a defined chain of command becomes increasingly important as the project crosses organizational boundaries. Figure 6.1 is an organization chart for an internal project in which all the stakeholders report to the same person. It spells out who will make decisions and which superior to refer a problem to. Since customers also make decisions, it is often useful to include their reporting structure in the SOW as well.

### *Go Beyond the Minimum*

After including all the necessary content listed here, be sure to add any other assumptions or agreements that are unique to this project. But be careful. Putting everything you can think of into the SOW will make it unmanageable. Remember that its purpose is as a tool to manage stakeholders.

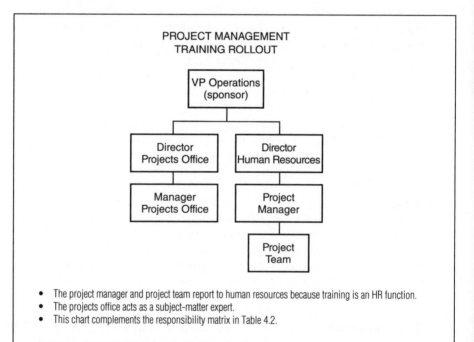

FIGURE 6.1 *Example: Organization chart.*

### Write the Statement of Work First

You, as project manager, need to write out the statement of work and then present it to the stakeholders. Even though you may not know all the answers, it is easier for a group to work with an existing document than to formulate it by committee. The stakeholders will have plenty of chances to give their input and make changes once the SOW is presented to them. (Experience has shown that after all the storm and fury of group discussion is over, you may find that as much as 80 percent of your document remains as you wrote it.)

### The First Change Control Tool

The statement of work is a tool for managing expectations and dealing with change. Should there be disagreements once the project has started, these can often be solved by simply reviewing the original agreement. It is also true that the original agreements and assumptions may change during the course of a project. In this case, all stakeholders must understand and agree to these changes, and the project manager must write them into the SOW. The SOW that remains at the end of the project may be very different from the original document. The amount of this difference is not important; what is important is that everyone has been kept up-to-date and has agreed to the changes.

### The Foundation of the Statement of Work

The basic content of the project proposal described in Chapter 4 overlaps the content found in the statement of work. That makes sense, because both are used to move a project from an inspiration to a tangible, achievable goal. Since the proposal is written first, any overlap with the statement of work represents an opportunity either to verify an earlier assumption or to develop that topic in greater detail.

## RESPONSIBILITY MATRIX

A statement of work answers many questions about a project, including the purpose, scope, deliverables, and chain of command. There is, however, a need for another document that precisely details the responsibilities of each group involved in a project. It is known variously as a responsibility assignment matrix (RAM), RACI (responsible, accountable, consulted, informed) chart, or simply *responsibility matrix*. The importance of this document is growing as corporations reengineer themselves and form partnerships and virtual companies. In these kinds of environments, many groups that otherwise might have nothing to do with each other are brought together to work on projects.

A responsibility matrix is ideal for showing cross-organizational interaction. For example, when a truck manufacturer creates a new cab style, it requires changes in tooling for the supplier as well as on the assembly line. The inevitable questions then arise: Who will make design decisions? Will the supplier have a voice in these decisions? When does each group need to get involved? Who is responsible for each part of the project? The responsibility matrix is designed to answer questions like these.

### Setting Up a Responsibility Matrix

A responsibility matrix lays out the major activities in the project and the key stakeholder groups. Using this matrix can help avoid communication breakdowns between departments and organizations because everyone involved can see clearly who to contact for each activity. Let's look at the steps involved in setting up a responsibility matrix:

1. *List the major activities of the project.* As shown in Table 6.2, only the major project activities are listed on the vertical axis; detailed task assignments will be made in the project plan. (Table 6.2 is a sample responsibility matrix for the training project described in Table 6.1.) Because the responsibility matrix shows interaction between organizations, it needs to emphasize the different roles required for each task. In highlighting the roles of the various stakeholders involved in the project's major activities, the matrix in Table 6.2 uses the same level of detail as the scope statement in Table 6.1.

   On very large projects it can be useful to develop multiple responsibility matrixes with differing levels of detail. These matrixes will define subprojects within the larger project.

2. *List the stakeholder groups.* Stakeholder groups are listed on the horizontal axis of the matrix. Notice how groups such as project team and user council can be named rather than individual team members; these individual team assignments are documented in the project plan. It is appropriate, however, to put individual names on the matrix whenever a single person will be making decisions or has complete responsibility for a significant part of the project.

3. *Code the responsibility matrix.* The codes indicate the involvement level, authority role, and responsibility of each stakeholder. While there are no limits to the codes that can be used, here are the most common ones:

   R—Responsible for execution. This person or group will get the work done.

**TABLE 6.2  Responsibility Matrix for Project Management Training Rollout**

| Activity | Training Team Project Manager | Project Office | VP Operations | Site Coordinators | HR Director |
|---|---|---|---|---|---|
| Develop training objectives | R | C/A | A | A | A |
| Outfit training rooms | R | | A | R | |
| Acquire the rights to use/modify training materials | R | C | A | | C |
| Modify training materials | R | I | | | |
| Establish materials production process | R | | A | | C |
| Recruit qualified trainers | I | C/A | A | | R |
| Train and certify instructors | R | | | | I |
| Promote training to divisions | R | R | R | R | R |
| Schedule classes, instructors | R | I | I | R | |
| Administer travel | R | | I | | I |
| Standardize project management practices | I | R | A | I | |
| Identify training participants | | | R | R | |
| Administer site training logistics | I | | | R | |

*Legend: R = responsible for execution; A = final approval authority; C = must be consulted; I = must be informed.*

• *The training team and project manager report to the director of human resources.*

• *The project office is not managing the project; they are the subject-matter experts.*

• *Notice how this responsibility matrix defines major tasks in much the same way as the scope statement in Table 6.1.*

• *The task level emphasizes the interaction among these stakeholders during the project.*

A—Approval authority (usually an individual). This person has the final word on decisions or on acceptance of the work performed (i.e., has final accountability for this activity).

C—Must be consulted. This group must be consulted as the activity is performed. The group's opinion counts, but it doesn't rule.

I—Must be informed. This group just wants to know what decisions are being made.

Notice how decisions can be controlled using A, C, and I. Specifying clearly these different levels of authority is especially useful when there are different stakeholders who all want to provide requirements to the project. For example, in Table 6.2, the project office has a say in selecting the basic course materials and instructors, but is only informed about modifying the training and is left out of certifying the instructors. By using the responsibility matrix to specify these responsibilities, the project manager (in the training department) has successfully managed the role of the project office.

4. *Incorporate the responsibility matrix into the project rules.* The matrix becomes part of the project rules, which means that once it is accepted, all changes must be approved by those who approved the original version. The advantage to this formal change management process is that the project manager is always left with a written document to refer to in the event of a dispute.

### Clarify Authority

When writing out the responsibility matrix, you need to leave no doubt about who must be consulted and which stakeholder has final authority. This will have the effect of bringing out any disagreements early in the project. It's important to make all these distinctions about authority and responsibilities early, when people are still calm. It's much more difficult to develop a responsibility matrix during the heat of battle, because people have already been acting on their assumptions and won't want to back down. Disagreements on these issues later in the project can escalate into contentious, schedule-eating -conflicts.

### END POINT

Each project is a new beginning, with new opportunities and new pitfalls. Making the project rules will put it on a firm footing and point it toward three of the five project success factors.

1. *The project team, customer, and management must all agree on the goals of the project.* Write down the goals and constraints in

the statement of work and let the stakeholders demonstrate their agreement by signing it.

2. *The size (scope) of the project must be controlled.* Listing the deliverables and writing the scope statement are the first steps for controlling scope. Once the statement of work is signed, it can be used as a tool to refocus all the stakeholders on the legitimate responsibilities of the project.

3. *Management support.* Tangible support from management starts with issuing the project charter and signing the statement of work.

The project definition activities in Chapters 4, 5, and 6 are the foundation of project management. The activities in the next two stages—planning and control—rely on the agreements made in the project rules. The project plan will depend heavily on the responsibilities, scope, and deliverables defined during this stage.

Making the project rules is also the first opportunity for the project manager to exercise leadership. Successfully bringing the stakeholders to an agreement about the fundamental direction of the project will establish your role as the leader.

## FAST FOUNDATION IN PROJECT MANAGEMENT

Start the project with a strong foundation. The *project proposal* assembles the information necessary for a sponsor or project selection board. The template for a proposal can be found in Chapter 4. The downloadable forms listed below address the key actions required to initiate the project with clear goals, effective communication, and management support.

- A project sponsor can use the *charter* template to formally authorize the project and project manager.

- The *statement of work* represents the formal agreement between project stakeholders about the goals and constraints of the project.

- The *responsibility matrix* clarifies the role and authority of each project stakeholder. See an example of this in Table 6.2.

- As you initiate the project, use the *definition checklist* to guide the team.

Download these forms at www.VersatileCompany.com/FFMBAinPM. Use these documents as the foundation of your own project management standards.

## PMP Exam Prep Questions

1. The pharmaceutical company is in the planning stages of a critical project and the project management team is finalizing the responsibility assignment matrix. How will this document benefit the team?

   a. The team will know who does what work and when they are to do it

   b. The team will know the sequence in which the resources are to perform the activities

   c. The team will know who is responsible for what work

   d. The team will know the location in which the work is performed

2. The project team has just started planning as a result of the charter being signed. Of the following, which does the charter not provide?

   a. Defines the scope statement

   b. Outlines the project manager's authority

   c. Contains or makes reference to the product description

   d. Gives the project existence

3. What can a responsibility matrix eliminate?

   a. Confusion about what order tasks come in

   b. Confusion about who is responsible for doing what

   c. Confusion about how long the tasks are

   d. Confusion about who is on the team

4. A new call center is being built to support a new product at a national telephone company. The company doesn't have any data on how long it will take to sign up customers via the call center. This data is important because it will help determine the number of employees needed in the call center. The company performs some tests to try to determine how long it will take to sign up customers. This test data is then incorporated into the projections and planning. What has the company just created?

   a. Team development

   b. Staff acquisition

   c. Assumptions

   d. Constraints

Answers to these questions can be found at www.VersatileCompany.com/FFMBAinPM.

## PART 3

# The Planning Process

*I keep six honest serving men*
*(They taught me all I knew);*
*Their names are What and Why and When*
*And How and Where and Who.*
*—Rudyard Kipling*

Was Kipling talking about project management? Maybe not, but his rhyme makes a good case for planning. Developing realistic cost and schedule commitments—and actually meeting them—requires detailed planning.*

The ultimate challenge in project management is *doing it right the first time*. But how can we be expected to produce accurate estimates when we're producing a unique product, one that hasn't been built before? How can we win cooperation from team members who don't really report to us? How can we manage stakeholder expectations so they get what they want *and* want what they get?

Accurate, organized information is the foundation of our ability to overcome these seemingly impossible obstacles. There are certain planning techniques that organize information in ways that enable us to make good decisions. There are a few ways that a project plan helps to organize a project:

*My thanks to Walter Derlacki, an experienced project manager and instructor, who introduced me to this project management rhyme.

- A plan analyzes in detail how to balance costs, schedule, and quality, providing data that the project manager uses to manage stakeholder expectations.

- A plan becomes the basis for evaluating progress during the project.

- A plan includes comparisons among possible strategies for executing the project, allowing the team to choose the approach with the best chance of success.

- The resource projections contained in the plan for each project can be combined to create resource projections for the entire department or company.

Like Kipling's honest serving men, the plan contains the *what*, *who*, and *when* of the project. Remember the five project success factors identified in Chapter 1: *clear goals, strong communication, management support, scope control*, and *a plan used to measure progress*. Every one of these relies on the kind of information found in the basic project plan, as described in Figure P.1. In Chapters 7 through 12 you will discover the tools for building the plan and the process for balancing it against reality.

The planning techniques in the next six chapters are the tools that seasoned project managers have used for decades to organize information to make better decisions. Like the rudder of a ship, information alone is not enough; but without it, the vessel and the project both recklessly wander out of control.

| ID | Task Name | Labor | Resource Names | Jun 15 | | | | | | | Jun 22 | | | | | |
|----|-----------|-------|----------------|--------|---|---|---|---|---|---|--------|---|---|---|---|---|
| | | | | S | M | T | W | T | F | S | S | M | T | W | T | F |
| 1 | Acquire lawn materials | 32 hrs. | Homeowner | | | | | | | | | | | | | |
| 2 | Remove debris | 256 hrs. | Teens, youth group | | | | | | | | | | | | | |
| 3 | Prepare soil | 32 hrs. | Teens, rototiller | | | | | | | | | | | | | |
| 4 | Plant lawn seed | 64 hrs. | Teens | | | | | | | | | | | | | |
| 5 | Plant shrubs | 32 hrs. | Teens | | | | | | | | | | | | | |

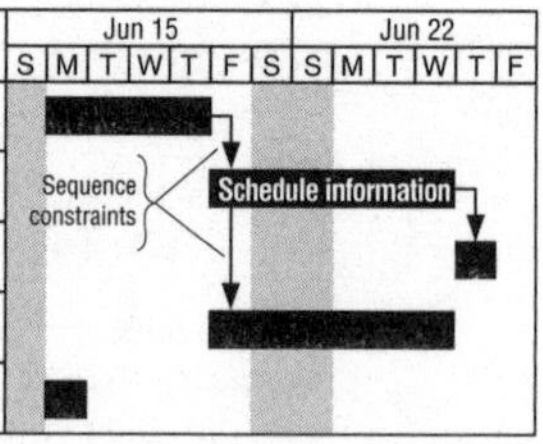

FIGURE P.1 *Essential project plan information.*

## CHAPTER 7

# Risk Management: Minimize the Threats to Your Project

## INTRODUCTION

Life is full of uncertainty. Project managers call that *risk*. Consider the following scenarios:

- A Silicon Valley software company subcontracts part of a product development effort to a software shop in Los Angeles. How will the project manager in San Jose make sure the subcontractor produces the right product on time?
- To reduce administration costs and streamline admissions, a hospital is considering reengineering its process for creating and storing patient records. How can hospital administrators accurately estimate the cost of the change when they aren't even sure what the change will entail?
- In the design to build a completely new fighter aircraft, a defense contractor specifies lightweight composite materials. How can the contractor be sure the new materials will hold up under the pressures a fighter jet endures?

In these projects, there is uncertainty about the schedule, the costs, and the quality of the end product. How can this uncertainty be managed?

*Risk management* is the means by which uncertainty is systematically managed to increase the likelihood of meeting project objectives. The key word is *systematically*, because the more disciplined the approach, the more we are able to control and reduce the risks. This chapter presents a framework for transforming the uncertainty inherent in projects into specific risks and developing strategies for managing them.

## The Risk Management Advantage

All projects experience the unexpected; but some project managers are ready for it. Impossible? The language of project risk management explains this phenomenon:

- *Known unknowns* represent identified potential problems, such as the possibility of a strike when a labor contract expires, or enough rain to stall a construction project during winter in Seattle. We don't know *exactly* what will happen, but we do know it has a potential to damage our project and we can prepare for it.

- *Unknown unknowns* are the problems that arrive unexpectedly. These are the ones you honestly couldn't have seen coming. But seasoned project managers do expect them, because they know something unexpected always happens.

The risk management advantage is that fewer problems catch the project team off guard. For every surprise thunder shower, the project manager just happens to have an umbrella handy.

The ability to prepare for and reduce uncertainty is well illustrated within the insurance industry, where risk management has become a sophisticated science. Actuaries are continually researching the probabilities of various calamities, and this research helps them set insurance premiums. Not only do insurance companies charge us for assuming risks, but they actively try to avoid risks by encouraging their policyholders to avoid risky behavior. Premiums are reduced for nonsmokers and for automobile owners with good driving records. The insurers even send representatives into businesses to advise them how to avoid accidents—and reduce the clients' premiums when they follow the advice.

## ALL PROJECT MANAGEMENT IS RISK MANAGEMENT

Insurance companies understand and practice risk management better than most project managers because they realize that it is their primary business. Not many project managers realize that it is

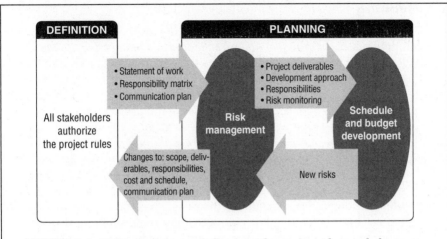

FIGURE 7.1 *Risk management influences the project plan and changes assumptions in the project rules.*

also *their* primary task, but those who do have an edge: They are constantly on the outlook for uncertainty that could lead to project failure.

Risk management is the primary job of a project manager? Yes, it's true, especially if you look at it this way: Every technique in every chapter of this book is really a risk management technique. Some techniques reduce the risk of being late. Others reduce the chances of overrunning the budget. A few address the process for ensuring the quality of the end product. And all techniques try to increase the satisfaction of every stakeholder and improve the chances of success.

All project management activities can be construed as managing risk, but the risk management process is a specific set of activities you'll consciously perform to identify and manage risks on the project. Like project definition, these are outcomes of the risk management process (see Figure 7.1). Let's consider the ways in which risk management activities relate to *project definition, project planning*, and *project control*.

### Definition

The first risks surface as the project is conceived, the business case is constructed, and the goals for cost, schedule, and product scope are developed. Initially, these risks may be listed as assumptions, but as it becomes clear that they represent specific threats, they become the first documented risks.

### Planning

Figure 7.1 shows the function of planning as having two major components: *risk management* and *schedule and budget development*. Schedule and budget development are the detailed plans required for day-to-day management of the project. Techniques for creating these detailed plans are described in the next three chapters. Risk planning represents the formal, conscious activities of the project manager and team to identify risks and to formulate strategies for managing the risks. *It cannot be overemphasized that risk planning happens repeatedly throughout the project.* Risk planning analyzes the project's deliverables, environment, and stakeholders from a critical perspective to find any weaknesses. The project team identifies risks and develops strategies for neutralizing the risks. Those strategies, in turn, will affect the detailed action plan and may require changes to the statement of work, responsibility matrix, or communication plan.

Risk management and detailed planning have a symbiotic relationship and are iterated two to four times before project execution begins. With each iteration, the assumptions are more fully exposed and the risk management plan and the detailed schedule and budget become a more accurate reflection of reality.

### Control

As the project is monitored for progress, known risks are watched and new risks are identified. Risks that don't materialize are removed from the risk plan, new risks are added, and the process of risk planning is repeated. All of these activities result in updates to the statement of work, budget reserves, progress reports, work breakdown structure, and the many other project management deliverables.

### Business Risk Versus Project Risk

The City of Seattle acquired a beautiful new office tower in the early 1990s after the lender foreclosed on the original developers. The city government was able to buy the building at a huge discount because so much of it was vacant. The developers had taken a risk in building the tower, and when the downtown office market hit a slump, they began to lose money. There was no evidence of cost overruns during construction; demand for office space simply didn't materialize.

This is an example of a successful project (a beautiful building, on time and on budget) that turned out to be an unsuccessful business venture. Business risk is inherent in all business activities, but it is seldom the project manager's job to manage it; that responsibility lies with the owner of the project. *Selecting the right project is business risk. Managing uncertainty to meet the stakeholders' objectives is project risk.*

### THE RISK MANAGEMENT FRAMEWORK

**CONCEPT** Figure 7.2 describes a risk management process that is repeated throughout the project:

- *Identify risks.* Systematically find all the factors that threaten project objectives.
- *Analyze and prioritize.* Assess each risk in terms of its possible damage and likelihood of occurrence. Most projects have an enormous number of potential risks. Quantifying the potential damage and the probability that a risk will occur enables the team to prioritize the risks, focusing their attention where it does the most good.
- *Develop a response.* Create strategies for reducing the possible damage and/or probability the risk will occur.

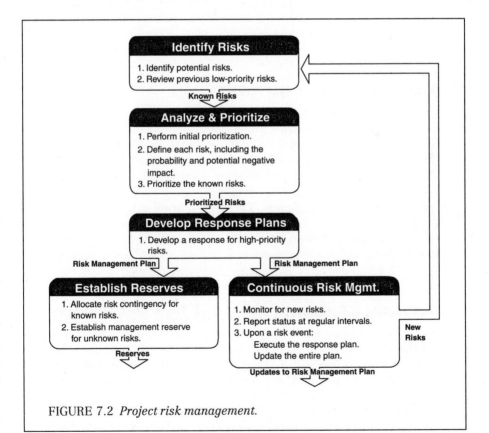

FIGURE 7.2 *Project risk management.*

- *Establish reserves.* Set aside additional funding for the project that will be used in case specific risks occur—the known risks—as well as funding for the unknown risks.

- *Continuous risk management.* Implement the strategies and monitor the effects of these changes on the project. Risk strategies may require fine-tuning as they are put into effect. Communicate with the stakeholders as new risks are found, known risks are avoided, and risk reserves are spent.

### Plan for Ongoing Risk Control

If it is smart to proactively plan for risk at the beginning of a project, it is even smarter to continuously plan for risk *during* the project. In the process of working through a project, new risks—both large and small—will usually emerge. Risk management is successful only if its steps are consciously repeated and applied to all risks throughout the life of the project. Planning for ongoing risk management is part of risk control and is usually documented either in the communication plan or in a specific risk management plan (to be discussed later).

### STEP ONE: IDENTIFY THE RISKS

One of the scenarios at the beginning of this chapter involved a defense contractor concerned about the strength of the new material the contractor was building into fighter planes. In this example, the first critical step of risk management was performed: The risk was identified. Identifying risk involves skill, experience, and a thorough knowledge of project management techniques—both the art and science of project management. There are four techniques for identifying risk: asking the stakeholders; making a list of possible risks (a risk profile); learning from past, similar projects; and focusing on the risks in the schedule and budget. We now look at these four techniques in detail, along with tips for making them work better.

### Gathering Information About Risk from Stakeholders

If you want to know what could possibly go wrong on a project, just ask the people on the team—they've probably been making their own lists since they were assigned to the project. Here are two ways to involve the team in identifying project risks.

1. *Brainstorming sessions.* Everyone's favorite method for generating ideas works well for identifying risks. Gather the stakeholders

and any others involved in the project and follow basic brainstorming rules:

- Generate as big a list of potential risks as possible. Don't try to evaluate the risks as they are named; let the creativity of the group flow.
- After generating a list of potential risks, combine similar risks and order them all by magnitude and probability. Risks that have little chance of affecting the project can be crossed off.

Don't try to solve all the risks at the meeting. If there are easy answers, be sure to capture them, but keep the session focused on *risk identification, not response development.*

2. *Interviewing.* Interviewing individuals about risk requires a more structured approach than brainstorming. Using a risk profile with specific questions will help stimulate the person being interviewed to think about all aspects of the project.

### Murphy's Risk Management Law

The art of identifying risk begins with a critical attitude. Because we're trying to find problems before they emerge, it's appropriate at first to adopt the attitude that "anything that *can* go wrong *will* go wrong." Later, after we've developed solid strategies for managing the risks, we can be optimistic again. There is, however, a big difference between a critical examination of the project to identify risks and plain old griping. It's up to the project manager to set the tone.

### Include All Perspectives

People bring different perspectives to the project depending on their project roles. Be sure to include customers, sponsors, team members, subcontractors, functional management, and people who have worked on similar projects. They all have a stake in the project and they'll gladly take this chance to help ensure its success.

### Using a Risk Profile

One of the best ways to ensure the success of a project is to apply the lessons learned from past projects. This is done by using a risk profile. A risk profile is a list of questions that address traditional areas of uncertainty on projects (see Table 7.1). These questions have been gathered and refined from previous, similar projects. Creating a risk profile is an ongoing process: At the end of this project, what has been learned will be incorporated into the profile.

### TABLE 7.1 Example: Risk Profile Questions

**Project Team**

1. How many people are on the team?
2. What percentage of the team is fully dedicated to the project?
3. Which team members will spend 20 percent or less of their time working on this project?
4. What is the experience level of the team?
5. Have team members worked together before?
6. Is the team spread out geographically?

**Customer**

1. Will the customer change current processes to use the product? (No) (Minor changes) (Major changes)
2. Will the project require the customer to reorganize? (No) (Minor changes) (Major changes)
3. Are the customers in different departments? In different companies?

**Technology**

1. Will there be technology that is new to the development team?
2. Will there be technology that is new to the users or customers?
3. Is there any new or leading-edge technology in the project?
4. Are the product requirements clearly documented and signed by all necessary stakeholders?
5. Are the product requirements stable?

**Executive Support**

1. Is there a known project sponsor who is actively involved in the project?
2. Is there sufficient recognition, support, and involvement from all the senior management required for the success of the project?
3. Is senior management setting deadlines or budget limitations independent of the project manager's schedule and budget estimations? If so, are these constraints realistic?

- Develop categories of risk; then list several questions for each category.
- Each question probes at a possible weakness.
- Add new categories and questions over time.

Good risk profiles follow these basic guidelines:

- *They are industry-specific.* For example, building an information system is different from building a shopping mall.
- *They are organization-specific.* While industry-specific profiles are a good place to start, the profiles are even better when they address risks specific to a company or department.

- *They address both product and management risks.* Risks associated with using or developing new technology are *product risks*. Management risk addresses project management issues, such as whether the team is geographically dispersed. Table 7.1 has examples of both product and management risks.

- *They predict the magnitude of each risk.* Even simple, subjective indicators of risk such as high, medium, or low contribute to a clearer assessment of specific risk factors. More specific quantitative indicators offer the opportunity for greater refinement and accuracy over many projects.

Risk profiles are generated and maintained by a person or group independent of individual projects. (See discussion of the project office in Chapter 18.) The keeper of the risk profile participates in post-project reviews to learn how well the risk profile worked and to identify new risks that need to be added to the profile. These profiles, when kept up-to-date, become a powerful predictor of project success. The combined experience of the firm's past projects lives in their questions.

It is even possible to buy good risk profiles. Consulting firms will sell them as part of their project management services. The Software Engineering Institute offers a detailed list of questions for evaluating risk on software projects in its *Continuous Risk Management Guidebook*.

## Historical Records

History continues to be the best predictor of the future. In addition to the history incorporated in the risk profile, a project manager can investigate what happened on similar projects in the past. There may be useful risk-related information already written down that you can tap into, such as:

- Planned and actual performance records that indicate the accuracy of the cost and schedule estimates.

- Issue logs that portray the unexpected challenges and relate how they were overcome.

- Post-project reviews that generate the lessons learned from the project; while these lessons are often ignored, they may be critical to the success of your project.

- Customer satisfaction records. Records like these are increasingly available in our service-oriented economy. You can mine them for the pitfalls or triumphs of your predecessors, particularly when a previous project generated either glowing praise or mountains of complaints from the customer.

### Be Your Own Historian

You can be your own source of historical records in the future. Organize project documentation in such a way that it will be easy to reference long after the project has been finished. Risk logs from previous projects will be particularly useful!

### Estimating Schedules and Budgets

Risk management contributes to detailed planning, but detailed planning is also an opportunity to discover risks (see Figure 7.1). As part of the plan, each low-level task will require a cost and schedule estimate. When you are involved in this process, watch for those tasks that are difficult to estimate; this usually means that there is some uncertainty associated with them. Treat these individual tasks the same way you would any other risk: Identify the reason for the uncertainty and create a strategy for managing it. (Chapter 11 deals in detail with estimating.)

The risks identified during scheduling and budgeting usually affect smaller parts of the project, but they are important just the same. Managing the small risks as well as the big ones means that little things are less likely to trip you up.

Recognizing detailed planning as a risk management opportunity further emphasizes the iterative and unbreakable relationship between risk planning and schedule development.

### STEP TWO: ANALYZE AND PRIORITIZE THE RISKS

Not every risk will jeopardize a project. Some are no more than pebbles in a pond; they cause a ripple that quickly subsides. But others resemble an underwater earthquake that causes a tsunami. Project managers must recognize the difference between the two. They must know how to discern the magnitude of the risk in order to develop an appropriate strategy to deal with it. There are three steps:

1. Define the risk, including the severity of the negative impact.
2. Assign a probability to the risk. How likely is it that this problem will occur?
3. Rank the risks according to probability and impact. This prioritized list focuses the project team on which risks they'll manage.

### Initial Risk Prioritization

If performed energetically, these risk identification activities will have created a long list of potential risks. However, many of these risks won't be worth managing—they'll have a low impact, a low probability, or both. Even without performing detailed analysis of these risks, the project manager and team will nonetheless be able to use their intuition to quickly sort through and winnow out the risks it doesn't pay to worry about. That means the outcome of the risk identification process is a list of known risks that are worth studying further.

## Defining the Risk

Being able to concisely describe the risk is essential to understanding it. The Software Engineering Institute offers this simple but effective format for recording a risk.

*Condition:* A brief statement describing the situation that is causing concern or uncertainty.

*Consequence:* A brief statement describing the possible negative outcomes that may be caused by the condition.

The more clearly the condition can be described, the more accurately the impact (consequence) can be predicted—and the better chance there will be of effectively managing the risk. Here's an example of a poorly defined risk:

*The project requires the use of technology that is new to the project team.*

This statement doesn't give any clues to how badly the cost and schedule might be affected. The new technology should be named, and why it is causing uncertainty should be explained.

Here's a statement that does it better:

*The state agency requires that all diagrams be developed using a software tool that our technical writers have not used before. In addition, the only boring machine that can handle the soil conditions is a complex product that has been used only a few times by our company.*

Now that's getting more specific. In fact, we see that there are two separate risks associated with new technology. Each should be addressed separately. That will also make it easier to assess the impact, or consequence, that attempting to use the new technologies could have on the project.

After you have successfully defined the risks, you need to record the consequence of these risks in terms of cost, schedule, and possible damage to the project. Cost and schedule affects are tangible and can be matched against the original cost-benefit analysis, while damage refers to the intangible negative effect of a risk.

### TABLE 7.2 Risk Analysis Example 1

| | |
|---|---|
| **Definition** | **Condition:** The soil conditions in the area where the pipeline crosses the river require a complex boring machine with which we have little experience. |
| | **Consequence:** Incorrectly operating the machine will damage it and/or the riverbank. Damage to the machine could cost from $50,000 to $250,000 in repairs and two to four weeks in lost time. Damaging the riverbank may result in landowners or environmental groups trying to prevent us from obtaining permits for future pipelines. |
| **Probability** | Probability of $75K equipment damage—20%<br>Probability of $200K equipment damage—20%<br>Probability of no equipment damage—60%<br>**Probable cost of equipment damage—$55K**<br>Probability of riverbank damage—25% |
| **Strategy** | The equipment provider will supply an experienced operator for an estimated cost of $10,000. Using its operator reduces the chance of equipment damage to less than 5% and the provider will bear the cost of repair. The probability of riverbank damage is also reduced to 5%. |

- The probability was determined from the experience of this company and interviews with two other companies that use the product.
- Probable cost of damage = ($75K × 20%) + ($200K × 20%)
- The strategy adds $10,000 to the project cost, but reduces the risk of cost damage to zero and the schedule risk to less than 5%. The risk of intangible cost due to riverbank damage is also reduced.
- The strategy is described in two project management tools:
  1. Communication plan—Includes increased monitoring and coordination activities with the equipment vendor.
  2. Project plan—Shows the equipment vendor as the resource on the task and the additional $10,000 in labor.
- This risk strategy is referred to as *risk transfer*, because the project pays the equipment operator to take the risk.

Tables 7.2 and 7.3 are examples of risk statements in which the condition and the consequence have been clearly defined. You'll find a Risk Analysis form online that can be used to document a risk in this way.

Just as the first rule of problem solving is to thoroughly understand the problem, the first rule of risk analysis is to thoroughly describe the risk.

## *TABLE 7.3* Risk Analysis Example 2

| | |
|---|---|
| **Definition** | **Condition:** The state agency requires that all diagrams be developed using a software tool that our technical writers have not used before. |
| | **Consequence:** All diagram generation and document management tasks will take longer. Limitations of the tool will cause rework. |
| **Probability** | On average, the slower work and the rework will add up to 25% more effort on documentation tasks.<br>Probable labor cost: $1.25 \times 20 = 25$<br>Probable schedule: $1.25 \times 4$ months $= 5$ months |
| **Strategy** | Send all the technical writers to a two-day course on the new tool. The training cost is $2,200. This will reduce the productivity factor to 1.1. |
| | Make one of the technical writers the tool expert. It will be his or her job to spend an average of one day each week to exercise the tool to find its limitations and to create standards and templates to build on its strengths. This will bring the productivity factor down to 1.0. |
| | The tool expert will spend five labor days to create document management strategies that ensure a smooth production process and eliminate rework. |

- The probability is a subjective estimate based on the average normal productivity of a junior technical writer versus a senior technical writer. Since all writers will be new to the tool, all are assigned the junior productivity factor.
- The normal cost for the required documentation is 20 labor months and the normal duration is 4 months.
- The strategy is to shorten the learning curve. It will cost 2 days of training (duration), and the time spent by the tool expert on experimentation adds a cost of 21 days (1 day a week for 4 months plus 5 days). So the new tool's duration consequence is cut to 5 days and the cost consequence is 21 days' labor plus the cost of training.
- The strategy is shown in the project plan, which shows the cost and duration of training and who will attend. Tasks are added for experimenting with the tool and developing tool standards. These additional tasks result in increased labor costs.

## Using Probability Theory in Risk Management

What are the chances of getting a six when rolling a single die? The math is pretty simple: There are six sides and all have an equal chance of being on top, so the probability is one out of six, or 0.167. How many houses in a specific area are likely to have flood damage in a year? An insurance company will count the number of houses in the area that have had flood damage in the past to predict flood damage in the future. What are the chances of falling behind on your project because a subcontractor doesn't come through? That's a little bit harder to quantify, but it's part of our job when we're analyzing risk.

Predicting the likelihood that a problem will occur contains the same difficulties as making any estimate. Many of the same rules apply to both. (See the golden rules of estimating in Chapter 11.) Looking at historical data will generally give the best indication of possible problems. But even when experienced project managers use all the tools at their disposal, assigning probabilities to a risk remains as much an art as a science. The sheer number of possible problems, including those that are intangible and impossible to quantify, requires that a project manager use creativity and intuition as well as knowledge and experience in assessing risks.

There is a temptation to flee from the hard work of developing a probability estimate for each risk. Often the hard data that makes statistical analysis possible just doesn't exist. Why worry about the infinite number of possible problems your project could encounter? That is exactly the point: Because there are an infinite number of possible risks to your project, it is necessary to quantify the known risks in order to prioritize them and establish a budget for managing them.

Assigning a probability to the risk helps to assess the consequences of the risk. If you multiply the probability of a risk by the negative consequences, you will begin to see how bad the risk really is. This is often referred to as the *expected value* of the risk:

$$\text{Probability} \times \text{Impact} = \text{Expected Value}$$

The example in Table 7.2 defines probability in terms of percentages to predict the probable cost of the damages. That means the expected value of the risk is $55,000. Understanding the expected value will influence the amount spent reducing the risk.

Even when there is absolutely no hard data available about a risk, the project manager can distill the intuition of the team to provide useful assessments of probability and impact. A common method (illustrated in Figure 7.3) is to use a consistent probability and impact matrix throughout the project. It uses subjective assessments to place risks in one of nine quadrants. Key components of using this subjective assessment are

- The same matrix must be used throughout the project, since the method relies on subjective judgment. This allows team members to adjust their thinking to a consistent reference point.
- It is okay to make a larger matrix. Again, make sure the same matrix is used throughout the project.

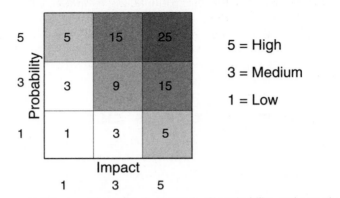

Team members can assign a ranking of 1, 3, or 5 to both probability and negative impact. Any risk whose total score is 5 or above should be analyzed further.

FIGURE 7.3 *Probability/impact matrix.*

- Continue to use objective data to quantify both probability and impact whenever possible; then place that risk in one of the quadrants. Using objective data for reference points makes the subjective judgments more consistent.
- Have a diverse group of project stakeholders assess the risks and then merge their assessments. If only the project manager is rating probability and impact, the ratings will be skewed by his or her unique perspective and risk tolerance.

Some risks have less to do with a specific event and more to do with the project's environment and its effect on productivity. For instance, the entire risk profile developed by the Software Engineering Institute addresses environmental risk factors such as the possible changes in requirements for a project, how skilled the project team may be, and the diversity of the user community.

Assigning a probability to risks from the project's environment relies on intuition and experience. You need to ask the right questions: How good are the team's skills, and how much faster or slower will this make them? How strong is the business case for the project, and how many major changes in requirements will happen? Because these factors are intangible, they are hard to assess; but if risk management is practiced systematically on all projects, at least there will be a record of how skillfully a manager used his or her intuition. This feedback will aid in making future risk assignments more accurate.

Finally, realize that assigning probabilities to risks is done for a very practical reason: You need to be sure that the size of the solution matches the size of the problem. The combination of subjective and objective assessments of known risks enables the team to rank the risks. The risks at the top will receive attention first, and the risks at the bottom of the list will be addressed later.

## STEP THREE: DEVELOP RESPONSE PLANS

Up to now, we've concentrated on assessing and quantifying the risks to a project's success. The time has come to develop strategies for dealing with these risks. This is the hard part, because there are as many ways to reduce risks as there are potential risks.

What is the best way to reduce a risk? The answer lies in the method we have discussed for assessing a risk: Reduce the impact, the probability, or both. For instance:

- If an event is out of my control but I can prepare for that event, then I have reduced the impact. That is why I take a first aid kit on a camping trip.
- In the risk example shown in Table 7.2, hiring an expert to operate a complex machine reduces the *probability* of an accident. In addition, because the risk is transferred to the owner of the equipment, the cost *impact* of an accident is reduced.

### Risk Response Strategies

There are basically five categories of classic risk response strategies: *accepting the risk*, *avoiding the risk*, *contingency plans*, *transferring the risk*, and *mitigating the risk*. Let's look at these in detail.

### 1. Accept the Risk

Accepting the risk means you understand the risk along with its consequences and probability, and you choose to do nothing about it. If the risk occurs, the project team will react. This is a common strategy when the consequences or probability that a problem will occur are minimal. As long as the consequences are cheaper than the cure, this strategy makes sense.

### 2. Avoid the Risk

You can avoid a risk by choosing not to do part of the project or by choosing a lower-risk (more predictable) option for meeting project objectives. This deletion of part of the project could affect more than the project—the business risk could also be affected. Changing the

**TABLE 7.4   Risk Beyond the Project's Control**

| | |
|---|---|
| **Definition** | **Condition:** The product design calls for a computer operating system that is yet to be released, and the manufacturer has a reputation for releasing unreliable products late.<br><br>**Consequence:** If the product doesn't meet specifications, custom software will have to be written. If the product is late, the entire project will be delayed. |
| **Probability** | Probability of the product having defects that affect the project is 15%.<br><br>Probability of the product being one month late (enough to negatively impact our project) is 30%. |
| **Strategy** | 1. **Avoid.** Choose a new design that relies on stable<br><br>2. **Monitor.** Get on the beta test team to have early access to the software and thoroughly test the features that affect the project. Two months prior to the planned project release, assess the probability of the risk and have an alternate design ready. |

Two possible strategies are listed. Each results in changes to project documentation.
1. Avoid
 • Project plan — Shows the new design and development tasks and the associated increase in cost and schedule.
 • Product requirements — Document any changes in the product's capability.
2. Monitor
 • Communication plan — Includes monitoring the beta test results and reporting them.
 • Project plan — Shows the additional activities for the beta test and development of the contingency design.

scope of the project might change the business case as well, because a scaled-down product could have smaller revenue or cost-saving opportunities (see Table 7.4). *Risk/return* is a popular expression in finance—if you want a high return on an investment, you'll probably have to take more risk. Avoiding risks on projects can have the same effect—low risk, low return.

### 3. Contingency Plans

When you can't influence the probability but can at least reduce the negative impact, monitor the risk and have an alternative course of action ready. Monitor a risk by choosing some predictive indicator to watch as the project nears the risk point. For example, if you are concerned about a subcontractor's performance, set frequent status update points early in the project and inspect his or her progress. The risk strategy in Table 7.4 is to monitor the risk by being part of the test team.

Contingency plans are alternative courses of action prepared before the risk event occurs. The most common contingency plan is to set aside extra money, a *contingency fund*, to draw on in the event of unforeseen cost overruns. It's important to make sure that this fund is used only for unforeseen cost overruns—not to make up for underestimating or substandard performance. Table 7.4 contains an example of a contingency—the project team is betting on a new technology, but they are also creating an alternative design that uses more stable technology. If it looks like the new technology isn't going to be workable, the team will have an alternative in place. It's important to note here that creating the alternative design probably costs a substantial amount. Contingency plans can be looked on as a kind of insurance and, like insurance policies, they can be expensive.

When using this "monitor and be prepared to act" strategy, two factors should be included in the risk response plan: *detectability* and *trigger events*.

1. A tricky factor in monitoring a risk is the ability to detect the risk in time to respond. For example, hurricane response procedures rely on the fact that most hurricanes can be tracked for several days as they develop over the ocean. Knowing the speed and intensity of the storm gives authorities time to broadcast instructions to local residents. Conversely, a tornado can form, touch down, and wreak havoc virtually without notice. For a known risk within the project, the team should assess the detectability using a subjective scale (such as 1 to 5, where 5 is "very difficult to detect"). The effort invested in monitoring the risk will reflect the probability, impact, and ability to detect. If a risk is particularly difficult to detect and the impact and probability are large, it probably justifies plenty of mitigation as well as contingency preparation.

2. Trigger events define the line we cross between monitoring the risk and implementing the contingency plan. Trigger events are described as objectively as possible, so it is clear when we've arrived at one. The reason for trigger events is illustrated in a well-known story: If a frog jumps into a pan of boiling water, it will immediately jump out. But if a frog is sitting in a cool pan of water that is placed on a stove, it will stay in the water until it is boiled to death. Trigger events help us recognize when the water in our project is too hot and we need to take action. The monitoring strategy in Table 7.4 has a trigger date set to monitor the risk and make a decision about whether to implement the contingency.

### 4. Transfer the Risk

Even though paying for insurance may be expensive, assuming all the risks yourself could cost a great deal more. Many large projects purchase insurance for a variety of risks, ranging from theft to fire. By doing this, they have effectively transferred risk to the insurance company in that if a disaster should occur the insurance company will pay for it.

While purchasing insurance is the most direct method of transferring risk, there are others. For example, hiring an expert to do the work can also transfer risk. In the example in Table 7.2, the project manager was concerned that a piece of heavy equipment operated by the project team would be damaged—or would damage the job site. The solution was to hire an operator from the company leasing the equipment. Because this operator works for the equipment leasing company, the leasing company would pay for any damage to the equipment or to the site.

Another way to transfer risk is to use a contract for service, in this case, a fixed-price contract. A *fixed-price contract* states that the work will be done for an amount specified before the work begins. Fixed schedules may also be added to such a contract, with penalties for overruns. With fixed-price contracts, project managers know exactly what the cost of this part of a project will be. They have effectively transferred the cost and schedule risks from the project to the subcontracting firm; any overruns will be the responsibility of the subcontractor. (The only downside to this scenario is that the subcontractor, knowing it will be held to the original bid, will probably make the bid higher to make up for the risk it is assuming.)

Another type of contract for service is called a *reimbursable*, or *cost-plus*, contract. Reimbursable contracts pay subcontractors based on the labor, equipment, and materials they use on a project.[4] The risk of cost and schedule overruns is borne completely by the project on these contracts. The project is not able to transfer risk with this kind of contract, but when the work to be performed is poorly defined, or the type of service is open-ended, a reimbursable contract is the only type a subcontractor will sign.

Clearly, transferring risk to another party has advantages, but it also introduces new risks. A major component of this strategy is effective contracting and subcontractor management—topics beyond the scope of this chapter.

### 5. Mitigate the Risk

*Mitigate* is jargon for "work hard at reducing" the risk. The risk strategy in Table 7.3 includes several ways to mitigate, or reduce, the productivity loss associated with using a new software tool. Mitigation covers nearly all the actions the project team can take to overcome risks from the project environment.

### Identify Which Risks You Can Control

The first step in determining a response to a possible problem is to identify those risks that are within the control of the project team—and those that are not. Here are a few examples of each kind of risk:

- Federal laws and regulations that affect your project are beyond your control. Labor disputes that cause some or all of your team to walk off the job are up to the company to handle. Who controls the weather? When the risk is beyond your control you generally have two options: Avoid it, or monitor it and prepare a contingency plan.

- The behavior of the project team is within the team's control. For example, a breakdown in communication can be solved by changing the way the team communicates. Other challenges, such as design or staffing problems, can also be overcome by changing the way the team works.

### Record Risk Management Strategies

**CONCEPT** The insights gained during risk planning must be documented. Complete your risk response planning by summarizing your risk analysis in a risk log and updating other project management documents.

The previous examples demonstrate how individual risks may be analyzed. Keep this analysis organized so you can review it later. Summarize the risks using a risk log. Table 7.5 is an example of a risk log that's updated weekly. (To create your own, see the Risk Log available online.) When you update such a log, do the following:

- Make sure there is someone responsible for every risk.
- Rank risks by severity and probability. Life doesn't give us time to expunge every risk from the project, so keep the most important ones at the top of the list where they won't be ignored.

### Consider Risk Strategies Carefully

Sometimes it seems that for every risk problem solved a new risk appears. For instance, if you contract out specialized work, this can reduce risk by transferring it to the subcontractor. But subcontracting can reduce control over the project and increase communication difficulties. In addition, you will need to develop a strategy for managing the subcontractor. What all this means is that you need to weigh

**TABLE 7.5 Examples: Monitor Risks Using a Risk Log**

| Risk ID | Priority | Date Found | WBS | Responsible Person | Description | Strategy | Current Status (As of 6/12) |
|---|---|---|---|---|---|---|---|
| 7 | 1 | 5/12 | 3.2 | J. Daniels | The product design calls for a computer operating system that is yet to be released, and the manufacturer has a reputation for releasing unreliable products late. | 1. Get on the beta test team. Test features affecting the project. 2. Assess the probability of the risk on 7/14. 3. Have an alternate design ready. | 1. Beta versions are very unpredictable. New beta due 6/15. **Risk: High.** Meeting scheduled. 2. Have identified alternative software. Design will be ready on 7/14. |
| 2 | 3 | 5/7 | 4.6.3 | F. Oak | The state agency requires that all diagrams be developed using a software tool that our technical writers have not used before. | 1. Send all tech writers to training. 2. F. Oak is creating standards and templates to build on its strengths. 3. F. Oak will create document management strategies. | 1. Completed 6/2. Improving learning curve. 2. Completed 6/10. Templates and standards are effective. 3. Having trouble with document merging. Working with product rep to solve. **Risk: Medium.** |
| 12 | 5 | 7/7 | 2.1 | J. Barnes | Soil conditions require a complex boring machine we are likely to damage. | The equipment provider will supply an operator for an estimated cost of $10,000. | Operator and equipment are contracted and scheduled. **Risk: Low.** |

the advantages and disadvantages of each proposed risk strategy very carefully.

## STEP FOUR: ESTABLISH CONTINGENCY AND RESERVE

The notion of a rainy-day fund is an old one. On a regular basis we set aside money—usually a small amount—in a sugar bowl or bank account, earmarked for that rainy day when things go wrong. When the car suddenly needs a new transmission, the refrigerator dies, or some other unpredictable malady strikes, we have the funds available to handle it. Some consider it the act of a cautious person; others maintain it is just common sense—something any responsible person would do. In project risk management terms these are called *contingency funds* and *reserve funds*, and it is absolutely the responsibility of the project manager and the sponsor to establish these accounts.

We have established that the risks recorded in our risk log are known unknowns; we know about them but we can't predict with certainty what will happen to them. To prepare for these risks we have several strategies available, some of which call for preparing a contingency plan—a plan that we will execute if the risk materializes. It makes sense that these contingency plans must be funded in advance, but it is not clear how much money should be set aside— after all, it is statistically unlikely that every contingency plan will be executed. Here are four steps you can follow to produce a reasonable contingency budget:

1. Identify all the risks in the risk log, where your strategy is to monitor the risk and prepare a contingency plan.

2. For each of these risks, estimate the additional cost of executing the contingency plan. If you total the cost of all the contingency plans, that is the amount you'd set aside if the probability for each of these risks is 100 percent. But the probability for each risk isn't 100 percent, so derive an expected value of the contingency for each risk by multiplying the probability the risk will occur times the cost of the contingency plan (expected value of contingency = cost of contingency × probability of risk event).

3. Sum the expected value of contingency for each of these risks. That will produce a number that executive management will choke on because nobody could conceive of so many things going wrong on a project. This is where the negotiation begins.

4. There is no good guy or bad guy in this negotiation. Set aside too much money, and you are denying funds to other legitimate projects from which the firm could benefit. Set aside too little money, and when known risks materialize you won't be able to

fund a response. All parties to this negotiation should have the same goal in mind—to prepare for the known risks. All parties face the same challenge—forecasting the future.

Contingency reserves account for identified risks, *known un-knowns*. Management reserves account for the *unknown unknowns*. As we've said before, the unknown unknowns are the events that we didn't see coming. No project, no matter how diligent the risk identification actions, will avoid the unknown unknowns. Therefore, like our rainy-day fund, we set aside a specific amount, earmarked to be spent on reacting to unforeseeable obstacles that arise during the project. How much do you budget for the unknowns? Firms that consistently establish a management reserve for projects will tell you that, over time, a certain percentage of the performance budget (the budget based on the work breakdown structure) emerges as the right amount. High-risk industries such as software development may add as much as 30 percent to the budget. More predictable projects will use an amount closer to 5 percent of the performance budget. The key to establishing management reserve is to do it consistently for every project and at the end of the project to determine how much was spent. Over multiple similar projects, an acceptable range will appear.

## STEP FIVE: CONTINUOUS RISK MANAGEMENT

No matter how rigorous, thorough, and diligent the initial risk planning activities, it is the ongoing risk management activities that produce results.

Our risk plan is based on the best information available when the project begins. As the project is performed, new information emerges— some favorable and some unfavorable. From a risk management perspective, we want to know how that affects our known risks and whether any new risks emerge. Stay ahead of the risks by scheduling the following activities on a regular basis:

- Monitor known risks with a risk log. Each risk in the risk log can be updated before every project status meeting to reflect the most recent information—even if that means "no change."

- Check for new risks at regular status meetings. This activity won't have the same level of thoroughness that the first risk identification activities had, but by routinely asking for new risks the project develops a climate of risk awareness. When team members do sense a risk, they'll know where and when to report it.

- Repeat the major risk identification activities at preplanned milestones within the project. These can be temporal, such as every six to nine weeks, or at the beginning of a new phase. The key is that these be planned in advance and that they are actually performed; otherwise risk identification isn't likely to happen. If there is reluctance on the part of project team members to repeat these activities during the project, remember that investing in risk identification is the "ounce of prevention."

- When new risks are identified, prepare response plans and check whether sufficient contingency or management reserve exists.
- Some risks don't materialize. When that happens, retire them from the risk log, but be sure to record why they didn't materialize—was it good luck or good risk management?

Continuous risk management is essentially the practice of repeating the major risk management processes throughout the life of the project. Through constant vigilance, we continuously root out risks before they become problems.

### Make Your Own Luck

The optimist's twist on risk management is to apply all these techniques to opportunities. An opportunity has a probability and a positive impact. If your team also scans for possible good fortune, maybe you'll be able to take steps to increase the probability that good things happen.

 **UNEXPECTED LEADERSHIP**

After reading this chapter, it should be clear that risk management can make a dramatic impact on a project. Despite that, identifying and managing risks is not appreciated by people who have not been educated in project management. Your team and management may not understand why you want to dwell on what might happen and may view it as some sort of "analysis paralysis." Don't be deterred. You will need to persuade them of the benefits of avoiding problems rather than fixing them. It might be necessary to introduce the risk process in small chunks, rather than all at once. And it will be critical to applaud the team's success when a potential threat is eliminated through forethought.

Your unexpected ability to use risk management to see over the horizon and your persistence applying techniques that were previously unfamiliar to the group will contribute to your reputation as a leader.

Projects, like life, are full of uncertainty. The risk management techniques in this chapter attempt to manage that uncertainty. From one perspective, everything a project manager does involves a type of risk management.

Risk management begins and ends with attitude. Skepticism and critical analysis expose lurking dangers. Then rational assessment, balanced by historical data, judges the probability and severity of the risk. Next, positive, creative problem solving forms a strategy to remove the hazard, and vigorous, energetic execution overcomes the obstacle. Finally, persistent, systematic vigilance reveals new perils, and the cycle begins again. Throughout this contest, we are confident and relentless.

## FAST FOUNDATION IN PROJECT MANAGEMENT

Continuous, systematic risk management uncovers problems before they damage the project. The downloadable forms described below provide a starting point for your own systematic risk management process:

1. The *risk analysis* template should be completed for every risk that has a reasonable chance of threatening the project.
2. The *risk log* offers a simple, systematic method for tracking active risks. Once the risk has been retired it can be moved to the bottom of the list.

See examples of these forms on page 490. Download these forms at www.VersatileCompany.com/FFMBAinPM. Use them to form the foundation of your own risk management process.

## PMP Exam Prep Questions

1. As part of a project to increase revenues from construction lending, a financial services company is reviewing an in-process construction loan for the development of an office and shopping complex just north of a rapidly expanding suburb. The project manager is adept at taking an exploit approach to risks and points out an opportunity to the functional manager. Of the following, which is the best example of an exploit type of risk response strategy the finance company could take in connection with this project?

   a. The finance company could delay construction loan payouts so they can continue to earn interest on that money

   b. The finance company could sell information about prospective tenants to marketing firms

   c. The finance company could purchase 100 acres of land abutting the development land based on its projections that the area will appreciate in value upon completion of the project

   d. The finance company could charge every fee and interest penalty in its arsenal

2. There is $150,000 allocated for management reserves. One of the stakeholders is a newly hired vice president who comes from a small company where project management was not formalized, so he is unfamiliar with this term. The project manager explains the specific reason for which management reserves are created. Of the following, what is the reason?

   a. Project risk events you know can occur

   b. Project risk events that do occur with a cumulative cost greater than the amount set aside in contingency reserves

   c. Project risk events that do occur with a cumulative cost greater than the amount set aside in management reserves

   d. Project risk events that cannot logically be forecasted

3. During the Identify Risk Process, the project manager and the team categorize risks in an effort to determine risks they may have missed. Of the following, which is the best example of risk categories?

   a. Quality, schedule, budget

   b. External, internal, technology, personnel

   c. Scope, time, cost

   d. Initiating, planning, executing, monitoring and controlling, closing

4. The project to develop a proprietary custom support system for a major mortgage company is underway. This is the largest project E-TEK has ever undertaken and E-TEK is concerned about possible liability due to failure to meet the schedule or to perform the work in accordance with the agreement. E-TEK responds to these concerns by obtaining Professional Liability Insurance. Of the following, what best describes the type of risk response represented by this response?

   a. Risk mitigation, which mitigates negative risk by taking actions to lessen its impact

   b. Risk avoidance, which avoids negative risk by taking actions to prevent it

   c. Risk acceptance, which accepts negative risk and has a plan to deal with it if it occurs

   d. Risk transference, which avoids negative risk by transferring or reassigning responsibilities

5. Of the following, which is the most comprehensive definition of project risk?

   a. Risk is a positive or negative event that may or may not have occurred

   b. Risk is a negative event that may or may not occur

   c. Risk is a positive event that may or may not occur

   d. Risk is a positive or negative event that may or may not occur

Answers to these questions can be found at www.Versatile Company.com/FFMBAinPM.* Copyright Eric Verzuh 2015. Original purchasers of this book are permitted to photocopy or customize this page by downloading it from www.VersatileCompany.com/ FFMBAinPM. The document can then be opened, edited, and printed using Microsoft Word or other word processing software.

# Work Breakdown Structure: Break Your Project into Manageable Units of Work

## INTRODUCTION

If you take a car trip to a town less than 100 miles away, it may not take much planning. Just hop in the car, check the gas gauge, and go. But if you were going to drive from the Florida Keys to Anchorage, Alaska, you'd probably spend some time looking at maps and researching your route. Somehow you'd break the big trip down into pieces. Maybe you would do this with geographic borders, such as states. Or you could plan it by how far you might go each day. But whatever approach you use, the only way to accurately plan a trip of this size is to break it down.

The same is true for projects. At a high level, you may understand a project well enough to balance its cost-schedule-quality equilibrium, but you also need to be able to break it down—to understand the whole project by understanding its parts. The *work breakdown structure* (WBS) is the tool for breaking down a project into its component parts. It is the foundation of project planning and one of the most important techniques used in project management. If done well, it can become the secret to successful project management. The WBS is perhaps the most powerful technique in this book.

## DEFINING THE WORK BREAKDOWN STRUCTURE

The work breakdown structure identifies all the tasks in a project; in fact, a WBS is sometimes referred to simply as a *task list*. It turns one large, unique, perhaps mystifying piece of work—the project—into many small, manageable tasks. The WBS uses outputs from project definition and risk management and identifies the tasks that are the foundation for all subsequent planning (see Figure 8.1).

Work breakdown structures can be set up in either graphic or outline form (see Figures 8.2 and 8.3). Either way, they list the various tasks involved. For example, designing and putting in a new lawn with a sprinkler system, surrounded by a new fence, involves a number of different tasks. The graphic WBS paints a picture that makes it easy to understand all the parts of a project, but the outlined WBS is more practical because you can list hundreds of tasks on it—far more than can be listed using the graphic approach.

The WBS clarifies and provides necessary details for a number of project management activities. Building a WBS helps to:

- *Provide a detailed illustration of project scope.* Though the statement of work defines scope at the conceptual level, a comprehensive look at a project's scope can be accomplished only with a WBS.

- *Monitor progress.* The tasks on the WBS become the basis for monitoring progress, because each is a measurable unit of work.

- *Create accurate cost and schedule estimates.* The WBS will detail costs for equipment, labor, and materials on each task.

- *Build project teams.* Every team member wants clear work assignments and a sense of how his or her work fits into the overall effort. A good WBS does both. You can also increase the team's commitment to the plan by having them participate in building the WBS.

### Understanding the WBS

The WBS breaks all the work in the project into separate tasks (tasks may also be referred to as *activities*). There are two kinds of tasks on a WBS: *summary tasks* and *work packages*.

"Install sprinkler system" for a lawn is a summary task, because it includes several subordinate tasks. Installing a sprinkler system might include several of these distinct, subordinate tasks, such as digging trenches or installing pipes. Each of these separate tasks is called a *work package*. By performing all these simple work packages, you accomplish a summary task (see Figure 8.3).

Note that a summary task is not actually executed; rather, it *summarizes* the subordinate work packages. The work packages are

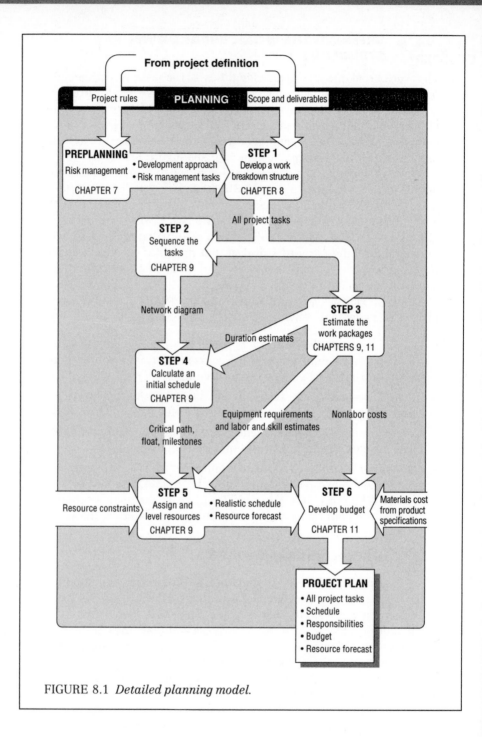

FIGURE 8.1 *Detailed planning model.*

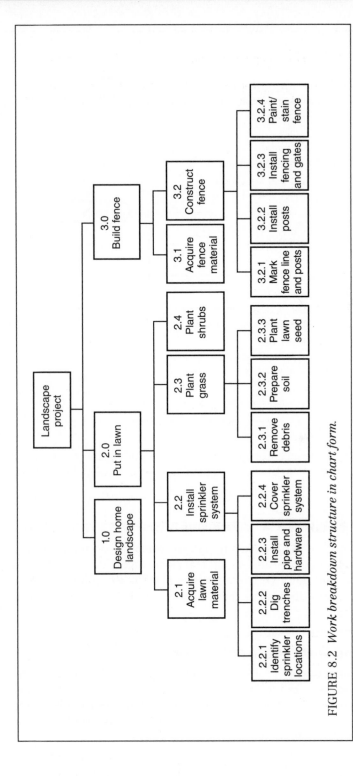

FIGURE 8.2 *Work breakdown structure in chart form.*

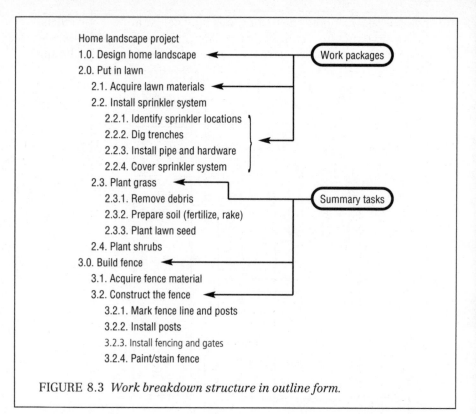

FIGURE 8.3 *Work breakdown structure in outline form.*

the ones that are actually executed. Understanding the relationship between summary tasks and work packages is fundamental to building a good WBS.

## BUILDING A WORK BREAKDOWN STRUCTURE

A good WBS makes it easy for everyone on the project to understand his or her role—and it makes managing the project much easier, too. But don't be fooled; it isn't always easy to build a good WBS. There are three steps that provide a guideline to developing a useful WBS.

### WBS Step One: Begin at the Top

A WBS breaks down a project into descending levels of details, naming all the tasks required to create the deliverables named in the statement of work (SOW). You can begin the breakdown process by listing either the major deliverables or the high-level tasks from the scope statement on the first tier.

Figure 8.3 demonstrates listing the major deliverables, or products, as the first step in making a WBS. The three major deliverables—design, lawn, and fence—are on tier one. Notice that the landscape design is listed as a major deliverable, even though it isn't an end product, like the lawn and fence. The statement of work can list many intermediate deliverables as well as end deliverables. All deliverables from the SOW appear on the WBS.

The other approach to getting started is to use the high-level tasks described in the scope statement as the tier-one tasks. Since the WBS shows all project work, it is essentially a detailed illustration of the processes involved in the project. Therefore, tier one can be set up as a view of these processes, representing the major phases or stages of a development life cycle. But even when using this approach, tier one still shows a deliverable for each phase. Either way, your WBS will be linked to the statement of work.

### Getting Started on the WBS

Sometimes the hardest part of making a work breakdown structure is getting started. The WBS includes so much that it can appear overwhelming. A good way to begin is to review the work you've already done during project definition and risk management.

### WBS Step Two: Name All the Tasks Required to Produce Deliverables

A task name describes an activity that produces a product. For example, if a WBS in a landscaping project lists "lawn" or "shrubs," you will need to add verbs to each task name: "lawn" becomes "put in lawn," "shrubs" becomes "plant shrubs," and so on. The next step is to break down each task into the lower-level, detailed tasks required to produce the product. Figures 8.2 and 8.3 illustrate how the WBS looks with multiple task levels.

This sounds easy, doesn't it? Don't be deceived. Breaking down the WBS can be the most difficult step in the planning process, because it's where the detailed process for building the product is defined. For example, a high-level task may seem easy to understand, but upon breaking it down, the project manager may find that he or she is unable to list all the detailed tasks required to complete it. At this point, it's time to invite more team members, with diverse skills, into the planning process.

In fact, when planning a large, multidisciplinary project, it makes sense to get a small team to create the top two tiers of the WBS, then give each task to an expert in the subject to break it down into work packages. When these experts are through, they can be brought together with the core team to construct the entire WBS. This kind of participative planning not only creates more accurately detailed work breakdowns, it can also encourage higher levels of commitment to the project.

A WBS may be especially difficult to create if the project covers new ground. Here's an example: Tom, a human resources manager for a company of about 10,000 people, was leading a project to create a new process for forecasting the firm's workforce requirements over a three-year time span. When he began to put together his WBS, he quickly realized that he wasn't sure what steps to follow in developing the new process. Because there was no precedent for this kind of project in his company, Tom and his team had to spend time devising a new strategy.

The resulting plan was presented to the customers, which, on this project, were the high-level managers who would use the system to forecast their personnel needs. This management group approved the plan, but in this case they weren't approving just the schedule or budget, they were also approving the new strategy that Tom and his team had devised. And, since much of the plan outlined how this management group would participate in designing the new system, they were also accepting their roles as defined in the plan.

When Tom's team had completed its plan, he commented, "We spent at least two weeks planning this project and most of that time was spent on the WBS. That was about two weeks longer than I originally intended. But by spending the time to get a detailed strategy worked out, I can see we actually saved a lot of time. If it took us two weeks to figure out how to handle this project, imagine how many blind alleys we would have run down without this plan."

## WBS Step Three: How to Organize the WBS

Once all the work packages are identified, it is possible to rearrange them in different ways. For example, it can be useful to place work packages under different summary task headings; in this case, the overall project will remain the same even though the work packages are grouped differently. Figure 8.4 demonstrates how it's possible to have two different breakdowns of the same project tasks. The same work packages are reorganized under different summary tasks.

Different ways of organizing work packages may emphasize different aspects of a project. For example, one grouping of work packages might highlight the various components of a new product, while another arrangement might emphasize the major phases of the product's release. This kind of difference is illustrated in Figure 8.4, where the first WBS provides high-level visibility on the widget's two main components. By contrast, the second WBS provides high-level visibility on the major phases of the new release. Both may be useful when communicating with the various groups

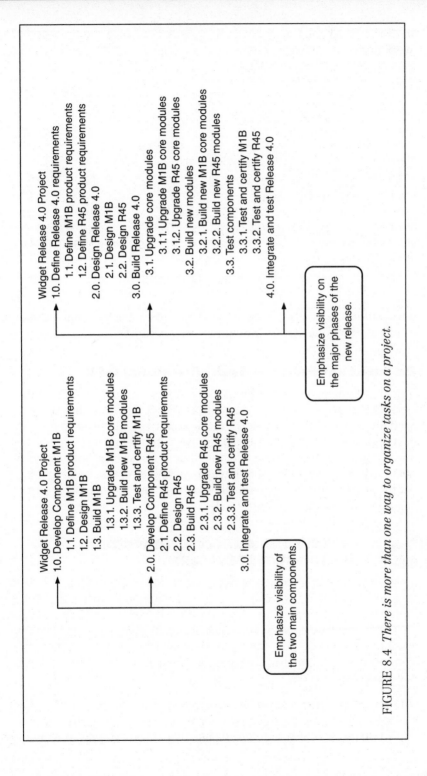

Widget Release 4.0 Project
1.0. Develop Component M1B
   1.1. Define M1B product requirements
   1.2. Design M1B
   1.3. Build M1B
      1.3.1. Upgrade M1B core modules
      1.3.2. Build new M1B modules
      1.3.3. Test and certify M1B
2.0. Develop Component R45
   2.1. Define R45 product requirements
   2.2. Design R45
   2.3. Build R45
      2.3.1. Upgrade R45 core modules
      2.3.2. Build new R45 modules
      2.3.3. Test and certify R45
3.0. Integrate and test Release 4.0

Emphasize visibility of
the two main components.

Widget Release 4.0 Project
1.0. Define Release 4.0 requirements
   1.1. Define M1B product requirements
   1.2. Define R45 product requirements
2.0. Design Release 4.0
   2.1. Design M1B
   2.2. Design R45
3.0. Build Release 4.0
   3.1. Upgrade core modules
      3.1.1. Upgrade M1B core modules
      3.1.2. Upgrade R45 core modules
   3.2. Build new modules
      3.2.1. Build new M1B core modules
      3.2.2. Build new R45 core modules
   3.3. Test components
      3.3.1. Test and certify M1B
      3.3.2. Test and certify R45
4.0. Integrate and test Release 4.0

Emphasize visibility on
the major phases of the
new release.

FIGURE 8.4 *There is more than one way to organize tasks on a project.*

Widget Release 4.0 Project

| | |
|---|---|
| 1.0. | Define M1B product requirements |
| 2.0. | Define R45 product requirements |
| 3.0. | Design M1B |
| 4.0. | Design R45M |
| 5.0. | Upgrade M1B core modules |
| 6.0. | Upgrade R45 core modules |
| 7.0. | Build new M1B modules |
| 8.0. | Build new R45 modules |
| 9.0. | Test and certify M1B |
| 10.0. | Test and certify R45 |
| 11.0. | Integrate and test Release 4.0 |

FIGURE 8.5 *WBS with no summary tasks. The Widget Release 4.0 Project has the same amount of work required, even though the summary tasks are removed.*

involved in the project, because the focus of each arrangement may speak to the concerns of individual stakeholders.

### Be Sure That Summary Tasks Are Meaningful

When organizing the work breakdown structure, remember that the sole purpose of summary tasks on the WBS is for communication or visibility. (Recall that summary tasks aren't actually executed, they just summarize work packages.) So every summary task should be meaningful to some stakeholder (including the project manager). If there are summary tasks that have no audience, erase them. As long as the work packages remain, the scope of the project is the same (compare Figure 8.5 to Figure 8.4).

### CRITERIA FOR A SUCCESSFUL WORK BREAKDOWN STRUCTURE

Because a good WBS is easy to read, people often assume that it's also easy to write. This, however, is a false assumption; there are large numbers of inaccurate and poorly developed work breakdown structures produced every year. However, if your WBS meets the following evaluation criteria, you can be sure it will be useful in planning, communicating, and tracking your project. Here are three criteria for a successful WBS:

1. *The WBS must be broken down starting at the top.* It is a top-down decomposition. You need to make sure your work packages are subsets of your summary tasks. The test is simple: Start with

Landscape Project

1.0. Design home landscape
2.0. Put in lawn                           *2.0 is a subset of the project.*
  2.1. Purchase lawn materials
  2.2. Install sprinkler system               *2.2 is a subset of 2.0.*
    2.2.1. Identify sprinkler locations
    2.2.2. Dig trenches                  *2.2.2 is a subset of 2.2.*
    2.2.3. Install pipe and hardware
    2.2.4. Cover sprinkler system        *2.2.4 is a subset of 2.2.*
  2.3. Plant grass
    2.3.1. Remove debris
    2.3.2. Prepare soil
    2.3.3. Plant lawn seed
  2.4. Plant shrubs
3.0. Build fence                            *3.0 is a subset of the project.*
  3.1. Acquire fence material
  3.2. Construct the fence            *3.2 is a subset of 3.0.*
    3.2.1. Mark fence line
    3.2.2. Install posts
    3.2.3. Install fencing and gates     *3.2.3 is a subset of 3.2.*
    3.2.4. Paint/stain fence

FIGURE 8.6 *Evaluation rule 1: The WBS must be a top-down decomposition.*

any work package and work your way up the hierarchy, asking, "Is this task a subset of the task above it?" (Figure 8.6 illustrates this rule.) Following this rule allows you to:

- *Use standard project management software.* Do it any other way and the software will give you nothing but nonsense at the summary level.

- *Present meaningful project information at the summary task level.* For example, costs for summary tasks are derived simply by adding up the costs of all subordinate tasks. This enables you to track the project at the work package level, yet present the status of the project to your sponsor using more meaningful information from the summary tasks.

2. *Work packages must add up to the summary task.* One of the most frustrating planning mistakes is to omit necessary tasks. You can avoid this problem by taking extra care when adding up the products of all the work packages below any summary task. All together, these subordinate tasks should produce the outcome named by the summary task. See Figure 8.7 for a further illustration of this point.

**173**

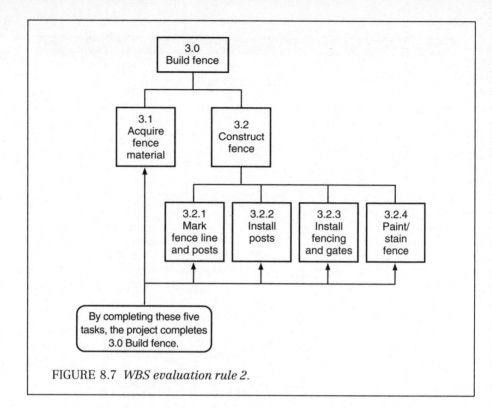

FIGURE 8.7 *WBS evaluation rule 2.*

3. *Each summary task and work package must be named as an activity that produces a product.* This means giving each task a descriptive name that includes a strong verb—the *activity*—and a strong noun—the *product*. Without these, the task becomes ambiguous. Two cases in point:

- *Open-ended tasks.* "Perform analysis" or "Do research" are activities we understand, but since there is no hard product being produced, they are activities that could go on indefinitely. Better task names include the products of the analysis or research, such as "Define hardware requirements," "Write a problem statement," or "List candidate vendors." The focus on producing a product gives the task—and the team—a clear ending, which makes it easier both to estimate and to track the task.

- *Open-ended activities.* "Database" is a task that will show up in thousands of projects this year, but what is the action required? It could be many things, from design to load to test. That's the point—it is unclear what is meant by this task. Clarify the task by including an activity, as in "Test the database."

## WBS: The Key to Success

Apply the following rule to any work breakdown structure and you will find yourself in absolute control of your project. This is the secret of successful project management: *Break the project into small, meaningful, manageable units of work.*

## WORK PACKAGE SIZE

The most common problem with projects that extend dramatically beyond their schedule is that work packages are so large that they can spin out of control. If a task is estimated to be eight months long and 3,800 labor hours (i.e., three people working full-time on the task), it's not a task—it's a subproject! This is the kind of task that is right on schedule for seven months, suddenly hits a rough spot in the eighth month—and ends up taking 12 months. The size of this task has made it unmanageable. If the entire project were to be planned in the same manner, the trouble would be multiplied many times over. To ensure that the work packages are the correct size, follow these common rules of thumb.

- *The 8/80 rule.* No task should be smaller than 8 labor hours or larger than 80. This translates into keeping your work packages between 1 and 10 days long. (Obviously, this is a guideline and not an ironclad law.)
- *The reporting period rule.* No task should be longer than the distance between two status points. In other words, if you hold weekly status meetings, then no task should be longer than one week. This rule is especially useful when it is time to report schedule status, because you will no longer have to hear about task statuses that are 25, 40, or 68 percent complete. If you've followed a weekly reporting rule, tasks will be reported as either complete (100 percent), started (50 percent), or not started (0 percent). No task should be at 50 percent for two consecutive status meetings.
- *The "if it's useful" rule.* As you consider whether to break tasks down further, remember that there are three reasons to do so:
  1. *The task is easier to estimate.* Smaller tasks tend to have less uncertainty, leading to more accurate estimates.
  2. *The task is easier to assign.* Large tasks assigned to many people lose accountability. Breaking down the task can help to clarify who is responsible. Another potential benefit is that having smaller tasks assigned to fewer people can give you greater flexibility in scheduling the task and the resource.

3. *The task is easier to track.* The same logic applies as in the reporting period rule. Because smaller tasks create more tangible status points, you will have more accurate progress reports.

If breaking down a task in a certain way is not useful—that is, if it doesn't make it easier to estimate, assign, or track—then don't break it down!

## When Very Small Tasks Make Sense

Is it possible that tasks broken down into one-hour increments could be useful? Talk about micromanagement! While projects spanning months probably wouldn't benefit from such small tasks, it is common to plan to this level for complex projects of short duration. Preventive maintenance for manufacturing plants can require the entire operation to be shut down for a day or a week. In order to minimize the time the plant is down, these projects are often planned out in hourly increments, which allows close coordination among many people and quick identification of any behind-schedule work that could delay reopening the plant.

While many managers might balk at having to reduce a large project into relatively small increments, the results can be rewarding. Consider these examples:

- An upgrade to a municipal wastewater treatment plant had a project budget of more than $500 million. In spite of the size of this project, contractors were required to plan and report work packages in units of no more than two weeks or $50,000. By requiring this detailed level of information, the municipal government's project office could identify any problems within a matter of weeks—no small feat for a project of this size. The project finished on time and under budget.

- In an article in *Sloan Management Review* on Microsoft, Michael Cusumano observed, "Managers generally allow team members to set their own schedules but only after the developers have analyzed tasks in detail (half-day to three-day chunks, for example) and have agreed to commit personally to the schedules." Yet, in a company the size of Microsoft, hundreds of people may be required to develop a new product. While working with these small increments will produce an enormous amount of detail, it dramatically increases the accuracy of estimating and tracking a project.[1]

## Put Project Management into the WBS

You can benefit by putting project management activities into the work breakdown structure. List them under a summary task called "Project management" (as shown in Figure 8.8). Though some of the tasks will be finite, such as hiring a subcontractor, the majority will

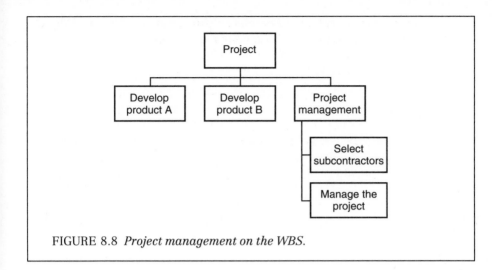

FIGURE 8.8 *Project management on the WBS.*

consist of everyday work, such as communication and problem resolution. These everyday duties may be grouped under a heading called "Manage the project." Now you have a place to assign all the time spent on project management duties.

## PLANNING FOR QUALITY

Common sense tells us that it is cheaper to design a product correctly than to fix it after it is built. Whether it is an airplane, an ad campaign, or a piece of software, the earlier an error is detected in the development life cycle, the cheaper it is to fix. In his excellent book, *Rapid Development*, Steve McConnell develops some general conclusions about the cost of fixing mistakes, in this case, on software projects.

> If a defect caused by incorrect requirements is fixed in the construction or maintenance phase, it can cost 50 to 200 times as much to fix as it would have in the requirements phase.
>
> Each hour spent on quality assurance activities such as design reviews saves 3 to 10 hours on downstream costs.[2]

How do we make sure that we catch problems early in the development life cycle? The answer is different for every industry. Aircraft designers use different techniques than software developers. Architects use different techniques than manufacturing engineers. But what does project management have to offer in this search for possible problems? It offers the risk management techniques we have already discussed; it also offers a process for setting standards for completion of the product. These standards, called *completion criteria*, form our next topic.

## Completion Criteria

Completion criteria answer these two critical questions about each work package: (1) What does it mean to be complete with this task? (2) How will we know it was done correctly? As McConnell's statistics illustrate, the time to ask these questions is early in the development life cycle. Yet these may be the tasks with the most intangible results. How do you test a problem statement or a business case? It may not be easy, but it is important. Determining completion criteria demands that the project manager and team look to the best practices in their industry. Here are some examples of completion criteria:

- *Peer reviews.* These are common in many industries in the early part of a product development life cycle when there is nothing tangible to test. Peer reviews, also known as *walk-throughs*, are based on the premise that three to six heads are better than one. Passing the review doesn't guarantee the product will be perfect, but experience has shown that subjecting tasks to peer reviews results in dramatically better results in the front end of the development life cycle—and this leads to more cost-effective work in the construction phase.

- *Checklists.* For instance, an engineering group at an aerospace company has developed checklists for evaluating new drawings. The checklists cover the standard tests each drawing must pass, and a lead engineer will use the checklist to evaluate another engineer's drawing. In this case, completion criteria for a drawing involve "passing the checklist."

- *Systematic testing.* There are almost always tests to run later in a product's life cycle. For example, airplane manufacturers have extensive test labs that simulate the stresses experienced by aircraft in flight. Passing rigorous, systematic testing can be defined as completion criteria.

In addition to improving quality, completion criteria improve our understanding of each task, which results in more accurate estimates and higher rates of success.

## The Acceptance Process: Begin with the End in Mind

One of Stephen Covey's seven habits of effective people is to "begin with the end in mind."[3] This is particularly good advice for project managers, who need to consider early on the process for delivering the final product. This process is called the *acceptance process*. Considering the acceptance process might add a few tasks to the WBS, such as turnover tasks at the end of the project. These might include training, initial start-up of the new product, or a post-implementation assessment.

## BREAKING DOWN LARGE PROGRAMS

**KEY CONCEPT**

A program manager responsible for a billion-dollar contract will not immediately break the program down into one-week increments. He or she will break the contract into projects, which in turn will be broken down into subprojects. Eventually, the work will be broken into small work packages, requiring between 8 and 80 hours in labor. This project within a project within a program approach is based on the top-down nature of the work breakdown structure.

### WBS Guidelines Vary

**DANGER!**

The terms introduced in this chapter—*summary task* and *work package*—are commonly used. Likewise, naming all tasks with strong nouns and verbs is a common practice. But the wide range of project types and sizes also means you'll find other guidelines. Here are two to be aware of:

- *The deliverable-oriented WBS.* Rather than using nouns and verbs to describe every component of the WBS, this school uses only nouns. Figure 8.9 shows a partial WBS for a jet fighter program. The WBS is clearly a representation of the components of the end deliverable, and in this program it also represents the organization

Airframe
    Airframe analysis and integration
    Midfuselage
    Empennage (tail)
    Edges
    Wings
    Forward fuselage
    Aft fuselage
Avionics
    Avionics analysis and integration
    Electronic warfare
    Core processing
    Radar
Utilities and subsystems
    Armament
    Hydraulics
    Fuel
    Electrical
    Landing gear

FIGURE 8.9 *Partial WBS from a fighter aircraft program.*

chart. Advocates of this approach include defense contractors and the Project Management Institute.

- *Work packages as subprojects or groups of activities.* When a project costs $50 million, $500 million, or $5 billion, it can make a lot of sense to decompose it into chunks that are still very large—far more than 80 hours! On these projects, a work package can be worth $100,000 and up. In this case, the work package itself can be decomposed using all the WBS guidelines found in this chapter.

## CONTRACTORS OR VENDORS CAN PROVIDE A WBS

If your project employs contractors or vendors to do some of the work, you can make a WBS part of the bid requirement. (You can also make it a reporting requirement for the winning bidder.) This can be a good tool for evaluating bids, particularly if there are wide variations in the cost and schedule estimates of the bidders; tying the bid to a WBS will show clearly when one contractor is making different scope assumptions than another.

When managing vendors, it is useful to require them to manage and report against a detailed WBS; this will often reduce the likelihood of unpleasant surprises later in the project. (Figure 8.10 shows how requiring a WBS as part of a bid can be used on a large project requiring multiple subcontractors.)

## END POINT

A project can best be understood by a thorough understanding of its parts. The work breakdown structure breaks the project down into many small, manageable tasks called *work packages*. The process of deciding who will perform these tasks and how they will be arranged provides the structure for the actual work of the project.

Most books on project management devote between one-half to two pages to work breakdown structures. "What's the big deal?" people say. "It's just a task list." It's a big deal because so much of a project manager's job relies on the WBS. Estimating, scope management, subcontracting work, tracking progress, and giving clear work assignments all depend on a well-defined breakdown of the tasks that make up a project. For every problem a project manager encounters, there is probably some way that he or she can use the WBS and its work packages to help solve it.

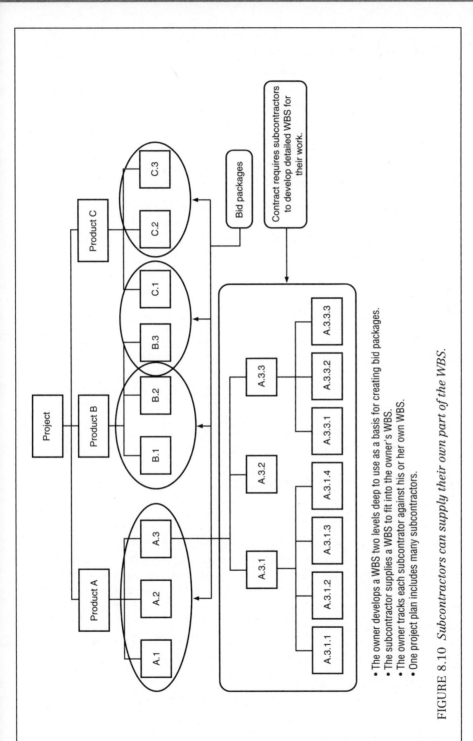

- The owner develops a WBS two levels deep to use as a basis for creating bid packages.
- The subcontractor supplies a WBS to fit into the owner's WBS.
- The owner tracks each subcontrator against his or her own WBS.
- One project plan includes many subcontractors.

FIGURE 8.10 *Subcontractors can supply their own part of the WBS.*

## PMP Exam Prep Questions

1. The project manager always involves the team in the creation of the work breakdown structure. What is the most significant benefit derived from this approach?

   a. Generation of a more accurate schedule
   b. Establishment of the project manager's authority
   c. Generation of a more accurate budget
   d. Buy-in from the team doing the work

2. The team is in the process of completing the work breakdown structure of the project. Once they have completed this, which of the following can they begin to work on?

   a. Estimating costs
   b. Developing schedule
   c. Estimating activity durations
   d. All the answers

3. The team has had five meetings to decompose the work of the aircraft carrier project. They are making progress and in a few more meetings should have all the decomposition complete for the multi-year project. Which of the following is not a benefit of using a WBS?

   a. Describes the deliverables of the project
   b. Helps the project team understand their role and buy-in on the project
   c. Provides the justification for staff, cost, and time
   d. Identifies special work packages that can be created outside the WBS, but within the project

4. The project to provide an organizational restructuring of the company to increase operational efficiency and provide clearer lines of communication and development opportunities for managers has been initiated. During the planning processes, the project manager is determining the milestones. Of the following, what is a key element of a milestone definition?

   a. It has a duration of zero (0)
   b. It defines a phase of the project
   c. It has a duration of one day
   d. It has value in the project charter but not in the plan

Answers to these questions can be found at www.VersatileCompany .com/FFMBAinPM.

# Realistic Scheduling

## INTRODUCTION

If you ask people what makes a project successful, "a realistic schedule" usually tops the list. But ask them to be more specific, and several characteristics of a realistic schedule emerge. A realistic schedule:

- Includes a detailed knowledge of the work to be done.
- Has task sequences in the correct order.
- Accounts for external constraints beyond the control of the team.
- Can be accomplished on time, given the availability of skilled people and enough equipment.

Finally, a realistic schedule takes into consideration all the objectives of the project. For example, a schedule may be just right for the project team, but if it misses the customer's completion date by a mile, then it's clear that the whole project will need to be reassessed. Building a project plan that includes all the necessary parts and achieves a realistic balance among cost, scheduling, and quality requires a careful, step-by-step process.

Chapter 8 dealt with the first step in planning the project: the work breakdown structure. This chapter explains planning steps two through five. Each planning step relies on the one preceding it, and each adds a new element to the plan. You can use the diagram in Figure 8.1 (see page 166) as a guide in this chapter.

## PLANNING OVERVIEW

Here is a quick recap of the steps involved in planning a project. The first two actions prepare the groundwork for planning and so can be considered preplanning activities. The remaining five steps develop the detailed plan.

## Preplanning Activities

- *Create the project definition.* The project manager and the project team develop the statement of work, which identifies the purpose, scope, and deliverables for the project and defines the responsibilities of the project team (Chapters 5 and 6).

- *Develop a risk management strategy.* The project team evaluates the likely obstacles and creates a strategy for balancing costs, schedule, and quality (Chapter 7).

## Planning Steps

1. *Build a work breakdown structure.* The team identifies all the tasks required to build the specified deliverables. The scope statement and project purpose help to define the boundaries of the project.

2. *Identify task relationships.* The detailed tasks, known as work packages, are placed in the proper sequence.

3. *Estimate work packages.* Each of these detailed tasks has an estimate developed that includes the amount of labor and equipment needed and the duration of the task.

4. *Calculate initial schedule.* After estimating the duration of each work package and figuring in the sequence of tasks, the team calculates the total duration of the project. (This initial schedule, while useful for planning, will probably need to be revised further down the line.)

5. *Assign and level resources.* The team adjusts the schedule to account for resource constraints. Tasks are rescheduled in order to optimize the use of people and equipment used on the project.

These steps generate all the information required to understand how a project will be executed. The steps are systematic, but they don't necessarily come up with the "right answer." It may take several iterations of these steps to find this answer, which is the optimal balance among cost, schedule, and quality. Chapter 12 will address the challenge of finding the optimal cost-schedule-quality equilibrium for a project, but right now, we will look at the step-by-step instructions for creating a project plan. Step One is the creation of a work breakdown structure, which was covered in a previous chapter. We start here with Step Two, which involves identifying the relationships between the different tasks.

# PLANNING STEP TWO: IDENTIFY TASK RELATIONSHIPS

The sequence in which detailed tasks—work packages—are performed is determined by the relationship between the tasks. To illustrate this point, consider the following five tasks from the landscaping project described earlier. These tasks constitute a subset of that project:

1. Acquire lawn materials
2. Remove debris
3. Prepare soil
4. Plant lawn seed
5. Plant shrubs

As the homeowner and the teenage children who will be working on this project contemplate these tasks, the question arises: What is the proper sequence? Any time a series of tasks is performed, there will be *sequence constraints*—that is, certain tasks that must be performed before others. Sequence constraints are governed by the relationships of different tasks. For instance, rocks, weeds, and other debris must be removed before the lawn seed can be planted. Performing these tasks in the reverse order doesn't make sense because the seed would be lost when the weeds were removed. Figure 9.1 shows both a predecessor table and a network diagram, two different ways of recording sequence constraints. A predecessor table is a common way to display task relationships. (In fact, this is exactly the way most project management software records the relationships.)

Notice that Tasks 1 and 2 have no predecessors. Either one can be done first, or, if there are enough people, they could be done at the same time. Tasks that can be performed at the same time are known as *concurrent tasks*.

There are just two basic rules when graphing task relationships with a network diagram:

1. *Define task relationships only between work packages.* Even though a project might have hundreds of work packages and several levels of summary tasks, keep the sequence constraints at the work package level. Summary tasks, remember, are simply groups of work packages, so it wouldn't make sense to put a task relationship between a summary task and its work package. (The only exception to this rule occurs occasionally on very large projects, where networks can be created to illustrate project relationships at the summary level.)

## PREDECESSOR TABLE

| | Task | Predecessor | Resources |
|---|---|---|---|
| 1 | Acquire lawn materials | | Homeowner |
| 2 | Remove debris | | Teens and youth group |
| 3 | Prepare soil | 1, 2 | Teens |
| 4 | Plant lawn seed | 3 | Teens |
| 5 | Plant shrubs | 2 | Teens |

**Correct**

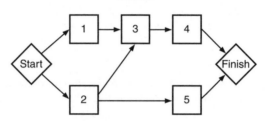

- Network diagram with milestones at the start and finish.
- This network has two *concurrent* paths.

**Incorrect**

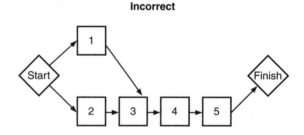

- The most common network diagram mistake is removing all concurrent tasks for the same resource.
- Resource constraints may prevent tasks 4 and 5 from being performed at the same time, but that shouldn't change the network. The network represents only task sequence constraints.

FIGURE 9.1 *Network diagram developed from a predecessor table.*

2. *Task relationships should reflect only sequence constraints between work packages, not resource constraints.* Changing a network diagram because of resource constraints is the most common error in building network diagrams. The fact that there aren't enough people or other resources to work on multiple tasks at the same time is irrelevant here. Regardless of resources, the

tasks will still have to be performed in the same order. (Figure 9.1 demonstrates the mistake of rearranging the network because the same resources, in this case, the teenagers, are working on Tasks 4 and 5.)

## Milestones Are Useful Markers

In setting up the sequence of events, many project managers find it useful to mark significant events in the life of a project. These markers—called *milestones*—are often used in work breakdown structures and network diagrams (see Figure 9.2). Milestones have zero duration, so adding them to a project doesn't affect the schedule at all. There are three great reasons to use milestones:

1. *Project start and finish milestones are useful anchors for the network.* The milestones don't change anything on the project, but many people find that they make the network diagram easier to read.

2. *Milestones can be used to mark input from one party to another.* Many projects are dependent on inputs from certain external sources (they have *external dependencies*). For example, a government agency might release an environmental impact report for an electric utility on a certain date. A project in that electric utility can use that release date as a milestone. Figure 9.2 shows a milestone representing an external dependency.

3. *A milestone can represent significant events that aren't already represented by a work package or summary task.* For example, if

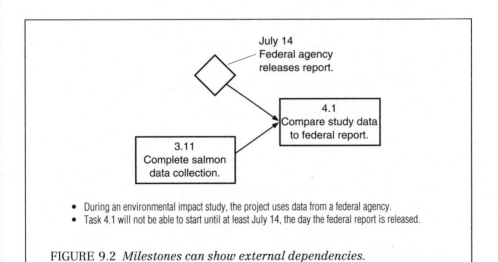

- During an environmental impact study, the project uses data from a federal agency.
- Task 4.1 will not be able to start until at least July 14, the day the federal report is released.

FIGURE 9.2 *Milestones can show external dependencies.*

a firm receives progress payments based on work accomplished, these payment points could be shown with milestones.

Milestones are useful to show major progress points, but the real progress indicators remain the detailed work packages. Every work package has specific completion criteria and a tangible result—which is the ultimate progress indicator.

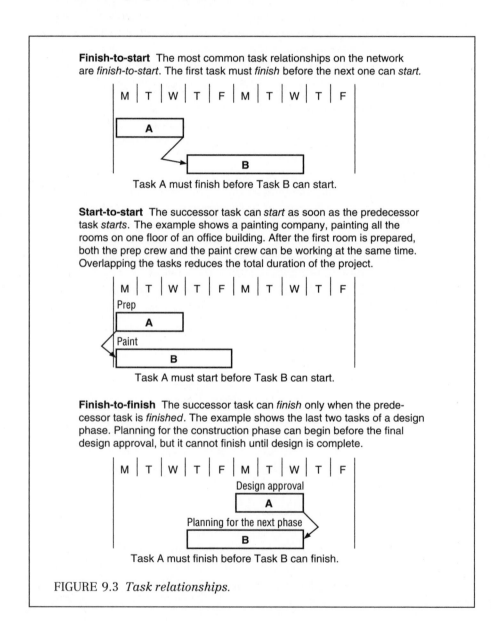

FIGURE 9.3 *Task relationships.*

## Finish-to-Start Relationships

The finish-to-start relationship states that one task must be completed before its successor task can begin. The network diagrams in this chapter all follow this simple assumption because it is the most common, but there are other types of relationships. Tasks with start-to-start (SS) relationships allow the successor task to begin when the predecessor task begins. Finish-to-finish (FF) tasks can start independently of each other, but the successor cannot finish until the predecessor finishes. Figure 9.3 shows the value of using these other types of task relationships.

**KEY CONCEPT**

## PLANNING STEP THREE: ESTIMATE WORK PACKAGES

In order to determine the cost and duration of an entire project, it's necessary to build a cost and schedule estimate for each work package; this is called *bottom-up estimating*. A lot of information is generated in the estimating process, so it is critical to record it in a systematic manner. (Table 9.1 shows the work package estimates for the home landscape project. Tables 9.2 to 9.5 illustrate some of the variables that affect work package estimates.)

The schedule estimate for a task measures the time from initiation to completion. This estimate is usually referred to as *duration* of a task. When building a schedule estimate, it's important to include *all* the time the task will span. For instance, it may take only one day to order materials, but if it takes 10 days for delivery, the total duration of the task will be 11 days. Similarly, while a certain decision might take only two hours to make, it might be more realistic to estimate duration at five days if the decision maker is likely to be busy at that time.

Cost estimates come from four sources:

1. *Labor estimates.* These project how much human effort will be put into a task. If three people work eight hours a day for three days, the total labor estimate will be 72 hours. On small work packages, labor is estimated in hours. (At the project level, labor can be such a large item that it is sometimes expressed in years.) In addition to recording the labor estimate, you will need to record the skill requirement. For example, a task might specifically require an electrician eight hours a day for three days. If more than one skill type is required, list them all.

2. *Equipment estimates.* Equipment requirements need to be identified at the work package level. These estimates then become the basis for estimating the total equipment cost for the project. Equipment, in this case, includes the tools necessary to perform

**TABLE 9.1  Home Landscape Project Work Package Estimates**

| Task | | Labor | Resource | |
|------|------|------|------|------|
| ID | Name | Duration | Hours | Names |
| 1 | Design home landscape | 5 days | 80 hrs. | Homeowner [0.5], Teens [1.5]* |
| 2 | Put in lawn | | | |
| 3 | Acquire lawn materials | 2 days | 64 hrs. | Homeowner, Teens [3] |
| 4 | Install sprinkler system | | | |
| 5 | Identify sprinkler locations | 1 day | Fixed fee, 8 hrs. | Contractor, Homeowner |
| 6 | Dig trenches | 2 days | Fixed fee | Contractor |
| 7 | Install pipe and hardware | 3 days | Fixed fee | Contractor |
| 8 | Cover sprinkler system | 1 day | Fixed fee | Contractor |
| 9 | Plant grass | | | |
| 10 | Remove debris | 4 days | 256 hrs. | Teens [3], Youth Group [5] |
| 11 | Prepare soil | 4 days | 96 hrs. | Teens [3], Rototiller |
| 12 | Plant lawn seed | 1 day | 16 hrs. | Teens [2] |
| 13 | Plant shrubs | 6 days | 96 hrs. | Teens [2] |
| 14 | Build fence | | | |
| 15 | Acquire fence material | 2 days | 16 hrs. | Homeowner |
| 16 | Install fence | | | |
| 17 | Mark fence line | 1 day | 32 hrs. | Homeowner, Teens [3] |
| 18 | Install posts | 5 days | 80 hrs. | Teens [2] |
| 19 | Install fencing and gates | 6 days | 144 hrs. | Teens [3] |
| 20 | Paint/stain fence and gates | 3 days | 72 hrs. | Teens [3] |

*On task 1, both the homeowner and teens are working 4 hours per day.

the task, from cranes to specialized software. (Don't bother to list common tools such as word processors, copy machines, or hammers.) Like labor, equipment use should be estimated in hours.

3. *Materials estimates.* Materials for the project can be a major source of project cost—or virtually nonexistent. While a construction project may have a significant portion of its total cost represented by raw materials, a project to institute new hiring guidelines will have no raw materials. Software development projects have no raw materials, but an information system project to install commercial off-the-shelf (COTS) software will have to include the cost of the software. *Even though materials costs can*

---

### *TABLE 9.2* Work Package Estimate: Example 1

*Task description:* During an environmental study, a power company counts salmon during a 40-day salmon run.

*Assumption:* The federal agency overseeing the power company dictates the length of the study.

*Duration:* 40 days

*Materials:* None

**Labor and Equipment Table**

| Type | Average Use | Total |
|------|-------------|-------|
| Salmon specialist | 1 @ 10 hrs./day | 400 hrs. |
| Field technician | 2 @ 10 hrs./day | 800 hrs. |
| Truck | 1 all day | 40 days |

*Increasing the number of people on this task does not change the duration, but it could increase the accuracy of the study.*

---

be a major portion of the project's cost, total materials cost should be estimated from the product specifications—not estimated from the bottom up using the work breakdown structure. (Chapter 11 covers project budget development in greater detail.) Including materials in the work package estimate helps to identify exactly when each of the materials will be needed; these schedule requirements, in turn, will determine order and delivery dates.

4. *Fixed-price bids.* Fixed-estimate costs can replace the three previous cost sources. For example, a vendor or subcontractor might make a fixed-price bid that includes labor, equipment, and materials. Fixed-price bids mean that the vendor takes responsibility for costs; should there be overruns, the cost to the project will not change. (The landscape project in Table 9.1 includes fixed-price bids by the sprinkler contractor.)

Is it really necessary to concentrate on costs when trying to build a realistic schedule? It is, because each cost represents a resource constraint. Costs such as hiring subcontractors and purchasing materials will constrain the schedule. Later on, the schedule will be adjusted to account for these resource constraints (this is the fifth step of planning), but before adjusting the schedule we need to identify all the resource requirements, one work package at a time.

## TABLE 9.3 Work Package Estimates: Example 2

*Task description:* During a training project, software is upgraded on 20 workstations in a training room.

*Assumption:* The average time to install the software is 2 hours per workstation. Testing is 1 hour per workstation. Only 1 person can work on one workstation at a time.

**First Estimate**

*Duration:* 5 days                                        *Materials:* 20 copies of the new software

**Labor and Equipment Table**

| Type | Average Use | Total |
|------|-------------|-------|
| Computer technician | 1 @ 8 hrs./day | 40 hrs. |
| Tester (user or technician) | 1 @ 4 hrs./day | 20 hrs. |
| Software test kit | 1 per tester | 1 test kit |

The training manager does not want the training room out of use for a whole week. In fact, he wants the upgrade done over a weekend so the training room doesn't lose any availability.

**Revised Estimate**

*Duration:* 2 days                                        *Materials:* 20 copies of the new software

**Labor and Equipment Table**

| Type | Average Use | Total |
|------|-------------|-------|
| Computer technician | 2 @ 10 hrs./day | 40 hrs. |
| Tester (user or technician) | 1 @ 10 hrs./day | 20 hrs. |
| Software test kit | 1 per tester | 1 test kit |

By adding 1 computer technician and working longer days, the duration is cut from 5 days to 2.

## How the Amount of Labor Relates to Duration

How long it takes to perform a task usually depends on how many people are assigned to do it. When you estimate the duration of a task, you will normally figure in the amount of available labor. In the example in Table 9.3, when a training manager added one more technician to a task involving a software upgrade, this addition, plus longer working days, cut the duration of the task from five days to two.

The work package estimates for the home landscape project in Table 9.1 include an example of using extra people to reduce the duration of a task. When the project team (the homeowner and the family's three teenagers) estimated Task 10, "Remove debris," they agreed it would be a long, unpleasant task if they worked on it alone. So they recruited some of the members of their local youth group to

## TABLE 9.4   Work Package Estimates: Example 3

*Task description:* A government agency is mapping a forest. Aerial photography of the entire area is the first step in creating the maps.

*Assumption:* An aerial photography subcontractor rents airplanes (complete with pilots and photographers). The agency has one scientist ride with every airplane. The forest is broken into 60 squares. They can photograph one square per day. During the flight, a ground technician stays in radio contact with the scientist to answer mapping questions.

### First Estimate

*Duration:* 60 days
*Materials:* None

### Labor and Equipment Table

| Type | Average Use | Total |
|------|-------------|-------|
| Scientist (in plane) | 1 @ 8 hrs./day | 480 hrs. |
| Airplane | 1 @ 8 hrs./day | 480 hrs. |
| Ground technician | 1 @ 8 hrs./day | 480 hrs. |

The forest area traditionally has so much cloudy weather that the agency estimates there will be only one clear day out of every three, but the photography needs to take place during the three months of summer when there is no snow.

Given this requirement, they decide to fly two airplanes every clear day. On days they can't fly there is no airplane cost and the scientist and ground technician can work on other things. A single ground technician can stay in contact with both airplanes.

### Revised Estimate

*Duration:* 90 days
*Materials:* None

### Labor and Equipment Table

| Type | Average Use | Total |
|------|-------------|-------|
| Scientist (in plane) | 2 @ 2.7 hrs./day | 480 hrs. |
| Airplane | 2 @ 2.7 hrs./day | 480 hrs. |
| Ground technician | 1 @ 2.7 hrs./day | 240 hrs. |

Since one ground technician can talk to both airplanes, the total labor for that person is cut in half. The expected hours for the scientist and the airplanes stay the same.

The average use estimates are used during the resource-leveling step to indicate the average amount of time the scientists and ground technician will have available to work on other projects during this 90-day period.

## *TABLE 9.5* Work Package Estimates: Example 4

*Task description:* A systems analyst is working on three projects at the same time. One of her project managers asks her to estimate the design of a subsystem.

*Assumption:* She will continue to work on all three projects simultaneously.

**First Estimate**

*Duration:* 40 days
*Materials:* None

**Labor and Equipment Table**

| Type | Average Use | Total |
|---|---|---|
| Systems analyst | 1 @ 2.5 hrs./day | 100 |

Her project manager needs the design performed much faster and suggests he could get another analyst to work with her part-time.

**Revised Estimate**

*Duration:* 30 days
*Materials:* None

**Labor and Equipment Table**

| Type | Average Use | Total |
|---|---|---|
| Systems analyst | 2 @ 2.5 hrs./day | 150 |

Adding people to a design task can speed up some of the work, but much of it will be done together so it results in an increase in the total labor cost. It is possible the resulting design will be better, but that is another assumption.

Then the project manager asks her what it would take to get it done the fastest. She responds, "Talk to my other project managers and arrange to get me completely off those projects for a few weeks so I can concentrate 100 percent on yours."

**Revised Estimate**

*Duration:* 10 days
*Materials:* None

**Labor and Equipment Table**

| Type | Average Use | Total |
|---|---|---|
| Systems analyst | 1 @ 8 hrs./day | 80 |

Not only is she able to spend more time per day on this task, but she knows if she is able to concentrate on it 100 percent she will be more productive.

help them for a few days. With eight people working on the task, it can be accomplished in four days.

## How Productivity Relates to Duration

When estimating the number of people needed for a task, you will need to consider their productivity. Adding people to simple tasks always reduces the duration. Productivity is said to be constant when the total labor hours do not change as the number of people assigned to the task changes. (The productivity of the technicians in Table 9.3 was constant; so was the "Remove debris" task in Table 9.1.)

However, in the case of tasks involving knowledge workers, adding more workers does not always result in greater productivity and shorter duration for a task. For example, if two engineers are working on a complex problem, adding three more may actually slow the task and produce no recognizable change in product quality. The result is a measurable decrease in productivity because the cost for labor increases while the product stays the same. (The first revised estimate in Table 9.5 is another example of this factor.)

Another point to consider when measuring productivity is that people who spend all their time on one project are usually more productive than people who spread their time across multiple projects (again, see Table 9.5). The analyst estimates that the most productive way for her to work—requiring the fewest hours and fewest days—is to be able to devote 100 percent of her attention to one project.

When calculating hours for your part-time project workers, it is usually unnecessary to figure out exactly what hour of which day they'll be working on your project. By assigning a resource-level assumption, such as "two hours per day," to all their tasks, you proportionally increase the estimates for the duration of the task. This approach allows each individual team member to decide for himself or herself when to actually work on the task. It doesn't matter whether they get started on it as soon as it's scheduled or work on it the last day. All you need to do to prepare a detailed plan is to give them a start time and a completion time.

As you can see, there is much to be considered when estimating the costs and duration of work packages. Chapter 11 discusses the subject further, with many more tips and techniques.

## PLANNING STEP FOUR: CALCULATE AN INITIAL SCHEDULE

Calculating a schedule may be one of the most well known, but unappreciated, of all project management techniques. It can be particularly tedious and time-consuming when done by hand for large projects. Yet it is the key to establishing realistic schedules and meeting them. (The tedium involved is a compelling reason to use project management software.)

As discussed earlier, the initial schedule is calculated by using the network diagram and the duration of each work package to determine the start and finish dates for each task, and for the entire project. Figure 9.4 shows how the network and task duration can work together to produce an initial schedule. Schedule calculation provides a set of detailed schedule data for every work package, as shown in the following:

*Early start* —The earliest date a task can begin, given the tasks preceding it.

*Early finish* —The earliest date a task can finish, given the tasks preceding it.

*Late start* —The latest date a task can begin without delaying the finish date of the project.

*Late finish* —The latest date a task can finish without delaying the finish date of the project.

Calculating the schedule to determine these four dates is a three-step process. Referring to Figure 9.4 will help to clarify this process.

### Step One: Forward Pass

The forward pass will help you determine the early start (ES) and early finish (EF) for each task. It is so named because it involves working through a network diagram from start to finish. (The next step will involve the reverse—a backward pass.) In Figure 9.4, we follow a forward pass through the diagram, step by step.

Figure 9.5 shows another way of displaying this information. It's called a *time-scaled network* because it uses a time scale across the top and each task is laid out across the calendar. Notice that all the early start dates are the same in Figures 9.4 and 9.5.

### Step Two: Backward Pass

The backward pass determines the late start and late finish dates. All of us have made this calculation hundreds of times—whenever we set an alarm clock. The goal of the backward pass is literally to work backward from the project finish date to determine how late any task can begin or end. The late start (LS) and late finish (LF) are calculated in Figure 9.4.

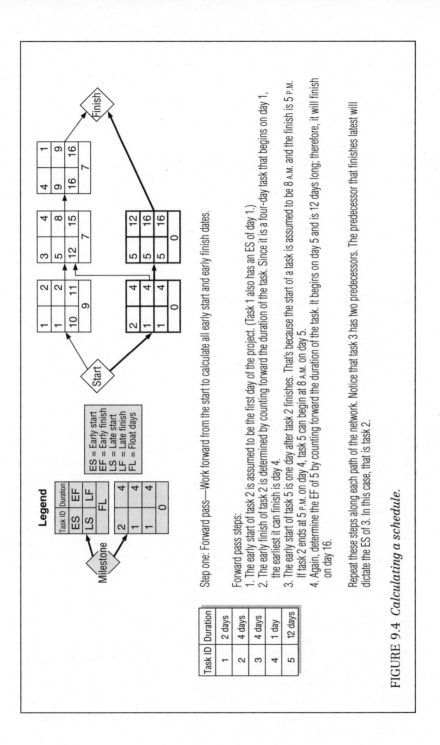

**Legend**

| | | |
|---|---|---|
| Task ID | Duration | |
| ES | EF | |
| LS | LF | |
| | FL | |

ES = Early start
EF = Early finish
LS = Late start
LF = Late finish
FL = Float days

| Task ID | Duration |
|---|---|
| 1 | 2 days |
| 2 | 4 days |
| 3 | 4 days |
| 4 | 1 day |
| 5 | 12 days |

Step one: Forward pass—Work forward from the start to calculate all early start and early finish dates.

Forward pass steps:

1. The early start of task 2 is assumed to be the first day of the project. (Task 1 also has an ES of day 1.)
2. The early finish of task 2 is determined by counting forward the duration of the task. Since it is a four-day task that begins on day 1, the earliest it can finish is day 4.
3. The early start of task 5 is one day after task 2 finishes. That's because the start of a task is assumed to be 8 A.M. and the finish is 5 P.M. If task 2 ends at 5 P.M. on day 4, task 5 can begin at 8 A.M. on day 5.
4. Again, determine the EF of 5 by counting forward the duration of the task. It begins on day 5 and is 12 days long; therefore, it will finish on day 16.

Repeat these steps along each path of the network. Notice that task 3 has two predecessors. The predecessor that finishes latest will dictate the ES of 3. In this case, that is task 2.

FIGURE 9.4 *Calculating a schedule.*

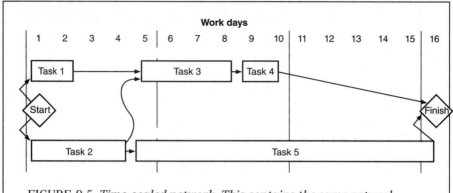

FIGURE 9.5  *Time-scaled network. This contains the same network information as Figure 9.4, but the format is different.*

### Step Three: Calculate Float

Some tasks have flexibility in when they can be performed in the schedule, and others have no flexibility. The term for this schedule flexibility is *float*. (Another common term is *slack*.) Float is calculated by subtracting early start from late start. (How to calculate float is demonstrated graphically in Figures 9.4, 9.6, and 9.7.)

 **Critical Path**

When the initial schedule has been calculated, the project schedule begins to take shape. One of the key features of the initial schedule is the critical path. The term *critical path* is one of the most widely used—and most widely misunderstood—of all project management terms. But the concept is simple: The critical path is defined as all of the tasks with zero or negative float. When outlined on a network diagram, the critical path is the longest path through the network (the *longest path* means the longest duration, not necessarily the most tasks). The critical path is boldly outlined in Figures 9.4 and 9.6.

The tasks that have zero float must be completed at their early finish date, or the project finish will be delayed. Making sure that all critical path tasks begin and end on time is the surest way of making the project end on time. That's why you'll hear a project manager motivating someone to complete a task by telling the person, "It's on the critical path!"

Since it is the longest path through the network, the critical path is one measure of schedule viability. This is because it demonstrates the *minimum* time the project will take. Sometimes it takes a network diagram with the critical path outlined to show stakeholders that their optimistic schedule estimate is unrealistic.

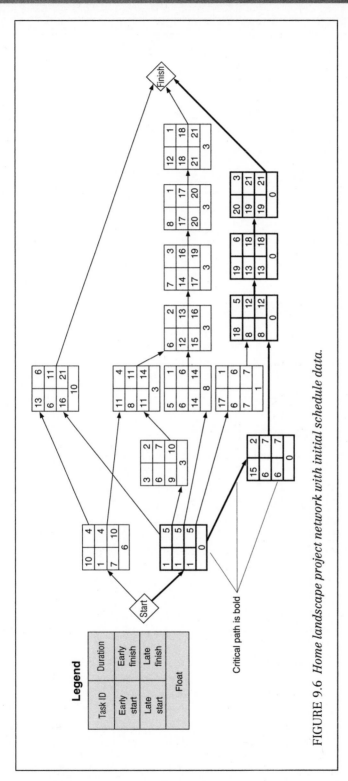

FIGURE 9.6 *Home landscape project network with initial schedule data.*

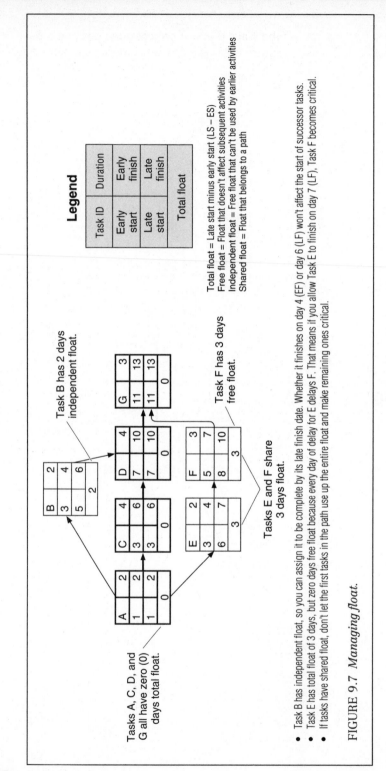

FIGURE 9.7 *Managing float.*

Tasks A, C, D, and G all have zero (0) days total float.

Task B has 2 days independent float.

Task F has 3 days free float.

Tasks E and F share 3 days float.

**Legend**

| Task ID | Duration |
|---|---|
| Early start | Early finish |
| Late start | Late finish |
| Total float | |

Total float = Late start minus early start (LS − ES)
Free float = Float that doesn't affect subsequent activities
Independent float = Free float that can't be used by earlier activities
Shared float = Float that belongs to a path

| A | 2 |
| 1 | 2 |
| 1 | 2 |
| 0 | |

| B | 2 |
| 3 | 4 |
| 5 | 6 |
| | 2 |

| C | 4 |
| 3 | 6 |
| 3 | 6 |
| 0 | |

| D | 4 |
| 7 | 10 |
| 7 | 10 |
| 0 | |

| G | 3 |
| 11 | 13 |
| 11 | 13 |
| 0 | |

| E | 2 |
| 3 | 4 |
| 6 | 7 |
| | 3 |

| F | 3 |
| 5 | 7 |
| 8 | 10 |
| | 3 |

- Task B has independent float, so you can assign it to be complete by its late finish date. Whether it finishes on day 4 (EF) or day 6 (LF) won't affect the start of successor tasks.
- Task E has total float of 3 days, but zero days free float because every day of delay for E delays F. That means if you allow Task E to finish on day 7 (LF), Task F becomes critical.
- If tasks have shared float, don't let the first tasks in the path use up the entire float and make remaining ones critical.

These are just two of the ways that the project manager might use the critical path. Several more are described later in this chapter and in Chapters 12 and 17.

## Shop Early and Avoid Negative Float

Not every project has a critical path. If a project has an externally imposed finish date that allows more than enough time to complete the project, all tasks will have float. A simple example is Christmas shopping. December 25 is the externally imposed finish date. Early in the year, when there are 200 shopping days until Christmas, nobody is stressed—because there is still plenty of float. Like Christmas shopping, most projects with no critical path are put off until all the float is used up.

When all the float has been used up, a new term emerges to describe the situation: *negative float*. Negative float results when externally imposed finish dates are impossible to meet (such as 10 presents to buy at 6 p.m. on December 24). Figure 9.8, for example, shows a network diagram with a critical path that is longer than the allotted schedule. When there is negative float, it means that adjustments will have to be made to bring the schedule in line with the critical path. This is the kind of information you will need when you renegotiate the cost-schedule-quality equilibrium.

## Gantt Charts and Time-Scaled Networks

A picture is worth a thousand words. The network diagram is essential in calculating the schedule, but it can be terribly difficult to decipher on a large project. Thankfully, there are two very good alternatives, which display both the schedule information and the task relationships.

Gantt charts, named after Henry Gantt, who developed them in the early 1900s, have become the most common method for displaying a project schedule. Figure 9.9 is a Gantt chart for the home landscape project. It has the same schedule dates as the network in Figure 9.6. Notice that all the tasks are currently scheduled at their early start date—you can tell that because all noncritical tasks display float. The great advantage of the Gantt chart is its clarity: The horizontal axis shows the schedule and the vertical axis lists the work breakdown structure.

Another excellent graphic for displaying a schedule is the time-scaled network (as shown in Figures 9.5 and 9.10). One advantage that this diagram has compared to the Gantt chart is the ability to condense the network onto less paper. On large projects, the Gantt charts can grow too large to print, whereas the time-scaled network, because it combines many tasks on one line, can be made one-half to one-tenth the height of the Gantt.

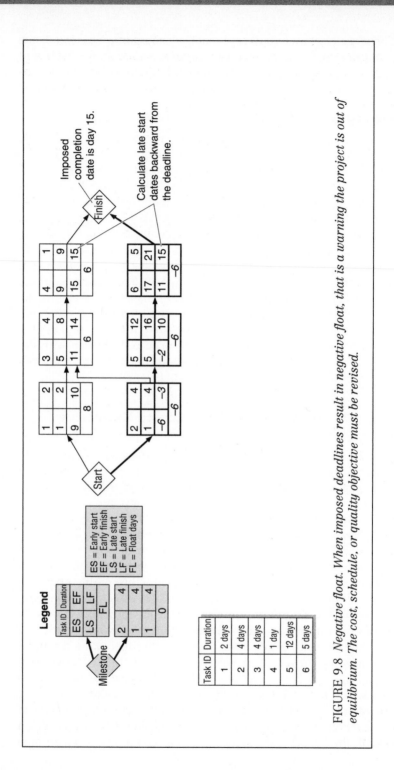

FIGURE 9.8 *Negative float. When imposed deadlines result in negative float, that is a warning the project is out of equilibrium. The cost, schedule, or quality objective must be revised.*

The initial schedule represents the combination of task sequence and task duration, but it's called an *initial schedule* because it hasn't taken into account people and equipment limitations. The next planning step uses the initial schedule as a starting point and balances it against the resources available to the project.

## PLANNING STEP FIVE: ASSIGN AND LEVEL RESOURCES

The goal of resource leveling is to optimize the use of people and equipment assigned to the project. It begins with the assumption that, whenever possible, it is most productive to have consistent, continuous use of the fewest resources possible. In other words, it seeks to avoid repeatedly adding and removing resources time and again throughout the project. Resource leveling is the last step in creating a realistic schedule. It confronts the reality of limited people and equipment and adjusts the schedule to compensate.

Using the home landscape project as an example, we can see how resource leveling makes a project schedule more realistic. The network (Figure 9.6) shows, in terms of task scheduling, that it's possible to put in the lawn and build the fence at the same time. But when we consider that the family has only the three teenagers available to work on the project, that means they have just a total of 24 labor hours available each day (3 teens × 8 hours per day). Trying to put in the lawn and build the fence concurrently is unrealistic because it would require each teen to work far more than eight hours a day for more than half the project. (The resource spreadsheet on the Gantt chart in Figure 9.11 indicates clearly how unrealistic the schedule is.) Resource leveling will adjust the schedule to keep the teens busy at a consistent, reasonable rate. (Figure 9.12 shows the same project as Figure 9.11, but with the resources leveled.) Not only does resource leveling take unreasonable overtime out of their project, but it also keeps the teens employed for a longer time at a steady rate. That's usually an advantage for any project team.

Let's consider a few of the problems faced by project managers in this process of leveling resources.

Every project faces the reality of limited people and equipment. The idea is to avoid both over- and under-allocation. As the home landscape project demonstrates, too many concurrent tasks can call for more resources than are available. For example, as discussed, the initial schedule had the teens working on the fence and the lawn during the same period, and this resulted in the teens being over-allocated during the first half of the project (they would have had to work more than eight hours a day to meet this schedule).

Project managers need to remember that whether it's teenagers planting the lawn, bulldozers, or programmers, there are rarely a bunch of spares sitting on the shelf. This over-allocation problem can become

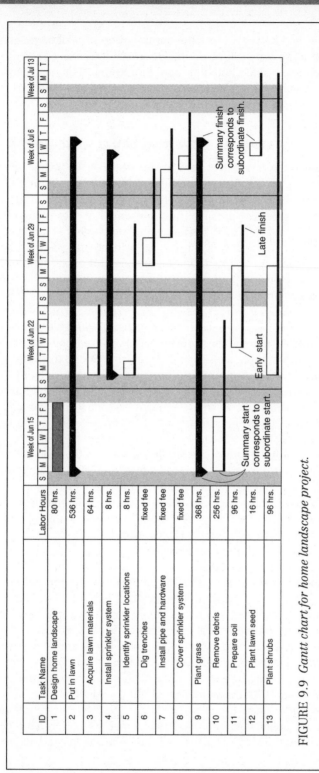

FIGURE 9.9 *Gantt chart for home landscape project.*

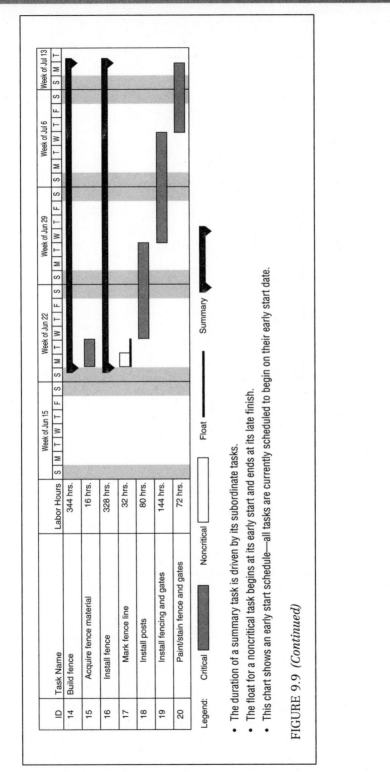

| ID | Task Name | Labor Hours |
|---|---|---|
| 14 | Build fence | 344 hrs. |
| 15 | Acquire fence material | 16 hrs. |
| 16 | Install fence | 328 hrs. |
| 17 | Mark fence line | 32 hrs. |
| 18 | Install posts | 80 hrs. |
| 19 | Install fencing and gates | 144 hrs. |
| 20 | Paint/stain fence and gates | 72 hrs. |

Legend:  Critical ▓▓▓  Noncritical ▢  Float ▭▭▭  Summary ▮▬▮

- The duration of a summary task is driven by its subordinate tasks.
- The float for a noncritical task begins at its early start and ends at its late finish.
- This chart shows an early start schedule—all tasks are currently scheduled to begin on their early start date.

FIGURE 9.9 *(Continued)*

205

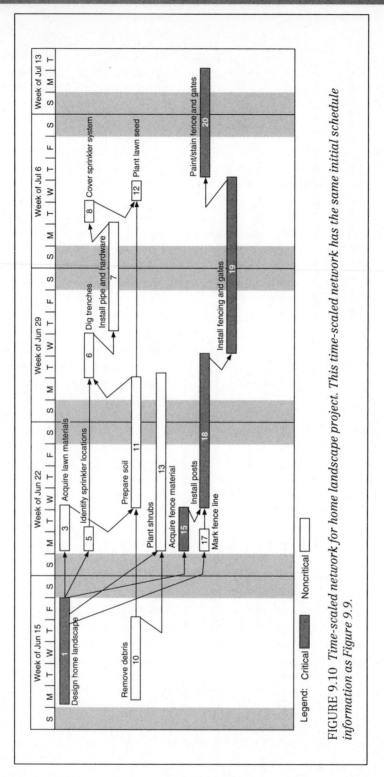

FIGURE 9.10  *Time-scaled network for home landscape project. This time-scaled network has the same initial schedule information as Figure 9.9.*

Legend:  Critical ▮   Noncritical ▯

especially acute if project managers imagine that they have a large supply of a rare resource, such as the unlimited time of the only subject-matter expert in the company. In this case, not only has the schedule become unrealistic, but the manager may have overloaded a key resource.

The other side of the problem is under-allocation. If the project team isn't busy on your project, it will likely be reassigned to other projects and be unavailable when the next peak comes. In the worst case, during lulls in the project some of the unassigned people may get laid off, becoming permanently unavailable and taking valuable knowledge about your project with them.

A further problem arises if people working on this project are also working on several others at the same time. If every project in the firm has wild swings in its resource requirements, it is almost impossible to move people smoothly between projects. Instead, people are yanked off one project to help another catch up, only to be thrown at yet another that is even further behind.

### The Process of Resource Leveling

It is important to remember how we are defining the term *resources*. Resources are the people, equipment, and raw materials that go into the project. Resource leveling focuses only on the people and equipment; the materials needed for the project are dictated by the specifications.

Resource leveling begins with the initial schedule and work package resource requirements (see Table 9.1). The leveling follows a four-step process:

1. *Forecast the resource requirements throughout the project for the initial schedule.* The best tool for this process is a resource spreadsheet such as the one portrayed in Figure 9.11. This spreadsheet, correlated to the schedule, can forecast all the people and equipment needed on each day of the project. The initial schedule is sometimes called an *early start schedule*. At first, this might seem like good project management, that is, getting as early a start on everything as possible. But an early start schedule usually has a lot of uneconomical resource peaks and valleys. For example, the over-allocation of the teens during the first half of the home landscape project is the kind of misallocation common to early start schedules.

2. *Identify the resource peaks.* Use the resource spreadsheet (Figure 9.11) and the resources histogram (Figure 9.13) to find the periods in the project where there are unrealistic or uneconomical resource amounts.

3. *At each peak, delay noncritical tasks within their float.* Remember that float is schedule flexibility. Tasks with float can be

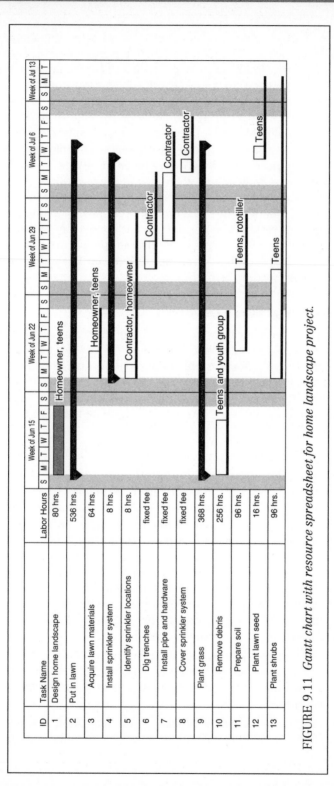

FIGURE 9.11 *Gantt chart with resource spreadsheet for home landscape project.*

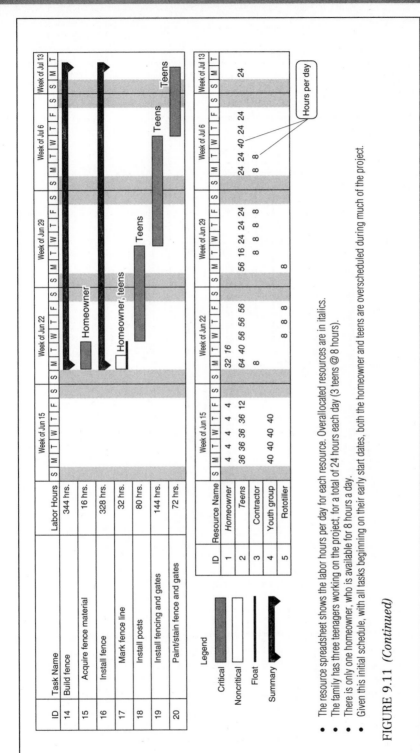

| ID | Task Name | Labor Hours |
|---|---|---|
| 14 | Build fence | 344 hrs. |
| 15 | Acquire fence material | 16 hrs. |
| 16 | Install fence | 328 hrs. |
| 17 | Mark fence line | 32 hrs. |
| 18 | Install posts | 80 hrs. |
| 19 | Install fencing and gates | 144 hrs. |
| 20 | Paint/stain fence and gates | 72 hrs. |

Legend

Critical

Noncritical

Float

Summary

| ID | Resource Name | Week of Jun 15 S M T W T F S | Week of Jun 22 S M T W T F S | Week of Jun 29 S M T W T F S | Week of Jul 6 S M T W T F S | Week of Jul 13 S M T |
|---|---|---|---|---|---|---|
| 1 | *Homeowner* | 4 4 4 4 4 | 32 16 | | | |
| 2 | *Teens* | 36 36 36 36 12 | 64 40 56 56 56 | 56 16 24 24 24 | 24 24 40 24 24 | 24 |
| 3 | Contractor | | 8 | 8 8 8 8 | 8 8 | |
| 4 | Youth group | 40 40 40 40 | 8 8 8 | | | |
| 5 | Rototiller | | | 8 | | |

Hours per day

- The resource spreadsheet shows the labor hours per day for each resource. Overallocated resources are in italics.
- The family has three teenagers working on the project, for a total of 24 hours each day (3 teens @ 8 hours).
- There is only one homeowner, who is available for 8 hours a day.
- Given this initial schedule, with all tasks beginning on their early start dates, both the homeowner and teens are overscheduled during much of the project.

FIGURE 9.11 *(Continued)*

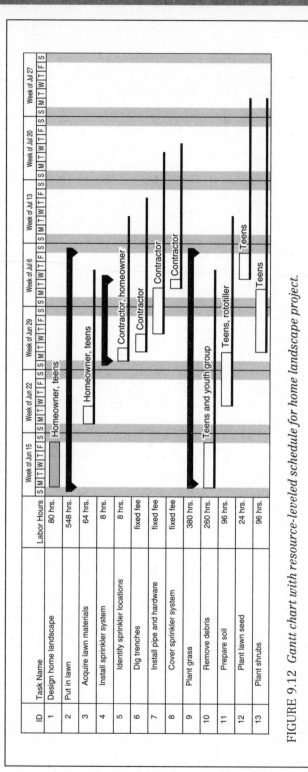

FIGURE 9.12 *Gantt chart with resource-leveled schedule for home landscape project.*

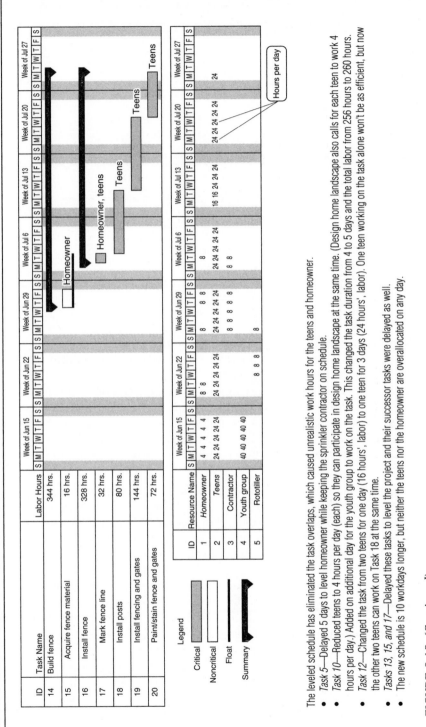

FIGURE 9.12 *(Continued)*

The leveled schedule has eliminated the task overlaps, which caused unrealistic work hours for the teens and homeowner.

- *Task 5*—Delayed 5 days to level homeowner while keeping the sprinkler contractor on schedule.
- *Task 10*—Reduced teens to 4 hours per day (each) so they can participate in design home landscape at the same time. (Design home landscape also calls for each teen to work 4 hours per day.) Added on additional day for the youth group to work on the task. This changed the task duration from 4 to 5 days and the total labor from 256 hours to 260 hours.
- *Task 12*—Changed the task from two teens for one day (16 hours', labor) to one teen for 3 days (24 hours', labor). One teen working on the task alone won't be as efficient, but now the other two teens can work on Task 18 at the same time.
- *Tasks 13, 15, and 17*—Delayed these tasks to level the project and their successor tasks were delayed as well.
- The new schedule is 10 workdays longer, but neither the teens nor the homeowner are overallocated on any day.

211

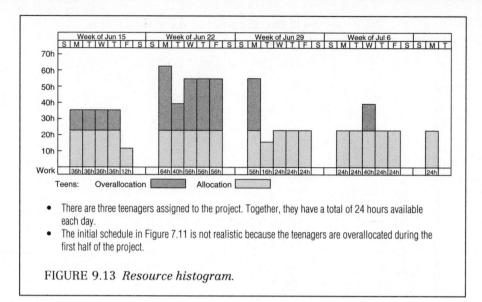

- There are three teenagers assigned to the project. Together, they have a total of 24 hours available each day.
- The initial schedule in Figure 7.11 is not realistic because the teenagers are overallocated during the first half of the project.

FIGURE 9.13 *Resource histogram.*

delayed without changing the project deadline. By delaying these tasks, you'll also be filling in the valleys of the resource histogram, that is, moving tasks from periods of too much work to periods when there is too little work. This means that you will need fewer people and they will be more productive, but the deadline will stay the same. (A comparison of the initial schedule in Figure 9.11 with the leveled schedule in Figure 9.12 demonstrates how Task 5 was delayed within its float, thus removing a resource peak for the homeowner on June 24.)

4. *Eliminate the remaining peaks by reevaluating the work package estimates.* Using the project float in Step 3 may not be enough to eliminate all the peaks and valleys. For example, instead of having two or three people working together on a task, consider whether just one person could do the work over a longer period of time. (Task 12 in Figure 9.12 was changed from two teenagers for one day to one teen for three days.) Alternatively, available people might be added to a task to shorten its duration. When performing these changes, take note that each change to a work package estimate is going to change the amount of float, or time flexibility, for that task. In other words, after changing a work package estimate, you will need to return to step 4 and recalculate the initial schedule. Then you will also need to repeat the first three steps of resource leveling. (This kind of recalculation is made much easier by using project management software.)

## KEY CONCEPT

### What to Do If the Resource-Leveled Plan Is Still Unrealistic

Re-estimating work packages and delaying tasks within their float can remove the worst resource peaks and valleys, but the plan might still contain unrealistic or uneconomic resource peaks. At that point, your next option is accepting a later project completion date.

On the home landscape project, the schedule had to be extended by two weeks to balance the available labor with the amount of work. This can be a difficult decision, but that's what it means to create a realistic cost-schedule-quality equilibrium. In Chapter 12, there will be further discussion of the factors that balance the schedule against cost and quality.

## DANGER!

### Computers Will Not Do Everything

Some of the tedious calculations described here are easily performed by project management software, but don't be fooled. Computers really perform only two tasks: data storage and calculations. Even if you employ a good software package, you will still have to understand each one of the steps in this chapter. (The Appendix at the back of the book summarizes the planning steps using the home landscape example.)

## KEY CONCEPT

### SMALL PROJECTS NEED SMALLER PLANS

Every project benefits from an action plan. The five steps of planning covered in Chapters 8 and 9 provide an analytical thought process as well as an approach to organizing and communicating the details of how we'll do the work. Small projects benefit from the analytical thought process even if they don't need all of the artifacts of planning. Every project, no matter what size it is, needs a clear understanding of the basic elements of a plan:

- *The list of tasks* to be performed (the work breakdown structure).

- *The proper sequence of those tasks*, particularly so people who are trying to coordinate their actions understand who needs to get their piece done so others can start theirs.

- *Key schedule goals.* Small projects with part-time teams may not need specific start and finish dates for every task. But project team members do need to know when their tasks are due and the impact on the team if they are late.

The need to efficiently coordinate work exists for all sizes of project teams. That coordination relies on clear task responsibilities and due dates that reflect sequence constraints.

### END POINT

The detailed planning techniques presented in this chapter are often downplayed as mere scheduling techniques. However, not only do they build a realistic schedule, but these techniques also form the foundation of the science of project management.

The planning model in this chapter portrays the step-by-step method of building a detailed plan. Laying out a detailed plan may not solve all the problems you'll face as a project manager, but it does provide a tool set for solving many of them. Every one of these planning techniques will be referred to again in later chapters. They are the entry point to the science of project management; without them it's impossible to practice the art.

### FAST FOUNDATION IN PROJECT MANAGEMENT

Large or complex projects can follow the advice in Part 3 together with project management software to build detailed action plans. Simpler projects may call for a simpler format.

The action plan template is simply a spreadsheet formatted with standard headings for recording the basic information of a plan and tracking actual performance. Fill in the calendar portion by shading the cells to create a Gantt chart. This template is available for download at www.VersatileCompany.com/FFMBAinPM.

See an example of this action plan template on page 490.

## PMP Exam Prep Questions

1. You are the project manager on a defense project and are creating a network diagram. Activity A (7 days) and Activity B (12 days) can start immediately. Activity C (3 days) can start after Activity A is complete. Activity D (4 days) and Activity F (3 days) can start after Activity B is complete. Activity E (5 days) can start after Activity C and Activity D are complete. Activity G (6 days) can start after Activity D and Activity F are complete. When Activity E and Activity G are complete, the project is done. What is the critical path?

   a. BDE

   b. ACE

   c. BFG

   d. BDG

2. Using the original network diagram question, what is the slack of Activity F?

   a. Two days

   b. One day

   c. Four days

   d. Not enough information

3. In the original network diagram question, if Activity D increases from four to five days, what is the critical path, and what is the length?

   a. BDE, 33 days

   b. ACE, 15 days

   c. BFG, 21 days

   d. BDG, 23 days

4. To determine the float, which formula should you use?

   a. Late finish-early finish (LF-EF) or late finish-late start (LF-LS)

   b. Late start-early start (LS-ES) or late finish-late start (LF-LS)

   c. Late finish-early finish (LF-EF) or late start-early start (LS-ES)

   d. Late start-early start (LS-ES) or early finish-early start (EF-ES)

Answers to these questions can be found at www.VersatileCompany .com/FFMBAinPM.

# 10

# Managing Agile Development with Scrum

## INTRODUCTION

If you could travel back to 1999, the end of the twentieth century, log on to the Internet and visit Amazon.com, you'd find a much simpler website and business than exists today. Yet, if you have been a regular Amazon user since that time, there is probably no point that you remember when "everything changed." Instead, they changed their services and the site operation *incrementally*.

Incremental delivery has many characteristics that are similar to a traditional understanding of projects. Something new and valuable is delivered by a team working together under a timeline. But there are also differences. In the Amazon example, one can envision many independent teams that relentlessly improve the features and functionality of the website and the associated customer-facing services. The change is so constant and never-ending that it doesn't fit the traditional paradigm of a project that can be approved, defined, planned, executed, and closed out.

In Chapter 3 we established the advantage of incremental delivery as an approach that made sense for developing products where high uncertainty exists. Each increment of delivery creates a feedback and course-correction opportunity. In these cases, there can eventually be an end to the project, when the customer decides that what has been delivered is sufficient for meeting the business goal.

So how do we manage these not-quite-projects? Agile is a framework for incremental delivery, particularly in software. It consists of techniques that allow for repeating the cycle of requirements-design-develop-test-deliver. One of these techniques is Scrum. Scrum is a management approach designed for incremental delivery.

Scrum belongs in a book on project management because more organizations are managing changes with incremental delivery, and not just software projects. The principles and techniques of Scrum have been proven in purely agile, incremental development efforts. In a world of increasing change, any practitioner of project management that understands Scrum will see opportunities where these techniques present an alternative approach to planning and managing work.

### Scrum Focuses on Team Management and Customer Feedback

In Chapter 3, Alan Shalloway provided the overview of Agile on pages 57 to 64. He lists five key questions that agile attempts answer:

1. How do we deliver value quickly to our customers?
2. How do we discover as early as possible what is needed?
3. How can we accelerate the learning of the development team?
4. How can we ensure that the software written will be able to grow and be extended effectively when new requirements are introduced?
5. How do we accurately gauge the progress we're making in our project?

Notice that only the last question is related to project management. The other questions are about *requirements analysis* and *product design.*

Scrum is focused on how a team works together and interacts with the customer. Scrum addresses some of these questions, but not all of them. That suggests that organizations that are adopting agile methods embrace both Scrum techniques (work management) and make sure that developers understand agile analysis, design, and development methods. As Alan's questions indicate, this is a highly iterative, discovery-oriented methodology. To make it work requires the techniques to design and build products that can be delivered incrementally. (See www.NetObjectives.com and www.agilealliance.org for more on agile methods for building software.)

### SCRUM IS A FRAMEWORK

The Scrum community is careful to describe Scrum as a *framework*, not a methodology. The framework consists of roles, artifacts, activities and guidelines. Scrum is a good example of the discipline required in agile development. While it may seem simple, the benefits of agile and incremental delivery are directly proportional to the rigor with which the Scrum framework is applied.

This chapter presents the Scrum framework as it has emerged over the past 20 years and is promoted by the Scrum Alliance (www .scrumalliance.org).

## Scrum at a Glance

To deliver a product incrementally requires three activities:

- A decision about what increment of a product to deliver.
- A team to build and deliver that increment quickly.
- Feedback from the customer on whether the incremental product is useful.

Scrum encompasses all of these elements.

The actual development of the increment occurs in a "sprint." As the name implies, this is a focused product development activity that takes place over a short time, normally one to four weeks. Scrum teams string several sprints together, each producing incremental value. Each sprint is the same duration.

The decision about what increment to develop during the sprint takes place before the sprint. A customer representative, called a "product owner," describes the most important potential improvements to the development team. This list of potential improvements is called a "product backlog." The development team talks among themselves and makes a commitment to the product owner about what they can deliver by the end of the sprint.

At the end of the sprint, the team shows the product owner what they've just built. The product owner can choose to accept it, or to reject it and explain why.

The Scrum framework defines the responsibilities of the product owner, the development team, and a key facilitator, the "Scrum master." These are the key Scrum roles. The key Scrum activities include the sprint and specific meetings before, during and after the sprint: sprint planning, daily Scrum, sprint review, and sprint retrospective. During the activities, the Scrum team uses specific artifacts, such as the product backlog.

## Scrum Roles

A principle of Scrum is to enable the development team to perform focused, productive work at a pace chosen by the development team. To accomplish this goal, Scrum defines three specific roles: product owner, development team, and Scrum master. Together, these three roles comprise the Scrum team.

### Product Owner

The product owner's job is to maximize the value of each sprint by providing clarity about what the product should do and to prioritize the list of potential improvements. Therefore, the product owner must be in a position to thoroughly understand the desires of the product's customers and end-users. In addition, the product owner must be an individual—not a committee—with the authority to set the priority in the product backlog.

### Development Team

The work of creating the product is done by the development team. Since incremental delivery assumes each increment must be understood (requirements refined), designed, developed, and tested, the development team must contain all the skills required to perform that work. The Scrum development team is also focused: they are working on one Scrum team and one sprint at a time. This team is mature enough to make and keep commitments to the product owner and the members are accountable to each other. (See more on attributes of high performance teams in Chapter 13.) Scrum guidelines call for development teams to be large enough to contain the cross-functional skills required, yet small enough for informal communication and coordination—in effect, fewer than ten people.

### Scrum Master

The first and most important job of the individual playing the role of Scrum master is to understand and promote the Scrum roles and practices both within the Scrum team and within the larger organization. The role is perhaps paradoxical—the "master" is the servant of the product owner and development team. Scrum masters focus on enabling others, facilitating communication and meetings, coaching the development team, and removing impediments to productivity. A key responsibility of the Scrum master is protecting the development team from being distracted or losing focus due to communication from stakeholders or management. All communication to the development team goes through the Scrum master or product owner.

Each of these roles will be further explored within the context of Scrum activities.

### Stakeholders

The Scrum team is not operating in isolation. Scrum recognizes that many other people interact with these three core roles. However, Scrum asserts that together these three roles working within the guidelines of Scrum make a powerful unit of productivity and therefore focuses all of its guidelines on what the Scrum team does. Anyone outside the Scrum team that has an interest in the project is simply referred to as a stakeholder.

## KEY CONCEPT — Scrum Activities: Before, During, and After the Sprint

Agile development increases flexibility and responsiveness, yet Scrum itself insists on adherence to some specific structures and disciplines. This paradox is revealed in the core activity of Scrum, the sprint, and in the activities that surround the sprint.

### A Release Is a Series of Sprints

To put a sprint in context, remember the first two goals quoted from Alan Shalloway's article in Chapter 3:

1. How do we deliver value quickly to our customers?
2. How do we discover as early as possible what is needed?

Using a series of sprints accomplishes this goal because every sprint produces a product that the customer can inspect and use. Each sprint has the potential to change the understanding of what will be most useful to the customer. So a series of disciplined sprints provides multiple value delivery points and multiple course-correction points. Delivering a substantial change may require several sprints, a 'release' in the language of Scrum.

### The Sprint

A sprint follows very careful guidelines.

- The duration of the sprint is established at the start of the sprint and there are no conditions for allowing the duration to change. This is known as a "time-box." A sprint should last between one and four weeks. The duration is a planning horizon: the farthest into the future the development team can realistically forecast. Since iterative development applies to projects with high uncertainty, attempting to plan more than a month at a time is unrealistic.
- A sprint has an established scope. The first action of the sprint is the sprint planning meeting, described below, which produces a sprint goal. All work in the sprint is focused on the sprint goal, which does not change during the sprint.

- During the sprint, the development team works to accomplish the scope. The product owner is available to clarify requirements as needed.
- Every sprint begins with a sprint planning meeting and ends with a sprint review and sprint retrospective. As with the sprint itself, these meetings are strictly time-boxed.
- As soon as one sprint is accomplished, another can begin.

The four Scrum meetings described below create an effective, focused effort within the sprint.

## Sprint Planning

Every sprint must begin with a clear commitment and a plan for meeting the goal. That is the purpose of the sprint planning meeting. The Scrum team works together, each with a special contribution.

- The product owner establishes the priority of the product backlog and is the sole authority for what are the most important products to be produced during the sprint.
- The development team has the sole authority for deciding how much scope should be taken on during the sprint. They accomplish this by discussing the highest-priority products with the product owner so that they are able to estimate the effort required for each product.
- The development team then turns its attention to planning their work: breaking products into small tasks, usually less than a day in duration, and identifying any of those tasks which must be performed prior to others.
- The Scrum master's key contribution in sprint planning is facilitation, coaching the development team and product owner.

As a result of the sprint planning meeting, the development team is able to show the product owner and Scrum master what they'll produce and how they'll go about it. The time box for sprint planning is proportional to the duration of the sprint itself: a two-week sprint is planned within four hours and a four-week sprint is planned in a maximum of eight hours.

## Daily Scrum

The daily Scrum illustrates a core premise of Scrum: the development team is capable of coordinating work and does not need to be given direction by anyone in a position of greater authority. The meeting occurs daily at the same time and the time box for the daily Scrum is fifteen minutes. That is just enough time for the development team members to report to each other and collaborate on setting the focus for the day's work. During the meeting each member addresses three topics:

- Accomplishments since the previous meeting
- Task focus for the coming day
- Any impediments that were encountered

The Scrum master should not have to facilitate this meeting; that is the job of the team. However, the Scrum master ensures the meeting takes place and can coach the team if necessary. The Scrum master also attends the meeting in order to learn about obstacles to the team's productivity and can leave with a list of impediments to resolve.

### Sprint Review

The sprint review provides the customer feedback element to incremental delivery. Every sprint ends with a sprint review and sprint retrospective. The review is for delivering the result of the sprint to the customer and for the customer to either accept or reject it and provide feedback to the team. The retrospective, described next, is a forum for the Scrum team to reflect on their effectiveness and make adjustments prior to the next sprint.

The review has a time box whose length is proportional to the sprint: a one-week sprint has a one-hour review; a four-week sprint has a four-hour review.

This is the most inclusive, most open meeting in Scrum. In addition to the Scrum team, participants in the review include any interested stakeholder, particularly those who can provide feedback on the direction of the product.

When the development team presents, they show the actual product that has been developed, emphasizing that incremental delivery really means delivering an actual product. Each product from the product backlog that was accepted for this sprint is demonstrated, giving the product owner the option to accept the product or reject it and return it to the backlog for the next sprint.

After all the products are either accepted or rejected, there is also time for stakeholders outside the Scrum team to ask further questions or bring new information to help shape the product. Involvement in the review gives these stakeholders a realistic view of overall progress measured by what has been delivered and what remains in the product backlog.

### Sprint Retrospective

The end of each sprint is an opportunity for reflection by the Scrum team to discuss their own effectiveness. This principle of continuous learning and improvement is also discussed in more detail in Chapter 13. For the first few sprints, a Scrum master may need to take a larger role in leading this discussion.

The time box for this meeting is also proportional to the duration of the sprint. Expect the retrospective to last about three-quarters as long as a sprint review, using a three-hour meeting for a four-week sprint.

Every facet of team productivity can be discussed at this meeting, including interpersonal communication, tools, and team processes. One important topic is always how much of the sprint product commitment was reached and what factors contributed to or impeded productivity. The result of the retrospective is a list of changed behaviors to adapt in the next sprint.

## MANAGING THE PRODUCT BACKLOG

Return to a central principle of agile for a moment: deliver value quickly. The product backlog is the primary tool for defining the increments of value and for prioritizing these so that the most valuable are delivered first.

## A Product Backlog Is the List of Requirements

What do we want the product to do? How will a user interact with the product? In a traditional, linear (waterfall) system development process, the answers to these questions are defined as much as possible during the requirements phase. But as agile practitioners regularly point out, the list of requirements grows as the product is designed and developed. Even in the waterfall model, some requirements are left out as "nice to have" and are saved as candidates for future enhancements.

Rather than fight the challenge of ever-changing requirements, agile methods embrace this reality. Since the product is going to be delivered incrementally, the requirements really only need to be crystal clear for the product increments that the team is working on during the current sprint. The lower the priority a requirement is, the more acceptable it is for it to be general and abstract.

Agile requirements are defined through "user stories." While there are a variety of standards for user stories among different agile practitioners and advocates, they all generally agree that a user story describes a specific interaction or activity the user will have with the product. User stories take many forms, but a practical and popular format is as follows:

As a <type of user> I want to <take an action> so that I can <achieve a result>.
For example:

As an online banking customer I want to store the contact information of my regular payments so that I can save time when paying my monthly bills.

Notice that this format is similar to the business requirements that drive a project proposal (business case) as it is described in Chapter 4. It is focused on the user and the value the product will produce. It is not written about the technology. While the format is similar, user stories are much more narrowly focused on a very specific user desire.

Therefore, a product backlog represents all of the types of users that are expected and describes what each of them wants to accomplish in business terms that the users themselves should understand. Through discussion and negotiation with all the stakeholders, the product backlog is prioritized constantly to represent the most current view of what would make the product most valuable.

### Focused User Stories Fit into a Single Sprint

Another indicator of the narrow focus of a user story is that Scrum expects several user stories to be accomplished within a single sprint. Narrowly focused user stories also make it easier to decompose the user story into tasks that require a day or less to complete.

### An Evolving View of the Product

Agile assumes a product can be continually improved; therefore the list of requirements in the product backlog can be always growing. Not only does the list of stakeholder desires grow, but stakeholders may also eliminate user stories as their understanding of how the product will be most useful evolves.

In sprint planning meetings, the development team asks questions of the product owner to clarify the purpose and acceptance criteria of each user story at the top of the product backlog. This dialogue refines everyone's understanding. During the sprint review, as each user story is presented the product owner and stakeholders see the product emerging. Therefore, a sprint review may produce new, high priority user stories.

## The Product Owner Manages the Product Backlog

There is only one person who has the authority to add user stories or change the priority of user stories: the product owner. The product owner derives an understanding of requirements and the product vision from the stakeholders outside the Scrum team, but it is the product manager's responsibility to negotiate, prioritize and clarify requirements. The product owner must have the skill and fortitude to synthesize the interests of all stakeholders while holding the line on reality: only the most important user stories make it into a sprint.

**KEY CONCEPT**

## MAKE THE PLAN VISIBLE: TASK BOARDS AND BURNDOWN CHARTS

Chapter 9 shows how network diagrams and Gantt charts make a plan visible. Scrum also makes plans visible using task boards and burndown charts.

## Task Boards Record the Sprint Backlog and Work In Process

As a result of sprint planning, the development team has chosen user stories and decomposed those stories into tasks. Throughout the sprint, these tasks have three possible states: Not Started, In Process, and Complete. The task board shown in Figure 10.1 shows a common method of representing this information. The task board should be updated at the daily Scrum. As people report in, they move their tasks on the task board.

Visibility of work is key, so task boards are routinely physical spaces on a wall, using sticky notes or index cards. Teams also modify the task board to make it meaningful for themselves, so they add color to distinguish user stories from tasks, or add in process columns to represent particular kinds of work. It is very common to have a column labeled "Verify" between In Process and Complete. This column shows that one team member or the product owner is verifying the work of another team member before it is considered complete.

## Co-Location Increases Collaboration But Is Not a Requirement

**TIP**

Every element of Scrum benefits from a team that is seated together on a daily basis. But geographically dispersed teams are a reality that doesn't prevent teams from using Scrum. In this case, the task board is stored on an easily accessible digital location. There are many

| User Story | Task (Not Started) | in Process | Complete |
|---|---|---|---|
| | | | User Story A |
| | | | Task 1 |
| | | | Task 2 |
| | | | Task 3 |
| User Story B | Task 4 | Task 2 | Task 1 |
| | Task 5 | Task 3 | |
| | Task 6 | | |
| User Story C | Task 4 | Task 2 | Task 1 |
| | Task 5 | Task 3 | |
| | Task 6 | | |
| User Story D | Task 1 | | |
| | Task 2 | | |
| | Task 3 | | |

FIGURE 10.1 *A task board illustrates the sprint backlog and work in process. This task board shows User Story A as complete. Tasks are grouped by user story.*

web-based products that support Scrum, proving that this is a common situation.

## Sprint Burndown Charts Demonstrate Productivity Trends

The development team made a commitment at the beginning of the sprint, and they want to know whether they are on track to meet that commitment. The sprint burndown is a simple visual that shows whether they are on track to meet the goal.

The burndown chart in Figure 10.2 has two axes. The vertical axis represents total hours of effort for the team. The horizontal axis is time, and represents the total duration of the sprint. The chart is constructed during the sprint planning session by the Scrum master.

During sprint planning, as each task is identified it is assigned an estimate of work hours. The team is not encouraged to over-commit, so a general rule of thumb is to take on seven hours worth of work per team member per day. The team also subtracts the planning, review, and retrospective meetings from their capacity, so a ten-day sprint has only nine working days. In the example, a four-person team on a ten-day sprint has a total capacity of 252 hours, so they accept tasks that total up to 252 hours.

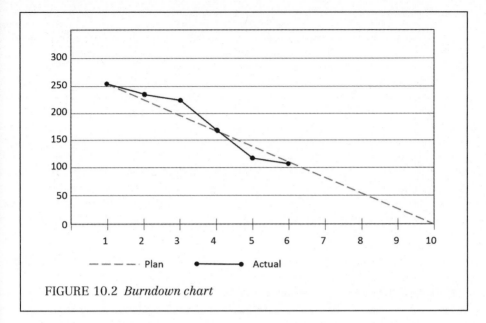

FIGURE 10.2 *Burndown chart*

Every day at the daily Scrum, tasks are shown as completed. The remaining backlog is recalculated, and mapped on the burndown chart. Within a few days a trend emerges. If the trend is not close to the planned productivity, then the team can see they are in danger of not meeting their commitment, and can decide what to do about it. Figure 10.3 demonstrates a sprint that has added tasks during the sprint. As with any project, a team can discover new work within a sprint. If the tasks are necessary to accomplish the user stories, then they are added to the sprint.

## KEY FACTORS FOR SCRUM TO BE EFFECTIVE

This overview of the Scrum approach to managing agile development has laid out the key roles, activities, and artifacts that make up Scrum. For all of these to work, certain environmental factors must also exist: mature, self-managing teams, a product that can be delivered incrementally, and an organization that has accepted the agile, incremental approach to product development.

**KEY CONCEPT**

### Self-Managing Teams Are Mature

From the sprint planning meeting through to the retrospective, the development team is expected to have the maturity to work cohesively, to be accountable to their commitments, and to maintain

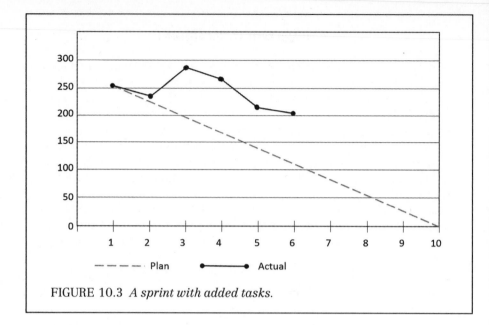

FIGURE 10.3 *A sprint with added tasks.*

respectful, productive relationships. Not all teams begin this way. A Scrum master can coach behaviors, but there is no "boss" to deal with any team member who doesn't play well in the group. Scrum assumes that, given the framework described here, a team has the ability to learn to manage itself and to improve its own productivity.

### A Product That Can Be Delivered Incrementally

The agile software development methods that have grown up in the past 20 years include approaches to design, coding, and testing. Figuring out how to actually build and deliver a product incrementally is every bit as important as managing the team with Scrum. The pioneers of agile and Scrum worked in software development. As these methods grow in popularity, new industries are finding ways to apply them. The trick is re-imagining how the product can be broken down into smaller elements that can be designed, built and tested in days or weeks.

 ### Scrum Must Be Embraced by Everyone

CONCEPT    The Scrum practices described in this chapter work well for the Scrum team, particularly the developers. But for Scrum to really work, all the stakeholders have to buy in to the agile premise: the benefits of incremental delivery outweigh the loss of a fixed date, fixed budget, and fixed specification.

---

### SCRUM AND PROJECT MANAGEMENT

Project management is a discipline that has evolved over the past seven decades through practice in a wide range of industries. Scrum, as described in this chapter, can trace its roots as far back as the mid-1980s, but only saw substantial growth with the advent of agile software development since 2001. Project management practitioners who don't work in agile software development will recognize some of the methods, but also be left with some questions about how Scrum fits with project management.

According to the strict definitions of Scrum as it is described by the Scrum Alliance, there is no project manager role in the Scrum framework. To reconcile this statement for yourself, reflect on the activities, roles, and artifacts described in this chapter and ask whether scope, schedule, cost, risk, and resources are being managed.

Scrum is quite focused on delivering incremental value through sprints. But what happens before the first sprint? Who decides whether there should be a project or when it should start? How are the people playing the Scrum roles assigned? Clearly, Scrum is not sufficient to manage the entire development lifecycle.

Scrum is the most well-known agile technique, but it is not the only one. It fulfills the critical role of *managing the development work* once that work begins. To truly understand Scrum, one must expand the focus to understanding agile software development.

---

### END POINT

When faced with uncertain requirements, traditional waterfall development lifecycles have often failed to deliver value, regardless of whether they were on time or budget. As a result, agile techniques evolved within the software development community. Scrum is a framework for managing the people and the process of an iterative, incremental product delivery process.

The roles, activities, and artifacts of Scrum create a highly disciplined work pattern that embraces the need to evolve a product vision. Scrum, coupled with agile design, development, and testing techniques, allows a team to experiment and learn rapidly, which are the hallmarks of agile methods.

Any project manager should understand the fundamental principles of Scrum in order to reap the potential benefits when faced with the challenge of uncertain requirements and the possibility of incremental delivery exists.

# The Art and Science of Accurate Estimating

## INTRODUCTION

"Kris, how long will it take to implement this new design?"

"If you mean how long until we produce a product with the new design feature, I'd guess eight months."

"You guess? Come on, we need something firm."

"All right. I *estimate* it will take eight months."

"Great. Let's do it."

This kind of dialogue is exchanged on thousands of projects every year. Simple as it is, it points up some of the key issues in accurate estimating. First, notice how Kris tried to clarify what was being requested before venturing a guess. Second, note that guessing wasn't acceptable; it was only when he changed his guess to an estimate that it was taken seriously.

Estimating is forecasting the future, trying to predict the time and money necessary to produce a result. Because forecasting the future is an uncertain business, it should come as no surprise when an estimate turns out to be wrong. But a wrong estimate isn't good enough for most project stakeholders; customers, especially, want the product on time and within the promised budget. This means that we need to focus on estimating accurately; we need to be able to predict the future in an uncertain world.

Professional estimators—those people who make their living by developing cost and schedule estimates—have developed many methods of predicting the future. When you consider how many formulas and calculations these professionals work with, it would seem reasonable to define estimating as a science. We will see, however, that art plays a critical role in estimating. (It may be that those with extremely accurate methods for predicting the future have left the pedestrian field of project management and are applying their expertise in locales where the fruits of their labor are quicker and more tangible, such as Wall Street or Monte Carlo.) This chapter confronts the difficulty of forecasting the future. We examine the factors that make our estimates wrong and suggest techniques that can make them more accurate. You'll find a Planning Checklist online that you can use as you complete your project plan to ensure you've covered all the bases described in this chapter and the other chapters in Part 3.

## ESTIMATING FUNDAMENTALS

As we've observed many times, projects are unique. In fact, the more unique they are, the more difficult they are to estimate; the less unique, the easier to estimate. Research and development (R&D) projects, for instance, are extremely difficult to estimate, because they are attempting to solve new problems. But every project will produce a unique product, which means that a different combination of tasks will be employed. In addition, there are usually a number of other unique or unpredictable factors on any project:

- The people on the project team may be unknown to the manager. However, their particular skills and knowledge will affect their productivity, and the more complex the tasks are, the more this productivity factor counts.

- Projects that rely on new technology face questions about the reliability of the new technology and the learning curve of the team.

- Since estimates are used to coordinate activities and forecast resources, incorrect timing predictions will cost money. If the project is behind schedule when a subcontractor arrives, you may have to pay the subcontractor to sit around and wait. If it is so far behind schedule that the vendor must be sent away, then this vendor may not be available when needed.

**KEY CONCEPT**  **Avoid the Classic Mistakes**

Common sense is not all that common. There are certain mistakes that many of us seem to fall into, even though common sense may warn us to avoid them. Following are the most common.

## Making "Ballparks in Elevators"

Maybe it's their authority, or maybe it's that you're off guard, but whenever a high-level manager or customer catches you in an elevator, hallway, or break room and asks for an estimate, you inevitably respond with an optimistic, seat-of-the-pants guess that you regret the moment it escapes from your mouth. The problem is compounded if that manager happens to be on the way to a meeting where your "estimate" will be the topic of discussion. The trouble here is obvious: It's impossible to consider all the details required for an accurate estimate when you're riding between the fourth and tenth floors. But the question is how to avoid this optimistic guessing. Here are a few suggestions:

- Assume a thoughtful, concerned expression and respond to the manager, "There are a lot of factors that will impact the effort required . . ." Then list a few of these factors and add, "I wouldn't want to mislead you by offering a guess on that."

- Offer to get a sheet of paper and write down exactly what the manager is requesting. At the same time, start listing the questions that need to be answered before a useful estimate can be produced. If the manager has a hard time being specific about what he or she wants—and you can produce several questions he or she can't answer—this should help the manager to understand that there are too many unknowns to make a responsible estimate.

- If all this maneuvering fails and the manager or customer continues to press you, it's time for the art of "ballparking." There can be three possible responses when using this technique: (1) Respond with the best guess you've got, while trying to factor in everything that could make it wrong. This response is appropriate for people who can be trusted not to use this figure against you later on. (2) Take your very best guess and double it. Then double it again. This is obviously not a rational way to make estimates, but then again, the manager or customer is hardly being rational by asking you for an estimate in the elevator. (3) Refuse to give an estimate without further specifications and planning time.

## Estimating Without Complete Specifications

This is the type of mistake that a contractor might make if asked to estimate a construction project without a blueprint. In actuality, developers and contractors rarely make this mistake more than once. On the other hand, software developers and managers of information systems (IS) projects seem to make this mistake regularly. Someone has an idea, the idea is approved, with a budget and a deadline, and off they go! They don't seem concerned that the specifics of implementing the idea won't be known until they are halfway through the project. The allure of this mistake is that it seems as if team members are adopting good business practices; after all, they do have a budget and schedule attached to the new initiative. But without complete specifications, it isn't clear what the project will be producing, so there is no basis for an accurate estimate.

### Confusing an Estimate with a Bid

Bids and estimates are not the same thing. An *estimate* is a projection of how much and how long a project will take, while a *bid* is the schedule and budget a subcontractor offers to deliver the project. The bid will quite likely be made up of estimates, but it will also include *profit margins* for the subcontractor. The important distinction is that a bid is calculated to be both attractive to the customer and profitable to the bidder, while an estimate is a prediction of what it will really take to deliver. The best bidders—the ones who make both themselves and their customers happy—are also good estimators.

### Padding the Estimate

There are many legitimate reasons for adding time or money to an estimate. Contingency funds may be added for risks identified during the risk management process. Extra time is usually added to allow for inevitable delays due to illness or vacations. But padding the estimate is different. Adding time and money to the estimate solely for the purpose of bringing the project in early and under budget is neither legitimate nor productive. The best strategy is to offer honest, detailed estimates. Then, if they are cut, you can use the actual performance data during the project to fight for acceptance of the original estimate. Eventually, this kind of straight dealing will gain you a reputation as an honest estimator who delivers on promises.

Table 11.1 shows how adding to the cost and schedule just to be safe is counterproductive in two ways. First, a valuable project may not be approved because the artificially high estimate makes it look like a bad investment. Second, if the project is approved with an inflated budget, this means it is taking money away from other potentially valuable projects.

 **Follow the Golden Rules**

Just as there are classic estimating mistakes to avoid, there are certain golden rules that apply at all times to all projects. These rules emphasize the appropriate attitude toward estimating.

### TABLE 11.1 Artificially Inflating Project Estimates Can Hurt the Bottom Line

| Project | Priority | Best Estimate | Inflated 20% | Revenue Year 1 |
|---------|----------|---------------|--------------|----------------|
| Blue | 1 | $300,000 | $360,000 | $1,000,000 |
| Red | 2 | 150,000 | 180,000 | 750,000 |
| Orange | 3 | 200,000 | 240,000 | 750,000 |
| Green | 4 | 200,000 | 240,000 | 600,000 |
| Black | 5 | 150,000 | 180,000 | 500,000 |
| Total | | $1,000,000 | $1,200,000 | |

- The total budget for projects in a year is $1,000,000.
- Projects are prioritized by their return on investment over five years. The table contains the return in the first year.
- The best estimate is the project manager's most accurate estimate based on detailed specifications.
- Because every project manager inflated the best-cost estimate by 20% "just to be safe," the Black project was delayed a year.
- If all projects perform to their best estimate, $150,000 will not be invested, which reduces revenue the following year by $500,000.

## Have the Right People Make the Estimates

Three factors define who the right people are:

1. The estimators must be experienced with the work they are estimating. No matter which techniques are used, estimating is always based on an understanding of the work to be done.

2. The people who will actually perform the work should also be involved in estimating it. They will have the best grasp of their own limitations. They will know, for example, just how much time their schedule will allow them to work on this project; they will also know whether they will need a steep learning curve before they are productive. Most important, when people make an estimate for their own work, they are usually more motivated to achieve it than when the estimate comes from the outside.

3. The estimators must understand the goals and techniques of estimating. Even when people understand the task at hand, they should not be allowed to estimate their own work until they learn both *how* to estimate and the *goal* of estimating, which is to produce accurate estimates that will come true, not optimistic projections of the best possible performance.

## *Base the Estimate on Experience*

Even though no two projects are alike, there are often enough similarities that performance data from past projects are useful in estimating future ones. Professional estimators constantly use new performance data to refine their estimating models. Building this type of database is beyond the scope of the individual project manager; the organization must take responsibility for it. With this kind of database, project estimates can become more and more accurate. Without it, every project team must start from scratch and rely solely on each member's memories and gut feelings. Past performance data will make every estimating technique in this chapter more accurate.

## *Don't Negotiate the Estimate—Negotiate the Equilibrium*

**DANGER!**

There are effective ways of countering attempts to meddle with an estimate. Consider the following scenario.

A project estimate has been developed by experienced estimators using past performance data from similar projects and employing sound estimating techniques. The project manager brings the estimate to management or customers and they begin to whittle away at the schedule and budget. (Or perhaps they may even take out a cleaver and whack away a big part of both.) At first the project manager stands her ground, but under continuing pressure she begins to give up cost and schedule, slowly letting the finish date move earlier and the budget get smaller.

*Stop!* This estimate was built from the product specifications, and it represents a realistic balance of cost, schedule, and quality. Dickering over cost or schedule alone throws the entire estimate out of equilibrium. While no estimate will go unchallenged, the proper defense is to demonstrate how the estimate is tied to the product specification and work breakdown structure. When estimates are developed correctly, they can be reduced only by changing the product or the productivity of the workers.

## Three Levels of Accuracy

**KEY CONCEPT**

Everyone wants accurate estimates, but accuracy costs money. It makes sense, therefore, to use different estimating techniques for the different decision points in a project. For example, initial evaluation of a project idea shouldn't take as much time and effort (or money) as the detailed planning necessary for formal project approval. Let's look at three levels of accuracy at different stages in a project.

### Idea Evaluation or Ballpark Estimate

This is the estimate we all try to avoid giving. Ballpark estimates can be off by as much as 90 percent, yet they are still useful for initial sizing. These estimates take almost no time—they are the result of a gut feeling from an expert. Their accuracy relies on the estimator's knowledge. *The only function of a ballpark estimate should be to evaluate whether it would be useful to get a more accurate estimate.*

### Project Selection or Order of Magnitude

Also known as ROM for rough order of magnitude, this estimate also has a wide variance, but is based on extrapolations from other projects instead of the gut feelings of the ballpark estimates.[1] The main difference between a ballpark estimate and an order-of-magnitude estimate is represented by a few hours of effort comparing the proposed project to past projects. For example, a builder may find that a proposed building is about twice the size of a similar one he has built and will therefore estimate the new one at twice the cost. If he decides that the proposed site for the new building will be more challenging, he might add another 10 to 20 percent. If an order-of-magnitude estimate is acceptable, several actions may result: A project may be formally initiated, a project manager identified, account codes set up, and the work begun on defining and planning the project. This planning is where the real work of creating an accurate estimate will take place.

### Detailed Estimates

Detailed estimates are sometimes referred to as *bottom-up estimates*, because they are based on all the various steps involved in project planning. A detailed estimate includes all of the schedule and resource information (as discussed in Chapter 9) and a forecast of a project's budget and cash flow (described later in this chapter). This is the estimate that will be used to manage the project and evaluate its success.

There is a huge difference in accuracy between an order-of-magnitude estimate and a detailed estimate, because the latter assumes a detailed understanding of the product and is based on the availability of key resources. Enormous amounts of work specifying product requirements and design work take place between the order-of-magnitude estimate, when there are no specifications, and the detailed estimate, which is based on specifications. This work requires large expenditures of time and money, but this money is not spent until the inexpensive ballpark and order-of-magnitude estimates determine that the project is feasible.

## ESTIMATING TECHNIQUES

Good project managers realize that it takes time and effort to produce accurate estimates, so they choose among a variety of estimating methods to get the accuracy they need. There is no shortage of information in this field. A number of books have been written on estimating alone. Computer-based estimating models with proprietary algorithms cost thousands of dollars. There are entire seminars taught on estimating software projects, construction projects, and pharmaceutical development projects. This book cannot make an exhaustive presentation of all these estimating methods; instead, our purpose is to help you understand the dynamics of accurate estimating by presenting a variety of established estimating techniques—the basic building blocks used by all skilled estimators.

**KEY CONCEPT**

### Phased Estimating

Phased estimating is a favorite among project managers because it requires cost and schedule commitments for only one phase of the project at a time. The phased estimating approach recognizes that it is impractical to demand a complete estimate at the beginning of the product life cycle. Instead, it breaks down the full product life cycle into phases, each of which is considered a project (see Figure 11.1). If you recall from Chapter 3, the product development life cycle describes the work required to create a new product, while the project life cycle focuses on managing the work. There can be a number of projects involved in the development of a new product.

In Chapter 3, we introduced Stage-Gate™ as a product development approach that established specific product development phases (stages) separated by decision points (gates). Phased estimating takes advantage of this development approach.

There is an enormous amount of uncertainty at the beginning of every development life cycle, but this uncertainty is reduced as the project progresses and more information is gathered. This presents a dilemma, because the customer, more than any other stakeholder, wants an accurate time and cost estimate for the complete development life cycle. This demand is easy to understand because the customer is trying to make an investment decision. The problem is that there is so much uncertainty when the product development

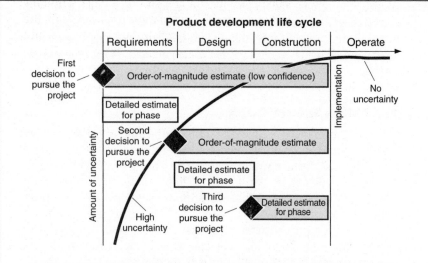

**Product development life cycle**

- At each decision point make two estimates: a cost and schedule commitment for the next phase, and an order-of-magnitude estimate for the remainder of the project.

- This example shows three decision points, but a product development life cycle could use 2 or 10 decision points—however many make sense to reduce the risk of overcommitting based on too little information.

- The amount of uncertainty is high at the beginning of the development life cycle—too high to make accurate estimates.

FIGURE 11.1 *Phased estimating.*

effort is first considered that an accurate cost and schedule projection is impossible to produce.

The phased estimating approach recognizes this impossibility and instead breaks down the full product life cycle into phases, each of which is considered a project. Here is what this process looks like:

- The first phase is initiated with an order-of-magnitude estimate for the full development life cycle combined with a detailed estimate for the first phase. This detailed estimate is considered a commitment by the project team; this commitment signals an end to the uncertainty that surrounds a new project. By agreeing to a detailed plan with a fixed completion date, the team becomes more focused and productive.

- At the end of the first phase, a new authorization for the second phase starts this cycle once more. A new order-of-magnitude estimate is developed for the remainder of the product life cycle together with a detailed estimate for the second phase. The new order-of-magnitude estimate will be much more accurate than the previous one because so much has been learned from the first development phase. This cycle of phase authorization will be repeated at each phase gate, and each time the order-of-magnitude estimate will become more accurate.

Project managers and teams like phased estimating because they are only required to commit to cost and schedule estimates for one phase at a time, what we call a "realistic planning horizon." The benefit to the people funding the project is not always so clear. To them, it appears that the project team just keeps asking for more money and time at every phase review, with no accountability to project budgets and schedules.

What this customer group needs to realize, however, is that phased estimating is a risk-reduction technique that also works in their favor. If the project team is required to commit to a cost and schedule estimate for the full product development life cycle before it has enough information about the product, this will place everyone at risk. This is because the team is likely to come up with an inaccurate estimate at this early phase.

Customers often believe that getting a firm commitment from the project team is their safeguard against runaway budgets, but, in this case, they are mistaken. Without a realistic budget, unforeseen costs are likely to crop up as the project progresses—and the customer will be the one to pay for them. This will be true even if the project team is an external firm with a fixed-price contract. If these overruns become too extreme, this team may simply leave, preferring damage to its reputation to bankruptcy. At this point, the customer will have lost money, and the project will still be incomplete. Without the accurate estimate, both sides will lose.

On the other hand, if the customer and project team work for the same organization—as is the case with many product development projects—then it is obvious who will pay for cost overruns: the company that both work for. If the original estimate was too low, no amount of pressure from above will get the project team to meet it. Again, both sides lose.

Customers will embrace phased estimating when they under-stand that every new phase gives them an opportunity to completely reevaluate the effort, or even cancel it if it looks too expensive. If they like the product but don't like the project team, then this is the obvious time to choose another. While it's true that canceling will mean that they have no end product to show for their money, at least they will have canceled an unrealistic project before it costs them even more.

Phased estimating is always used on construction projects. If you planned to build a house, no contractor would commit to a bid until you knew the location and had a blueprint. After the design was complete, you might find that the cost of the house was too high and decide not to pursue the project. This realization didn't come without cost, because you had to spend time and effort to find the location and pay for the design of the house. But it was smart to do your homework before you started digging a hole for a house you couldn't afford!

Successful project managers treat every phase of the development life cycle as a project. They use the phased estimate approach to formally review the cost-schedule-quality equilibrium several times during the product development life cycle. The great advantage to this method is that it allows the project to be directed by many small, informed decisions rather than one large, premature decision.

 **Apportioning**

Also known as *top-down estimating*, apportioning begins with a total project estimate, then assigns a percentage of that total to each of the phases and tasks of the project. The work breakdown structure provides the framework for top-down estimating (as shown in Figure 11.2). Making useful top-down estimates relies on some big assumptions, among them:

- Since apportioning is based on a formula derived from historical data of other, similar projects, the historic projects must be very similar to the project at hand for the formula to be accurate.

- Since apportioning divides a total project estimate into smaller pieces, it will be accurate only if the overall estimate is accurate.

Although apportioning is rarely as accurate as a bottom-up estimate, it is an appropriate technique for selecting which projects to pursue. Despite its wide accuracy variance, it allows a project selection committee to approximate the length of project phases; this information then helps the committee decide which projects can be initiated and executed during a given budget period (see Table 11.2).

Apportioning is a valuable technique when used in conjunction with phased estimating. During phase reviews, the formula for apportioning can use the figures from the actual cost/effort of completed phases to increase the accuracy of the order-of-magnitude estimate (see Figure 11.3). For instance, if the original top-down estimate dictated a phase-one cost of $75,000, and the actual phase-one cost was $60,000, this means that the overall project estimate should be reduced

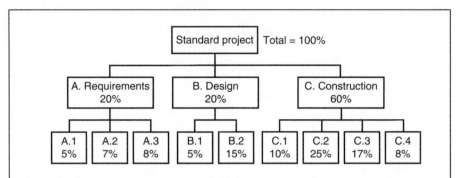

- Some types of projects break into consistent proportions.
- Firms that have developed standard work breakdown structure templates use past projects to create the apportioning formula.
- With a good high-level estimate, the formula shows how big each of the project phases and tasks should be.
- For example, if the total budget estimate is $40,000, that leaves $8,000 for requirements, $8,000 for design, and $24,000 for construction.

FIGURE 11.2 *Work breakdown structure as a basis for apportioning.*

by 20 percent. Again, notice the need for an accurate apportioning formula.

## Parametric Estimates

As the name implies, the parametric technique seeks a basic unit of work to act as a multiplier to size the entire project. The golden rules of estimating really apply with this technique: It is always based on historical data, and the estimator must develop a solid parametric formula. To see how parametric estimating works, consider the following examples:

- A cycling group in Dallas, Texas, was planning a cross-country bicycle trip, starting in Seattle, Washington, and ending in Miami, Florida. Based on their experience riding together every Saturday for two months, they figured they could average 80 miles per day comfortably. A road atlas put the total trip distance at 3,334 miles. Dividing 3,334 by 80, they estimated the total trip would last 42 days. At this point, the only parameter was this normal daily rate of 80 miles. But when one of the riders pointed out that all their practice rides had been on relatively flat terrain in dry weather, they made changes to their model. They reduced their average daily mileage to 30 for the mountainous parts of their route (the route had about 200 miles of mountain crossing), and they added 10 percent for weather delays. This changed the formula from

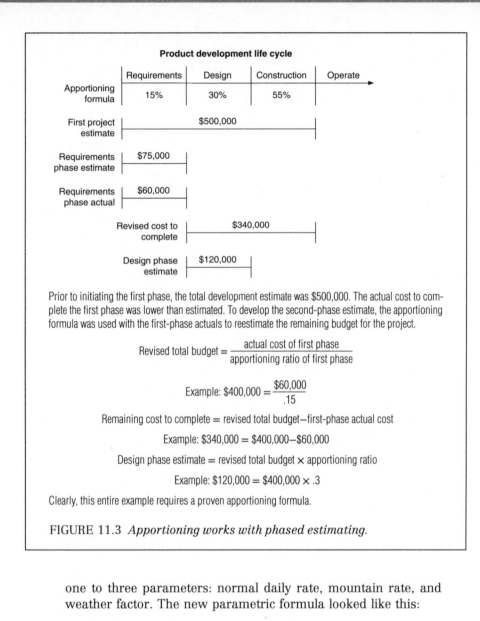

**Product development life cycle**

| | Requirements | Design | Construction | Operate |
|---|---|---|---|---|
| Apportioning formula | 15% | 30% | 55% | |

First project estimate — $500,000

Requirements phase estimate — $75,000

Requirements phase actual — $60,000

Revised cost to complete — $340,000

Design phase estimate — $120,000

Prior to initiating the first phase, the total development estimate was $500,000. The actual cost to complete the first phase was lower than estimated. To develop the second-phase estimate, the apportioning formula was used with the first-phase actuals to reestimate the remaining budget for the project.

$$\text{Revised total budget} = \frac{\text{actual cost of first phase}}{\text{apportioning ratio of first phase}}$$

$$\text{Example: } \$400,000 = \frac{\$60,000}{.15}$$

Remaining cost to complete = revised total budget − first-phase actual cost

Example: $340,000 = $400,000 − $60,000

Design phase estimate = revised total budget × apportioning ratio

Example: $120,000 = $400,000 × .3

Clearly, this entire example requires a proven apportioning formula.

FIGURE 11.3 *Apportioning works with phased estimating.*

one to three parameters: normal daily rate, mountain rate, and weather factor. The new parametric formula looked like this:

Trip duration

$$= \left( \frac{\text{total miles} - \text{mountain miles}}{\text{normal daily rate}} + \frac{\text{mountain miles}}{\text{mountain rate}} \right) \times \text{weather factor}$$

$$\text{Trip duration} = \left( \frac{3,334 - 200}{80} + \frac{200}{30} \right) \times 1.10$$

Trip duration = 50 days

**TABLE 11.2  Apportioning Supports Annual Budget Development**

| Project | Total Schedule | Total Cost | Description | Requirements | Design | Construction | Total Cost Year 1 |
|---|---|---|---|---|---|---|---|
| A | 2 years | $500,000 | % schedule completion in 1 year | 100% | 66% | 0% | $166K |
| | | | Phase budget | $100K | $100K | $300K | |
| | | | Amount of phase budget spent in 1 year | $100K | $66K | $0 | |
| B | 2 years | $300,000 | % schedule completion in 1 year | 100% | 66% | 0% | $99.6K |
| | | | Phase budget | $60K | $60K | $180K | |
| | | | Amount of phase budget spent in 1 year | $60K | $39.6K | $0 | |
| C | 4 years | $400,000 | % schedule completion in 1 year | 83% | 0% | 0% | $66.4K |
| | | | Phase budget | $80K | $80K | $240K | |
| | | | Amount of phase budget spent in 1 year | $66.4K | $0 | $0 | |
| D | 6 months | $100,000 | % schedule completion in 1 year | 100% | 100% | 100% | $100K |
| | | | Phase budget | $20K | $20K | $60K | |
| | | | Amount of phase budget spent in 1 year | $20K | $20K | $60K | |
| E | 1 year | $300,000 | % schedule completion in 1 year | 100% | 100% | 100% | $300K |
| | | | Phase budget | $60K | $60K | $180K | |
| | | | Amount of phase budget spent in 1 year | $60K | $60K | $180K | |
| | | | Total project budget required for fiscal year | | | | $732K |

A company has five projects that will begin in its next fiscal year. Based on past experience, it has developed apportioning ratios for its standard projects.
- The requirements phase uses 20% of the total budget and 30% of the total schedule.
- The design phase uses 20% of the total budget and 30% of the total schedule.
- The construction phase uses 60% of the total budget and 40% of the total schedule.

Based on order-of-magnitude cost and schedule estimates and the apportioning formula, the company was able to estimate the total project budget required for the next fiscal year.

- A manufacturing company needs to have its 340-page user manual localized into several languages. Based on past localization projects, the staff has created a parametric estimating model. The basic unit of work is a page. On average, 15 pages per day can be localized into the target languages. This parameter assumes two people working together on every target language. If the number of people is increased or decreased, the parameter changes. But if they add a new language and therefore new members to the team, the parameter of 15 pages a day is probably too optimistic for the first document.

  Localization project duration (per language) = 23 days = 340/15

- To estimate the carpet allowance on a house remodel, the project manager figured a cost of $5 per yard for purchasing the carpet and $4 per yard to install it, or $9 total cost. Then he measured the length and width of all the rooms, calculated the area in square yards, and multiplied by $9. Construction projects are full of parametric estimates of this kind.

- On a defense program to build a new jet fighter, the total number of engineering drawings required was estimated from a conceptual model of the proposed aircraft. Thousands of drawings would be created from this model, and, based on past experience, the staff estimated that the average drawing would take 200 engineering hours. With the drawing as the basic unit of work, this simple parametric model allowed them to estimate the total engineering effort. By dividing the total number of hours by the number of engineers they assigned to the project, they set the high-level schedule. Obviously, this was not sufficient detail for managing all the work, but because their parametric model allowed them to accurately estimate both the number of drawings and the average time per drawing, at least the engineering phase was accurately sized.

Three lessons can be distilled from these examples:

1. While it's possible to use parametric models to create either project-level or task-level estimates, the estimates will be more accurate at the lower level. Nevertheless, high-level parametric estimates make excellent order-of-magnitude estimates and are accurate enough for the process of project selection.

2. When building detailed estimates, greater accuracy is achieved by first estimating the low-level tasks (work packages) using parametric models, then combining all these work package estimates to build the project or phase estimate. It is useful to employ

parametric modeling at all decision points (phase gates) in the phased estimating approach, both to create the high-level estimate and to ensure the next phase commitment.

3. The variables in the parametric formula almost always require detailed product specifications. The more accurate the specifications, the more accurate the model. For example, the translation project required a completed user guide in the original language. Construction projects require blueprints. Both of these examples make one important point: Parametric estimating is usually applied to the *construction phase* of a product life cycle.

**KEY CONCEPT**

### Bottom-Up Estimating

Bottom-up estimating requires the most effort, but it is also the most accurate. As the name implies, all the detailed tasks are estimated and then combined, or rolled up (see Figure 11.4). Bottom-up estimating is another name for the planning model presented in Chapters 8 and 9 (see Figure 8.1). The final component of that model, building a project budget and cash flow, is described at the end of this chapter.

Within the planning model, step three calls for estimating work packages. (Recall that work packages are the lowest-level tasks on the project.) The accuracy of the entire model is dependent on the accuracy of these work package estimates. (Recall from Chapter 8

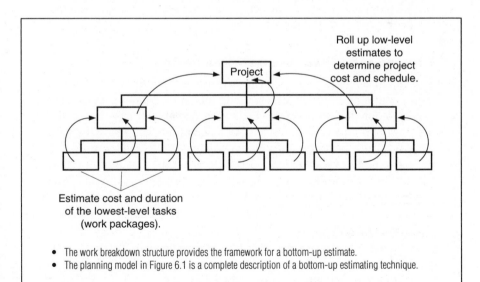

FIGURE 11.4 *Bottom-up estimating.*

the rules for work package size and from Chapter 9 the many variables that affect work package estimates.)

If bottom-up estimating is so accurate, why isn't it always used? It would seem the accuracy justifies the additional time to build the schedule. The answer is that at the very beginning of a product development life cycle, there just isn't enough information to develop a detailed bottom-up estimate for the entire life cycle. So bottom-up estimating works only to build the detailed phase estimates.

## BUILDING THE DETAILED BUDGET ESTIMATE

**KEY CONCEPT** Project budget estimates can be "ballparked," calculated with parametric formulas, and determined through apportioning. While these high-level estimates are useful in the process of selecting projects, they are not accurate enough for managing a project. Once the project is approved, there is a need for a detailed, accurate cost estimate.

The detailed cost estimate becomes the standard for keeping costs in line. Everyone—customer, management, project manager, and team—is better served when a cost target is realistically calculated from a detailed plan. The team understands how the goal was created, and customers and management can be more confident that the project will stay within budget. Forecasting cash flow enables the project's funding to be planned and available when needed. And finally, during the course of the project, this detailed cost information will help in controlling the project, monitoring the progress, identifying problems, and finding solutions.

### Sources of Data for the Detailed Budget

The actual calculation of a budget is pretty straightforward; it simply involves adding up figures. Just about any spreadsheet program is a good tool for the total budget calculation. What isn't easy is creating the numbers that go into the overall calculation. The following categories are the basis for the budget calculation. (Keep in mind that these are high-level categories. Depending on the size and nature of any project, some categories may be eliminated or may need to be broken down to be more specific.)

### *Internal Labor Cost*

Internal labor costs represent the effort of people employed by the firm. The planning model discussed in Chapters 8 and 9 forms the basis for estimating the total labor costs (see Figure 8.1).

The detailed source for all labor estimates comes from estimating the individual tasks. Including the sequence constraints and leveling the resources presents a realistic view of how many people are required. The resource projection represents the total effort. All that remains is to multiply each resource by its hourly (or daily, weekly, or monthly) rate to derive the total internal labor cost for the project. Figure 11.5 shows the total resource projection derived from the detailed schedule, the labor rates, and the total project labor cost.

### Use the Burdened Labor Rate

The actual hourly pay of salaried employees varies from person to person, often for no discernible reason. But it is rare to have to worry about actual pay when estimating labor costs. Instead, look to the finance department to establish a standard burdened labor rate for each labor type. A *burdened rate* is the average cost of an employee to the firm. It includes wages, benefits, and overhead. Overhead represents the many fixed costs that are spread over all projects, such as functional management, workplace facilities and equipment, and non-project costs like training. It's not necessary for a project manager to figure out this rate; nearly every company has an established burdened labor rate on record.

### Don't Leave Out the Cost of Staffing the Project

A big mistake—which, unfortunately, is made on a routine basis—is leaving out the cost of internal staff in the project budget. The usual justification for this folly is that "these workers are free to the project because their salary is a constant." But this statement would be true only if salaried employees had infinite hours available to work on projects. Including internal labor cost in a project budget is necessary to build the kind of realistic budget that will allow management to choose among multiple project opportunities.

### Internal Equipment Cost

Internal equipment costs apply to special equipment that is not routinely available. They do not apply to the kind of equipment that is standard or assumed for all workers. Technical writers, for example, are assumed to have computers with word processing software; street repair crews are assumed to have shovels. But if that street repair crew needs a backhoe, the cost for this special equipment needs to be estimated separately. This separate estimate allows the purchase and maintenance costs of the internal equipment to be passed on to the customer.

These internal equipment costs can be estimated using the same steps used in estimating internal labor costs. Figure 11.6 shows equipment use on the resource plan.

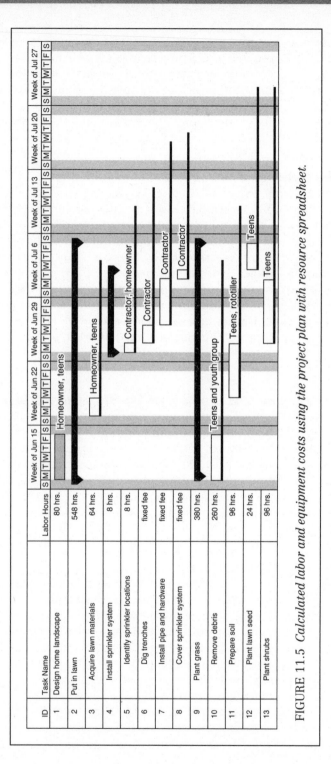

FIGURE 11.5 *Calculated labor and equipment costs using the project plan with resource spreadsheet.*

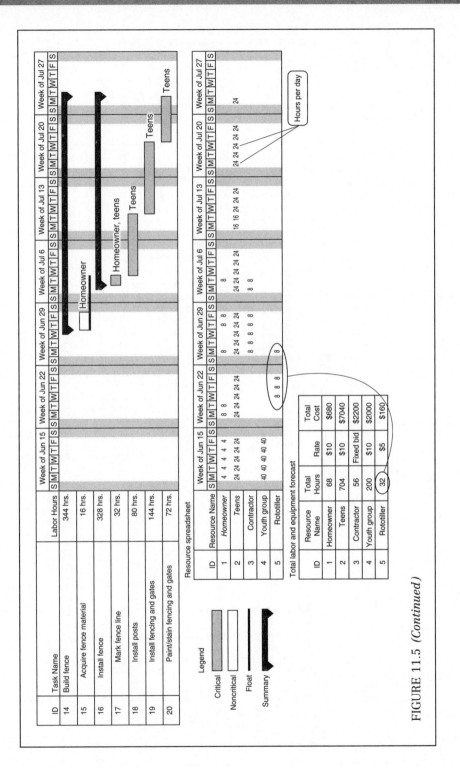

| ID | Task Name | Labor Hours |
|---|---|---|
| 14 | Build fence | 344 hrs. |
| 15 | Acquire fence material | 16 hrs. |
| 16 | Install fence | 328 hrs. |
| 17 | Mark fence line | 32 hrs. |
| 18 | Install posts | 80 hrs. |
| 19 | Install fencing and gates | 144 hrs. |
| 20 | Paint/stain fencing and gates | 72 hrs. |

Legend

Critical
Noncritical
Float
Summary

Resource spreadsheet

| ID | Resource Name | Total Hours |
|---|---|---|
| 1 | Homeowner | 68 |
| 2 | Teens | 704 |
| 3 | Contractor | 56 |
| 4 | Youth group | 200 |
| 5 | Rototiller | 32 |

Total labor and equipment forecast

| ID | Resource Name | Total Hours | Rate | Total Cost |
|---|---|---|---|---|
| 1 | Homeowner | 68 | $10 | $680 |
| 2 | Teens | 704 | $10 | $7040 |
| 3 | Contractor | 56 | Fixed bid | $2200 |
| 4 | Youth group | 200 | $10 | $2000 |
| 5 | Rototiller | 32 | $5 | $160 |

FIGURE 11.5 (Continued)

**249**

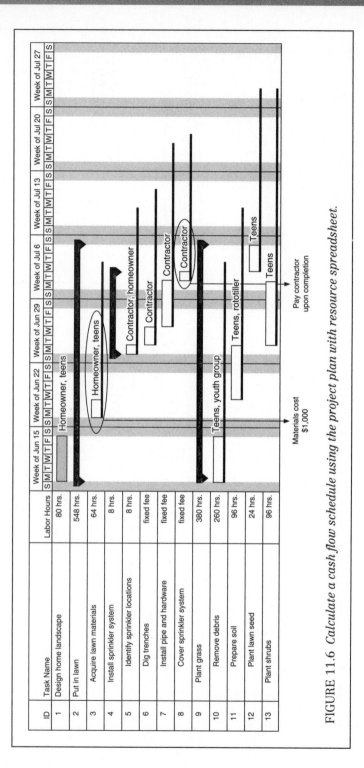

FIGURE 11.6 *Calculate a cash flow schedule using the project plan with resource spreadsheet.*

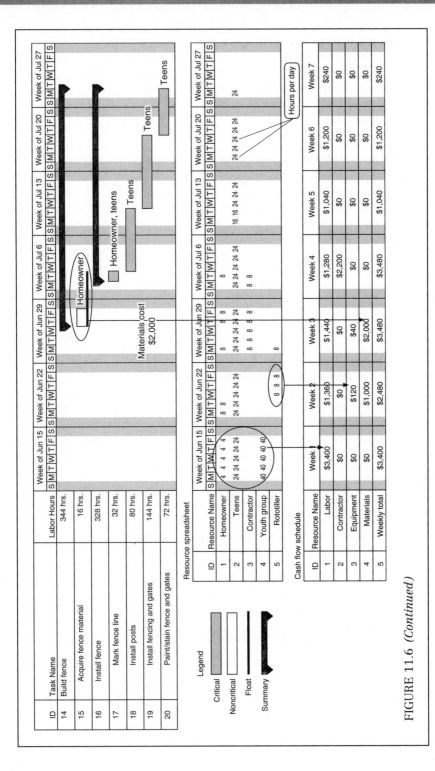

| ID | Task Name | Labor Hours |
|----|-----------|-------------|
| 14 | Build fence | 344 hrs. |
| 15 | Acquire fence material | 16 hrs. |
| 16 | Install fence | 328 hrs. |
| 17 | Mark fence line | 32 hrs. |
| 18 | Install posts | 80 hrs. |
| 19 | Install fencing and gates | 144 hrs. |
| 20 | Paint/stain fence and gates | 72 hrs. |

Resource spreadsheet

| ID | Resource Name | Week of Jun 15 | Week of Jun 22 | Week of Jun 29 | Week of Jul 6 | Week of Jul 13 | Week of Jul 20 | Week of Jul 27 |
|----|---------------|----------------|----------------|----------------|---------------|----------------|----------------|----------------|
| 1 | Homeowner | 4 4 4 4 4 | 8 8 | 8 8 | 8 | | | |
| 2 | Teens | 24 24 24 24 | 24 24 24 24 | 24 24 24 24 | 24 24 24 24 | 16 16 24 24 | 24 24 24 24 | 24 |
| 3 | Contractor | | | 8 8 8 8 | 8 8 | | | |
| 4 | Youth group | 40 40 40 40 | | 8 | | | | |
| 5 | Rototiller | | 8 8 8 | | | | | |

Cash flow schedule

| ID | Resource Name | Week 1 | Week 2 | Week 3 | Week 4 | Week 5 | Week 6 | Week 7 |
|----|---------------|--------|--------|--------|--------|--------|--------|--------|
| 1 | Labor | $3,400 | $1,360 | $1,440 | $1,280 | $1,040 | $1,200 | $240 |
| 2 | Contractor | $0 | $0 | $0 | $2,200 | $0 | $0 | $0 |
| 3 | Equipment | $0 | $120 | $40 | $0 | $0 | $0 | $0 |
| 4 | Materials | $0 | $1,000 | $2,000 | $0 | $0 | $0 | $0 |
| 5 | Weekly total | $3,400 | $2,480 | $3,480 | $3,480 | $1,040 | $1,200 | $240 |

Legend

Critical
Noncritical
Float
Summary

FIGURE 11.6 (Continued)

### Estimating Equipment That Will Be Used Up

If equipment will be purchased and used up on a single project, then all you will need to do is add up the pieces of equipment and the cost of each (a parametric estimate). For example, a boring machine used to dig utility tunnels uses up drill bits at the rate of 1 every 50 feet. So a 1,300-foot tunnel will require 26 drill bits (1,300 divided by 50).

### Estimating Equipment Used on Multiple Projects

Use a unit cost approach to estimate equipment purchased for one project but expected to be used on many others. Here's an example.

R&D engineers for an aerospace company needed an expensive computer to run complex tests. At $50,000, the computer would double the project budget, and this extra cost would probably prevent the project from being approved. But since they could identify five other potential projects that would use the machine in the immediate future, they were able to justify the cost of the new computer by spreading its cost over the expected use for the next two years. The formula used to spread the cost across several projects gave them a unit cost (hourly rate) that they could apply to their project estimate.

### External Labor and Equipment Costs

It's possible to use the same approach in estimating external labor and equipment costs as in estimating internal labor and equipment. The only differences will stem from the type of contract negotiated with the external contractor or vendor. Under a cost-plus contract, the labor and equipment rates are written into the contract, and the vendor bills the project for the amount of labor, equipment, and materials supplied to the project. In this case, either the project manager or the vendor can estimate the work and arrive at the total cost by using the same bottom-up method described for internal costs. In the case of a fixed bid, however, the vendor will estimate the total cost of labor and equipment for its part of the project and will be held to this figure (that's why it's called a *fixed bid*). In this latter case, the vendor has performed the necessary estimating; all that's needed is to add this estimate into the total labor and equipment costs. (See Chapter 7 for more on the difference between fixed bids and cost-plus contracts and their impact on estimating accuracy.)

### Materials Costs

Materials are the "things" that go into a finished product. For some projects, materials represent half or more of the total costs, while for others, materials costs are inconsequential. A software development project, for example, may produce millions of lines of code, but no tangible materials are required. Materials can be raw, such as plywood, concrete, or welding rod, or materials can be subcomponents of your product, such as computer hardware, telephone switches, or air-conditioning units.

Until now, we've stressed the value of the work breakdown structure as the basis for identifying all costs. When it comes to materials costs, however, the WBS is relegated to second place. The first place to look is the product specification. For example, the blueprint for a building is the basis for calculating how much concrete, plywood, plumbing, or flooring to purchase. It shows the number of sinks, doors, windows, and elevators to order. Similarly, the network design will determine the number of workstations, routers, hosts, and telephone switches required for a computer network.

The work breakdown structure can be used to ensure that every task that requires materials will have them. This is done by planning order and delivery tasks. Include the payment dates as tasks, and you'll have all the information you need to build a cash flow schedule for the project.

## KEY CONCEPT — GENERATING THE CASH FLOW SCHEDULE

Knowing *when* money will be spent is almost as important as knowing *how much* will be spent. Companies that depend on operations to generate the cash to fund projects need to control the rate at which money goes into the project. Let's look at a couple of operations that depend on cash flow schedules:

- A small housing developer plans to build five houses, sell them, and build five more. By keeping his rate of production constant, he intends to keep all of his employees busy at a steady rate. By staggering the starting dates of all the houses, he can move crews from one house to the next and, he hopes, sell house number one before it's time to start house number six. Timing is everything in his plan. If there are too many people on a framing crew, the job will get done too fast and the next house may not have the foundation ready for the crew. If the completed houses don't sell within his planned time frame, he won't be able to fund new houses and will have to lay off workers.

- A municipal engineering department spreads all street maintenance projects across its fiscal year in order to keep its use of people and equipment steady. Large engineering projects that span fiscal years are also carefully timed. The department heads make sure that they spend only the amount of budget allotted per year, but they need to stretch out this budget to the very end of the year so a project doesn't have to stop and wait for the new fiscal year to begin.

Once the project's schedule and costs have been estimated, generating a cash flow projection is pretty simple. Figure 11.6 shows the information from the project schedule that determines the cash flow. It's easy to see how project management software can readily calculate cash flow from all the other data that has been entered.

## END POINT

Estimating will never be a science that produces results that are 100 percent accurate. In all the estimating techniques presented in this chapter there are consistent lessons:

- It takes time and costs money to develop accurate estimates.
- Every technique gives better results when it is used consistently. The lessons of the past improve the forecasts of the future.
- Comparing actual performance to estimates is essential to refining the estimating model. Without this comparison there is no science in the process, only gut feelings.

Perhaps the most important lesson we can learn about estimating is that all the stakeholders are responsible for accurate estimates. Customers, sponsors, and management, for example, have more control than the project team over factors such as the stability of the specifications, the availability of personnel, and the deadline pressures. A cooperative approach among these stakeholders will yield positive results. When estimating becomes an adversarial game between the project team and the customer, there will always be a loser. On the other hand, if all stakeholders understand the dynamics of estimating and work honestly to reduce the uncertainty of the project, everyone will win.

## FAST FOUNDATION IN PROJECT MANAGEMENT

A thorough project plan is the foundation of a strong project. Download a Planning Checklist to guide your team and yourself to ensure you've covered all the bases.

The planning checklist is available for download at www .VersatileCompany.com/FFMBAinPM. As you and your colleagues use this checklist, you'll find new items to add, customizing it to better fit your projects.

# *Stellar Performer: Tynet, Inc.*

Installing computer networks is a high-risk, competitive business. Thousands of companies, large and small, offer the services to tie together local area networks, telephone equipment, and Internet service providers. Bids for the service required to put the networks together need to be accurate, because any underestimated labor quickly eats up profits for the job. Tynet, Inc., identifies project management as its competitive edge.

Brian LaMure is the director of network services for Tynet and a certified project management professional. He credits dramatic increases in revenue and profitability to Tynet's emphasis on project management. "We began using the project life cycle as the basis for our entire network services business, from initial sales through implementation and follow-up. Before that time, nearly 80 percent of our projects were late and/or over budget, meaning we lost money. By focusing on some of the basics, we've reduced failed projects to almost zero." In Tynet's case, the basics include using a phased estimating model, parametric estimating, more customer involvement in managing the project, and more detailed project planning.

## PHASED ESTIMATING

One of the reasons Tynet had so many late or over budget projects in the past was the way it bid them. A Tynet sales representative would visit a prospective client to understand the problem and develop a proposal. Since there were often technical issues that the sales representative didn't understand completely, it was easy for the representative to underestimate a project. "Now we use a phased estimating model based on a standard project life cycle," explains LaMure. "The previous model was a no-win scenario for the sales reps, because they couldn't be expected to understand all the components of a job, but they were under pressure to get the business."

Tynet's phased estimating model follows six phases. (See Figure 11.7.)

1. *Business analysis.* This is where a sales representative spends time most productively. The sales reps qualify clients to make sure the client and Tynet are a good fit, and if they aren't, they'll refer the client to someone else. If it looks like Tynet could help the customer solve a problem, the sales representative sets a time for a design engineer to evaluate the project.

2. *Concept.* Together, the design engineer and sales representative spend between 4 and 12 hours learning the client's business objectives for the network and developing a detailed estimate. This is work the client doesn't pay for, but it builds the customer's confidence that Tynet will be able to deliver the right solution. The bid for time and materials will vary up to 25 percent for the design phase and from 50 to 100 percent for the actual implementation of the entire project. If the customer accepts the bid, the design phase begins.

3. *Design.* During design, the design engineer works with a project manager and, if necessary, a lead engineer to develop a complete network design and detailed project plan for the remainder of the project. They also re-estimate the project based on this additional information and submit a new bid to complete the project. This bid is accurate within 10 to 25 percent. If the customer accepts the bid, the hardware and software are ordered and the service is scheduled. If the client's company doesn't like the bid or the design work, it pays Tynet for the design phase and the contract is over. If the bid is more than the customer wants to pay, even though the customer

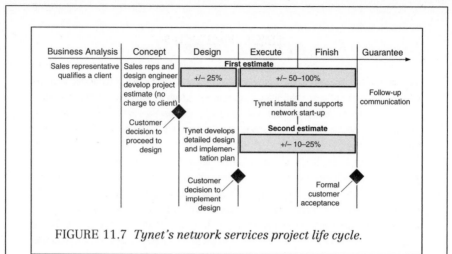

FIGURE 11.7  *Tynet's network services project life cycle.*

realizes it is realistic, the detailed project plan can be used as a tool for finding work the client can do in-house, thus decreasing the hours Tynet puts into the project.

4. *Execute.* The system solution is installed. The project manager uses the detailed plan to make sure everything stays on track.

5. *Finish.* The project manager and the original design engineer meet with the client to make sure the system is operating effectively. All of Tynet's work is unconditionally guaranteed, so they want to make sure the client is completely satisfied.

6. *Guarantee.* Sales representatives continue to stay in touch with clients after the project is over so that any problems can be quickly resolved. The reps also help clients recognize new opportunities for improving their business based on their new network capabilities. These activities are Tynet's way of supporting customers to grow both their business and their network capacity over the long term.

The increased time and expertise Tynet spends on developing proposals still sometimes result in estimates that are off by as much as 100 percent; it is easy to see, therefore, why the previous bidding process often produced proposals that were impossible to deliver. With bids offered at both the concept and design phases, both Tynet and its clients reduce their risks. Tynet is less likely to dramatically underestimate a job, and the client has two opportunities to evaluate the bid.

## PARAMETRIC ESTIMATING

When the project manager and design engineer build their detailed estimates in the design phase, they use a parametric model that has been refined over many projects. Each component of the system, whether it's installing hardware, installing software, or delivering training to the client, is estimated separately. Since a network project is typically composed of a unique set of known components, LaMure and his team have created a list of all the components they've used on past projects and an estimate for each. By continually comparing their project performance to the parametric estimating tables, they refine the estimates, making future project bids more accurate.

## DETAILED PROJECT PLANS

The detailed parametric estimating model lends itself to detailed planning and control. Every task has a person and a schedule assigned, so accountability is clear and tracking more effective. LaMure estimates that overall delivery time has decreased by 50 percent through more effective execution, which is a result of better plans. Another cost benefit to the client is that breaking the tasks down into smaller increments makes it easier to put the person with the right skill on each job. That means a senior technician isn't working on jobs that a more junior team member could accomplish at a lower billing rate.

## CUSTOMERS INVOLVED IN PROJECT MANAGEMENT

Before instituting the phased life cycle model, Tynet bid work on a fixed-price basis; this meant that if Tynet was wrong, it paid the price. By giving the customers two opportunities to accept its bid and by using detailed project plans and parametric estimates, Tynet has increased the customer's involvement in managing the project. This has enabled Tynet to change its bids to a time-and-materials basis, reducing its risk. "With more detailed information, the customer gains more control of the project and has better cost-schedule-quality results," explains LaMure. "They can see that they're better off than forcing us to add contingency factors into a fixed-price bid."

Tynet is proof that project management isn't just a discipline that improves efficiency. The company has used it to restructure its entire network delivery process, and the results speak for themselves.

Source: Interview with Brian LaMure.

# *Stellar Performer: Adobe Systems*
## Developing a Calibrated Model for Estimating Project Time

### John Gaffney

Today, Adobe Systems is known for sophisticated desktop software products such as Adobe Photoshop, but in fact the company got its start in 1982 by developing PostScript, the first device-independent page description language. I joined Adobe as a software developer in 1984 when Adobe was developing the Apple LaserWriter, the first PostScript printer.

After Apple introduced the LaserWriter in 1985, many new customers signed up with Adobe to license PostScript software for their products. Adobe grew quickly; by 1990 it had developed many PostScript printers, but had an admittedly marginal track record in accurately estimating its project times. In an attempt to improve that track record, I developed a simple estimating formula based on actual development time of completed projects. The formula predicted total projected time, given the printer complexity and the assumption that only one software developer would work on the project—which was the norm. The formula soon became known inside Adobe printer engineering as the "Gaffney Meter," a name invented by my colleagues. This model proved to be reasonably reliable, so I later modified it for estimating multiple-developer project time.

#### CREATING THE SINGLE-DEVELOPER MODEL

A half-dozen or so completed printer projects were analyzed for clues. It was no surprise that the more complex projects took longer, so it seemed appropriate to use a simple count of product features and custom development tasks to measure the project's complexity. This complexity count accounted for special printer features such as color printing, duplex (two-sided) printing, and Japanese fonts.

One completed project was a relatively simple printer whose development tasks were in common with all other projects; it had taken five months from the time the developer received the hardware until the printer was certified. This project was used as the baseline, or *zero-complexity*, project against which more complex projects were compared.

A simple plot of all the complexity counts against their project times showed an expected exponential growth in time as the number of complexities increased. The project time $T$ as a function of its complexity count $C$ behaved something like this:

$$T = 5 \text{ months} \times G^C$$

where $G$ was some uncalibrated *time growth factor*. For a zero-complexity ($C = 0$) project, this model yielded the expected five-month development time for the "simple" printer. A couple of trial-and-error calculations showed that $G = 1.2$ matched the plot of completed projects fairly well.

## SINGLE-DEVELOPER TIME ESTIMATION MODEL

Refer to Figure 11.8. The single-developer project time $T$ (in months) for a project with a complexity count $C$ is:

$$T = 5 \text{ months} \times 1.2^C$$

One way of looking at this model is that *every complexity added to a project increases the project time by 20 percent*. This compounding effect is not surprising. Adding another product feature to an already complex product takes longer to develop and contributes more uncertainty than adding it to a simpler product.

### Some Nuances of the Model

Applying the model to a new project is more of an art than a science, especially in determining the project's complexity count. For example, some product features are more complex than others; the easy ones are sometimes counted as 0.5 and difficult ones as 1.5 or 2. In reality, the average complexity weight is 1, especially for highly complex projects, so it does not matter too much how the complexities are weighted.

Some projects, such as maintenance releases or upgrades, reuse much of the code developed for earlier versions of the product, so a simplification that has a complexity value of −1 is sometimes used. Another simplification involves assigning an especially skilled developer to the project.

In spite of these subtleties, analyzing a project's complexities and calculating the estimated project time provide a valuable tool for meeting customer expectations. If the model indicates that a project is going to be too late to hit a market window, negotiating with the customer to simplify the project sometimes enables the product to ship on time.

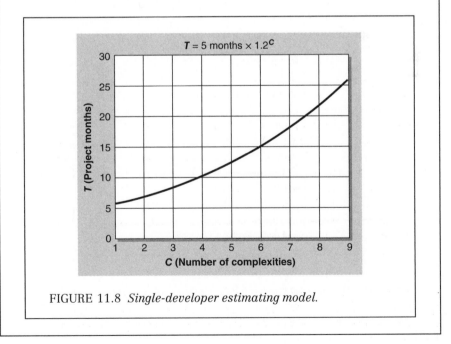

FIGURE 11.8 *Single-developer estimating model.*

## CREATING THE MULTIPLE-DEVELOPER MODEL

Eventually, more and more printer projects at Adobe became so complex that assigning only one software developer was not appropriate. The complexity/time relationship of the single-developer model appeared to be correct, so it seemed reasonable to analyze how the overall project complexity changes when multiple developers are assigned. Adding developers helps reduce the task-related complexity, simply because more developers share the task load; however, adding developers also adds a complexity of its own.

For example, Figure 11.9 shows the effect of adding developers to a complexity 9 project: For one developer, a complexity 9 project would take roughly two years, due mostly to the fact that the lone developer must work serially on the project tasks. Assigning a second developer significantly reduces the project time to about 13 months, thanks mostly to sharing the task load. In other words, the task-related complexity has been reduced by half while adding a comparatively small people-related complexity. Adding a third developer does not reduce the project time as much because there are fewer tasks to share. In addition, with three developers assigned, the people-related complexity becomes more significant. Notice from the graph that the project time increases if you add too many developers.

Using fewer developers than optimal may be cost-justified. Project managers need to evaluate this by comparing the estimated lost revenue from a later product introduction with the cost of additional developers, who could perhaps be assigned to other, higher-priority projects. In this example, maybe that third developer could be assigned to a different project where one more person would shorten the schedule much more.

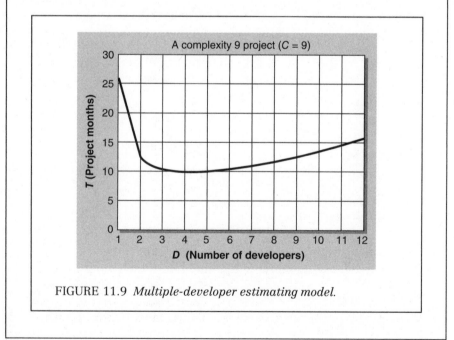

FIGURE 11.9 *Multiple-developer estimating model.*

## MULTIPLE-DEVELOPER TIME ESTIMATION MODEL

The model for estimating the project time $T$ (in months) for a project of complexity $C$ with multiple developers $D$ is:

$$T = 5 \text{ months} \times 1.2^{C/D + 0.5 \times (D-1)}$$

The $C/D$ term says that the task-related complexities $C$ are divided among the number of developers $D$, and the $0.5 \times (D - 1)$ term adds one-half complexity for each additional developer. Note that this model becomes the single-developer model when $D = 1$.

## HOW WELL DID THE MODEL REALLY WORK?

In general, the model had a good track record. Some critics said that it was too easy to adjust the complexities during the project to make the end date come out right, but the model was usually accurate to within a month or two for projects lasting about a year. One engineering manager quoted a 15 percent variance, but no one has done any rigorous model verification.

Some customers did not like the model because there was no way to express the notion that working harder would move up the project completion date. They missed the point that the model was calibrated against projects whose developers worked very hard, often including nights and weekends. Such is the nature of printer development.

Today, the model is rarely used in Adobe printer engineering because most printer development takes place at customer sites with software kits delivered by Adobe.

## MAKING YOUR OWN TIME ESTIMATION MODEL

The ability to devise your own model relies on these factors:

- You can define a simple project that has development tasks in common with all others.
- There are past project records to use for calibration, including the simple project described here.
- Your projects are similar to one another, yet vary in complexity.
- There are countable tasks or features that represent the complexity of the projects.

### Step 1: Establish a Baseline Project

Find a completed simple project whose tasks or features are in common with all other projects. This project can have one or more developers. Use its project time to set $T_0$, the duration, and $D_0$, number of developers, of a zero-complexity project.

### Step 2: Calibrate the Time Growth Factor

In your project records, find 6 to 10 other projects that have the same team size as the simple project but have more complexity and took longer.

For each of these projects, identify and count the complexities, such as product features or custom work. Make a plot of complexity count against project time and compute a value for $G$, the growth factor, which most accurately describes how your project times increase with increasing complexity.

### Step 3: Calibrate the People Penalty Factor

If you can, find 6 to 10 projects that have the same moderate complexity but a different number of developers. Plot the number of developers against the project times for these same-complexity projects and compute a value for $P$, the people penalty, which will probably be somewhere in the range of 0.4 to 0.6.

### Step 4: Validate Your New Model

Once you calibrate the model, you should validate it by applying it to new projects or other completed projects. If the model is not working, feel free to recalibrate it with different completed projects, or invent your own model from scratch.

John Gaffney is a senior engineering director for Adobe Systems.

## PMP Exam Prep Questions

1. The project manager is creating an estimate for building a warehouse and distribution center. It is a project similar to those he executes about three times a year. He is using the rule of thumb of $100 per square foot to calculate the estimate. What type of estimate is this?

   a. Parametric           c. Gut feel

   b. Analogous           D. Bottom-up

2. The construction team is building a new design for their company and the market for the product is extremely unstable because of current interest rates. According to the site manager, a key to success will be to have an extremely accurate estimate of the resource needs for the project, especially because the company is resource constrained. Which type of duration estimating approach is the most accurate?

   a. Parametric estimating

   b. Bottom-up estimating

   c. Analogous estimating

   d. Fast tracking

3. The management team is calculating the cost range for a project to develop a product that targets an unfamiliar market. What is the key principal that governs the cost range tolerance?

   a. The less known, the wider the range

   b. The more known, the wider the range

   c. The earlier in the project, the narrower the range

   d. −50 percent to +50 percent

4. To ensure that all the project work is considered, the project manager and his team create a bottom-up estimate. Of the following, which is not an advantage of creating such an estimate?

   a. The estimate provides team buy-in since the team is involved in its creation

   b. The estimate takes a great amount of time to create

   c. The estimate provides supporting detail

   d. The estimate has a greater degree of accuracy than other estimates because of the detail

Answers to these questions can be found at www.VersatileCompany .com/FFMBAinPM.

# Balancing the Trade-Off Among Cost, Schedule, and Quality

## INTRODUCTION

As I prepared to write this chapter I received an e-mail that ended this way:

> *I have recently changed job focus. I work part-time from home while caring for my six-week-old girl. Parenthood has consumed more of my personal resources than I budgeted. Consequently, I am behind schedule on this project.*

This new father is not only learning about the demands of parenthood, he has aptly summed up a dilemma of life: limited resources. Whatever we do, we are faced with limited time, limited money, and a shortage of the people, equipment, and materials we need to complete our jobs. This problem of limited resources goes beyond issues of efficiency or productivity. No matter how efficient they may be, new fathers and project managers alike must realize their limits and make choices.

But doesn't good project management mean we get more done, in less time, for less money? This is a valid question. Good project management *does* deliver more for less (particularly when compared to bad project management). But there are still limits. The best predictor of project success remains realistic stakeholder expectations. The project manager needs to rein in any unreasonable demands by the customer, as well as any unreasonable hopes of the project team. If these hopes and demands are allowed to drive a project, the result will almost certainly be cost and schedule overruns—and painful disappointment later in the project. Instead, project managers must establish realistic expectations through rational analysis of the facts. They must employ the definition and planning techniques described in previous chapters to balance the project scope against these three most common project constraints:

1. *Time.* The project, as defined, won't be finished in the time originally envisioned in the project rules.

2. *Money.* The project can deliver the desired outcome on schedule, but the cost is too high.

3. *Resources.* The projected cost is acceptable, but the schedule calls for people, equipment, or materials that aren't available. You could afford them, but there aren't any to hire.

If one or more of these constraints is a factor, the project will need to be balanced; that is, the balance among the cost, schedule, and quality of the product will have to be reconsidered. This balancing can take place at several different levels.

## THREE LEVELS OF BALANCING A PROJECT

Balancing a project can take place at one of three different levels of authority in an organization, depending on the kind of change needed:

1. *Project.* Balancing at the project level requires making changes that keep the project on track for its original cost, schedule, and quality objectives. Since these three parts of the project equilibrium won't change, the project manager and team should have authority to make these decisions.

2. *Business case.* If the project cannot achieve its cost-schedule-quality goals, then the equilibrium among these three factors must be reexamined. This means that the business case for the project must be reevaluated. Changing any of the goals of the project puts this decision beyond the authority of the project manager and team. To understand why the decision to change the cost-schedule-quality equilibrium has to be made at the business level, consider that:

   • Cost goals are related to profitability goals. Raising cost targets for the project means reevaluating the profit goals.

   • Schedules are closely linked to the business case. Projects that deliver late often incur some profit penalty, through either missed opportunities or actual monetary penalties spelled out in the contract.

- Changing the features and performance level of the product affects the quality—and therefore the value—of the end product.
- Balancing the project to the business case requires agreement from all the stakeholders, but most of all, from those who will be affected by changes to cost, schedule, or quality.

3. *Enterprise.* When the project and business case balance, but the firm has to choose which projects to pursue, it is then balancing the project at the enterprise level. The enterprise could be a department within a firm, an entire company, or a government agency. This decision is absolutely beyond the power of the project manager and team, and it may even exceed the authority of the sponsor and the functional managers, although they'll be active participants in the decision. Choosing which projects to pursue and how to spread limited resources over multiple projects is primarily a business management decision, even though it requires project management information.

## BALANCING AT THE PROJECT LEVEL

There are as many ways to balance projects as there are projects. This chapter presents the best-known alternatives for balancing at the project, business case, and enterprise levels. Because determining the right alternative depends on which balance problem exists, each alternative is listed with its positive and negative impacts and the best application—the best way of applying the technique. Following are a number of ways of balancing the project at the project level.

### 1. Re-Estimate the Project

This is the "optimist's choice." This involves checking your original assumptions in the statement of work and the work package estimates. Perhaps your growing knowledge of the project will allow you to reduce your pessimistic estimates. Here are the possible impacts of this kind of checking.

*Positive.* If certain estimates can be legitimately reduced, the project cost, and perhaps the schedule estimates, will shrink, and the accuracy of your estimates will have increased.

*Negative.* Unless there is new information to justify better estimates, don't fall prey to wishful thinking.

*Best application.* Always check your estimates. Make sure your estimating assumptions about productivity, availability of skilled people, and complexity of tasks are consistent and match all available information. While you are making changes, however, it's important not to succumb to pressure and reduce the estimates just to please management or customers. If anything, the second round of estimating should create an even firmer foundation of facts supporting cost, schedule, and resource estimates.

## 2. Change Task Assignments to Take Advantage of Schedule Float

This is a straightforward resource allocation maneuver, particularly if you're using project management software (see Figure 12.1). It involves moving people to critical path tasks from tasks that are not on the critical path in order to reduce the duration of the critical path. The noncritical tasks—those with schedule flexibility (float)—will finish later.

*Positive.* The beauty of this trick is that the schedule can be reduced with no change in the total labor cost. If labor or equipment is pulled from a task with sufficient float, that task will just be performed later for the same cost (see Tasks 7 and 8 in Figure 12.1).

*Negative.* The original work package estimates may have had the optimal number of people assigned to the task. By adding people to a task, the duration may be reduced, but the actual labor costs might go up if efficiency is compromised (certain tasks are not performed as efficiently with more people). The noncritical tasks, from which workers were removed, may also suffer a loss of efficiency.

*Best application.* There are three considerations when moving people from noncritical tasks to critical tasks:

1. They both need the same resource type. (Pulling attorneys off a task to help a bricklayer won't work.)
2. The noncritical task needs enough float to allow it to be delayed without delaying the entire project. Don't forget that shortening tasks on the critical path will take float away from all noncritical tasks. You may find that reducing duration on a few critical path tasks changes the critical path.
3. You must be able to reduce the duration of the critical path tasks by applying more people. (See Tables 9.2 and 9.5 in Chapter 9 for examples of tasks that don't decrease in duration by adding people.)

## 3. Add People to the Project

This is an obvious way to balance a project because it reduces the schedule. Adding people to the project team can either increase the number of tasks that can be done at the same time or increase the number of people working on each task.

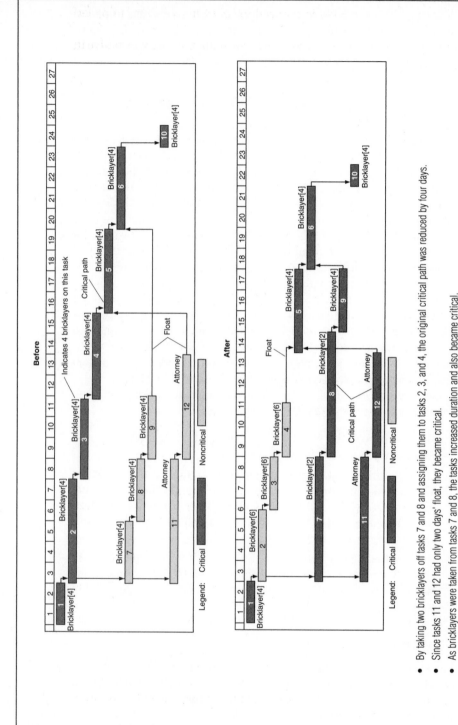

FIGURE 12.1 *Change task assignments to take advantage of schedule float.*

- By taking two bricklayers off tasks 7 and 8 and assigning them to tasks 2, 3, and 4, the original critical path was reduced by four days.
- Since tasks 11 and 12 had only two days' float, they became critical.
- As bricklayers were taken from tasks 7 and 8, the tasks increased duration and also became critical.

*Positive.* The schedule is reduced because more labor is applied every day of the project.

*Negative.* Fred Brooks[1] summed up the danger of this alternative in the title of his landmark book, *The Mythical Man-Month.* Pouring more people onto the project may reduce the schedule, but it increases the cost of coordination and communication. Economists refer to this effect as the *law of diminishing marginal returns.* (As an example, you can refer to the Stellar Performer profile of Adobe Systems in Chapter 11. It demonstrates how each person added to a software project has a diminishing impact on schedule performance.)

You can't just add another warm body to a project; this option requires *qualified* resources. Many project managers have asked for more people, only to have the most available people (which usually means the least competent) sent to their projects. Weighing the project down with unskilled workers can create such a drag on productivity that it is almost certain to drive up both cost and schedule.

*Best application.* Certain work lends itself to piling on, that is, adding more people to get the job done faster. Task independence and product development strategy are both factors to consider when adding people to a project. The greater the independence of the concurrent tasks, the more constant the advantage of adding people.

For instance, a highway department plans on repaving a 100-mile stretch of highway. They could break down the repaving into 10 10-mile subprojects and perform them all at the same time, assuming they had enough qualified contractors to run 10 projects concurrently. (If shortening the schedule were really important and there were enough road paving contractors, they could even break it into 20 five-mile subprojects.) The independence among all the subprojects makes it possible to overlap them. Trying to coordinate that many people and that much equipment would require extra project management effort, but even if it took 10 times as many supervisors from the highway department to coordinate the project, these costs would remain constant because the duration would be cut by 90 percent. There are other realities to consider on a project like this, however, such as whether all the various contractors will use the same roads, gravel pits, and equipment parking. But these are only resource constraints (resource constraints can be analyzed using the resource-leveling technique described in Chapter 9).

Fred Brooks also points out that a software development schedule is not strictly divisible by the number of people on the project. But developing software products can require huge teams. Likewise, producing a new commercial aircraft requires thousands of engineers. Projects that use knowledge workers can usefully add people to reduce their schedules by following good product development practices such as these:

- The project team organization reflects the product design. The overall project must be broken into teams and/or subprojects the same way the overall product is broken into components or sub-products. Manufacturing companies refer to this organizational style as *integrated product teams* (IPTs), because all of the disciplines required to develop a component of the product are teamed together.

- The product is designed from the top down, and the schedule contains design synchronization points. Top-down design means establishing the product's overall design parameters first, then repeatedly breaking the product into components and subcomponents. Scheduled synchronization points are times to focus on component interfaces and reevaluate how the entire product is meeting the overall product design requirements (see Figure 12.2).

- Actual construction of any part of the product begins only after the design for that component has been synchronized and stabilized

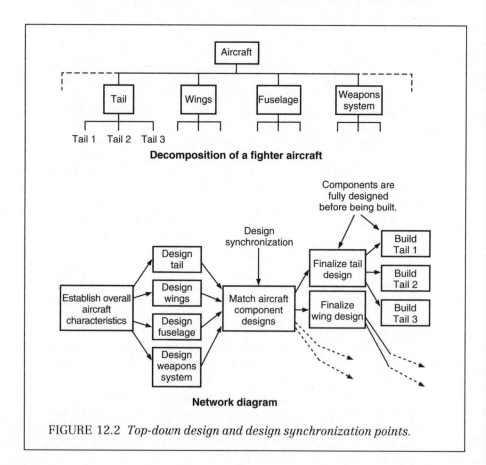

FIGURE 12.2 *Top-down design and design synchronization points.*

against the design for interfacing components. Aircraft manufacturers commonly use three-dimensional engineering software that actually models the interaction of different components, eliminating the need for physical mock-ups of the aircraft. Figure 12.2 demonstrates how useful a network diagram is for identifying concurrent tasks. These concurrent tasks are opportunities for adding people to the project in order to reduce overall duration.

- Component construction includes unit testing and frequent integration testing. Unit tests refer to testing the functions of individual components as they are built. Frequent integration tests pull together the most up-to-date versions of completed components to make sure they work together. Frequent integration testing has emerged as a required development technique for products with many components because the sheer number of possible interface failures is beyond the ability to test and effectively debug (see Figure 12.3).

Finally, don't forget that by adding people to the project to reduce schedule, you are increasing cost risks. The more people who are idled by unexpected delays, the higher the cost per day of any delay.

## 4. Increase Productivity by Using Experts from Within the Firm

It's no secret that some people are more productive than others. I've seen top computer programmers turn out 10 times as much as the weakest member of a team. Though it may not be at a 10:1 ratio, every industry has people who are just more capable. So why not put as many of them as you can on your project? These high performers have technical competence, problem-solving skills, and positive attitudes. After they've re-estimated your project, it will probably meet or beat all the original assumptions about cost and schedule performance.

*Positive.* Not only will this team deliver the best possible schedule performance, it will also be cost-effective. These high performers might double the output of the average team member, but it's rare that they get paid twice as much for doing it. On top of that, their expertise is likely to produce a better product.

*Negative.* This can be an inefficient strategy for the firm. Putting all these stars on one project means that they'll probably be doing work that's well below their ability levels—something a junior staff member could do as well, even if not as fast. Another negative is that when other projects begin to suffer, the stars will be reassigned and the stellar project will slowly fall behind schedule.

*Best application.* Top people are spread around many projects so their ability and expertise can make other people more productive.

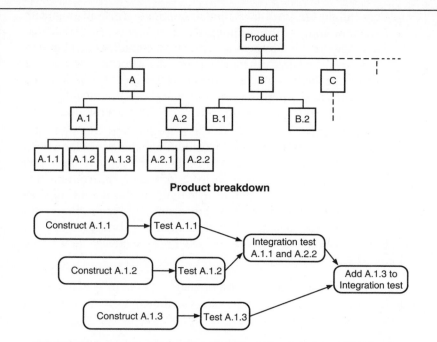

**Product breakdown**

**Network diagram showing an incremental approach to integration testing**

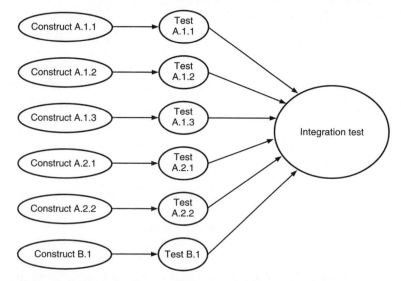

**Network diagram showing an all-at-once approach to integration testing**

FIGURE 12.3 *Component construction phase includes frequent unit and integration tests.*

You'll have a better chance of getting the optimal mix of average and star players when you do two things.

First, create experts within the team by putting the same people on related tasks. For instance, when a team of business analysts was working with a hospital to redesign the hospital's methods for keeping records of patients, the project leader assigned one person to be responsible for decisions affecting the maternity ward, another for the pediatric ward, another for the pharmacy, and so on. Even though these assignments didn't necessarily increase their skill level as analysts, each person did become the subject-matter expert for his or her part of the project. This strategy is even more important when there are many people who won't be working full-time on the project, because it keeps specialized knowledge in one place.

Second, using the work breakdown structure, network diagram, and work package estimates, identify the tasks that benefit most from top talent. Here are some indicators that you'll get a big payback from a star:

- *Cost.* The most complex tasks produce the highest returns from top performers. These are the kind of tasks that produce productivity ratios of 10:1.
- *Schedule.* Put the top performers on critical path tasks, where their speed will translate to a shorter overall project schedule.
- *Quality.* Top performers make good technical leads by making major design decisions and spending time discussing work with junior team members.

Most important, involve top performers in project management activities such as risk management, estimating, and effective assignment of personnel.

## 5. Increase Productivity by Using Experts from Outside the Firm

The same logic for the preceding alternative applies here, except that this option seeks to pull in the best people from outside the firm. Whether you hire individual people as contract labor or engage a firm to perform specialized tasks, the process is similar: Use the work breakdown structure to identify the best application of their talents and manage them like one of the team.

*Positive.* Some work is so specialized that it doesn't pay to have qualified people on staff do it. The additional costs incurred by hiring the outside experts will be more than offset by the speed and quality of their work. Just as with the experts from within the firm, assign them the time- or quality-critical tasks to get the most leverage from their work.

*Negative.* There are two downsides to this option: vendor risk and lost expertise.

1. *Vendor risk.* Bringing an outsider into the project introduces additional uncertainty. Unfortunately, not every expert delivers; he or she may not live up to the promises. By the time you find out your expert isn't productive, you may find, in spite of the added costs, that the project is behind schedule. In addition, locating a qualified vendor or contract employee can be time-consuming; if it takes too much time, it can become a bottleneck in the schedule.

2. *Lost expertise* Every contract laborer or subcontractor who walks out the door at the end of the project takes some knowledge along—and this problem intensifies if the work is "brain work." In this case, the project manager needs to make sure that the work has been properly recorded and documented.

*Best application.* Hiring outside experts is useful when it appears that their specialized skills will move the project along faster. You should expect these experts to attend team meetings and participate in product development discussions; don't let them become islands, working alone and avoiding interaction with long-term employees. Like the inside experts, they should be included in project management and other high-leverage activities. Before they leave the project, whatever they produce should be tested and documented.

The added productivity that outside resources bring to the project must outweigh the effort to find and hire them. The ideal situation is to have a long-term relationship with a special-services firm whose employees have demonstrated their expertise on past projects.

## 6. Outsource the Entire Project or a Significant Portion of It

This method of balancing a project involves carving out a portion of the project and handing it to an external firm to manage and complete. This option is especially attractive if this portion of the project requires specialized skills not possessed by internal workers.

*Positive.* This moves a large portion of the work to experts whose skills should result in greater productivity and a shortened schedule.

*Negative.* This shifting of responsibility creates more risk. The project manager will have less control over the progress of the work, and if the outside specialists prove to be less than competent, it may be too late to "switch horses." Even if it succeeds, an outside firm will leave little of its expertise with your firm at the end of the project.

*Best application.* Outsourcing is at the high end of the risk/return spectrum. When it works, it can be a miracle of modern business methods; when it doesn't, it can result in real catastrophes. The keys to successful outsourcing are finding qualified vendors and coming to clear agreements before the work begins. These agreements must be built using various tools from this book, including responsibility matrixes, work breakdown structures, network diagrams, and Gantt charts.

### ⚠️ DANGER! *Don't Underestimate the Risks of Outsourcing*

The full process for finding and hiring a qualified subcontractor involves many of the techniques in this book—and even more that you won't find here. Finding qualified subcontractors for large projects amounts to a major subproject in itself. Don't underestimate the risks and challenges of outsourcing major projects.

## 7. Crash the Schedule

When tasks are compressed on the critical path, the entire project is shortened.[2] But compressing task duration can be expensive. Crashing can employ any of the alternatives listed in this chapter to reduce the duration of critical path tasks, but it takes the extra step of producing a *cost/schedule trade-off table*, which is used to analyze the cost of reducing the schedule (see Figure 12.4).

*Positive.* The table makes it clear which tasks are the cheapest to compress.

*Negative.* The only potential negative is that the estimates in the table may turn out to be not completely accurate.

*Best application.* Any time that tasks on the critical path need to be compressed, a crash table points out the path where the payback will be the greatest.

## 8. Work Overtime

The easiest way to add more labor to a project is not to add more people, but to increase the daily hours of the people already on the project. If a team works 60 hours a week instead of 40, it might accomplish 50 percent more.

*Positive.* Having the same people work more hours avoids the additional costs of coordination and communication encountered when people are added. Another advantage is that during overtime hours, whether they come before or after normal working hours, there are fewer distractions in the workplace.

*Negative.* Overtime costs more. Hourly workers typically earn 50 percent more when working overtime. When salaried workers put in overtime, it may not cost the project more money, but sustained overtime can incur other, intangible costs. In *Peopleware: Productive*

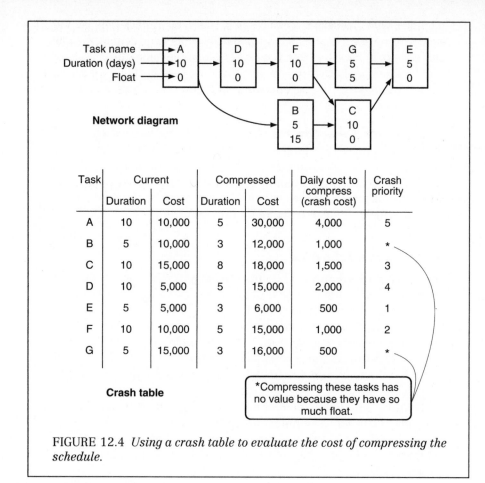

FIGURE 12.4 *Using a crash table to evaluate the cost of compressing the schedule.*

*Projects and Teams,* Tom DeMarco and Timothy Lister not only recognize the intangible cost of sustained overtime (divorce, burnout, turnover), they also call into question whether *any* overtime on projects involving knowledge workers is effective. They state: "Nobody can really work much more than forty hours [per week], at least not continually and with the intensity required for creative work. . . . Throughout the effort there will be more or less an hour of undertime for every hour of overtime," where *undertime* is described as nonwork activities such as "personal phone calls, bull sessions, and just resting."[3] Adding in overtime assumes that people are as productive during the ninth, tenth, and eleventh hours as they were the first eight hours of a day. Since this is rarely the case for any type of worker in any industry, the extra pay and intangible costs of overtime may not really buy much in increased output.

*Best application.* How much overtime is effective is debatable, but one thing is certain: Overtime is perceived by the project team as over and above the normal expected performance. Whether he or she demands overtime or allows people to voluntarily sign up for it, the project manager must demonstrate clearly the ways in which the extra work will benefit the project and the individual team members. The best rule is to apply overtime sparingly and only where it produces big paybacks.

## Reducing Product Performance Is Not an Option

**DANGER!**

As stated in Chapter 2, the two characteristics of product quality are functionality and performance. *Functionality* describes what the product does, while *performance* describes how well the functionality works. Reducing the performance of the product is another way of balancing a project. Time and money can be saved by cutting the testing and quality control tasks and by performing other tasks more quickly and less thoroughly.

*Positive.* The cost and schedule may very well be reduced because we're spending less effort on the project.

*Negative.* Philip Crosby[4] titled his book *Quality Is Free* on the premise that the cost of doing things twice is far greater than the cost of doing them right the first time. When performance is cut, costs go up for many reasons, including these:

- Rework (performing the same tasks twice because they weren't done right the first time) during the project will drive the cost higher and delay completion.

- Rework after the project finishes is even more expensive than rework during the project. Any potential development cost savings are wiped out by the high cost of fixing the product.

- Failures due to poor product performance can be staggeringly expensive. Product recalls always bear the expense of contacting the consumers as well as fixing or replacing the product. Product failures such as collapsing bridges and malfunctioning medical equipment can even cost lives.

- Poor product performance causes damage to the reputation of the firm and ultimately reduces the demand for its product.

*Best application.* Never! Crosby's argument is correct: It is cheaper to do it right than to do it twice. The only legitimate arguments in favor of cutting performance are presented in the next section under the first alternative, "Reduce the Product Scope."

## BALANCING AT THE BUSINESS CASE LEVEL

If, in spite of all attempts to balance a project at the project level, the cost-schedule-quality goals still cannot be achieved, then the equilibrium of these three factors needs to be reexamined. This means that the business case for the project must be reevaluated. Decisions relating to goals are beyond the authority of the project manager and team alone; this reevaluation requires the authorization of all the stakeholders. This section will look at the various ways that the business case for a project can be reevaluated.

### 1. Reduce the Product Scope

If the goals of the project will take too long to accomplish or cost too much, the first step is to scale down the objectives—the product scope. The result of this alternative will be to reduce the functionality of the end product. Perhaps an aircraft will carry less weight, a software product will have fewer features, or a building will have fewer square feet or less expensive wood paneling. (Remember the difference between product scope and project scope: *Product scope* describes the functionality and performance of the product; *project scope* is all the work required to deliver the product scope.)

*Positive.* This will save the project while saving both time and money.

*Negative.* When a product's functionality is reduced, its value is reduced. If the airplane won't carry as much weight, will the customers still want it? If a software product has fewer features, will it stand up to competition? A smaller office building with less expensive wood paneling may not attract high-enough rents to justify the project.

*Best application.* The key to reducing a product's scope without reducing its value is to reevaluate the true requirements for the business case. Many a product has been over budget because it was overbuilt. Quality has best been defined as "conformance to requirements." Therefore, reducing product scope so that the requirements are met more accurately actually improves the value of the product, because it is produced more quickly and for a lower cost.

Calculating the cost and schedule savings of reduced functionality begins with the work breakdown structure. Reducing the functionality means that certain tasks can be reduced or eliminated; these tasks need to be found and the estimates reduced accordingly (see Figure 12.5). As always, focusing on critical path tasks is the surest way to reduce a schedule.

If the project remains over budget or over schedule after you have reevaluated the requirements and scaled back the product scope, then it is time to focus on the customer's use of the product. Which

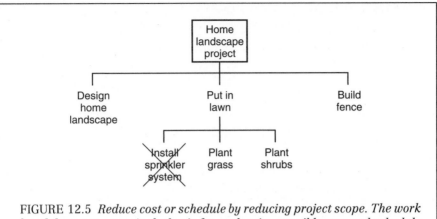

FIGURE 12.5 *Reduce cost or schedule by reducing project scope. The work breakdown structure is the basis for evaluating possible cost and schedule reductions to the home landscape project.*

requirements are absolutely necessary and which could be modified or eliminated? You can start by prioritizing the requirements, then analyzing the cost-benefit trade-off of each requirement. In particular, expensive requirements that add little benefit need to be identified. Again, the first tool used in evaluating the cost and schedule savings of each requirement is the work breakdown structure.

### 2. Fixed-Phase Scheduling

During the early days of a product development life cycle, it is difficult to pin down the cost, schedule, or product quality. But some projects, for very important reasons, need to be completed by a specific date. When fixed-phase scheduling is employed, the project phases are apportioned from the top down and scheduled according to the required completion date. (See "Phased Estimating" and "Apportioning" in Chapter 11.) At the end of each phase, the scope of the project is reevaluated (functionality is added or removed) to fit the remaining schedule (see Figure 12.6).

*Positive.* Since functionality can be added as well as removed, the project will meet the schedule with the best possible product because it was consciously rescoped several times. Quality (product performance) will remain high with this method, because quality-oriented tasks won't be sacrificed at the last minute to meet the schedule.

*Negative.* Not every product lends itself to functionality changes several times during the life cycle. The design for many products is holistic, encompassing all the functions. During construction of a house, for instance, it isn't appropriate to add another bedroom and bathroom just because the project is ahead of schedule or under budget.

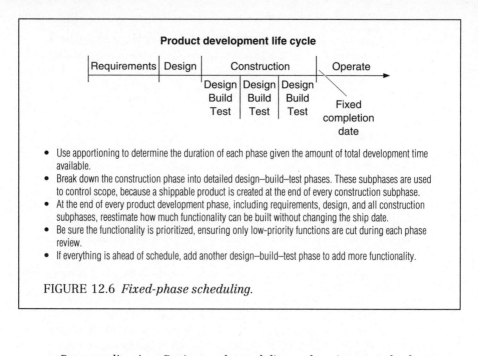

**Product development life cycle**

- Use apportioning to determine the duration of each phase given the amount of total development time available.
- Break down the construction phase into detailed design–build–test phases. These subphases are used to control scope, because a shippable product is created at the end of every construction subphase.
- At the end of every product development phase, including requirements, design, and all construction subphases, reestimate how much functionality can be built without changing the ship date.
- Be sure the functionality is prioritized, ensuring only low-priority functions are cut during each phase review.
- If everything is ahead of schedule, add another design–build–test phase to add more functionality.

FIGURE 12.6 *Fixed-phase scheduling.*

*Best application.* Projects whose delivery date is set and whose products can be scaled up or down during development without compromising design lend themselves best to this method. Software (including information systems) is probably the best candidate for fixed-phase estimating, because most software designs are modular. In addition, it's critical that these products meet their delivery date because their market success often depends on beating a competitor to the punch.

Iterative delivery was described in more detail in Chapter 3, in the Stellar Performer, The Agile Approach to Software Development, and in Chapter 10, Managing Agile Development with Scrum. Customers and the project team will re-prioritize the deliverables several times over the life of the project, which requires a customer to be as skilled in this process as the team.

### 3. Fast-Tracking

Fast-tracking involves overlapping tasks that are traditionally done in sequence. The best example of this balancing technique is beginning construction on a building before the design is complete. The argument for fast-tracking holds that you don't have to know where all the closets and doorways will be before you start digging the foundation.

*Positive.* Fast-tracking can decrease the project schedule significantly, sometimes by as much as 40 percent.

*Negative.* Overlapping design and construction is risky, and this is why the decision to fast-track a project must be made at the business level. All the stakeholders need to understand and accept the risk that, if initial design assumptions prove to be mistaken, part of the product will have to be demolished and built again. In the worst cases, the mistakes made in a fast-track environment can not only slow down the project to the point where there is no schedule advantage, but can also cause the costs to run far over the estimates.

*Best application.* The fundamental assumptions of fast-tracking are that only 15 to 30 percent of the total design work can provide a stable design framework and that the remainder of design activities can be performed faster than construction activities. For these assumptions to hold true, the product must be capable of modular, top-down design. (This type of design was described in the previous section under alternative 3, "Add People to the Project.")

Overlapping design and construction is becoming more common in software development, but in addition to overlapping these phases they also *repeat* each phase. Instead of increasing risk, this design-build-design-build approach actually lowers risk, because the product is developed incrementally. Because of the incremental development, this doesn't quite qualify as a fast-track example, but it does point up how this technique can be successfully modified.

The bottom line with fast-tracking is that it overlaps tasks that have traditionally been done in sequence. The overlap is the risk. The Stellar Performer profile of Safeco Field at the end of this chapter demonstrates how risky it can be.

## 4. Phased Product Delivery

In a situation in which the project can't deliver the complete product by the deadline, there is still the possibility that it might deliver some useful part of it. Information systems composed of several subsystems, for example, will often implement one subsystem at a time. Tenants can move into some floors in a new office building while there is active construction on other floors, and sections of a new freeway are opened as they are completed rather than waiting for the entire freeway to be complete.

*Positive.* Phased delivery has several benefits:

- Something useful is delivered as soon as possible.
- Often, as in the case of information systems, phased delivery is actually preferred because the changes introduced by the new system happen a little at a time. This longer time frame can reduce the negative impacts to ongoing business operations.
- Feedback on the delivered product is used to improve the products still in development.

- By delivering over a longer period, the size of the project team can be reduced; a smaller team can lead to lower communication and coordination costs. And, since the people are working for a longer time on the project, project-specific expertise grows. These factors should lead to increased productivity in subsequent project phases and to an overall lower cost for the project.

- Phased delivery allows for phased payment. By spreading the cost of the project over a longer time, a larger budget might be more feasible.

*Negative.* Not all products can be implemented a piece at a time. Phased implementation may also require parallel processes, in which old methods run concurrently with new methods, and this can temporarily lead to higher operating costs.

*Best application.* Modularized products, whose components can operate independently, can be delivered in phases. In order to determine how to phase a product delivery, you need to look for the core functionality—the part of the product that the other pieces rely on—and implement that first. The same criteria may be used in identifying the second and third most important components. When multiple components are equally good candidates, they can be prioritized according to business requirements.

Although consumer products such as automobiles don't appear to be good candidates for phased delivery ("You'll be getting the windshield in January and the bumpers should arrive in early March . . ."), a limited amount of phased delivery is possible for some consumer products. For example, software products can be upgraded cheaply and effectively over time by using the Internet, and current customers can download product updates directly onto their computers from company sites on the World Wide Web.

### 5. Do It Twice—Quickly and Correctly

This method seems to contradict all the edicts about the cost advantages of doing it right the first time (as in Philip Crosby's *Quality Is Free*). Instead, this alternative suggests that if you are in a hurry, try building a quick-and-dirty short-term solution at first, then go back and build the right product the right way.

*Positive.* This method gets a product to the customer quickly. The secondary advantage is that what is learned on the first product may improve the second product.

*Negative.* Crosby is right: It is more expensive to build it twice.

*Best application.* This is an alternative to use when the demand for the product is intense and urgent—when every day (even every hour!) it isn't there is expensive. The high costs of doing it twice are more than compensated for by the reduced costs or increased profits that even an inferior product offers. Military examples abound, such as pontoon bridges that replace concrete bridges destroyed by combat. In the realm of business, a product that is first to market not only gains market share, but may actually provide the revenue stream that keeps the company alive to develop the next product.

## 6. Change the Profit Requirement

If your project needs to cost less in order to be competitively priced, this method recommends reducing the profit margin. This means reducing the markups on the project and the hourly rates charged for the project employees.

*Positive.* Costs are reduced while schedule and quality stay constant. Perhaps the lower cost helps the company win a big project. Even if the project isn't as profitable, it may give a good position to the firm in a new marketplace. Or it may be that a long-term, lower-profit engagement gives you the stability to take on other projects with higher returns.

*Negative.* The project may not bring in enough profit to allow the firm to survive.

*Best application.* Reducing the profit margin is clearly a strategic decision made by the owners or executives of the firm. This is a viable option when a firm must remain competitive in a difficult market. But deciding whether to go ahead with a project with a reduced profit margin would be considered an enterprise-level decision for the firm bidding on the project.

## BALANCING AT THE ENTERPRISE LEVEL

Enterprise-level balancing mainly confronts the constraints of insufficient equipment, personnel, and budget. At the enterprise level, the firm decides which projects to pursue, given finite resources. Making these decisions requires accurate estimates of individual project resources, costs, and schedules (see the discussion on program management in Chapter 18).

Choosing between projects is difficult; there will always be important ones that don't make the cut. While it might be tempting to do them all, pursuing too many might be more costly than pursuing too few. When an organization tries to complete 10 projects with resources enough for only eight, it may wind up with 10 projects that are 80 percent complete. In spite of all the effort, it may not finish a single project.

The alternatives that are successful at the enterprise level are variations of the ones applied at the project and business case levels:

1. *Outsourcing* allows you to pursue more projects with the same number of people, if you have enough money to pay the outside firm.

2. *Phased product delivery* means that more projects can be run at the same time, with many small product deliveries rather than a few big ones.

3. *Reducing product scope* on several projects requires cost-benefit trade-off analysis among projects, rather than just among functions on a single product.

4. *Using productivity tools* can be a strategic decision to improve productivity across projects. The proper tools can bring great leaps in productivity increases; this may enable firms to pursue many more projects with the same number of people.

But no matter which alternatives the enterprise chooses or how successfully they are applied, there will always be more good ideas than time or money allows.

## END POINT

Balancing shouldn't wait until the end of the planning phase; it should be a part of every project definition and planning activity. Balancing involves reconsidering the balance among the cost, schedule, and quality of the product.

Although it is usually referred to as "course correction," balancing will continue to be present during project control, as the team responds to the realities of project execution and finds that the original plan must be altered.

It would be a mistake to see project management techniques as a tool set for proving that schedules or cost requirements cannot be met. Rather, they're intended to make sure projects are performed the fastest, cheapest, and best way. Balancing requires stakeholders to face the facts about what is possible and what is not. When a project is badly out of balance, it will do no good to fire up the troops through motivational speeches or threats. People know when a job is impossible. Instead, the project manager's job is to create a vision of what is possible and then to rebalance the project in such a way that the vision can become a reality. Balancing requires thought, strategy, innovation, and honesty.

# *Stellar Performer: Safeco Field*
## Fast-Tracking a Baseball Stadium

Baseball is full of surprises. In 2001, the Seattle Mariners won a record-tying 116 wins in regular-season play. But they were eliminated during the American League playoffs, so the winningest team in baseball didn't make it to the World Series. That up-and-down feeling characterized the building of Safeco Field, the Mariners' state-of-the-art stadium that opened in July 1999. The stadium's classic design and 11-acre, three-piece retractable roof made it an exciting project for the contractor, joint venture team Hunt-Kiewit. But the biggest challenge was the accelerated schedule.

In August 1998, the project was plunging forward on a fast-track schedule when J. C. Brummond, project manager for the new baseball complex, took time to explain how the intense schedule was affecting the project.

Prominently displayed in Brummond's office was a simple chart comparing the normal 50-month schedule for a ballpark of this size and the fast-track, 34-month schedule for Safeco Field. "This chart tells the whole story," said Brummond, a 25-year veteran of the construction industry who has built everything from an island at Prudhoe Bay to bus tunnels in Seattle and freeway bridges in Hawaii. As with most fast-track projects, the speed of construction came with a price. "There are a thousand reasons why the cost of this project is climbing, but they all come back—in whole or in part—to an aggressive schedule," said Brummond. (See Figure 12.7.)

*Fast-tracking*, the practice of beginning construction before design is complete, is inherently risky because it opens up the possibility of wrong assumptions and subsequent rework. At Safeco Field, fast-tracking led to many cases where design modifications and detail drawings were released the same day concrete for that part of the structure was poured. Brummond emphasized the unusual situation: "We accepted drawings up until the time of pour. I called it just-in-time design." Amazingly, the project stayed on schedule. But the relentless pace was balanced by predictable, but unavoidable, cost increases.

### OVERTIME

From the start, the men and women on the site worked overtime. Ten-hour days were common, and work often continued over weekends. With the average overtime rate at time and a half (50 percent more than the regular wage), it's easy to understand why these costs increased.

### INEFFICIENCY OF OVERTIME

The theory of overtime is that one person can accomplish 80 hours of work by working either two 40-hour weeks or by working 12 hours a day for seven days straight. The reality is different, particularly when it's physical labor. "Bricklayers are a good example," Brummond explained. "Bricklaying is exacting, hard work. You can't speed brickwork with overtime, because you wear out the laborers. The law of diminishing marginal returns applies to everyone on this site. So all the extra overtime helps the schedule, but the overtime hours aren't as productive."

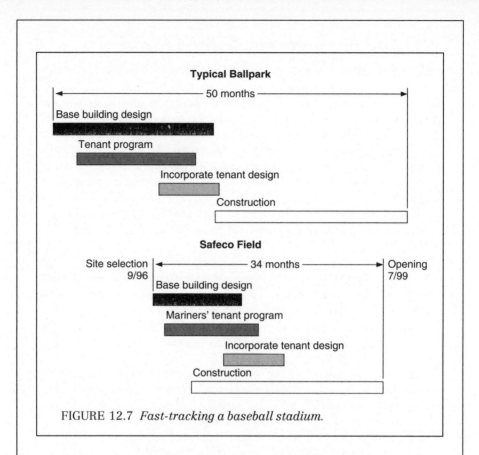

FIGURE 12.7 *Fast-tracking a baseball stadium.*

## LATE DESIGN PRODUCED MORE CONCURRENT WORK

"Ideally, we would have started with the most complex part of the structure, the area behind home plate," explained Brummond, "and then worked both left and right around the park, meeting in center field." But with design still in progress, construction began in center field instead. Then last-minute changes to the scoreboard design forced construction to begin in right center field and proceed clockwise around the park in one direction only. "There are limits to how many people you can stack on any part of this park before they start to get in each other's way. If we could have worked two directions at the same time, there would have been many more opportunities for efficiency. Concrete, for instance. We could have had the pouring and finishing crews alternating between the two sides of the stadium, keeping both of them busy and out of each other's way."

## SCHEDULE PRESSURE CUT TIME TO PLAN FOR COST SAVINGS

Normally, the engineers and architects have an opportunity to scrub the design for constructibility issues—modifications that make the structure more efficient to build. With the intense schedule pressure, many constructibility issues weren't identified until they had already become obstacles on the job. For example:

- The computer-assisted design optimized every concrete beam in the stadium, designing each one to the minimum size for its structural requirements. While that reduced the total amount of materials (concrete and reinforcing steel) needed to build these beams, it resulted in over 900 beam sizes, some of them only fractions of an inch in difference. "They should have standardized all the beam sizes in the design stage, because standard sizes make it more efficient to build the forms," said Brummond. "In this business you focus on labor to cut costs." Again, a fast-track schedule called for building part of the structure before design for other parts was complete—leaving out the time necessary to reevaluate the design for constructibility cost savings.

- The anchor bolts used to tie the structural steel to the cast-in-place concrete structure had a similar problem. Again, the concrete columns, beams, and shear walls were optimized for materials, producing a design where the reinforcing steel was so tightly packed there was barely room for the lag bolts that stick up from the tops of the columns, beams, and slabs. This made it impossible for the craftsmen setting the lag bolts to put them in exactly the right place—a problem that became apparent every time a crane lifted a piece of structural steel to be attached and its holes didn't match the bolts. "So then you have a bunch of steelworkers standing around while the old anchor bolt is cut off and a new one is installed in the right position. We hit this problem over and over throughout the erection of the steel."

## NO TIME TO PLAN FOR EFFICIENCY

Part of keeping the costs down on a big construction project is thinking through how all the different subcontractors will work together—for example, which subcontractor needs to deliver materials to an area before another puts up the walls. But on a fast-track project, with everyone working as fast as they can, this type of planning often falls by the wayside, with predictable results. For instance, during the August 1998 tour, a number of 20- and 40-foot copper pipes, four inches in diameter, sat in a hallway outside of rooms that they should have been in. When they were delivered only days before, there had been no hallways or rooms because the walls hadn't been built. It cost extra labor to get the pipes into the right rooms to be installed.

## REWORK

Fast-tracking's most predictable risk is rework, and Safeco Field saw plenty. Since the schedule demanded that the structure's concrete be poured before the commercial tenants had designed their spaces, holes had to be cut through the concrete for many of the drain lines, water pipes, cables, and other service lines. When a huge air duct was installed after the fire sprinkler lines had been hung from the ceiling, the duct was blocked by some of the sprinkler lines. Brummond pointed this out as just one more example of the cost of building before completing design, then recorded it in a notebook he carried with him constantly. "When they installed it, there was no way the people who put in that sprinkler line could know that vent would come through here. But now they have to move that line."

## SPECIAL EQUIPMENT

To speed the schedule, four large tower cranes were placed at the four corners of the ballpark, allowing the exterior structure and the seating structures to be raised at the same time. This strategy cut as much as six months off the schedule, but the tower cranes were significantly more expensive than conventional track-mounted mobile cranes.

Not every innovation was more expensive. Rather than building wooden forms for some of the stairs and other concrete structures in the stands, the construction team decided to pour the concrete over Styrofoam blocks. "The Styrofoam is lighter-weight, won't rot, and it takes a guy about five minutes to cut the blocks. It's a lot faster than plywood."

The decision to fast-track a project is always a risky one, and it always comes down to one question: Which is more important, cost or schedule? For the Seattle Mariners, moving to their new stadium immediately following the All-Star break in 1999 was the dominant factor. The construction team, architects, engineers, and the public agency overseeing construction of the ballpark all walked into this fast-track project with their eyes open, aware of the risks. In August 1998, halfway through the construction schedule, the budget for the stadium had been raised from $417 million to $498 million; this was due to many factors, including increased scope and underestimating the original job. But there is no denying that a portion of the budget increase was due to the pace of the work and the inevitable inefficiencies that came with it.

When the stadium opened, on time, in July 1999, the final budget had been revised to $515 million. Safeco Field has been filled ever since, with fans who love to watch baseball in this beautiful park.

*Sources:* Interview with J. C. Brummond, Project Manager, Hunt-Kiewit Joint Venture, August 25, 1998; "M's Will Pay Overruns," *Seattle Times*, July 21, 1998, A1, A11.

# Stellar Performer: Boeing 767-400ER Program
## Integrated Schedule Development

The Boeing Company of Seattle, Washington, is known for its ability to deliver huge, complex projects on time. The challenge of building a new-model commercial aircraft includes optimizing the efforts of thousands of people while building a complex product that requires integrating hundreds of design decisions. To meet these challenges, Boeing's 767-400ER program rigorously applied classic schedule integration techniques.

### SETTING THE DELIVERY DATE

Launched in April 1997, the 767-400ER program put together an aggressive schedule to deliver the first airplane to Delta Air Lines in May 2000. But an aggressive schedule isn't worth much if it can't be met. "The program used right-to-left scheduling," explained Fred Black, the manager responsible for program planning and schedule integration. Using parametric estimates from previous derivative programs, the program tied airplane requirements to a high-level schedule. *Right to left* means that they set a delivery date and worked backward to figure out all other project milestones. Once they had a delivery date and a launch customer, the program was under way. "Right-to-left scheduling works only if it's based on a realistic overall estimate, but because we had the performance data from other recent models we knew we would meet our commitment to Delta." The 767-400ER planned on shaving several months off recent airplane development schedules.

### TOP DOWN AND BOTTOM UP

With the delivery date set, the program schedule was developed from the top down and from the bottom up. Top-down scheduling broke the overall schedule into major phases. Within those phases, *integrated product teams*, cross-functional teams often known as IPTs, decomposed the airplane requirements into specific *part identification numbers* (PINs). In other words, the entire aircraft was decomposed into 2,600 groups of drawings. A schedule was developed for each PIN, and then the PIN schedules were tied to the major development milestones. Keeping the program-level schedule milestones constant, the resources required to meet the PIN-level schedules were developed from the bottom up, that is, using bottom-up resource estimating.

### A REQUIREMENTS-DRIVEN PROGRAM

It's one thing to determine that it will take an army of engineers to deliver on schedule, but how do you integrate the hundreds of design decisions required to optimize the new aircraft? Fred Black described the complexity of the major design reviews that were necessary throughout the program schedule. "The basic requirement of airplane weight is a good example. The aircraft's weight is one of the prime factors affecting range. A target weight determined by the range requirement is established at the beginning of the design effort. Of course, all the components of the aircraft add weight, and the weight of one component often affects the design of another. The weight of the wing impacts the design of the fuselage attach points for the wing. The weight of the landing gear impacts both the fuselage and the wing. The weight of the engines impacts the design of the engine pylon structure. All of the integrated product teams for these areas work together to manage the weight of the airplane to the target weight at periodic reviews throughout the design process. Thus, one of the major contributors to the eventual range of the airplane is managed to that requirement. During design reviews, we constantly refer back to the requirements, because we are a requirements-driven program."

### 767-400ER MEETS CUSTOMER COMMITMENTS

767-400ER is using classic project management techniques to remain focused on the business requirements of the aircraft. For example:

- The high-level schedule is based on performance data from similar programs. Launch customer Delta Air Lines and other early customers can be confident their airplanes will be delivered when they need them.

- The work breakdown structure for the entire program is a decomposition of the business requirements, ensuring that all the needed work will be performed to deliver the right aircraft.

- Bottom-up resource estimating means taking an honest look at the effort required to meet all the program requirements.

- Cross-functional design reviews bring integrated product teams together to make sure that all of their decisions are driven by the aircraft's business requirements.

Boeing understandably emphasizes the aircraft's new technological advancements, such as a raked wingtip that reduces airplane weight while increasing performance. But behind all the twenty-first-century technology, proven project management techniques kept the program on track, delivering the first airplane to Delta as promised.

*Sources:* Interview with Fred Black, Manager, Program Plan and Schedule Integration, 767-400ER Program, June 12, 1998; Boeing press release, www.boeing.com/news/releases/1998/news_release_980507.html, www.boeing.com/commercial/767-400ER/background.html.

## PMP Exam Prep Questions

1. The sponsor of a project to move the loan processing system from C++ to the intranet is deciding whether the project should continue or be scrapped. The project has been plagued with issues. So far, $1M has been spent on the project. Of the following, what best describes the $1M that has been spent so far?

   a. Opportunity cost

   b. Budgeted cost of work performed

   c. Sunk cost

   d. Phase 1 cost

2. The construction team is behind schedule on its project. The customer is considering giving the project to another company if the project cannot be put back on track. The team is considering putting more resources on the critical path to accelerate the schedule. This is an example of what?

   a. Staff acquisition

   b. Crashing

   c. Re-planning

   d. Fast-tracking

3. The project to build an art museum for the city is in the planning stages. The project manager has determined that the installation of the marble water feature should be outsourced because his company does not have the necessary expertise. The vendor proposals specify different contract types: cost-plus-fixed-fee, fixed-price, cost-plus-incentive-fee, and time and materials. Which of the proposals present the least probability of loss for the buyer?

   a. Proposals that use cost-plus-fixed-fee

   b. Proposals that use time and materials

   c. Proposals that use cost-plus-incentive-fee

   d. Proposals that use fixed-price

4. The software company is working with a staffing company to provide a technical writer for its newest project, accounting software for contractors and small businesses. The staffing company will provide an experienced technical writer for $75 an hour. The technical writer will work on the project until it is complete; then the contract will end. Which of the following best

describes the type of contract the software company is most likely to use?

a. Time and materials because it lends itself to small initiatives and staff supplementation

b. Fixed-price because it ensures that the cost of the writer does not increase during the term of the contract

c. Fixed-price because it lends itself to small initiatives and staff supplementation

d. Time and materials because it ensures that the cost of the writer does not increase during the term of the contract

5. The network diagram for the project to create logical e-mail groups has three paths that have a duration of 29 days and two paths that have a duration of 10 days, respectively, the longest and shortest durations for the project. Which of the following is a true statement?

a. If the shortest paths are the same length, the path with the least number of activities is the critical path

b. If the shortest paths are the same length, there can be multiple critical paths and the more critical paths there are on a project, the greater the increase of risk to the project

c. If the longest paths are the same length, the path with the greatest number of activities is the critical path

d. If the longest paths are the same length, there can be multiple critical paths and the more critical paths there are on a project, the greater the increase of risk to the project

Answers to these questions can be found at www.VersatileCompany .com/FFMBAinPM.

# Controlling the Project

*There is a time in the life of every problem*
*when it is big enough to see,*
*yet small enough to solve.*
—*Mike Leavitt*

During the first two phases of a project, as presented in Parts 2 and 3, the focus is on creating a project environment that will lead to efficient work through careful planning. Now, in Part 4, Chapters 13,14,15,16 and 17, the project is under way, and the focus has shifted to keeping the project on track—controlling the project.

Controlling a project blends the art and science of project management—building a strong, committed team at the same time you are making progress against the plan. Controlling also involves discovering and solving problems while they are still small, measuring progress, and ensuring continued agreement on goals and expectations. The key to these control activities is communication—making sure that the right people have the right information at the right time. Strong communication among all stakeholders is what allows a project to evolve in an ordered way, instead of veering out of control.

# 13

# Building a High-Performance Project Team

## INTRODUCTION

As we have detailed the science of project management in previous chapters, there has been an unspoken assumption: that the people on the project team would work together in harmony to build plans, manage risks, perform tasks, and commit themselves to achieving the clearly stated goals of the project. But that is not always the case.

Despite detailed plans and frequent status meetings, some teams don't work well together. Most of us, at one time or another, experience the frustration of teamwork that is characterized by bickering, unproductive meetings, and a joyless plodding as the project falls further and further behind. If that challenge isn't enough, consider that project teams are temporary, existing only for the duration of the project—how can we expect the team members to commit to the success of *this* project? It is no secret that the science of project management cannot create successful projects without the committed, cooperative work of a cohesive team.

To discuss this topic thoroughly, we must begin with a basic definition of a *team*: "a group of people working interdependently to produce an outcome for which they hold themselves mutually accountable." Project teams have another characteristic: They will be temporary, formed specifically for the purpose of achieving the goal, after which they will disband.

Our purpose in this chapter is to provide guidelines for building a cohesive project team. It is a large topic, which leads to it being a long chapter. Therefore, a brief explanation of the structure of the chapter will make it easier to assimilate all the information. The introduction establishes how project team dynamics contribute to project success. In these first few pages we'll also begin to solve the problem of building a cohesive team by understanding the two major obstacles that all project teams face. Next, to explain the factors that contribute to a high-performance team, we'll use a model, or framework. That framework is initially described at a high level. After that, the remainder of the chapter explores each of the components of the framework in detail.

There have been scores of books written on the topics of leadership and team performance—one chapter cannot attempt to address the breadth of the topic. Therefore, we limit the scope of this chapter to the challenge of forming a cohesive team from a collection of individuals assigned to a project. We will present a framework for building a high-performance project team by describing specific traits the team must possess and the steps a project leader must take to build the team. Despite the fact that one or two disruptive individuals can derail an entire team, we will not address managing individual people or individual performance problems.

## The Importance of Project Team Dynamics

A weak, uncooperative team isn't just *unproductive*; it can make your job a daily grind of frustration and resentment. People burn out, blow up, or quit their jobs because of negative interpersonal dynamics on teams. Conversely, many people cite the strength of a team or their terrific teammates when recounting how they survived a project when everything seemed to go wrong. Of all the topics in this book, this chapter has the greatest potential to change the daily work experience for you and your team.

## Team Building Is Every Project Leader's Responsibility

Every project team needs its leader to consciously invest in building a strong, cohesive, capable team. Whether the project manager gets to choose the team members or not, it is his or her responsibility to optimize their performance. Team building is every bit as essential as project definition and planning.

## When a Team Is Not a Team

Accomplishing the work of a project can require the effort of several people without requiring them to work as a cooperative unit. For example, hosting a major conference can require hundreds of people to perform in the right place at exactly the right time, but many of the performers won't interact with each other at any time before, during, or after the conference. Caterers, conference speakers, audiovisual equipment technicians, and trade-show vendors all play a key role; yet each is typically managed directly by the conference management team, with no communication among themselves.

In other cases, the project team does need to meet and talk periodically, but individuals are able to accomplish their own responsibilities *independently* of other team members. To test your own team's cohesion requirement, consider these two variables.[1]

1. Individuals must cooperate in order to complete their tasks.
2. The team has a whole product or service to produce rather than individual components.

To the degree that these are true, your team benefits from all the factors described in this chapter. If these factors don't exist, you'll still need to follow the science of project management—knowing the goals and constraints, tracking progress, and coordinating activities—but cohesion isn't as important. As a project leader, gauging the interdependence of the team members helps you calibrate the degree of effort you should invest in team unity.

## The Challenge of Building Project Teams

Why is it so difficult to get a team to jell? To the novice project manager it can seem mysterious, the result of luck, and certainly unpredictable. But the productivity and joy that come with a high-performance team are too important to rely on luck. In reality, every project team faces two central challenges, two obstacles to becoming a high-performing team.

1. Project teams form to solve complex problems, and they must solve those problems together.
2. Project teams are temporary and so they must *learn to work together*.

Understanding these two challenges reveals why some teams work while others never do. Teams that learn to work together to produce effective decisions with efficiency become increasingly bonded and productive throughout a project. The framework presented in this chapter addresses these two obstacles. Before we present the framework, it is worthwhile to clearly understand the two obstacles our teams face, for by understanding these challenges we are better prepared to overcome them.

## A Series of Problems to Solve

Viewing your project as a series of problems to solve may surprise you, but consider these typical activities you find on large and small projects:

- Determining the goals and success criteria for the project
- Making trade-offs among cost, schedule, and scope
- Designing a product, or even a sub-subcomponent of a product
- Setting a time and a place for a milestone celebration event

Each task requires a group of people to arrive at a conclusion. Some of these decisions may be easy to make, others more difficult. But viewed in this way it is clear that projects are filled with problems to solve.

The challenge is multiplied for so-called knowledge workers—anyone from engineers to attorneys to administrators—who *think* for a living rather than use their bodies to perform work. Knowledge workers often tackle complex, abstract problems. Designing an ad campaign, an aircraft wing, or a compensation and benefits plan is actually a series of decisions.

As individual humans we tend to work through problems in a variety of ways. Some of us are linear thinkers, others intuitive. Some study the details, while others focus on the big picture. Some of us are comfortable discussing problems and solutions out loud, forming our views as we speak, but others won't utter a word until they've thoroughly evaluated the information and formed a position. All of these approaches can be effective for us as individuals, but when mixed together in a team they can create chaos that results in frustration and distrust.

As a project leader, your challenge is to harness the problem-solving power of a diverse team. The guidelines and techniques in this chapter will help you build a team that thrives on solving problems and produces truly synergistic results: decisions and products that are superior because they are made by a team with diverse talents and styles.

## Temporary Teams

Projects begin and end, and so, therefore, do project teams. Not only are teams temporary, but the trend toward teams that cross functional, corporate, and even national boundaries increases the likelihood that a new project team will be made up of people who haven't worked together previously. Developing trust, respect, effective communication patterns, and the ability to maintain positive relationships despite disagreements takes time. Most important, it takes a conscious effort by the project team leader. This chapter describes specific activities you can take to move a team from a loose collection of individuals to a cohesive unit.

### Understanding the Problem Lays the Foundation

The chapter thus far has established why we need to pay attention to the health of the project team and has outlined the challenges we face in building a strong team. Next we present an overall framework for understanding the desirable components of a team. The remainder of the chapter is broken into examining each of those components in greater detail. As you read the chapter, refer to the model in Figure 13.1 to maintain the context of each topic.

## A FRAMEWORK FOR BUILDING HIGH-PERFORMANCE TEAMS

So far we've established the importance of a strong team and the challenges of creating one. But what, exactly, do we mean by a *high-performance team*? In this section we examine the attributes of such a team and present a model that will help us build one.

High-performance teams are more than merely highly productive. A team composed of experienced, capable people can be very productive until those people hit an obstacle or are confronted with an unexpected challenge. This is the point at which the team either shows its strength or reveals its limitations. Teams that successfully persevere tend to have certain characteristics described by the model in Figure 13.1.

As the diagram suggests, we can break the components of a strong project team into three areas that work together in the same way that an arch works to support a bridge. Our teamwork arch shares the same properties as a structural arch:

1. A strong team requires each of the individual components.
2. The strength of the arch lies in the way the pieces work together.
3. Weakness in one component cannot be compensated for by strength in another component.

Envision the goal of your project team as getting from point A to point B. In the model, the project team forms the bridge, spanning from A to B. For simple projects, you could simply grab a handful of people, drop them onto the project, and they'd somehow get from A to B without a lot of special attention to team building. Similarly, you might throw a couple of strong boards across a small ditch to make a simple bridge—quickly and easily. That works fine for simple projects and simple bridges, but if that bridge has to hold up the weight of a complex project, it must be strong. That's the purpose of the arch—to provide the strength and support to a team with a heavy load.

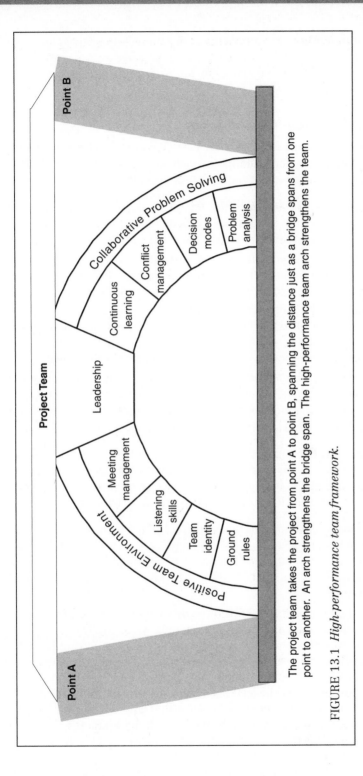

The project team takes the project from point A to point B, spanning the distance just as a bridge spans from one point to another. An arch strengthens the bridge span. The high-performance team arch strengthens the team.

FIGURE 13.1 *High-performance team framework.*

The three primary components in our model—*positive team environment, collaborative problem solving*, and *leadership*—are introduced here with their component parts. Each part is described in detail later in the chapter.

### A Positive Team Environment

A positive environment promotes trust and respect among team members and increases performance through more productive work habits. Creating this environment requires four specific elements:

1. *Ground rules that describe the work patterns and values of the team.* Ground rules are explicitly stated expectations about personal behavior that reflect the team's values.
2. *A team identity built on commitment to a shared goal.* This commitment relies on goal and scope clarity, demonstrated support from the project sponsor, and understanding the strengths and contributions of all team members.
3. *The ability to listen.* Problem solving demands an exchange of ideas, which is possible only if team members actually work hard to listen to perspectives that are different from their own.
4. *The ability to effectively manage meetings.* Much team work is accomplished in meetings (or at least it should!). Just like a project, a meeting needs to begin with goals and a plan, and it must be actively steered toward the goals.

Broken into these elements, we see that a positive environment is not merely an abstract feeling; it is a set of observable skills that a project manager can instill. Further, this positive environment produces two important characteristics of the high-performing team:

1. *Personal ownership of the team goal.* Each team member interprets his or her own success in terms of the team's goal. When team success becomes a matter of personal and professional pride, we've tapped a powerful source of motivation and determination.
2. *Strong interpersonal relationships based on trust and respect.* For many who have worked on high-performance teams, the camaraderie during the project was far more satisfying than the act of achieving the goal. This element is the most essential and most elusive, because it begets itself. Trust builds trust and respect breeds respect. Trust and respect are essential for people working interdependently because they allow us to rely on one another, which is absolutely necessary if the whole is going to be greater than the sum of the parts.

### Collaborative Problem-Solving Capability

We have established that project teams solve a series of problems and that they need to learn to work together to solve those problems. Build this collaborative capability by focusing on four team abilities:

1. *Problem-solving skills tied to an accepted problem-solving process.* A team made up of individuals with diverse skills and styles must agree on the process they'll follow for working through problems, both large and small. A commonly accepted problem-solving process enables all team members to flex their styles because each understands and trusts the process.

2. *Understanding and applying multiple decision modes.* Some decisions are made solely by the project leader; other decisions are made by the entire team. These are only two examples of decision modes. Efficient decision making requires that a team understand the possible decision modes and consciously choose which are appropriate for any decision.

3. *Conflict-resolution skills.* Producing superior decisions demands creativity, which necessarily produces disagreement. Mature teams accept and value the inevitability of conflict. They have the skills to leverage conflict to achieve the best decisions while maintaining strong relationships.

4. *Continuous learning.* When innovation and breakthrough solutions are required, the team's culture must embrace a certain amount of risk taking and have the ability to improve its own performance throughout the project by learning from *both* success and failure.

Each of these capabilities can be developed by the team, although not all are simple. Together they create a truly synergistic result: decisions and products that are superior because they are developed by a team with diverse styles and talents.

### Leadership

The keystone of our high-performance framework is the leader who ties the team together as he or she embodies the skills and characteristics found in the two legs of the arch. No team will reach its potential without one or more people consciously attending to the health of the team.

The key focus of the framework is the abilities that the *team* possesses. For that reason, we will limit our discussion on leadership to the actions a leader must take to nurture and establish these capabilities.

### Competence Matters

In 1980, the U.S. Olympic hockey team upset the dominant Soviet Union team in the medal rounds of the Winter Olympics and went on to win the gold medal. It was a perfect story of the power of a united, cohesive team, as the much younger, all-amateur U.S. team beat a veteran Soviet team that was overwhelmingly favored to win. Commenting years later on what became known as the "Miracle on Ice," coach Herb Brooks had this to say: "We could not beat the teams we beat just on talent. If we forgot about the team-building aspect and just relied on talent we wouldn't have been able to do it."

Underdog stories exist in every industry—stories in which the power of a united team produces unexpected, even miraculous, results. Each story is a testament to the themes of this chapter. We must never forget that, although these underdog teams were not made up of acknowledged stars, neither were they made up of novices, incompetents, or those with attitude problems. The high-performance team framework leverages the talents of your team, but if the talents don't exist, don't expect a miracle. Make a realistic assessment of the skills required for the project, and make sure the team either has these skills or can gain them during the project.

### Framework Summary

A positive team environment, collaborative problem solving capability, and leadership—these are the three primary components of a high-performance team. The model in Figure 13.1 demonstrates how these pieces fit together. In the remainder of the chapter we will explore the skills and capabilities that make up each of these components, beginning with leadership.

## LEADERSHIP RESPONSIBILITIES

> What you are stands over you and thunders so,
> I cannot hear what you say to the contrary.
> —*Ralph Waldo Emerson*

Leadership is difficult to define but critical to project success. Every topic in this book is a leadership topic, because the actions the project manager takes—or fails to take—influence every stakeholder on the project. In this section of the chapter, we focus on leadership—the keystone of our high-performance team arch—in the context of how a project manager influences the performance of the core team.

We lead through our actions. The ideals and attitudes we carry in our heads mean nothing to our teams because their only experience is our action. The leadership actions that contribute to a high-performance team fall into the five categories discussed in this section.

## Attending to the Health of the Team

The first required leadership action is to allocate the time of the leader and the team to building the capabilities described in this chapter. The concept is simple, but the action is difficult.

As project leaders, our days are full of status meetings, responding to problems, and completing our own assignments. Our sponsor and customers may demand the tangible products of the science of project management: a work breakdown structure (WBS), a schedule, or a risk management plan. Our success is measured by being on time and on budget and adhering to specifications. There is no space on our status report to indicate whether our team atmosphere fosters learning and creativity, no measurable statistic on team unity. Virtually no one will ask for your plan to build and maintain a high-performance team—or demand that you devote time and resources to building one.

Faced with these apparent priorities, team building requires personal conviction that team health actually affects the project's result. We demonstrate this conviction by allocating the time of the leader and the team to monitoring and improving the building blocks of team performance.

## Maintaining the Strategic Vision

While team members focus on the near-term problems and tasks, the project leader maintains a steady focus on the final outcome of the project and the path toward the goal. This steady focus informs our actions as we engage in day-to-day activities with the team, ensuring that tasks are performed and problems solved in the context of the overall goals of the project. The science of project management makes an obvious contribution to this leadership responsibility as the statement of work, the work breakdown structure, and other planning techniques provide structured methods to understand both the forest and the trees.

## Attending to the Team Members

For better or worse, our team members are human beings with feelings, egos, non-work interests, and career goals beyond the project. Their personal performance will vary according to their motivation, confidence in project leadership, and the respect with which they are treated. Recognize their efforts and accomplishments. Beware of working them to the point of burnout. Treat them with a little more respect than you would want for yourself. When the project demands an above-and-beyond effort, your demonstrated concern for them as human beings will be a deciding factor in whether that effort materializes.

### Exhibiting and Demanding Accountability

Successful projects rely on execution. Plans are meaningless if the team does not carry through. Leaders set the tone by keeping their promises and delivering on their responsibilities, and they expect the same of every team member. Holding team members accountable can require some tough conversations and real consequences for non-performance. It is not the best part of a leader's duties, but we owe it to the team to make sure the efforts of some are not diminished by the nonperformance of others.

### Personal Energy That Inspires the Team Through Example

Teams need leaders. Somebody must put the group in motion, focus the goals, facilitate the plan, and maintain forward momentum. Every project management action described in this book is a visible signal of our personal commitment to create a successful team and to meet the project goal. The energy, attitude, and commitment of the team rarely rise above those of the leader. In the words of Emerson, "What you are stands over you and thunders so, I cannot hear what you say to the contrary."

 ### Leadership Styles

**CONCEPT**    What kind of a leadership style makes a project team kick into high gear? Should you be laid-back? Hard-driving? Participative? Autocratic? The options and strategies fill books, yet there is no single best way. There is, however, a well-accepted model for team development that should inform whichever leadership strategy we choose. The model articulated in 1967 by Bruce Tuckman, which has been referenced and expanded upon ever since, identifies five stages of team development—stages that every team will pass through as it evolves from a collection of strangers to a cohesive unit to the point at which the team disbands. The stages, and how each informs our leadership style, are summarized in the box on the subsequent pages. The benefit of understanding these stages is that at each stage of development a team has different requirements of its leader. Under-standing these stages enables us to flex our style to the needs of the team.

## STAGES OF TEAM DEVELOPMENT

### Forming

The team begins as a collection of individuals. Initial reactions reflect the uncertainty everyone feels at the outset: pride at being selected for the team, excitement about the work ahead, yet a cautious or tentative attachment to the team. At this stage team members act as most people do when introduced into a roomful of strangers: They are polite and avoid conflict, seeking to find common ground and common purpose, and each wants to be accepted as a member of the group.

*Leadership Style for Forming Stage.* Respond to the uncertainty of the group by providing structure and clear direction. Provide background information to help them understand the goals and purpose of the group. The general desire to avoid conflict means that group decision making may not be comfortable or effective. Establish team expectations using ground rules. (Ground rules are explained later in this chapter.)

### Storming

As the team digs in and goes to work, conflict is inevitable. The team hasn't yet learned to trust each other. Greater awareness of the work ahead can cause feelings of anxiety, even a desire to leave the group. Some are impatient to progress. Others are confused about tasks and responsibilities. A sense of thrashing emerges and may produce power struggles. Amidst this seeming chaos, the team is actually gaining clarity about goals and roles. They are starting to make decisions together, albeit somewhat painfully.

*Leadership Style for Storming Stage.* This stage is rarely fun, but it is natural. Respond to the chaos with structure and clear direction. Recognize early accomplishments. Be willing to engage the group in participative decision making to address their concerns. Facilitate group decisions, demonstrate effective listening, and ensure equitable participation among all team members. Your example will be setting the tone that moves them to the next stage.

### Norming

During this stage team members begin to trust each other and trust the group. People can help each other and focus on team goals because their own need for role clarity has been met. They are capable of making team decisions, though they may try to avoid conflict in order to maintain harmony. Ground rules have become accepted and internalized.

*Leadership Style for Norming Stage.* The strength of the group enables the leader to shift to a facilitative style, giving increasing authority to the team. Don't let the team's new harmony cause them to avoid necessary conflict (learn the value of conflict later in this chapter under "Conflict Management"). Build momentum from the group's unity by reviewing and improving team processes.

### Performing

Not all teams reach this stage, but those that do enjoy the power of a united, effective work group. A hallmark of a team in the performing stage is the ease with which it handles changes and obstacles.

Personal relationships are strong, enabling high trust. Team skills for conflict resolution and problem solving enable the group to be highly productive. Team ownership of the goal results in a focus on task accomplishment. Commitment to the team keeps people helping each other, building confidence in the ability of the team.

*Leadership Style for Performing Stage.* As the team practically manages itself, the leader can focus on removing obstacles and improving team processes. Delegate leadership responsibility to members of the team, particularly as the team self-selects informal leaders. Don't abdicate your leadership role; just share it more widely.

### Adjourning

As projects end, teams disband. The satisfaction of accomplishment is tempered by the sadness of leaving the team. Closure rituals enable the team to say good-bye to the project and their team members.

*Leadership Style for Adjourning Stage.* Facilitate closure by setting up opportunities to review the team's performance. Recognize their successes and opportunities for improvement.

Teams progress through these stages and, at times, move backward into previous stages. Changes to team membership or team goals can cause a team in the norming stage to move back to the storming stage. Throughout all these stages, the team leader adjusts his or her style to address the needs of the group.

Bruce Tuckman originally addressed this topic in 1965 in the *Psychological Bulletin,* 63(6), 384–399, American Psychological Association.

## Leadership Summary

The leadership responsibilities we've described in this section form the keystone of the high-performance team framework. Without leadership, the other components of the framework are drastically diminished.

### BUILDING A POSITIVE TEAM ENVIRONMENT

Relationships among team members, the way meetings are conducted, role and goal clarity—all these factors form the daily environment of the team. People can fight a hostile environment and still make progress, but who wants to? We would rather put our energy into accomplishing tasks than wrangling with uncooperative coworkers or spinning our wheels because the goals and roles aren't clear.

Project leaders can influence the daily environment of their project team members. We can set expectations for conduct during meetings and create opportunities for team members to know and trust each other. In short, the project manager can consciously put into place the attributes that contribute to a *positive team environment*. This major component of our high-performance team was described earlier when we introduced the framework, and forms the left side of the arch in Figure 13.1. The next four topics describe specific skills and attributes that affect our team environment on a daily basis. Each is relatively simple, yet when any of them are absent it creates a negative drain on the energy of the team. Our goal in the following sections is to understand each attribute and identify actions we can take to build them into our team.

## GROUND RULES

Building a positive environment begins the first time the team gets together. As Tuckman pointed out, during the Forming stage the team wants structure. We meet that team need and begin establishing our team's culture by setting ground rules.

*Ground rules* are explicitly stated expectations about team behavior and values. Making these expectations explicit accomplishes three things:

1. Team members understand what is expected of them as a member of an interdependent group.
2. The team has an opportunity to form and own its culture.
3. You meet the team's need for structure.

Ground rules can cover a lot of territory, but generally fall into two categories:

1. *Team values.* Ground rules reinforce specific values by identifying behaviors or attitudes that support the value. An example can be found on a project to redesign a firm's compensation plan—the team may want to emphasize the importance of confidentiality.
2. *Meeting behavior.* Setting expected meeting behaviors is a classic application of ground rules. Since we often brainstorm solutions, debate alternatives, assign new work among ourselves, and perform other creative work, it is essential that our behaviors demonstrate respect for each other and, at the same time, make productive use of the time we are together.

Table 13.1 contains examples of ground rules in these two categories.

Although ground rules may seem to state the obvious, such as "listen to and respect other points of view," the reality is that such

## TABLE 13.1   Examples of Ground Rules

These examples show how ground rules create clear expectations for team member behavior. A team could have many more.

### Team Values

- *Confidentiality.* We do not discuss project information with anyone outside the project team or the project steering committee.
- *Team learning.* Be open to new approaches. It's okay to ask questions and to ask for help. Be curious.
- *Respect.* No personal attacks. Don't ridicule ideas or suggestions.
- *Accountability.* Follow through on commitments. Perform on time or alert others when you know you'll miss a deadline.

### Meeting Behavior

- *Use active listening.* Ask for clarification. Suspend judgment of the idea until it is understood. No side conversations.
- *Be solution focused.* Don't just criticize; bring new ideas. Attack ideas, not people.
- *Limit distractions.* No cell phones.
- *Begin and end on time.* Arrive before the meeting is scheduled to begin.
- *Challenge the group.* Explore the pros and cons of all ideas. Don't hold back just to avoid conflict.
- *Be prepared.*

obviously desirable behaviors don't always exist on teams. Ground rules provide a way for the team's leader to gain agreement on expected behavior, and they serve as a tool for reminding people of what behavior is expected. Post the rules for the first several project team meetings and refer to them during the meetings. Once it is clear that the team has internalized the rules, it may not be necessary to post this list of obvious rules.

## Prime the Pump

A team will take greater ownership over a set of ground rules that it develops, but starting with a blank sheet of paper can paralyze the group, particularly if many team members aren't familiar with the concept of ground rules. Prime the pump by bringing a starting list of ground rules to the first meeting. People will quickly understand the concept from the suggestions you've made. Then enlist the group to complete your initial set of ground rules.

## TEAM IDENTITY

When a colonel in the army was selected to lead a task force that consisted of members from each branch of the military, he knew his success would be limited if he could not convince the team members to put the goals of the team ahead of the goals of their individual branch. It is a problem common to all temporary teams: to gain each member's commitment to a common goal to which all will hold themselves accountable. A large part of creating this commitment is accomplished through the four elements of building a *team identity* that are described in this section. All work together to build one more component of the positive team environment.

### KEY CONCEPT Communicate the Goals and Scope of the Project

Chapter 6 of this book contains a detailed description of determining project goals and scope and recording them in the statement of work. In addition, Chapter 8 describes the work breakdown structure (WBS) technique for creating a detailed description of project scope. Share this information with the project team to give them a tangible description of why this project exists and where it is going. If the team members are assembled before the statement of work or project plan has been completed, their involvement in defining and planning the project will increase their sense of ownership for the goals and plans.

### We Learn Through Repetition

Announcing the project goals at the first team meeting gives all participants a vision of why the team exists. That is important, because the goal should be the North Star for the team, a reference point that influences all team activity. For the goal to have that level of influence, each team member must learn it deeply and internalize it, something that happens only with repetition. Here are a few simple actions you can take as a project leader to appropriately repeat the goal:

- Write the goal at the top of every meeting agenda. You won't necessarily even have to mention it, but seeing it there at every meeting will be a steady reminder.
- Start with the project goal when introducing the project to any new team member or involving any new stakeholder.
- Reference the goal frequently during early meetings, particularly when making a decision, as in: "Let's remember that our ultimate goal is to have the right products on hand and to decrease excess inventory; therefore. . . ." You will be showing the team how the goal is related to all team activity.

## Establish the Project's Organizational Alignment

Provide the context for the project within the organization. What relationship does this project have with other projects? How will this project affect strategic goals? If this project shares personnel and other resources with other projects, are there established priorities among these projects? Though as project managers we often consider our own project to be important, we need to be realistic about how it fits into the larger picture. The statement of work and business case will contain some information about the contribution this project has to the organization. Your sponsor will also be a source of information.

The organizational alignment of a project may be complex or abstract. As with the project goal, it may require time and repetition for the team to truly understand. In addition to your own explanation, you may enlist other project stakeholders to visit a project meeting to describe how the project will affect their operations. For example, information technology project teams typically benefit from spending time with the people who will be affected by their systems.

### Demonstrate Management Support for the Project

A project sponsor's job is to champion the project manager and the project team. As discussed in Chapter 5, a temporary project team needs the power and authority of a sponsor in order to overcome organizational obstacles. The team members also need to feel that their team is important to the organization—to know that the team is not alone in its pursuit of the project goal. The attention of a sponsor signals that both the project and the team matter.

As a project manager, look for opportunities to invite the sponsor or other involved executives into team activities. When working with your sponsor and executive management, ask them how they would like to participate in the project, particularly to demonstrate support for the team. Here are some classic sponsor activities:

- Attend the kickoff meeting to explain the purpose and importance of the project.
- Continue to attend project team meetings periodically throughout the project, particularly after significant accomplishments, to recognize the team's performance.
- Recognize individual performance with a phone call or visit to the team member.

As a sponsor displays interest in the project, enthusiasm will build within the project team. Early visible involvement by management builds excitement; sustained visible involvement builds commitment.

### Actions Speak Louder Than Words

**DANGER!**

Unfortunately, many of us can recall projects where sponsorship consisted of all talk and no action. *Management support* is one of our five project success factors. Teams know when they have management support, because they receive sufficient resources to accomplish their work and receive timely attention to problems.

### Build Team Relationships Based on Understanding Strengths and Diversity

**KEY CONCEPT**

Strong teams rely on positive, productive relationships between team members—relationships the project manager can consciously foster.

A project team with positive, productive relationships does not mean everyone on the team will be personal friends who choose to socialize outside of the work environment. Rather, these relationships recognize that, sharing a common goal as colleagues, all will be more successful by treating each other with respect, cooperation, and accountability to the team. These relationships are characterized by several factors that we can work to build.

- The team knows the strengths and contributions of each member. Each of us brings technical expertise, customer knowledge, business savvy, and a range of other talents to the project team. This awareness enables us to increase our reliance on each other.

- We understand our diversity of styles and the benefits and potential risks that exist when we bring together introverts and extroverts, detail-oriented and big-picture thinkers, people who are task oriented and those who are people oriented, and so on.

- We trust our teammates to keep their word and perform as they have promised.

- We see each other as human beings as well as co-workers. Human beings get sick, have honeymoons, celebrate birthdays, become stressed by family-work trade-offs, and generally have a range of emotions and experiences that go beyond the workplace.

These factors—particularly trust—can be difficult to build, but they begin with the team's leader creating opportunities for team members to get to know each other early in the project. Try some of these activities:

- Interview each team member as he or she comes on board to understand the person's background, strengths, and personal goals for the project. Then, at the next team meeting, introduce that person to the rest of the team. Alternatively, you could ask each person to be prepared to introduce himself or herself, as long as it is clear in advance what you'll be asking people to say at the meeting.

- Bring food to a meeting. Better yet, schedule a working lunch, with the project picking up the tab. Breaking bread together is a strong symbol, and the downtime for eating will provide a bonding opportunity.

- Meet regularly in person, if that is possible. While all meetings should have a purpose and be productive, remember that the act of coming together for a shared purpose builds identity and a sense of belonging to the group.

- If the group is geographically separated, the sooner they get together in person, the better. A single daylong planning session early in the project will accelerate relationship building far faster than teleconferences or any other electronic media.

These are all simple activities that can be done in the context of other project tasks. Each contributes to people getting to know and understand each other. Of course, there are many project teams whose challenges justify hours or even days spent on activities whose sole purpose is to build stronger working relationships. These examples show the depth and variety available to us:

- Many personality and behavioral assessment tools have been developed to help people understand their own preferences and styles in performing work. The Myers-Briggs Type Indicator is probably the best known of these tools, but there are many more to choose from. Each attempts to help us see ourselves and others, and to understand how our different approaches affect teamwork. As a team leader, we could devote a few hours to using such a tool within our teams.

- Physically challenging team-building events have been designed to focus teams on their interpersonal dynamics. Usually facilitated by experts, these events range from learning to sail a boat to rappelling down a cliff to crossing a rope bridge suspended 40 feet in the air. In particular, these exercises strive to reveal the importance and existence (or lack) of trust among team members. Ideally, the lessons the teams learn from cooperating in these extreme events will carry back to the workplace.

Focusing on team relationships early speeds the growth of the team, but relationships are not static. It is the project leader's job to pay attention to this factor throughout the life of the project and to address relationships that become negative.

## Summary of Building Team Identity

Forging a team identity is an organic process that benefits from repetition and attention. As you work to build these elements into your project team, recall Tuckman's stages of team development and adjust your style accordingly. The structure of your early attempts to clarify the goals and scope and provide a strong kickoff to the project will be welcomed when the team is Forming. Likewise, initial attempts to build relationships may be embraced and may seem productive, yet more attention may be necessary as the team reaches the Storming phase. If your investment in team identity pays off, you will find that your team progresses rapidly from Norming to Performing.

## TEAM LISTENING SKILLS

When teams form around common challenges and overcome them with creativity and perseverance, strong communication skills are at work. In such a dynamic problem-solving environment, no communication skill is more important than listening, because it is through listening that we gain the value of another person's insight. In addition, effective listening builds trust and demonstrates respect during the give-and-take of creativity. As I work to understand your idea, I show you respect that builds trust and increases the likelihood that you will treat my ideas the same way.

Listening is a personal communication skill. The work of group problem solving requires that every team member have this. Therefore, it is the job of project leaders to model, teach, and coach this skill. Here we highlight some well-known guidelines you and your team can follow. As your team members develop this skill, it will contribute to the overall goal of building a positive team environment.

**KEY CONCEPT** **Active Listening**

The term *active listening* implies that listening to others and actually understanding their intended message requires effort and skill. When you consider some of the naturally occurring obstacles to listening, it is easy to understand why.

- Physical distractions, such as a hot, stuffy conference room, telephones, or a computer screen with an e-mail in-box, can take our attention away from a speaker.
- Knowledge of the subject matter gives us preconceived ideas about what the speaker is saying. Whether we know a lot or a little, our own ideas might crowd out the idea the speaker is trying to transmit.
- The speaker's style or skill in speaking, when it is different from our own, can confuse us. Not everyone is good at clearly describing

ideas or speaking concisely. Idioms and jargon of one company or geographical area need to be translated to outsiders.

- Mental noise from other problems we are facing, past experience with the speaker, frustration, or impatience with the meeting may distract us. Our brains are capable of thinking roughly twice as fast as we speak, which often leads to mentally drifting off to other topics at the same time we are listening.

For a summary of active listening skills, see the box below.

---

### ACTIVE LISTENING TIPS

As you listen to others—whether in a one-on-one discussion or during a meeting—practice these six behaviors to maximize your ability to understand their message.

1. Focus yourself *physically*. To the degree possible, eliminate environmental distractions. Provide the speaker an environment conducive to listening.

2. Use nonverbal cues to show you are involved in what the speaker is saying, including nodding your head, making eye contact, and leaning forward.

3. Provide feedback, paraphrasing or summarizing the speaker's statements to ensure that you understand them as the speaker intended.

4. Ask relevant follow-up or clarifying questions.

5. Listen for the *idea* behind the facts and data.

6. Suspend judgment on the speaker's statements. Understand his or her point first. As you ask questions or acknowledge points, remain neutral in your responses. "So what you are saying is . . ." "From your point of view . . ." Demonstrate that you understand without revealing whether you agree or disagree.

During active listening, here are four behaviors you should work to avoid.

1. Don't try to solve the problem or give advice until it is asked for. Analyzing a problem with questions shifts the focus from the speaker to *your* hypothesis. "Have you tried . . . ?" "What happened before . . . ?" "Are you sure that is the issue?" You may be able to help the speaker solve a problem, but first you need to listen.

2. Don't judge what you are hearing, either positively or negatively. Particularly don't share a judgment, as in "That's not logical."

3. Don't shift the attention to yourself. This happens when we try to relate to the speaker, but end up talking about our own experiences, ideas, or emotions.

4. Finally, be aware of resistance and defensiveness by the speaker. Probing too deeply or playing psychiatrist may not be welcome.

These simple guidelines can get you started. As with any skill, your ability to listen will improve with practice.

For a thorough reference on the skills and value of listening, see Erik Van Slyke's *Listening to Conflict: Finding Constructive Solutions to Workplace Conflict* (American Management Association, 1999).

---

Listening during team meetings requires even more skill than listening during one-to-one conversations. Many natural obstacles to listening are typically present during meetings. Obviously, whoever is leading the meeting should also lead the active listening, but that may not be sufficient. An honest dialogue may require several participants to use active listening techniques, such as summarizing or asking clarifying questions, in order to understand just one person's point of view. That makes it all the more important for the entire team to have these skills.

## The Most Important Skill: Suspending Judgment

The physical activities just listed help us engage our bodies and demonstrate our attention, but listening truly takes place only when we suspend judgment on what we are hearing before we respond.

For example, someone makes the following statement: "The best vacation is Phoenix in the summer."

Does the voice in your head respond, "Hah! The temperature in Phoenix averages over a hundred degrees a day in the summer—it's a terrible place to vacation!" Or does the voice say, "Phoenix in the summer? I don't understand. I'd better listen closely."

If the voice in your head sounds more like the latter, you have just suspended judgment in an effort to understand. If your voice responds more like the former statement, you've made a judgment before you've heard all the facts. When you present a new idea to your team or a team member, which response would you like from them?

Suspending judgment is a personal discipline that requires conscious practice. By applying this skill, we are choosing to delay forming an opinion or response to what the speaker is saying. Instead, we practice the active listening behaviors until we have established that we do understand.

This skill has additional value when the speaker is having difficulty articulating his or her idea. Whether because it is a sensitive subject, because the speaker is uncomfortable speaking in front of the group, or because the speaker lacks the language skills, if we don't work at it, we won't understand. When people with positions of authority practice this skill, it is even more powerful. Our patience and respect will demonstrate that we value the speaker's contribution. Demonstrating our respect reinforces the positive atmosphere we are trying to establish for our team.

### Suspending Judgment Does Not Require Agreement

Once you have clearly understood the speaker, you are free to disagree. You have established, via summarizing or paraphrasing, that you understand the person's point. That was respectful. Now make your judgment and form your response.

### Teach Your Team to Listen

Effective listening is a habit that your entire team needs to develop. You can speed this development through several actions early in the project.

- Be aware of the skill level of the team. That will tell you how quickly and how formally you need to address the skill.

- Plan time to teach the skills. Over the course of the project, it is appropriate to spend some time attending to the team's effectiveness. Show a video, hand out and discuss a good article (or this chapter), or bring in a professional trainer to instruct the team.

- As the project leader, you can demonstrate effective listening, which teaches by example.

- Look for effective listening behaviors within the team. Point them out as you debrief a team meeting, emphasizing how active listening contributed to a better discussion.

- Add active listening as a desired behavior to your ground rules. Use the ground rules as a reminder during meetings if discussions start to degenerate into arguments.

Teaching the team to listen pays off rapidly. It is not a difficult skill, but it does take practice and a conscious attempt to improve.

### Listening Is a Team-Building Activity

Our project teams come together temporarily to solve a series of problems. As the group learns to work together and struggles to find new solutions, they are likely to disagree time and time again. Although such disagreement is a sign of a healthy dialogue, not everyone is used to or comfortable with this type of disagreement or conflict. The listening skills we have described here enable the people to use respectful conversations as they discuss ideas, maintaining relationships while pursuing the best solution. To the degree that a team leader can teach these skills, it can help the team move more quickly through Tuckman's storming phase.

Finally, listening skills have a special role in the high-performance team framework: All of the other capabilities depend on team members being able to listen effectively.

## MEETING MANAGEMENT

Much teamwork is accomplished in meetings. We gather and distribute information, coordinate activities, uncover new problems, assign tasks, and make decisions. Meetings also reinforce team identity, as we gather to make progress on common goals. Productive meetings demonstrate all the characteristics of a high-performance team and produce a result that is beyond what any team members working individually could achieve. *Meeting management* is the last of our four topics that address the high-performance component of a positive team environment.

Unfortunately, we have all attended ineffective meetings that produced nothing but boredom and frustration. As the team's leader, we set the guidelines for running project meetings, whether we lead the meeting or somebody else does. The box that follows highlights commonly accepted guidelines for running effective meetings. During the meeting itself, every component of the high-performance team framework is in play, and weakness in any component will show up as behavior that detracts from the value of the meeting.

### Meeting Structure and Stages of Team Development

The formality and structure of team meetings necessarily changes during the life of the project team. During the Forming stage, the team will welcome the structure provided by agendas, action items, and meeting minutes. As the team Storms, it is likely to become more challenging to run a meeting that stays on task—all the more reason to use these meeting management tools. Once the Norming stage begins, the benefits of structured meetings will start to appear as team members adopt effective meeting habits. Now you can begin to share the leadership of the meetings, a pleasure that will increase as the team reaches the Performing stage.

## SUMMARY OF BUILDING A POSITIVE TEAM ENVIRONMENT

We want the people on our teams to hold themselves mutually accountable to a common goal. The team members want to trust each other and to be treated with respect. They also want to accomplish something, to know their energy and talents are producing results. Ground rules, listening skills, meeting management, and the actions that build team identity all work together to create a positive team environment, as shown on the left side of the arch in our high-performance team model (see Figure 13.1). As the team's leader, it is your job to put each of these pieces in place.

### EFFECTIVE MEETING GUIDELINES

Meetings are held to accomplish work. Whether that is to coordinate tasks, distribute information, make decisions, or explore ideas, we expect specific accomplishments through attending the meeting. The guidelines here provide structure to make our meetings more efficient and productive. These guidelines are targeted to address meetings of anywhere from two to 20 people. When the group grows beyond that size, the dynamics change significantly, and some of these guidelines no longer make sense.

#### Before the Meeting

1. Send a meeting invitation specifying the purpose, planned start and finish times, and location of the meeting. Let everyone know in advance who else will be there.

2. Send out an agenda stating the purpose of the meeting and listing the major topics to be discussed. Assign a time frame and a topic leader for every topic. Frame each topic as specifically as possible, using a goal, so people know the objective of the discussion. "Goal: Agree on laptop performance requirements" is much clearer than simply "laptops." A strong agenda enables people to prepare for the meeting.

#### During the Meeting

1. Start on time. Reward promptness.

2. Review the process you expect to follow. If necessary, set ground rules and determine how decisions will be made (i.e., consensus, voting, or autocratic).

3. Have a recorder track decisions and the key points leading to the decisions. These will become the meeting minutes. Meeting minutes are not a transcript of the meeting, but a recap of the decisions made and their rationale.

4. Use the agenda to structure the meeting. If a topic appears to be too big to resolve within the time allocated, particularly if the entire group is not needed for resolution, develop an action item and handle it outside the meeting.

5. Drive topics to resolution. Summarize comments and bring the group to a decision.

6. During discussions, someone must monitor the group and control involvement. If you are seeking a group consensus, the meeting leader or facilitator must encourage fair participation.

#### Ending the Meeting

1. Summarize the meeting by reviewing the decisions and action items.

2. Be clear about the next meeting date.

3. Briefly wrap up each meeting with an evaluation of the meeting process. A simple method is to run a quick Plus-Delta exercise. On a chart put the headings + (*positive*) and $\Delta$ (*change*). Have meeting participants make two lists: what really worked about the meeting (the pluses) and what they would like to see changed (deltas).

4. End on time or get the group's permission to end later.

**After the Meeting**

1. Send out meeting minutes. The sooner these are issued, the more likely people will be to read and respond to them.

Following these simple guidelines demonstrates respect for your team by making all your meetings as productive as possible.

## COLLABORATIVE PROBLEM SOLVING

**KEY CONCEPT**

There is ample evidence that decisions made by a group are superior to decisions made by a single manager or executive in isolation. A group can bring more background, information, and creativity to a problem. In addition, if the group that made the decision is responsible for its implementation, its members are likely to be more committed to making it work.

The advantages are clear, but not always easy to achieve. Even a project that has established a positive team environment can become bogged down in consensus or spend endless meetings flogging a dead horse. The components of *collaborative problem solving* enable a project team to harness the strength of the group to generate *creativity and productivity.*

It is easier to understand this collaborative problem-solving capability if we break it into four team competencies: problem analysis, conflict management, continuous learning, and the ability to use multiple decision modes. In practice, these skills are interwoven so tightly they appear as one, and if any of these elements are missing, the effectiveness of the others is diminished. The remainder of this chapter explores each of these topics, which together comprise the right side of the high-performance team arch in Figure 13.1.

### PROBLEM ANALYSIS

As individuals we vary in our approach and ability when it comes to analyzing problems. When we come together as a team, this variation becomes both a strength and a weakness. My ability to maintain a view of the big picture and see how the big pieces fit together is complemented by your attention to detail. Another team member's creativity brings a fresh perspective, encouraging us to look beyond the same old solutions. The risk, however, is that I may grow impatient with irrelevant details and unrealistic options, and a detail-oriented team member may lose commitment to our decisions because he or she perceives the team as jumping ahead, skipping the hard work in favor of quick solutions. As individuals with different styles, each of us can become frustrated and begin to disengage from

**319**

the team because the group is not following a process that we personally consider practical or effective.

Minimizing the risks and maximizing the advantages of analyzing problems as a team requires an acknowledged problem-solving process and skill with problem analysis methods. As with all the topics in this chapter, entire books have explored these subjects. Our purpose here is to provide an understanding of the skills the team requires.

## KEY CONCEPT — Acknowledged Problem Analysis Method: Diverge and Converge

If you accuse me of jumping to a conclusion, it is not a compliment. The phrase suggests that I have not sufficiently understood the problem before I made a decision. It reflects the reality that problem analysis should be viewed as shown in Figure 13.2, diverging to gather facts and perceptions, then drawing conclusions to converge on a solution. Your accusation also reflects our different approaches to problem analysis—what you perceive as "jumping" may just be a different path of understanding the facts and options.

As a team, we all benefit when there is an acknowledged method of problem analysis, for three reasons:

1. We want to be sure the team is using sound problem analysis methods. Much study and practical experience has produced a field of generally accepted principles and techniques. Using these techniques will improve the quality of our decisions and, ultimately, our projects.

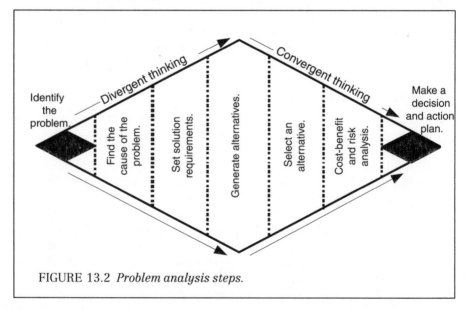

FIGURE 13.2 *Problem analysis steps.*

2. Having an acknowledged process provides a commonly accepted view of the correct steps for working through a problem. This reduces the frustration that results from being individuals with different styles and improves the group's unity and focus on each step.

3. An acknowledged process also provides a common language to describe the experience, which allows the team to improve the process. It enables us to talk about what we are doing. For example, "We agree we have developed a clear problem statement" or "We need to stay in the alternatives-generation step longer."

There is certainly debate over the right steps to follow to solve a problem. The steps provided in the box on the next page reflect generally accepted stages of analyzing a problem and correspond to Figure 13.2. You'll scale your use of this process depending on the complexity of the problem. For instance, you may follow these steps several times within a single meeting to address small problems. For a major problem, the process may take weeks or even months and will be reflected in the tasks of your work breakdown structure. Whether your team uses this one or invents its own, as a project leader you can make sure the team has an acknowledged problem analysis process.

## Problem Analysis Is a Discipline

Just as project management is a discipline made up of accepted techniques and processes, problem analysis has its own body of knowledge that is captured primarily in the quality management literature. The simple seven-step framework laid out in the box may be adequate for simple problems, but if your team is grappling with complex problems, you could benefit from exploring this field further.

As with other team skills we've described in this chapter, monitor the problem analysis skills of your team to determine whether they would benefit from additional training. The presence or absence of these skills will have a tremendous effect on the team's collaborative problem-solving ability.

## DECISION MODES

Groups have a variety of options available to them as they make decisions. Consensus, although often touted as the best mode, is only one. Teams can also decide by majority vote, delegate the decision to an expert or a subgroup, or allow the leader to make the decision after discussion. There are even times when the best decision is made by a leader without involving the group.

## PROBLEM ANALYSIS STEPS

1. *Identify the problem.* The team agrees on the problem, the severity of the problem, and the desired state. The way the problem is defined will influence the subsequent analysis, so a clear understanding of the problem by the entire team is important.

2. *Find the true source of the problem.* Root-cause analysis ensures we dig deeper than the symptoms to uncover the real problem. Many forms of investigation may be required to determine the root cause, including interviewing stakeholders, gathering past performance data, and conducting tests.

3. *Set solution requirements.* These requirements describe our ideal state after the problem has been solved. They'll be used to compare possible alternative solutions. Here is an example of a useful format for phrasing solution requirements.

The problem will be solved when:

We know _____.

We have _____.

We can _____.

We are _____.

4. *Generate possible alternative solutions to the problem.* We can't sufficiently emphasize the importance of this step. Finding breakthrough solutions is possible only when we devote time and energy to generating many potential solutions. During this step we must accept that many useless ideas will be generated in the process of finding some new useful ones. The team realizes there is inefficiency in creativity, enabling everyone to be more patient and focused on this step.

5. *Select an alternative.* Ideally, we've created several reasonable alternatives by this stage. Now we use the solution requirements to screen and prioritize the alternatives. There may be an obvious solution now, but if not, quantitative and qualitative comparison techniques help us sift through the options and select one.

6. *Perform risk and cost-benefit analysis on the selected option.* Risk analysis ensures that we have considered the disadvantages as well as the strengths of this option. Cost-benefit analysis checks to make sure the solution won't cost more than the problem. Based on the more detailed analysis of this step, the team may decide to consider another alternative that might be cheaper or have fewer risks.

7. *Make a decision and an action plan.* Put the actions and responsibilities to carry out the decision in meeting minutes or into the project plan. Organize and file the results of the problem analysis in case you need to revisit the problem again in the future.

Given these choices, understanding the decision modes available and deciding when each is appropriate comprise an essential part of a team's collaborative problem-solving capability.

A team functions best when members know which decision mode they are applying to any problem and why. If part of my team expects a consensus decision, yet I intend to make the decision myself after listening to the team, people will become confused, disappointed, or resentful. As a leader, I need to understand the implications of choosing one decision mode over another. The following list describes common modes for making decisions and offers the strengths and weaknesses of each.

- *Consensus.* The entire team participates in the decision together, including understanding the problem and creating alternatives. Performed correctly, consensus is a powerful way to leverage the capability of a group, because it builds a solution using ideas from the entire team.

  *Advantages:* The decisions made through consensus can be far superior, and because they are involved in making the decision, the commitment of the team to the decision is very high.

  *Disadvantages:* The consensus process can take a lot of time, particularly if the team doesn't have the requisite skills. (See the box on consensus guidelines later in this section.) Also, there is a physical limit to the number of people who can realistically be involved in a consensus decision. For a group much larger than 15 people, the pace becomes glacial.

  *Best application:* Consensus is a good choice for complex decisions with far-reaching consequences, where the quality of the decision and the commitment from the group outweigh the need for a speedy decision. A team in the Performing stage is likely to use consensus more frequently, both because they seek the best solution and because their consensus skills are mature enough to provide a reasonably quick decision.

- *Voting.* This method is completely democratic. It assumes the options are well understood, and a simple majority vote makes the decision.

  *Advantages:* It is quick and can include many people.

  *Disadvantages:* If the options are complex, it is less likely that they are well understood. Further, if there are more than two options, it can take multiple rounds of voting to identify a clear majority. Voting risks low commitment to the solution by the losing side.

  *Best application:* Voting is appropriate for well-understood options, particularly when there is a large group involved. Before using this technique, make sure that opposition to the decision by the losing side can't derail implementation. Voting is sometimes used as the fallback decision mode when a consensus process is bogged down and the time for the decision has arrived.

- *Delegating.* Allow one or a few of the team to make the decision because they are perceived to have the necessary information and expertise.

*Advantages:* It simplifies the decision process because it requires fewer people.

*Disadvantages:* The decision-maker(s) must have the trust of the entire group, and must have the knowledge and ability to work independently of the group.

*Best application:* Delegating works well when specialized knowledge is required and the decision makers are strong individual performers capable of managing themselves.

- *Autocratic.* The project manager makes the decision. The variable in this mode is the degree that the team is asked to contribute to the decision.

*Advantages:* One person can make a decision faster than a group can, particularly when that person is well informed. Often, the group leader has a perspective or responsibility that is different than the rest of the group's, which also makes it appropriate for the leader to make the final decision.

*Disadvantages:* A speedy, uninformed decision may be disastrous. Team commitment to the decision will depend on team commitment to the project manager. If the project leader always makes autocratic decisions and the team often disagrees with those decisions, trust in the leader and commitment to the team will disintegrate.

Ironically, strong teams need leaders who will make autocratic decisions. "Decisive" is an oft-cited characteristic of a good project leader. It's necessary when a choice must be made but there is insufficient information for the team to reach a consensus. At other times, the impact of the decision is small, so the time required for consensus building isn't justified. But the most important autocratic decisions are often those that have the biggest impact. The image of General Eisenhower setting the date for the Normandy invasion is one of a participative, yet still autocratic decision. Whether the team is Forming or Performing, asking for input to help make a decision is practical in order to make an *informed* decision, but the leader is the one who must make the call. The responsibility of leadership cannot always be shared with the team.

As the team leader, you can make the rest of the team conscious of the mode being used for any decision. For example, "The selection of our vendor will have such broad consequences that we will make this decision by consensus." Or, in the case of an autocratic decision, "I want each of you to give me your ideas and concerns about the layout for our new office space. I do value your views and I will take them into account as I make the decision."

## Decision Modes Reflect the Team's Maturity

Clearly, the decision modes of the team will reflect the leadership style of the project manager, which in turn is influenced by the development stage of the team. For example, arriving at a consensus for a complex problem may be too difficult for the team early in the project when they are still forming. During the Storming phase, the team is likely to challenge a leader who is not using participative decision styles. This need to change leadership styles during the project increases the need for the project leader to be clear about which decision mode is being pursued from problem to problem. Further, the team's ability to participate in choosing decision styles relies on the entire team's awareness of the factors that cause each mode to be appropriate.

---

### GUIDELINES FOR BUILDING A CONSENSUS DECISION

Building decisions through consensus can produce superior decisions, because we leverage the knowledge and skills of the team. Consensus is not the same as unanimity, where every participant agrees that the decision is the best choice. Rather, we reach a consensus when every participant can agree that the decision process was fair, that their perspective was heard and understood, and that each of them can support implementation of the decision.

Here are five leadership tips for reaching consensus in meetings:

1. *Follow a structured problem-solving process.* Begin with a clear understanding of the problem or decision to be made. Use the structure to create focus at each step of the process.

2. *Manage group participation.* Encourage people to use active listening skills. Ensure a balance of power—don't allow the most vocal to dominate or the least vocal to not participate. Use a method to ensure each person has been heard at each step of the process.

3. *Embrace conflict as a sign of creative thinking.* People should avoid changing positions just to avoid conflict. Examine differences of opinion thoroughly.

4. *Build consensus.* Seek alternatives that satisfy the goals of all members. Try to find ways to integrate multiple viewpoints.

5. *Know how you'll make the final decision.* Identify an alternative decision method in advance in case the team deadlocks.

The key to consensus is ensuring balanced participation and creating a decision everyone will support in implementation. To arrive at the final decision, Kristin Arnold (2001) offers the "Five L" scale.[2] Once it seems the group has come to a decision, the leader asks everyone to rank the decision on the Five L scale: You *loathe* it. You will *lament* it, complaining about the decision after the meeting. You can *live* with it. You *like* it. You *love* it! If there are people who will either loathe or lament the decision, then you aren't finished.

---

## CONFLICT MANAGEMENT

Conflict is an inevitable result of group problem solving. In any project where two or more people need to make decisions, there will eventually be disagreement—which is why conflict management skills are absolutely necessary to build the collaborative problem-solving capability of a team.

Though it isn't always comfortable, high-performance teams actually use conflict to solve problems. They know conflict is a natural, valuable source of energy for the group. It's often a product of legitimate differences of opinion that must be resolved in order to move forward on a project. Working through these differences involves real learning and often results in significant breakthroughs.

There are two risks in any decision where conflict exists: First, the wrong decision may be reached, particularly if conflict affects the problem-solving process. Second, relationships may be damaged as the issue is resolved. The terms *win-win* and *win-lose* refer to the ability for positive relationships to be maintained while achieving the best decision. In situations in which both sides will have to work together after the conflict is resolved—the reality for project teams—it is essential to both maintain the relationship *and* find a good decision.

Employing conflict to a team's advantage takes trust, respect, and lots of practice. Our own experiences with conflict can affect how we respond to it in team situations. Successful conflict resolution requires recognizing the common responses to conflict and understanding the techniques that allow you to make productive use of the conflict itself. The following list describes four common but *usually unproductive* approaches to conflict.[3] The team leader and team members should understand what these behaviors are and why they are unproductive. Then keep on the lookout for these approaches and head them off.

1. *Withdrawing from the conflict.* This approach avoids both the issues and the people associated with the conflict. The strategy relies on the belief that it is easier to avoid conflict than to work through it. If the issue is real, this approach just delays the inevitable and increases the tension as schedule pressure adds to the situation.

2. *Smoothing over the conflict.* This response focuses on the positive relationships and deemphasizes the areas of conflict. Smoothing prioritizes relationships over resolving disagreements, a short-term solution at best.

3. *Forcing resolution to the conflict.* This method attempts to over-power others into accepting a position or solution without

regard to the relationships within the group. Forcing behaviors include physical force, such as raising one's voice, ridiculing an idea, and the pure use of organizational authority: "I'm the boss, so do it my way." Although forcing does result in a decision, there may be very low commitment to the decision by those who perceive that it was forced on them. Clearly, forcing exhibits a lack of respect for other team members and threatens the positive relationships required in a high-performance team.

4. *Compromising, accepting a no-win solution.* This approach accepts that neither side will get what they want. Each side accepts less than they want, with the consolation that they got as much as the other party. Though this strategy attempts to respect both parties, compromise is considered lose-lose because the solution doesn't satisfy anyone and the disappointment can cause resentment.

There are times when each of these strategies can be the right choice. We may apply the old wisdom "Choose your battles" when we avoid or smooth over a conflict because the issue at stake just isn't worth the emotional energy required to confront the problem, or the relationship has been under a lot of strain. Likewise, there is a time for compromise, for accepting that no commonly acceptable solution exists and at least a compromise allows the team to make a decision and move on. The rationale for forcing a decision does not apply often, particularly on teams where respect for each other is important.

Understanding these responses to conflict allows team members to recognize when someone is choosing an unproductive method to handle conflict. When the symptoms become evident, you need to switch to a better approach, known as *confronting conflict*, or simply *problem solving*.

### KEY CONCEPT Confronting Conflict

Viewing conflict—disagreement among team members—as a source of *positive* creative energy doesn't make it fun or easy. The project team and the project manager should be on the lookout for conflict and steer its energy into productive problem solving by applying these guidelines.[4]

- *Prevent the conflict.* Even though we acknowledge that conflict will arise, we can avoid the stress of many conflicts by attending to the components of a high-performance team. Ground rules, effective listening, good meeting management, and a clear problem-solving process all contribute to a smoothly functioning team.

- *Acknowledge the conflict.* Point out the disagreement and recognize the emotions that are surfacing. Describing the conflict helps focus on the problem rather than on the people with whom we disagree. "We seem to disagree on the amount of memory these computers will need, and everyone is getting pretty excited about it."

- *Frame the conflict in reference to the project.* Make it clear how the decision being considered will ripple through other decisions. Understanding the context of the decision within the project also reveals the urgency to solve the problem: "Can we wait for more information, or do we need to make a decision now?"

- *Focus on interests, not positions.* Early life experience may have taught us that stubbornness wins arguments. That is a forcing response. Rather than digging in and defending positions, each side of the conflict should be explicit about their interest, goals, and requirements for the outcome. This focus reveals all that we have in common, a starting point for building a mutually satisfying solution.

- *Trade places.* Attempt to describe the situation from the other person's perspective. Understand that person's reluctance to embrace your proposal. Listen as he or she describes your perspective to you.

- *Separate identifying and selecting alternatives.* As described in the problem-solving method earlier, keep the group focused on identifying possible solutions first. Use clear ground rules that encourage generating many ideas, not evaluating them. As in brainstorming, this tactic leads to new thinking by combining ideas and allowing either side to offer unorthodox options to expand the thinking of the group.

- *Agree on process, if not outcome.* If the logjam continues with no mutually agreeable solution appearing and no way for either side to accept the other's position, shift the focus to creating a process for deciding that both sides can accept. For example, can we find a third party everyone trusts to make the decision?

These guidelines are designed to maintain trust and respect within teams while working through disagreements. They work because everyone on the team shares the same overall project goal. However, these guidelines are not necessarily the right rules to follow for negotiating in an adversarial setting.

### Conflict Management Requires Skill

**DANGER!**

Conflict management is not a natural talent for many people. Life and job experience may not have taught you the skills for confronting a conflict. If this is not your strength, enlist support from outside the project. Strong disagreement that polarizes the group or erupts into emotional arguments justifies involvement from a seasoned facilitator.

Conflict management is not just for project leaders; it is a team skill. If your team breaks down when facing disagreement, then it is time to focus on building this skill. This is one topic that the project leader probably shouldn't try to teach to the team. Unless you have been trained in this area, avoid the do-it-yourself approach. Most large organizations have human resources or organizational development professionals who are educated in conflict management. Invest in this skill early in the project to reduce Storming and speed the transition from Norming to Performing.

## CONTINUOUS LEARNING

Pioneering, innovating, and delivering breakthrough solutions means taking risks and learning from mistakes. Continuous learning means that we recognize the need for the team to learn and improve throughout the project. The final component of our collaborative capability contains both the culture and habits that promote continuous learning throughout the project.

### Create a Continuous Learning Culture

**KEY CONCEPT**

High-performance teams learn rapidly, but only if the project's culture makes it safe. No one has more influence on this factor than the project leader. Do we punish every failure? Do we quickly dismiss new or uncommon ideas? Are we willing to question our own perceptions in order to fully understand an opposing point of view? Do we recognize ineffective habits—our own as well as the team's—and consciously change them? Our daily actions set the tone for the team.

### Continuous Learning Habits

It may seem as though the habits that contribute most to continuous learning have been previously discussed: setting ground rules, conducting routine self-assessments, and following active listening and consensus decision-making guidelines to promote honest discussion. But teams can do all of these things and still not reach their potential. John Redding,[5] author of *The Radical Team Handbook*, notes that routine self-assessment by project teams is fairly common. What

## TEAM PROCESS ASSESSMENTS

You can buy into the importance of positive team dynamics, but unless you have a way to measure the team's health you can miss out on opportunities for improvement. According to Vicki Legman, who has spent more than 20 years coaching teams, "People 'get' that they should assess how the team is doing, but unless it is easy for them to do so, they won't. They might ask folks 'how's it going?' and they will only get task and maybe process feedback, but usually not on people and teaming issues." Legman recommends formalizing the approach to assessing team health. "It doesn't have to be complicated to be effective. But it does have to be specific and repeatable." She provides a four-step strategy any team can follow.

### Objectives

- To identify what's working and what can be improved.
- To make concrete steps to change team performance.

1. *Decide on a feedback tool.* Select the topics you'll assess and the format the team will use for evaluation. Be sure to include questions on all three areas of group behavior: People, Product (task), and Process. The feedback tool should let you check whether the team is adhering to your team's guidelines. If not, should the guidelines be changed, or can a specific new behavior be put into place to help you adhere to them?

2. *Set a timetable.* Establish how often you will use your feedback tool, when you will start, and when you will evaluate the tool to see whether it's valuable. Put these activities on the project calendar so they aren't forgotten.

3. *Evaluate the tool.* Evaluate the tool as described in Step 2. Make adjustments until the team agrees the tool is making a difference.

4. *Take concrete actions based on the feedback.* Take action steps and announce the actions as triggered by the feedback process. Know that if you conduct a feedback process and take *no action,* you will seriously damage morale.

The goal of this feedback process is to identify what's working and what can be improved, and to take concrete steps to change team performance. According to Legman, the questions on the tool can be as simple as these: "What is working, and what needs to be improved?" However, she offers her clients several examples of questions to ask:

*Example Feedback Question 1:* Rank our team on a scale of 1 to 5 for statements 1 through 8; then complete the sentence for statements 9, 10, and 11.

1. Our meetings are productive and organized.
2. People are contributing equitably in the meetings.
3. Everyone has contributed equitably to project work.
4. The project is on schedule.
5. We are dealing with conflict effectively.
6. I am comfortable in the team setting.
7. I feel my ideas and input are appropriately considered.

---

8. I am satisfied with the progress of the project.

9. The best thing about our team is _____.

10. A current challenge for our team is _____.

11. We need to change this form to better serve our purposes by _____.

*Example Feedback Question 2:* Rank our team on a scale of 1 to 5 for statements 1 through 6; then complete the sentence for statements 7 and 8.

1. The objectives of the project are clear.

2. Roles and responsibilities are clear.

3. Everyone is contributing a fair amount to the project.

4. Our processes are working well.

5. Our relationship issues are solid (I feel respected, listened to, and valued).

6. Conflict is dealt with effectively in our team.

7. What I really like about our team is _____.

8. Issues that need to be addressed immediately are _____.

Once a team process assessment is established, the team can monitor the scores on a regular basis for the same reason they will measure cost and schedule performance: We want to see the problems when they are still small, when they are easier to solve. These example feedback forms are part of the Fast Foundation in Project Management downloadable forms found at www.VersatileCompany.com/FFMBAinPM.

*\*The four-step process and examples of team feedback are copyright Legman Communication Training and used by permission.*

---

differs, he notes, is whether the assessments lead to new or deeper understanding of the problems the team is facing. Likewise, many teams use ground rules to set norms without developing the habits that create original solutions. What makes the difference?

Ground rules and self-assessments are designed to reinforce desired behaviors, so if you want outside-the-box thinking, ask for it! The following list describes the behaviors you can ask for with ground rules. As the project moves forward, when you debrief a meeting's effectiveness or run a periodic lessons-learned session, be able to cite specific examples of these actions.

*Actively identify and question assumptions.* Assumptions constrain our thinking, often unconsciously. When we define assumptions as "a premise not supported by objective evidence or concrete information," we may find we are using more assumptions than facts to drive our thinking.[6] If you can't find facts to support an assumption, then be willing to question the assumption, and be cautious about letting it drive decisions.

*Strive for honesty over conformance.* As discussed earlier in the chapter, some people avoid conflict in order to maintain harmony. That leads to suppressing bad news or new information that contradicts our plans. If the real problems are discussed in the hall after the meeting, it's a danger sign that people are avoiding the truth.

*Make learning a conscious goal on an ongoing basis.* When debriefing a meeting, ask these questions: What did we learn? What do we need to learn? What information could improve our understanding? As another example, Redding suggests that, when discussing an issue, team members should begin by asking questions rather than presenting solutions.[7]

*Be disciplined in creativity.* That may sound illogical, but finding the best answer for a complex problem often means viewing it from many perspectives and exploring many options. Employ techniques that force the team to dig deeper to uncover the root of a problem or cause more potential solutions to be produced. Brainstorming is a well-known example of disciplined creativity, but many other techniques exist. Finding specific techniques to promote idea generation and providing the time for creativity are signals to the team that new ideas and thorough analysis are valuable.

*Question the project's goal, scope, and plan.* These are the foundations of all activity for the team. They were set early in the project. Progress is likely to shed new light on the assumptions and facts that drove the original business case. Periodically question the premise for the project. To paraphrase common wisdom, if you are climbing a ladder and find it is leaning against the wrong wall, quit climbing and move the ladder!

Peter Senge's landmark book, *The Fifth Discipline*, introduced corporate America to the idea of a learning organization. In this book and its companion, *The Fifth Discipline Fieldbook*, Senge and others describe how a wide array of methods produce a culture that values curiosity, truth, and original thinking.[8] As a project leader, you can use these and other sources to educate your team on both the values and behaviors that promote continuous learning.

## Continuous Learning Unleashes Team Potential

Continuous learning values and behaviors tie our high-performance framework together in several ways. All of the previous components of both a positive team environment and collaborative problem solving must be in place for the continuous learning behaviors to function. Adding this final capability lifts the team out of the ruts of seeing problems and options in the same old way, thus releasing the true creativity of your united group.

## SUMMARY OF COLLABORATIVE PROBLEM SOLVING

Project teams cause change and deliver unique results, solving problems every step of the way. A mature high-performance team combines the four components described in this section to move through these problems with both efficiency and effectiveness: Using a structured approach to *problem solving* provides focus and a common language. The ability to switch among *decision modes* leverages the strength of group decisions while maintaining momentum. *Conflict management* skills enable individuals to bring contrasting perspectives to build better ideas and maintain team relationships. Finally, the culture and habits of *continuous learning* promote the creativity necessary to discover the best solutions.

As these skills increase, the benefits of a positive team environment are magnified. Commitment, unity, and perseverance combine with creativity and continuous learning to maximize the strengths of all team members. The team is more likely to meet its goal, and the journey is more exciting and satisfying.

## KEY CONCEPT    JOB SATISFACTION

We have framed our discussion of high-performance teams by focusing on the productivity benefits such teams produce. Productivity is important to our project-driven organizations because it brings down the total cost of delivering a project. But high-performance teams have another benefit, one that is harder to grasp but perhaps of even greater importance. When we work with people whom we trust and respect, when our individual efforts are multiplied by our teammates, when we overcome huge challenges and deliver to the best of our potential, we have pride and joy in the work we perform.

The satisfaction of delivering a project on time, on budget, and with a superior product is brief. Our daily work lives are filled far more with the journey to the goal than with the momentary enjoyment that comes from meeting the goal. When we devote our energy to building high-performance teams, we give our teammates and ourselves one of the greatest gifts available in the workplace: a job we can enjoy.

## END POINT

This chapter has emphasized that project team members are challenged to work interdependently to solve many problems. These problems can be simple or complex, but every project is, essentially, a series of decisions to make and problems to solve. Since project teams are temporary, each project team must *learn* to work together.

The topic of team leadership is large and covers far more than we can address in this single chapter.[9] For that reason, we have limited our scope to presenting a framework of specific skills and attributes that are necessary in a high-performing team.

The high-performance team framework identifies the factors that must be present for a team to reach its synergistic potential: to deliver more as a team than the individuals working alone ever could. A project manager helps the team establish a positive environment for daily interaction by setting ground rules for team behaviors, by ensuring the team uses good listening skills, by practicing good meeting management, and by building team identity. To enable the team to face problem after problem together, the project manager works to improve its collaborative capability, including leading the team to learn problem solving and conflict-resolution skills.

Leadership is the keystone of a high-performance team. Among the many important characteristics of a good leader, this chapter recognizes several as essential for leading a project team:

- Maintaining a strategic vision and keeping it attached to the tactical plan.
- Developing a culture that promotes learning during the project.
- Giving attention to individual team members to keep them bonded to the project.
- Consciously attending to the factors identified in the high-performance team framework.
- The ability to flex leadership style to the needs of the team.

The leadership actions and team factors described in this chapter take energy and effort. Although project managers are routinely asked for cost and schedule status, we are rarely asked for an update on the health of the team. That makes it easy to stay focused on task execution rather than team process. Investing in building a high-performance team requires the conviction that a cohesive team with mature problem-solving skills does make a difference to the team's productivity.

# Stellar Performer: Habitat for Humanity

Rod Pipinich

Project management skills are equally important to not-for-profit organizations, especially those that rely heavily on volunteers, such as Habitat for Humanity International, which has built more than 225,000 houses around the world. Each home is a project, managed with traditional project management tools. A major challenge for Habitat projects is relying on a constantly changing stream of volunteer workers with very different skills and abilities. Habitat's continued success offers valuable lessons for managing volunteers. You may recognize that these six lessons have implications for managing conventional projects as well.

1. *Provide a positive experience.* Habitat relies on volunteers, so it is important that the volunteer experience be a constructive one. Keep them coming back by taking a break from the usual intensity of the business world by going out your way to treat your project team with respect and gratitude. Volunteers appreciate a break from their regular routine of employment, so don't be afraid to show a bit of irreverence. For example, rework is expected on Habitat sites; crew chiefs state an unwritten Habitat motto as: "Do it right the last time."

2. *Remember that volunteers are stakeholders.* Local Habitat volunteers have a stake in improving their own community by helping to provide affordable housing. Volunteers work alongside the project's major stakeholders, the future homeowner families who put in sweat-equity hours. Everyone wants the project to succeed, so instill confidence through strong project management. Keep the work flowing by providing clear direction according to the project plan. By all means, prevent volunteers from standing around waiting for something to do.

3. *Be flexible.* Safety is the first priority at Habitat, so volunteers are never asked to perform tasks they find uncomfortable. Project managers usually meet their crew for the first time at the beginning of each day, so they must quickly align assignments with appropriate levels of skill, interest, and aptitude. The ability to reallocate resources on the fly helps the project team enjoy their work, reduce accidents, and improve productivity.

4. *Delegate.* Use the variety of volunteer experience to the project's advantage. Identify leaders early and assign them responsibility for a work package to be performed by a smaller team. This allows the project manager to better manage the entire project rather than focus on any single task.

5. *Provide learning opportunities.* Volunteers enjoy helping the community, but also desire to learn something new. Show volunteers how to do unfamiliar tasks, but don't do the work for them. Be prepared to let them fail in noncritical situations that will enhance the learning experience. Be patient, and check for quality to find any errors early, before they become irreversible.

6. *No overtime.* Make sure that the site is shut down early or on time (see Item 1).

### PMP Exam Prep Questions

1. Meetings to facilitate information sharing between the project management team and the customer have been unorganized and unproductive. What should be done to improve the meetings?

   a. The meeting leader should be established

   b. The team should receive communication training

   c. An agenda should be created and published and the meeting leader established

   d. An agenda should be created and published

2. Three team members have different solutions to a critical path related problem. What is the best method the project manager can use to resolve the conflict?

   a. Problem solving

   b. Reward

   c. Withdrawal

   d. Compromise

3. The project to develop a vaccine against bee colony collapse is experiencing conflict. To minimize this, what tools are available to the project manager?

   a. Interpersonal skills, ground rules, and project management practices

   b. Ground rules, networking, interpersonal skills, and project management practices

   c. Networking and project management practices, ground rules, and group norms

   d. Group norms, ground rules, and project management practices

4. Leadership and managerial style evolve within the project management life cycle. Of the following, which is the best description of that evolution?

   a. Directing, delegation, support, facilitation, and mentoring

   b. Directing, coaching, facilitation, and support

   c. Facilitation, directing, support, and coaching

   d. Mentoring, directing, facilitation, and support

Answers to these questions can be found at www.VersatileCompany.com/FFMBAinPM.

# 14

# Clear Communication Among Project Stakeholders

## INTRODUCTION

Communication ranks high among the factors leading to the success of a project. Specifically, what is required is *constant, effective communication among everyone involved in the project.*

Projects are made up of people getting things done. Getting the right things done in the right way requires communication among all the stakeholders. As project managers, we spend a great deal of our time communicating. This includes setting and gaining agreement on goals, coordinating people, discovering and solving problems, and managing expectations. (We've addressed these topics throughout this book.) What this means is that from the statement of work through risk management and detailed planning, every project management technique is a method of communicating.

This chapter presents several project-oriented techniques for ensuring that the right people have the right information to make the necessary decisions and carry them out. You will recognize some of these techniques from previous chapters:

- Creating a communication plan
- Change management

- Communicating within the team
- Closeout reporting

Communication is a vital skill for project managers. Project managers need to be able to write and speak well, lead meetings effectively, and resolve conflicts constructively. They also need to listen well, so that they really understand what's being said. Some of these topics are addressed in this chapter; others are addressed in Chapter 13; but to truly teach these essential communication skills is beyond the scope of this book. This chapter describes the communication *responsibilities* of a project manager without going into depth on communication skills. In addition, a Kickoff Checklist, Communication Plan, Task Assignment sheet, Meeting Agenda template, sample Status Report, Control Checklist, and Closure Report available online emphasize that structuring our communication on projects leads to greater consistency and effectiveness.

### EMBRACE YOUR ROLE AS A LEADER

A project manager is not merely a conduit for information distribution. Project managers are leaders. Remember that as we present all the communication mechanisms and responsibilities in this chapter. Every interaction with a stakeholder is an opportunity to set a tone, to manage expectations, to reinforce the strategy and direction, and to lead by example. You may use e-mail to send task assignments and post status reports on websites, but your job is not to interact with a computer; it is to focus the energies of a group of people on a common goal and promote their efficient, coordinated action.

When you interact with your team, you are literally onstage. The energy, integrity, optimism, respect, and accountability that you demonstrate will be reflected in the work of the team. Your management and customers are relying on you for advice. They need you to stand up for the facts, particularly when the facts tell an unpleasant story.

From the moment you accepted the responsibility to define and plan the project you have been in the role of leader. Now, as the project moves into execution, embrace that role anew. See yourself the way others see you. Be the leader your team, management, and customer are seeking.

### CREATING A COMMUNICATION PLAN

It is the job of the project manager to make other people more productive. Through agreements, plans, recommendations, status reports, and other means, a project manager coordinates and influences all the stakeholders while giving them the information they need

## WINNING COOPERATION FROM SUPPORTING TEAM MEMBERS

**Marlene Kissler**

It is rare for a project of any size not to rely on at least one person or group outside your department or even your company. Even in a minor role, these external players have the potential to loom large if they fall behind schedule. So be proactive in making them a successful part of your project. Even in the best of circumstances, with support from management, a competent contact person, and clearly defined specifications, things can go wrong. It seems as if this should be a simple relationship: All you need to do is make a phone call to introduce yourself, briefly explain your project and what the contact person needs to do, and give her the name of the contact within your group. Then you can tell her the major project milestones, invite her to call anytime she has questions or concerns, and ring off.

But if you only do that, it's likely that you'll find out a few weeks later that nothing has been done—that this apparently minor component of your project may limp along behind schedule for the rest of the project, perhaps eventually affecting your critical path. Or the component may have to be minutely tested for its impact on every function. In short, that small but now significant portion of the project has become a disaster. Why?

To answer this, you need to consider the situation from the contact person's point of view: Perhaps, on the day you called, she was distracted by another problem and didn't catch everything you said; then later on, when she looked at what she did write down, it didn't make any sense. To her, you were just a disembodied voice full of your own self-importance, and this rubbed her the wrong way. She may have felt that your assignment had been thanklessly dumped on her; perhaps her supervisor volunteered her without reducing her existing workload. She never called the contact you gave her because she didn't know where to begin and didn't want to appear foolish. And, because your project never came up in status meetings with her supervisor, the whole thing was easy to shuffle to the bottom of her things-to-do list.

The lesson here is that, when working with people outside your group, your department, or even your company, you need to overcome any tendency to assume too much and minimize contact; realistically, these are the people who need interpersonal contact the most.

Here are 11 tips to help you avoid the pitfalls described in this scenario:

1. Make personal contact. Whenever possible, arrange a face-to-face meeting with contact people. Don't interact solely over the phone or by e-mail, even if you work in different countries. Exchange pictures or use videoconferencing to establish rapport face-to-face.

2. Start with a short warm-up visit; this should be no more than a brief introductory meeting at a mutually convenient time. Send a friendly e-mail with a succinct overview of your project prior to the meeting. Don't blindside them with a cold call, filled with details they can't absorb. Instead, give them some more documentation and some time to prepare for the in-depth follow-up meeting. Allow them ample time to review it and bring their questions.

3. Ask for their help. Don't assume that they are already on board psychologically. The tone of your initial meeting should be "Will you help me?" not "You will do this." Ask whether they can meet the projected schedule. Give them an honest opportunity to say no. And make sure they have a realistic workload and support from their manager.

4. Personally introduce them to their contacts and technical resources in your company or department. Walk them to the office of each person they will need to work with or get information from, and introduce them. Sit in on high-level meetings if necessary. Make sure your group is accessible and helpful.

5. Provide an in-depth explanation in person, including documentation they can refer to later. Either personally review the project at the required level of detail with them or make sure the right person does. Don't force them to ask for everything.

6. Invite them to all meetings. That includes the kickoff meeting as well as all status and impromptu meetings. Treat them like full team members. Even though they may not choose to attend everything, give them the option.

7. Include them in the information loop. Make sure they are on all relevant distribution lists. They need to know project status, design changes, and schedule adjustments just as much as the other stakeholders.

8. Do milestone check-ins. The early ones are the most important. Personally review the deliverables. Be sure to catch miscommunications up-front. Be explicit in your feedback about what has been done right and what needs improvement. Once you're comfortable that the contact people are on track, you can then do high-level check-ins.

9. Include them in all acknowledgment meetings and accomplishment write-ups. Everyone likes to have his or her name associated with a successful project. Make the acknowledgments appropriate to their level of contribution.

10. Write them personal thank-you notes. Acknowledge that their contributions required effort above and beyond their regular assignments (if this was the case).

11. If the contribution has been substantial, include a report to their supervisor specifically describing their work. Be honest, fair, and timely with your report.

But why bother with all this time-consuming personal contact? There are several reasons.

The first is that it will ensure the success of your project. If you don't use your "soft" management skills, all the "hard" skills in the world won't get your project completed. Because people get the work done, people skills are what will encourage them to do it right.

The second reason relates to your product or service. Every component and every person on your project is important, and this includes interfaces with projects and people outside your project. If it fails in any area, your project and others will be negatively impacted, perhaps in ways you may not even be aware of until serious damage has been done.

The third reason to pay special attention to personal contact is that it is an investment in your career and your reputation. Yes, you got the job done and were efficient, were organized, and maintained positive rapport. But you can take it further. Be the project manager with whom people want to work. The people on your project are, after all, people. They will appreciate your courtesy, respect, and recognition of their contributions. And if you don't show courtesy, respect, or recognition of their contributions, they'll remember that, too.

This probably won't be the last project you lead. You may need cooperation from these supporting organizations for your next project. Some of these people may get transferred to your department, or you might get transferred to theirs. One of you may end up as the other's boss.

> Winning cooperation from supporting team members takes a little extra effort, but it pays off for your project and your career.
>
> Marlene Kissler earned her MBA at the University of Washington. She has been a project manager and systems manager for Fortune 500 companies.

to be more productive. He or she also manages customer expectations. But no matter what the task, every action of a project manager includes communication. Careful planning reduces the risk of a communication breakdown.

A communication plan is the written strategy for getting the right information to the right people at the right time. The stakeholders identified on the statement of work, the organization chart, and the responsibility matrix are the audience for most project communication. But on every project, stakeholders participate in different ways, so each has different requirements for information. Following are the key questions you need to ask, with tips for avoiding common pitfalls:

1. *Who needs information?*

   *Sponsor.* The sponsor is supposed to be actively involved in the project. There shouldn't be a question about who the sponsor is after writing the statement of work.

   *Functional management.* Many people may represent functional management. Their two basic responsibilities of providing resources and representing policy will dictate the information they need. Each functional manager's name or title must appear on the communication plan, though it may be appropriate to list several together as having the same information needs.

   *Customers.* Customers make decisions about the business case— what the product should be, when it is required, and how much it can cost. There are likely to be many different levels of customer involvement, so individual names or titles must be listed.

   *Project team.* The project team can be a particularly complex communication audience. It will be relatively straightforward to communicate with the core team, because they'll be tightly involved in the project. Other project team members, such as vendors, subcontractors, and staff in other departments, may have a variety of communication barriers to overcome, so each will need to be evaluated separately.

   *Project manager.* While the project manager is the source of much information, he or she will often be on the receiving end as well.

2. *What information is needed?* In addition to the obvious cost and schedule status reports, several other types of information are distributed during the project. Basically, the following categories classify how information is managed:

*Authorizations.* Project plans, the statement of work, budgets, and product specifications must all be authorized. Any document that represents an agreement must have an approval process, including steps for reviewing and modifying the proposal. Be specific about who will make the decision.

*Status changes.* Reports with cost and schedule progress fall into this category. So do problem logs. It is common to issue status reports, but the content of each report should be specific to the audience receiving it.

*Coordination.* The project plan helps to coordinate all the players on a project. It contains the tasks and responsibilities, defines the relationships between groups, and specifies other details necessary to work efficiently. When change occurs during the course of a project, coordination among teams or locations is often required on a daily basis. The communication plan should record the process for keeping everyone up-to-date on the next steps.

## Keep the Status Report Short

A common mistake is to include in the status report everything about the project that anyone might want to know. Instead of having the intended effect of informing everyone, these obese reports are overwhelming for a busy audience. When developing the report content, keep it practical. A department manager responsible for 250 projects made the point this way: "Some of our project leaders have 10 projects. If they have to spend two hours a week writing status updates, there won't be any time left for them to do work. They report to supervisors overseeing up to 80 projects. We need a way to identify and communicate the key information quickly so project leaders and supervisors can spend time solving problems and moving the projects ahead!"

## Make Information Timely

For information to be useful, it has to be timely. As part of the communication plan, the project manager needs to decide how often to contact each stakeholder and with what information. In fact, stakeholder response to the communication plan is a way of discerning the involvement level of each stakeholder. For example, a sponsor who won't sign up for frequent status meetings or reports is signaling his or her intention to support this project from afar. Table 14.1 uses a matrix to map which information needs to be communicated to each stakeholder and how often. Notice that a time for response is designated in Table 14.1; unless the stakeholder agrees to respond within this required time, his or her commitment to the project remains in question.

## Include Regular Meetings in the Communication Plan

It's best to have regularly scheduled progress meetings written into the communication plan. While everyone says they would rather be proactive than reactive, many sponsors or supporting managers want to have status meetings only as needed—meaning only when there is a big problem. They are willing to let the project manager handle everything as long as it is going smoothly (they call this type of uninvolvement "empowering the project manager"). In reality, when troubles occur, by the time these higher-level managers become involved, it is often too late for them to help. This is why scheduled meetings are important. If things are going smoothly, the meetings won't take long, but if a problem does arise, these meetings will give management the background information they need to be effective.

## How Will Communication Take Place?

There are now myriad ways to stay in constant communication. Internet and intranet technologies allow more people to share information simultaneously. Status reports are now posted on project websites, and videoconferencing enables project teams to be spread around the world and still meet face-to-face. But with all these options, the question still remains the same: What is the best way to deliver the information? One thing is certain: Technology doesn't have all the answers. Putting a project's status on a website, for instance, doesn't ensure that the right people will see it. You need to consider the audience and its specific communication needs. For example, because high-level executives are usually very busy, trying to meet with them weekly or sending them a lengthy report may not be realistic.

## Take a Tip from Madison Avenue

If you want to communicate effectively, why not take a lesson from the folks on Madison Avenue? Whether they are running ad campaigns for cars or computers, movies, milk, or sunscreen, they use both repetition and multiple media channels. You can mimic this by providing hard-copy reports at status meetings and then following up with minutes of the meeting. In the case of a video- or teleconference, providing hard-copy supporting materials becomes even more important.

**TABLE 14.1   Communication Plan**

| Stakeholder | What Information Do They Need? | Frequency | Medium | Response |
|---|---|---|---|---|
| Sponsor | High-level cost, schedule, quality performance<br>Problems and proposed actions | Monthly | Written report and meeting | Required in 3 days |
| PM's supervising management | Detailed cost, schedule, quality performance<br>Problems, proposed actions, assistance required | Weekly | Written report and meeting | |
| Customer executive | High-level cost, schedule, quality performance<br>Problems and proposed actions<br>Required action by customer | Monthly | Meeting with project sponsor<br>Published meeting minutes | Required in 5 days |
| Customer contact | Detailed cost, schedule, quality performance<br>Problems and proposed actions<br>Required actions by customers<br>Coordination information for customer action | Weekly | Written report and meeting<br>Include in project team meeting | Required in 3 days |
| Project team | Detailed cost, schedule, quality performance<br>Problems and proposed actions<br>Coordination information for next two weeks<br>News from customer and sponsor | Weekly | Project team meeting<br>Published meeting minutes | |

*Even a simple plan makes communication more deliberate and represents stakeholder commitment to attending meetings and responding in a timely manner.*

## Don't Miss Out on Informal Communication

While it is important to plan for communication, it is also true that some of the best communication takes place informally and unexpectedly. You can nurture the opportunities for informal communication. Be available. Get into the places where the work is being done or the team members are eating their lunch. Listen. Watch for the nonverbal, unofficial signs of excitement, confusion, accomplishment, or burnout.

## CHANGE MANAGEMENT: PROMOTE BEHAVIOR CHANGE IN AFFECTED STAKEHOLDERS

Projects make changes, and for many projects that means people will have to change their behaviors for the project to deliver results. But will they? Will people on the receiving end of a project embrace the new strategy, policy, or technology? Or will they shrug, duck their head and try to ignore it.

Experience has shown that without conscious attention to helping people change their behaviors, many people won't change. And that can ruin the Return on Investment for your project. The framework and techniques of *change management* address this critical need.

---

### CHANGE MANAGEMENT INCREASES THE PROJECT'S VALUE

**Tim Creasey**

#### Introduction

Projects come in all shapes and sizes. Some impact the entire enterprise while others may impact a single workshop. Some are disruptive while others are incremental. Projects can aim to improve processes, systems, tools and structures. But, despite all the wonderful variety in the project world, there is *one universal constant* in terms of both impact and contribution to success: the *people whose jobs will be affected* and changed as a result of the project implementation. The people side of change sits squarely along the critical path to delivering value above and beyond specifications. And, unfortunately, the people side of change is often the most overlooked, underserved, under-resourced and underfunded.

But there is a solution. *Change management* is the discipline focused on that people side component of your projects. It is ultimately about applying structure and rigor to support the "soft" side of change, which in reality is often the harder side of change. As a working definition of change management, we will use the following seven-word, concise definition: "catalyzing individual transitions to deliver organizational results." This brief introduction will provide an overview of change management, its desired outcomes, its required actions and how you can be more successful as a project manager if you integrate project management and change management on your efforts.

---

## Why the People Side Matters

The people side of change matters because, when projects are implemented, organizations don't change, people do. Consider the question: how much of my project's expected results and outcomes depend on employees adopting and using the solution? When I have asked this question, even at large technology-focused conferences, the answers are routinely in the 70 to 100 percent range. Employees embracing, adopting and using a solution is what bridges the gap between an effectively managed project and truly delivering expected improvement and meaningful results to the organization. Data from nearly a decade of research by Prosci shows that projects with excellent change management are six times more likely to meet or exceed objectives than those with poor change management (and simply moving from poor to fair yields a threefold increase).

There are also tangible costs and risks for ignoring the people side of change like resistance, delays, attrition and loss of productivity. One of the largest costs of ignoring the people side of change are the RE costs—like redo, revisit, re-scope, redesign, rework, retrain—and in some cases, retreat. When adoption and usage are only addressed at the end of a project, these RE costs are significant and prevalent. Although the people side of change is often underestimated and underserved, it is one of the largest and most critical steps along the project value chain.

## The Differences and Similarities of PM and CM

Project management and change management are certainly related but different disciplines. Some of the primary differences include:

- One focuses on the technical side of implementing change; the other focuses on the people side of implementing change.
- They have slightly different definitions of "done" and measures of progress.
- They require different mindsets, competencies, and skill sets.
- The have different histories in terms of both length (60+ years to 20+ years) and of origin.

While they do have some differences, project management and change management have some significant similarities that create a prime opportunity for a collaborative partnership:

- Both are disciplines.
- Both are process driven and tool rich.
- Both are applied to specific, discrete undertakings (i.e., projects).
- Both need skilled practitioners.
- Both share the ultimate objective of delivering successful change outcomes and value to the organization by helping it perform in a new, improved way.

Projects and initiatives are more successful when they apply both project management and change management, a phenomenon we describe as the "unified value proposition."

## The Unified Value Proposition of an Integrated Approach

When change management and project management are applied together, in unison, in an integrated manner, the result is what we call "the unified value proposition." The solution is BOTH "designed,

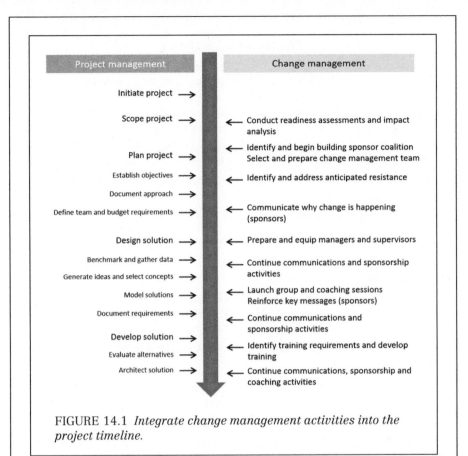

FIGURE 14.1 *Integrate change management activities into the project timeline.*

developed, and delivered" effectively AND it is "embraced, adopted, and used" by impacted employees. Organizational results and value come from solving both the technical side and people side of the puzzle through this unified value proposition.

The question that remains for many project managers newly exposed to change management is: What does it really mean to "apply" change management on a project? Effective change management requires two perspectives: (1) individual change management, which aims to answer how one person makes a change successfully, and (2) organizational change management, which provides the structure, process, and toolset for the project team to apply to support the individual transitions caused by and required for the project to yield value.

### Outcomes Desired: Individual Change Management

"The secret to successful change lies beyond the visible and busy activities that surround change. Successful change, at its core, is rooted in something much simpler: How to facilitate change with one person."

—Jeff Hiatt, Prosci Founder, in Chapter 1 of *ADKAR:*
*A Model for Change in Business, Government and Our Community*

The first step in applying change management is to understand how a single individual makes a change successfully, because, in the end, it is through individual employee adoption and usage that project and organizational value is created. Here, we will introduce the Prosci® ADKAR® Model, developed by Prosci Founder Jeff Hiatt. ADKAR describes the five building blocks of a successful individual change, whether that change is happening at home, in the community, or at work:

- **A**wareness of the need for change
- **D**esire to participate and support the change
- **K**nowledge on how to change
- **A**bility to implement required skills and behaviors
- **R**einforcement to sustain the change

Whether your project requires employees to follow new processes, use new tools, or interact with new systems, those affected employees need each of the ADKAR building blocks to be successful in their personal transition, which is what ultimately contributes to project and organizational success. Let's explore each of the ADKAR building blocks, along with specific "how to" suggestions for building and fostering each one.

## Awareness

Awareness is the first building block. It is important to note that this is not "Awareness that a change is happening," but rather a true understanding of the motivations and triggers for the change. In today's environment, where engagement and ownership have replaced predictability and control, employees being affected by a change expect an answer to "Why?" Prosci research indicates that the lack of a compelling case for change, that is, a lack of awareness, is the greatest source of employee resistance.

As a practitioner, you can begin by answering four simple but often neglected questions:

- What is the nature of the change?
- Why?
- Why now?
- What if we don't?

Awareness of the need for change is created through effective and well-crafted communication and sponsor messaging early in the project lifecycle. Examples of awareness-building activities include:

- Ensuring effective sponsor messaging
- Empowering manager conversations
- Communicating, communicating, communicating
- Providing access to readily available information
- Kicking off the project with an event

- Presenting data in a visual and compelling way
- Highlighting observable conditions or catastrophic events

You know you have built sufficient awareness when an impacted employee would say: "I understand why. . . ."

### Desire

The second step in ADKAR is desire to participate and support the change. Desire is ultimately the personal decision by an individual to take part in the change. Desire cannot be forced because it is a personal decision; however, desire can be motivated and encouraged. Building desire is founded upon the ability to highlight and make clear the personal and organizational motivating factors for the change, including:

- Expected gain or achievement (both personal and organizational)
- Fear of consequences of not changing (both personal and organizational)
- Importance of being part of something
- Importance of following a trusted leader

Building desire is tricky because it is so personal. However, there are specific actions that can be taken to help build desire, including:

- Ensuring active and visible support by sponsors
- Building a strong sponsor coalition
- Ensuring personal engagement by managers and supervisors
- Anticipating and proactively managing resistance
- Involving employees in the change process
- Providing opportunities for input and feedback
- Aligning incentive programs with the change

You know you have built sufficient desire when an impacted employee would say: "I have decided to . . ."

### Knowledge

Knowledge on how to change is the third building block, but is often the de facto and default that project teams jump to. When changes impact employees, the first response is often, "Let's send them to training." Knowledge is necessary, but not sufficient if the foundational awareness and desire are not in place. When thinking about knowledge, it is important that project teams account for:

- Knowledge requirements during the change
- Knowledge requirements after the change

Knowledge is often the least challenging of the five building blocks, given the history and prevalence of training and training departments as part of change efforts. However, there are several more tactics to consider when building knowledge, including:

- Delivering formal training
- Providing web-based educational materials

- Establishing mentoring relationships and opportunities
- Providing coaching in a one-on-one setting
- Leveraging experience
- Creating user groups and forums
- Making job aids readily available and accessible
- Providing specific troubleshooting guidance

You know you have built sufficient knowledge when an impacted employee would say: "I know how to . . ."

## Ability

After awareness, desire, and knowledge comes ability. Ability is when the change actually happens; it is when employees have and can demonstrate the capability to do their jobs in the new way. Knowledge does not ensure ability (see my golf game as an example), but project teams can provide specific support in creating ability, including:

- Providing opportunities to practice
- Creating the necessary time to commit to the change
- Coaching by managers or peers
- Accessing subject-matter experts
- Role modeling of the new behavior
- Delivering effective and timely feedback
- Providing support resources

You know you have built sufficient ability when an impacted employee would say: "I am able to . . ."

## Reinforcement

Reinforcement is the final building block of the ADKAR Model. As human beings, it is our natural, psychological, and physiological tendency to revert back to what we know. Without concrete measures and mechanisms to reinforce change, employees can slip back into old ways and the change will not stick. To be effective, reinforcement must be meaningful to employees. As a project team, reinforcement can take many different flavors, including:

- Celebrating successes
- Rewarding new ways of working
- Recognizing successful change
- Providing feedback
- Implementing corrective actions
- Sharing performance measurements

- Implementing accountability mechanisms
- Saying "thank you" and "job well done"

You know you have built sufficient reinforcement when an impacted employee would say: "I will continue to . . ."

## ADKAR Summary

The Prosci ADKAR Model is one of the most widely used models for managing change. Practitioners say that it makes sense, is easy to explain to others, and helps them see and unlock numerous and various types of change. Whether a change is impacting five, 50, 500, or 5,000 employees, the change will deliver better results when each employee has awareness, desire, knowledge, ability, and reinforcement. Since ADKAR describes the outcomes of a successful individual transition, the five building blocks can be considered the *milestones* of successful change at the individual level. So what can a project team do to support impacted employees through their own individual journeys?

## Actions Required: Organizational Change Management

Whereas individual change management and ADKAR describe the "outcomes desired" for change, organizational change management describes the "actions required." Over the past two decades, change management has evolved from primarily conceptual frameworks toward a rigorous, structured and documented process with formal *deliverables* and tools to support its application. While there are numerous approaches available, here we will explore the Prosci Three-Phase Process at a high level and call out specific activities and deliverables in each of the phases: Preparing for Change, Managing Change, and Reinforcing Change.

## Phase 1: Preparing for change

A "one size fits all" solution for change management is ineffective. The type and nature of change will be unique, and so will the people side impact and people side challenges. Phase 1 focuses on building the strategy, situational awareness, and supporting structures dictated by the change you are working to manage. Key activities of Phase 1: Preparing for Change include:

- Defining the individual level change required by the project
- Assessing the nature and type of project (change characteristics)
- Assessing the individuals and groups being impacted by the change (organizational attributes)
- Evaluating overall people side risk
- Developing risk mitigation tactics
- Anticipating resistance and developing mitigation tactics
- Creating a customized change management strategy
- Designing the sponsorship model needed to support realization
- Equipping the change team and project team

The outputs of building situational awareness in Phase 1 guide the development of the specific activities and deliverables in Phase 2 and Phase 3.

## Phase 2: Managing Change

The second phase in the process, Phase 2: Managing Change, covers the outward, employee-facing activities of change management. Based on the analysis in Phase 1, including the risk profile and customization based on situational awareness, the team creates five specific plans for supporting individual adoption and usage during the course of the project. These five plans are aligned to the ADKAR elements and integrated into a project plan for greatest impact. The five plans are:

- *Communications plan:* A "telling plan" merely informs employees about what the project team is doing; a communication plan answers the questions employees have and are delivered by preferred senders through preferred mediums.

- *Sponsor roadmap:* The sponsor roadmap provides specific direction and actions needed by senior leaders to fulfill their role as sponsor, namely active and visible participation, building a healthy coalition and communicating directly to employees.

- *Coaching plan:* The coaching plan presents the actions needed by front-line managers and supervisors throughout the organization to support their direct reports in times of change; their proximity to impacted employees makes them crucial allies.

- *Training plan:* The training plan details the efforts to build sufficient knowledge for both during and after the change, documenting requirements and positioning efforts within context.

- *Resistance management plan:* The resistance management plan lays out the approach for both proactive and reactive resistance management, including who the key players are for identifying and managing resistance.

Each of the five plans supports specific building blocks of the Prosci ADKAR Model. For example, you cannot train awareness, and you cannot communicate ability. ADKAR provides guidance that enables the team to leverage the right plans and tools at the right time during the change lifecycle. Formal deliverables are created for each of the five plans and they are integrated into the project timeline to ensure that affected employees have ability when it is time for "be live" on the project.

## Phase 3 : Reinforcing Change

The final "action required" in organizational change management is Phase 3: Reinforcing Change. As with individuals, the natural tendency of organizations is to revert. Specific, deliberate activities and mechanisms must be leveraged to ensure the change sticks and results are sustained. Key activities in Phase 3: Reinforcing change include:

- Proactively collecting feedback
- Listening to employees
- Auditing compliance
- Measuring performance
- Diagnosing gaps

- Identifying and managing resistance, particularly pockets of resistance
- Implementing corrective actions
- Celebrating successes
- Transitioning the change to operational owner

Many times, the project team is disbanded once the project ends, but reinforcement activities are still required to ensure sustainment. This requires a well-architected approach that transfers ownership and accountability for reinforcement into the organization.

### Conclusion

While projects come in all sorts of shapes and sizes, the universal constant is the affected employees who must change how they do their jobs. A significant portion of your project's expected results and outcomes rely on and depend on individuals making their own personal transitions successfully (even more so for strategic, critical, and integration-oriented projects). As a project manager, your ability to support and catalyze those individual transitions is a key driver of value creation and your own success. Change management provides the structured discipline, milestones and deliverables you need to manage the "harder" side of projects and initiatives.

### Learning More About Change Management

Visit www.prosci.com to access blogs, webinars, tutorials, and tools on how to effectively apply rigorous change management to projects and initiatives. Prosci provides role-based solutions for project managers, change management leaders, and business leaders and managers based on decades of research, including online tools, training, and the books *ADKAR: A Model for Change, Change Management: The People Side of Change,* and *Best Practices in Change Management.*

Tim Creasey, Prosci Chief Development Officer, is a dynamic thought leader and speaker whose focus is enabling change teams to deliver results by catalyzing employee adoption and usage. Prosci has researched change management for 20 years and provides holistic solutions to build organizational change competency.

## COMMUNICATING WITHIN THE PROJECT TEAM

Our project team gets the work done. We include vendors and part-time team members from supporting departments in the role of project team, as well as the usual full-time people. The larger your project, the more likely you'll be including people from outside your immediate department, and possibly outside your company. As you plan communication, realize that they all share four major communication needs:

1. *Responsibility.* Each team member needs to know exactly what part of the project he or she is responsible for.

2. *Coordination.* As team members carry out their work, they rely on each other. Coordination information enables them to work together efficiently.

3. *Status.* Meeting the goal requires tracking progress along the way to identify problems and take corrective action. The team members must be kept up to speed on the status of the project.

4. *Authorization.* Team members need to know about all the decisions made by customers, sponsors, and management that relate to the project and its business environment. Team members need to know these decisions to keep all project decisions synchronized.

Each technique in this section addresses two or more of these communication needs.

## Distributed Teams Are Real, Not Virtual

A lot of teams are no longer working side by side, seeing each other every day on the elevator and in the break room. Teams can be geographically separated across cities, time zones, and continents. But they are still real teams. The term *virtual team* is commonplace, but in this chapter we'll refer to these teams as *geographically distributed.* After all, they don't produce virtual deliverables and won't work for virtual money.

## Making Task Assignments Clear

Projects and project managers need clear direction if they are to succeed; this is why developing the statement of work is so worthwhile. Team members also need clear direction. Fortunately, all the work that's gone into project planning tells them just what they need to know. Every work package is like a mini-project, with time lines, dependencies, and deliverables. Whether you are assigning work to an individual performer or to a vendor, these basic rules should be observed:

- Explain the deliverables. Be sure they know exactly what they are supposed to deliver, including any completion criteria that will be used to judge it.

- Be clear about the level of effort expected and the due dates. The network diagram is a good tool to explain how their pieces fit into the whole project.

- If you know of any obstacles they can expect or special information they'll need, make sure they know it, too. Set them up for success.

- Hand out work assignments personally, allowing plenty of time for questions and discussion. These meetings should be considered an investment in team performance: The better you prepare them, the better they'll perform.

We can't overemphasize the importance of clear task assignments, but it doesn't have to be difficult. The Task Assignment form found online covers the basic information a team member needs.

## Individual Status Meetings

Plan on spending time with every member of the team on a regular basis. Remember, your job is to make them more productive, and you can't do that if you don't understand what they're working on—and what problems they're struggling with. The project status meeting just doesn't allow for this level of interaction. The project manager must take responsibility for setting up these meetings. Even though a manager might say, "I have an open-door policy; my team doesn't have to wait for a special meeting; they can find me anytime they want," this would be true only if the manager was always at his or her desk. In reality, project managers spend a lot of time in meetings and can be difficult to find. If you make team members seek you out, they may wait until their problems have grown too big to solve easily; the same problems might have been nipped early on if a meeting had been held sooner.

### Put the Meetings on the Calendar

Many project managers intend to spend a lot of time with team members, but as the project goes on they are just too busy. The best bet is to put time for every team member on your weekly calendar. That way you've planned in advance to be available.

### The Kickoff Meeting: Start the Project with a Bang

In football, the kickoff represents a clear, decisive start. Everyone knows the game is under way. Projects can start the same way. The kickoff meeting brings all the stakeholders together to look each other in the eye and commit to reaching the goals.

A kickoff meeting usually marks the beginning of the execution phase of a project. By this time, the statement of work and project plan have been approved and the team is assembled. It's an opportunity to celebrate initiation of the project. Here's a format for a kickoff meeting:

- The sponsor leads the meeting and takes the opportunity to explain the project's purpose and connection to the overall business.
- The customers are introduced; they offer an explanation of the project's importance to their business.
- The project manager is introduced and enthusiastically endorsed by the sponsor.

- Project team members are introduced, if there are not too many. Vendors and contractors also need to be introduced.

- The coffee mugs, T-shirts, or other project memorabilia are passed out. This is a good time to do this, rather than at the end of the project, because they can help in creating a sense of unity and team spirit.

- Celebrate. Everyone needs to get to know everyone else and all must communicate their enthusiasm for the project.

On big projects there are usually too many team members to introduce at the kickoff meeting. So have kickoff meetings for teams within the project, too. The hour or two spent on each of these meetings is an investment in team cohesion and performance. It will pay off.

## Project Status Meetings

Keeping a project on track requires regularly scheduled meetings to both share information and make decisions. A good project status meeting meets a lot of communication needs within the project team. Status meetings give the project manager an opportunity to:

- Increase team cohesion; status meetings are often the only time the entire team gets together.

- Keep the team informed about project developments from sources external to the team, such as from the sponsor, the customer, or management.

- Identify potential problems or share solutions to common problems.

- Ensure that the team understands the progress of the project and works together to determine any necessary changes to the project plan.

- *Make sure that the entire team shares the responsibility of meeting all the project objectives!*

Project status meetings rely on a participative management style. They build on the team's involvement in planning the project; the manager should encourage the same kind of involvement to keep it on track. This attitude is based on the philosophy that involvement leads to ownership, and ownership leads to greater commitment and accountability. In addition to the basic rules for running an effective meeting that were covered in Chapter 13, the following guidelines are useful for running a project status meeting:

- Be prepared. In addition to your agenda, everyone attending the meeting needs to have an open task report (OTR) *before* the meeting begins. (Table 14.2 shows an open task report.) An OTR is a subset

**TABLE 14.2   Open Task Report (OTR)**

OTR for a 10/14 Status Meeting

| ID | Task Name | Responsibility | Plan Start | Actual Start | Plan Finish | Actual Finish |
|----|-----------|----------------|------------|--------------|-------------|---------------|
| 7  | Task G    | Lee            | 10/5       | 10/5         | 10/12       |               |
| 8  | Task H    | Chris          | 10/8       |              | 10/14       |               |
| 12 | Task I    | Lee            | 10/17      |              | 10/25       |               |
| 15 | Task O    | Lee            | 10/20      |              | 11/2        |               |
| 22 | Task V    | Chris          | 10/25      |              | 11/7        |               |

The OTR acts as an agenda for progress reporting and near-term planning.
The OTR includes tasks that are incomplete but scheduled for completion and tasks in the next two reporting periods.

of the project plan listing any tasks that should have been completed but weren't, plus the tasks scheduled for the next two reporting periods.[1] (A *reporting period* is defined as the period between status meetings. If you have a status meeting every week, then a reporting period is one week.)

- Include the part-time team members who have been working on project tasks or who will be working on them during the next two reporting periods.

- Use the meeting to disseminate decisions made by management or customers. Be sure to pass on any positive feedback from these stakeholders.

- Using the open task report, find the status of every task that should have been started or completed since the last status meeting.

- Take advantage of the fact that the entire team is available to consider what action needs to be taken on any problems. If special action needs to be taken, be sure that you *write it down*. Either add a task to the project plan or an action to the issues log. Every action should have a due date and a person responsible for its completion. (An Issues Log is explained in Chapter 15.)

- Don't try to solve problems that are too big for the meeting or that don't include everyone present. If a problem takes more than five minutes to resolve, assign it as an action item.

- Review the readiness for future tasks on the OTR. Are the right people assigned? Are there any known obstacles to performing the tasks as planned?

- Review the issues log and the risk log. Are the issues and risks being resolved, or do they need to be escalated to higher management? (Read about issues in Chapter 15 and risks in Chapter 7.)

When team members participate in managing the project, they are more likely to take responsibility for its success. This participation changes the project manager from an enforcer to an enabler, and the team from individual performers to team members. If a member is behind on his or her work, peer pressure is more effective at boosting this individual's output than management pressure. A project manager at one software company takes it one step further: "We rotate leadership of the weekly status meeting. Everyone has a sense of ownership over the project."

### Face-to-Face Meetings Add Value

As collaboration and communication technology advance and team members are increasingly not working side by side, it may seem old-fashioned to bring people together around a conference table every week. Indeed, it becomes easier every day to share information, so why fight busy schedules and insist on a face-to-face discussion? Don't be fooled: Humans are complex animals, and communication happens in many ways. For example, reluctant bearers of bad news may first use their body language to report their feelings; a discouraged demeanor by several team members should be a signal for the project manager to probe deeper. In addition, problem solving and team building become more natural when people can look each other in the eye or slap each other on the back.

### Long-Distance Status Meetings Benefit from Formality

Project teams that are geographically dispersed don't get the benefit of informal communication of the kind that happens in the break room or hallway. Conference calls and videoconferencing bring people together, but they need an additional level of formality to make sure all the issues are raised and everyone is heard. The open task report provides the structure for keeping all parties on track and ensuring that all the details are discussed.

### Use the Fast Foundation in Project Management Templates

By going to www.VersatileCompany.com, you'll find some basic downloadable templates for planning a meeting and reporting status. In addition, you could use the basic action plan found at the end of Chapter 9 for communication on small projects.

# Stellar Performer: Lockheed Martin Aeronautics
## Communication on an International Team

Lockheed Martin Aeronautics, one of five core business areas of Lockheed Martin, is a global leader in the design, manufacture and support of military aircraft with a stated goal to provide a full spectrum of aeronautical resources to allow the U.S. and its allies to conduct air operations anywhere, any time.

Lockheed Martin Aeronautics produces the tri-variant F-35, which represents the pinnacle of more than 50 years of fighter development technology. Designed to dominate the skies, the F-35 combines the 5th Generation characteristics of radar evading stealth, supersonic speed and extreme agility with the most powerful and comprehensive integrated sensor package of any fighter aircraft in history. The F-35 family includes three variants – the F-35A conventional takeoff and landing (CTOL) variant, the F-35B short takeoff/vertical landing (STOVL) variant with a Rolls-Royce patented shaft-driven LiftFan® propulsion system and an engine that can swivel 90 degrees, and the F-35C carrier variant (CV) with a broad wingspan, arresting hook and ruggedized structures. Along with United States Air Force, Marine Corps and Navy, eight other international allies have partnered with the U.S. Government and Lockheed Martin to support development and eventually utilize the F-35 for their services. The noted allies include, the United Kingdom, Norway, The Netherlands, Denmark, Canada, Australia, Italy and Turkey.

### Continuous Innovation

Although Lockheed Martin's F-35 is now in production, the aircraft continues to generate opportunities for innovative projects to support evolving requirements, technology advancements, and new customer pursuits. Though the three variants provide a spectrum of landing options, some customers have other landing challenges which require a capability not originally designed into the aircraft. Northern countries such as Norway and The Netherlands as well as Canada have short runways with potential for icy conditions. A drag chute capability is being introduced for more stopping control than can be provided by standard aircraft brakes to aide in landing an F-35.

### International Cross-Functional Team Assembled

When Lockheed Martin was awarded the contract to design and develop a drag chute for Norway, a large, international geographically dispersed project team formed to take on the challenging task. Team members included the F-35 Joint Program Office technical team in Crystal City, VA; a F-35 Joint Program Office program manager based in Seattle, WA with his technical team located in Arlington, VA,.; BAE Systems in Salmesbury, UK, the production site of the F-35 aft fuselage; and the wing and final assembly and integration teams in Fort Worth, TX. Software development will also add Northrop Grumman in El Segundo, California. The Field and Training elements add Lockheed Martin Mission Systems and Training in Orlando, FL. Suku Kurien, a Lockheed Martin Senior Manager was selected to manage the drag chute program, partly due to his diverse background from years of rotational assignment across various business functions which broadened his understanding of developing new aircraft and new capabilities.

## A PROGRAM MANAGER COMMITTED TO DISCIPLINED PROJECT MANAGEMENT

Suku Kurien's experience across many programs has made him a believer in the value of project management. He consciously seeks out and engages stakeholders, invests in detailed requirements and schedules, and fosters communication across this international team.

Kurien's experience in sustainment, supply chain management, engineering, change management, and production has proved valuable in the management of project stakeholders. Kurien has been able to leverage his experience to gain greater acceptance from the cross-functional, cross-continent team by demonstrating a thorough understanding of the organizations which support the project. He also has built rapport and gained cooperation by involving teams in making decisions and is able to suggest options and approaches from his own background to help speed the project along. This is especially helpful to those stakeholders new to the program or new to their role within the project. Rather than directing stakeholders on how to best meet the needs of the project, Suku prefers to act in a mentoring and collaborative manner, which fosters stakeholders to be more engaged and empowered to make decisions. As a result, stakeholders are motivated to pursue quality solutions and support all needs of the project.

### Results Rest on Disciplined Fundamentals

The F-35 Norway Drag Chute team achieved a major milestone recently during the Critical Design Review (CDR), when the F-35 Joint Program Office and Norway customers agreed that Lockheed Martin is on track to meet design requirements. The team also successfully overcame the biggest technical challenge for the program: developing an aerodynamically clean pod to house the drag chute. The pod resembles a bump on the upper surface between the two vertical tails, which must not degrade the F-35's stealth capabilities and aerodynamics. The CDR is required for the customer to authorize manufacturing the initial development units for the drag chute system. Once manufactured and assembled, the drag chute will be ready for a ground test and flight test at Edwards Air Force Base, Calif. and additional testing in Alaska.

The project's success thus far can be attributed, in large part to Kurien's adherence to project management fundamentals. However, at the beginning of the project, the detailed, resource-loaded schedule was missing and stakeholders and customers had not agreed on requirements. Kurien made it a priority to establish the schedule and directed Lockheed Martin engineering to coordinate with their technical customer counterparts to complete the requirements.

Another important project management fundamental is to establish a positive relationship with the customer. For military aircraft development projects, the customer is usually actively involved to ensure expectations from a technical and schedule perspective are clear. Extra up-front effort was spent to help the entire team become more cohesive, internally and externally. A vision was provided to highlight the path forward and establish a solid foundation. Cooperation was enhanced when all stakeholders held a common understanding of the project elements as a whole. These efforts reduced misinterpretation of requirements and avoided the misalignment of customer feedback with Program Manager expectations that can be particularly detrimental to a team spread around the globe.

Also contributing to the teams' cohesiveness is the understanding that Kurien uses project management practices as intended, not to "go through the motions" according to procedure. Kurien emphasizes that when predictable aspects of project are under control, the team can better handle the inevitable unpredictable events, in order to achieve project commitments defined in the plan.

### Technology and Values Combine to Foster Trust and Cooperation

Above all, the best way to build trust and improve cooperation is through active and timely communication. Kurien holds periodic all-hands meetings with his internal development team, technical interchange meetings and weekly team leadership meetings including with the customer, and impromptu meetings whenever necessary. With Kurien's open door policy, impromptu meetings may also be called by his stakeholders from any of the global locations to share or resolve issues. Kurien notes that success to any project is regular, open communication via face-to-face or teleconferences on a tempo that supports timely engagement to address challenges.

Virtual collaboration with all international and widespread domestic team members is a necessity to keep the project on track. Kurien has become accustomed to be flexible in scheduling meetings and video conferences early into the morning when needed to accommodate European time zones. Customer reviews are easier even though there is a one hour time difference for some and a two hour time difference for others located around the United States. All applicable program and technical information is exchanged on a secure internal website.

### Project Management is a Platform for Enduring Customer Relationships

"The drag chute system is the first new capability to be contracted for the F-35 by one of the original eight international partners," notes Kurien. Lockheed Martin has partnered with Norway on a variety of global security programs for more than 30 years. With the disciplined use of project management tools to execute the drag chute program objectives, this relationship will continue to be strengthened for the long term.

## CLOSEOUT REPORTING

The most neglected project management activity is closing out the project. The reporting and accounting tasks associated with the closeout just aren't as exciting as developing the product, and on many projects they are completely ignored. This is unfortunate, because these activities can bring a very high return to the project manager's firm. A simple, downloadable project closure form is found on the Versatile Company website.

The end of a project may coincide with delivery of a final product or may simply be the end of a product development phase. In either case, the deliverables from project closeout serve two purposes: They finalize the project in the eyes of the stakeholders, and they present a learning opportunity. The customer's formal acceptance of the product, the reconciling of project accounts, closing out the change logs and issues logs—all these things bring the project to crisp completion. In addition, producing a lessons-learned report and organizing the project documentation present opportunities for process improvement or, in the case of the project manager, personal improvement.

The real proof that the project is finished comes from the customer. Formal acceptance of the finished product, or acknowledgment of phase completion, signifies that the work is complete. The project manager must plan for customer acceptance from the beginning. You need to be clear what form it will take and the work required to get it. The acceptance process may be lengthy, including extensive testing and evaluation that begin long before the final signature is given. To ensure that it goes smoothly, the customer's acceptance process should be on your work breakdown structure and in the project plan.

Some closeout activities may be classified as *transition tasks*. These include:

- Notifying all project participants of the new status of a project and whom to contact in the future. This is accomplished with a *project turnover memo*.

- Giving product improvement ideas that weren't used on the project to the team supporting the product. Some good ideas become even better when implemented in subsequent versions.

- Detailing any open tasks or unresolved issues by means of an updated project plan. Pass this on to the person taking responsibility for the next phase, and you'll make his or her job easier.

Finally, take the opportunity for organizational and personal improvement. Poll project participants—team, customers, vendors, management—on the effectiveness of the project management process. What was done well? What should be done differently next time? How could you improve communication, estimating, risk management, or change control?

When you document the results, be sure to both distribute them and store a copy where it can easily be found when you start your next project.

### END POINT

It's no mystery that good communication is cited as a factor common to all successful projects. When people work together to accomplish a unique goal, they need to coordinate their activities, agree on responsibilities, and reevaluate the cost-schedule-quality equilibrium. Put the project on a strong foundation by consciously setting up the mechanisms that enable communication, such as regular meetings, reports, and a plan for change management. The Control Checklist found on the website is an aid for keeping track of the many responsibilities of a project manager.

Along with the structures to enable communication, a project manager needs strong communication skills. Negotiating, listening, conflict resolution, writing, and many more skills affect our ability to work with the many people we encounter on every project. Even though these skills are not specifically addressed in this book (because they are not unique to project management), they are essential skills for project managers.

## FAST FOUNDATION IN PROJECT MANAGEMENT

Communication is the core of a project manager's role. The downloadable templates and checklists described below add to your toolbox for proactively engaging your team, management, customers and other stakeholders.

1. The *kickoff checklist* is a guide for putting all the pieces in place as you put the project in motion.

2. Effective communication is no accident. Use the *communication planning matrix* to identify who needs what information and how you'll be sure to get it to them. Remember that having more mediums of communication increases the likelihood your message will get through. See an example of this form in Table 14.1.

3. Use the *task assignment* to make sure each team member clearly understands his or her responsibility.

4. The *meeting agenda* is structured to help you prepare for a meeting and take useful meeting minutes.

5. A *status report* for your management should be brief and focused to help the audience read it quickly and identify any necessary action. This template will get you started.

6. Evaluate your project and your project management style with the *control checklist* on a regular basis. These are the activities that keep the project on track from beginning to end.

7. When the project is finished, the *project closure report* summarizes the outcome of the project and compares the original goal with what actually happened.

See examples of these forms on page 490. Download them at www .versatilecompany.com/FFMBAinPM. Use these documents as the foundation of your own project management standards.

## PMP Exam Prep Questions

1. All of the following interpersonal or soft skills are applicable to managing stakeholder engagement except . . .

   a. Building trust

   b. Minimizing conflict

   c. Active listening

   d. Overcoming resistance to change

2. The project to upgrade the accounting software in consideration of upcoming tax law changes is underway. The project manager is working with the chief information officer (CIO) and chief financial officer (CFO) to ensure regulatory compliance and requirements alignment. Where will these two stakeholders most likely fit in a power/interest grid?

   a. High power/low interest

   b. Low power/low interest

   c. High power/high interest

   d. Low power/high interest

3. An activity performed by the project manager on a daily basis is communicating with individual team members, the team, company personnel, vendors, and customers. What is the approximate percentage of the project manager's time dedicated to communicating?

   a. 100%

   b. At least 50%

   c. Not more than 70%

   d. Approximately 90%

4. The expansion project requires extensive communication with stakeholders. On what will the project manager rely to determine what information should be communicated and who should receive the communications?

   a. Communications technology, models, and methods

   b. Communications requirements analysis

   c. Communications management plan

   d. Stakeholder management strategy

Answers to these questions can be found at www.versatilecompany .com/FFMBAinPM.

# 15

# Control Scope to Deliver Value

## INTRODUCTION

Every kind of project faces changes. During a kitchen remodel, the customers might change their minds about appliances, or a certain type of window might be unavailable. During a software development project, the competition might release a product with some exciting new features, forcing the development team to add these features as well.

The big question for a project team is: How do these changes affect the value of the project? After all, a recurring theme is that successful projects deliver business value. The original equilibrium of cost, schedule, and quality defined at the beginning of the project was valuable—but how much can we change that before it is out of equilibrium and not worth the time and expense?

Let's look at what can happen when such a breakdown occurs. Dirk, a project manager for a consulting firm, tells this story:

> *We were assisting one of the biggest pharmaceutical companies in the United States with FDA approval for a new production facility they were building. Like most of our projects, the client requested a lot of changes as we proceeded. I followed the normal change control process outlined in our contract, getting the client project manager to sign off on any changes that would cause a cost or schedule variance with the original bid. Although the changes caused a 50 percent increase over the original budget, the client approved each one, and I thought I was doing my job right.*

*When we finished the project and sent the bill for the changes, our customer's president saw it and went ballistic. He came down to my office and chewed me out. He'd never heard of any changes to the original bid, and he sure didn't expect a 50 percent cost overrun. The president of my company flew out to meet with the customer's president. I spent two weeks putting together all the documentation to support our billing, including the signed change orders. We did get paid, but you can bet I didn't get an apology from their president. And we didn't bill them for the two weeks I spent justifying the bill.*

*I made the mistake of assuming the client's project manager was passing on the cost overrun information to his superiors. I don't make that mistake any more.*

This story illustrates the danger of incremental cost and schedule changes.

*Agreement on project goals*, is one of our success factors. So is *controlled scope*.

This chapter presents the guidelines and processes for making sure that the inevitable changes don't become a source of conflict, confusion, or failure while keeping all the key stakeholders aware of the most current expectations about cost, schedule, and quality – the value equation. The two primary points of focus are change control and configuration management.

 **THE CHANGE CONTROL PROCESS**

A project manager building a 90-mile gas pipeline meets every day with a customer counterpart to review the changes to scope that occurred that day. Once a week, the project manager is joined by his boss on a conference call with the customer's top management to discuss the impact of these changes on the budget and schedule. This process keeps everyone aware and synchronized on the facts. Whether it is the right process for your project is something for your team and customer to decide.

The specific change control process you follow should fit the size and complexity of your project; you will need to pay special attention to the number and diversity of your stakeholders. But every change process is based on the same fundamental model shown in Figure 15.1. Downloadable forms for requesting a change and tracking changes throughout the project can be found online.

There are two parts to the change control process: the steps leading up to the initial approval of a product and the process for controlling changes to that product. As Figure 15.1 shows, once the stakeholders

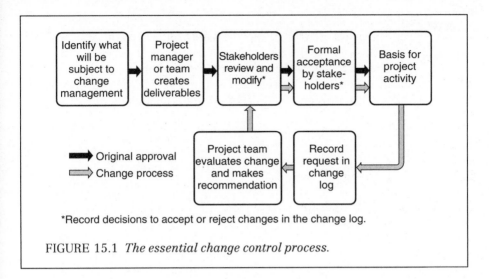

FIGURE 15.1 *The essential change control process.*

accept a product, it becomes controlled and any subsequent changes must pass through the change control process.

Change control planning—establishing how the process of change will take place—occurs during the project definition stage. You will need to select the members of the change board and decide how often meetings will be held. The intermediate products that will be subject to change control need to be identified and a configuration management structure created. (*Configuration management* means controlling the different versions of the product. It is explained later in this chapter.)

Figure 15.1 describes the eight basic components common to every change control process:

1. *Identification of deliverables.* Identify all the project deliverables that will be subject to change control. The list will include everything that all stakeholders must approve, including requirements descriptions, design documents, and, of course, the statement of work.

2. *Creation of the intermediate deliverables.* The project manager and team develop these intermediate deliverables as they execute the project. As each of these deliverables is created, it becomes a candidate for stakeholder approval.

3. *Stakeholder evaluation/modification.* Once the product is created, various stakeholders will evaluate it and may request modifications. This step, along with continued development of the product, is repeated until the appropriate stakeholders are satisfied with the documents.

4. *Formal acceptance.* Stakeholders formally accept the product, producing a record of who approved the product and the approval date. At this point, the record becomes a control document; it is now a basis for action, and project team members will begin to execute the decisions represented by the product. These approved products are now subject to configuration management.

5. *The recording of change requests.* As ideas for change come in from the stakeholders, a designated team member records all change requests in a change log, noting their source, the date, and a description of the change. Each change request will have a unique identifier, usually a number, so that it can be tracked and referenced.

6. *Evaluation of requests and recommendation.* On a regular basis, the project manager or a designated team member will evaluate all potential changes for their impact on cost, schedule, and product quality and make a recommendation to accept or reject the change. Both the evaluation and the recommendation are recorded in the change log.

7. *Ongoing stakeholder evaluation/modification.* Stakeholders consider the proposed change to the control documents and the recommendation from the project manager. There are three possible outcomes to this evaluation: (1) the change is accepted as recommended or with minor modifications; (2) if the request has merit, but the decision-maker(s) need(s) additional information, the request may be sent back to the project team with specific questions (this step may be repeated until the request is accepted or denied); (3) the request is denied and the reasons for denial are recorded in the change log. No matter what the outcome, the status of the request is updated in the change log and the originator is notified of the result.

8. *Formal acceptance.* When stakeholders formally accept the change, this acceptance will be recorded in the change log, including who approved the change, the date of the approval, and the impact. The change may also produce an update to the project plan in the form of added, changed, or deleted activities. If the change affects a control document, the document is updated and the new version becomes the basis for action.

## Control Documents

In Chapter 6, we described intermediate deliverables as essential products produced during the project that may not be part of the final product. These intermediate products vary from industry to industry—software development requires a list of product functions and features, while residential construction requires a list of the carpets, kitchen appliances, and other materials selected by the homeowner. Design documents such as blueprints are another example. Intermediate products such as these are both a record of decisions and a basis for action. Plumbers, electricians, and carpenters, for instance, carry out the engineering decisions represented on a blueprint. Therefore, it is critical that these documents be kept accurate and up-to-date, because they represent the series of decisions that lead up to the final product. They are called *control documents* because they are tools to maintain control over the product and project.

## Change Thresholds and Change Boards

While everyone admits the value of change control, we also want to avoid any drag it might add to decision making. Including all stakeholders in every decision just isn't necessary. Therefore, to balance the need for change control against the desire for flexibility and quick decisions, the project manager needs to separate changes into different categories, depending on how deeply they affect the project. These categories, called change thresholds, are as follows:

- The lowest threshold is for changes that the project team can approve. These changes typically don't affect the cost, the project schedule, or the way in which the customer will use the product. However, they can include design changes that make the product work better or last longer. Even though the team or project manager has the authority to approve these changes, they will still need to be documented.

- The second threshold, which involves changes that *will* affect cost, schedule, or functionality, requires more formal approval. This is the domain of the *change board.* Change boards meet on a regularly scheduled basis and consist of people representing the views of all stakeholders.

- Even though a change board may be authorized to approve cost and schedule changes, it is usually for a limited amount only. Above that designated amount, higher-level executives from the customer and project organizations must be involved. This is because these changes are usually large enough to threaten the business case for the project, fundamentally altering its profitability and market value.

Let's look more closely at the four categories making up a change board:

1. *Representatives from the project team.* These representatives offer the most expertise on the proposed change to the product

and its effect on cost, schedule, and functionality. Although the project manager often plays this role, it is also appropriate for other team members to represent the project team.

2. *The customer's representative.* This board member must not only approve changes to the cost and schedule, but must also understand how the change affects the product's usefulness.

3. *Representatives from groups with related products.* For instance, the change board for a redesign of a truck fender may include engineers responsible for other parts of the truck's cab. They will want to identify any changes that might alter the way their parts work.

4. *Representatives from functional management.* Management participates on change boards to represent company policy. If the project team for the fender redesign should recommend a change that would result in using a new vendor, the company's procurement representatives would have a say in this decision.

The larger the project, the more change control thresholds will exist—along with more change boards. Large programs have change boards operating at many levels. While this adds complexity, it is an appropriate strategy for controlling project decisions and pushing decision-making authority down as far as possible.

### Issues Are Problems We Haven't Resolved

Projects are regularly confronted with unexpected problems. When these problems aren't easily resolved, they begin to threaten cost, schedule, and quality goals. We call these unresolved problems *issues*.

As the number of issues grow, the potential is to lose track of these problems, causing their impact to grow worse. Issue management is the process of recording issues as they arise and systematically confronting the issue until it no longer poses a threat to the project.

The issue log in Table 15.1 looks surprisingly like a risk log. The process for managing risks and issues is very similar.

As problems arise that the project manager or team cannot resolve, the problem is added to the issue log. Someone is assigned to "own" the issue, meaning that person is responsible for resolving the problem. Issues have varying urgency and impacts on the project, so as the issue is recorded the size of the impact and the "resolve by" date help explain the seriousness of the problem. The impact and urgency contribute to the issue's priority, which is typically categorized as high, medium, or low.

---

**TABLE 15.1    Issues Log**

---

An issue is a problem or obstacle the project team doesn't have the power to resolve. Every issue is recorded and tracked with some basic information:

*Issue ID*—Unique identifier, probably a number, assigned as each issue is identified.

*Priority*—Typically a code for High, Medium, or Low indicates the severity and urgency.

*Status*—An issue is either open or closed. Keeping closed issues in the log is one form of project history.

*Description*—What is the issue and what is the impact if it is not resolved?

*Assigned to*—The project team member (or project manager) responsible for pursuing resolution.

*Date identified*—Date the issue was originally added to the log.

*Due date*—Resolve the issue by this date or the impact grows.

*Last action/current status*—The date of the last action, a description of the action, and the current status of the issue. Leave all the action/status lines in the log as a record of how the action was pursued.

---

A key difference between risks and issues is that risks are problems that might occur, while issues are problems that exist. In other words, the probability of an issue is 100 percent.

Monitor the issues log on a regular basis, such as at every project team status meeting. Ideally, the person responsible will be able to report back that a solution was identified and implemented and that the issue can be closed. However, if the problem is large enough, the proposed solution is expensive, it may exceed the authority of the team, requiring approval from the change board. Tough issues can also be escalated up the management chain, where the sponsor or another person with greater authority can solve the problem.

The issue log is a relatively simple tool. The power comes from regularly monitoring issues and escalating them quickly when the team can't find an answer.

### Vigilance and Discipline Make the Difference

**TIP**

Stakeholders make decisions throughout the project. They choose the size, speed, color, and strength of the product. They agree on the cost-schedule-quality equilibrium. They divide the work and accept responsibilities. But the fastest way for a project to degenerate into a confusing mass of expensive rework is to allow these decisions to be changed randomly and without record. The formal change control process guards against this anarchy of sudden decision changes. Even though it adds bureaucracy and overhead to the project, it remains one of the project manager's strongest tools, both for self-preservation and for managing expectations.

Every member of a project team can be vigilant for the individual changes that accumulate into higher budgets or extended schedules. The habit of being aware of changes and passing them to the project manager can be fostered in a team.

**KEY CONCEPT**

## CONFIGURATION MANAGEMENT

When the fifth revision is made to the blueprints, the electricians and plumbers may still be working from the third version, and the roofers from the first version. At this point, someone is bound to notice that the chimney and the fireplace are on different sides of the house. Configuration management prevents disasters like these by limiting the changes to control documents and other project deliverables. It is a subset of change control, which focuses specifically on how to implement approved changes. It keeps everyone in a project reading from the same sheet of music.

### What Products Are Subject to Configuration Management?

It is unlikely that a driveway or building foundation, once completed, will be lost or a second one will be mistakenly installed. But when products are less tangible, these kinds of mistakes are more likely to happen. The items that should be subject to configuration management come from a wide variety of sources (and many are every bit as tangible as a driveway). So what should be subject to configuration management? The answer is: any product that might have multiple versions during the project. This list includes many possible candidates.

- Control documents are obvious candidates for configuration management because they are the basis for project action.
- Any products produced by computer and stored on electronic files, including computer programs, word processing documents, drawings, and so on, are candidates.
- Prototypes or product mock-ups may be revised and upgraded many times during a project.
- Test environments are set up to simulate real-life product behavior. These can be costly to create and might lead to incorrect test results if changes were randomly introduced.

### How Is Configuration Management Accomplished?

Configuration management is practiced most robustly in the manufacturing of complex products, such as automobiles and aircraft. Each revision or upgrade to a component of the product is formally controlled by the product's configuration management process. The fundamental process for configuration management is the same at any level of complexity: Identify the items that will be controlled, set up the control structure, and assign responsibility for control. Let's look at the steps involved in this process.

### Step One: Identify Items/Products

There are two sets of items to control: the end products and the intermediate deliverables. Both types of products need to be identified by using the work breakdown structure. (As we mentioned earlier, the control documents are obvious candidates for configuration management.)

### Step Two: Establish the Control Structure

A number of questions must be answered in order to design the configuration management structure.

- How will access to the controlled item be restricted? If an engineering drawing is stored electronically on a computer file or on paper in a filing cabinet, how will you control who can update it?

- Do you need a record of the changes? At the end of the project, will it be useful to compare the first approved version of a design document to the final version? Will it be valuable to know not only the changes made along the way, but also the reasons for the changes? If the answer is yes, the next question is, how much are you willing to spend? If you need a record of the changes, the change log might be sufficient—or you may need a log for every controlled item. If, on the other hand, you don't need a record of the changes, or if the final product is the only one that matters, this will simplify your control structures (because each outdated version can be discarded or deleted).

- How will everyone know if they have the most recent version? This can be accomplished with version numbers or revision dates in electronic documents and files. Tangible products will require labels.

### Step Three: Assign Configuration Management Responsibility

Somebody, preferably not the project manager, needs to be responsible for implementing and administering the structure. This is an administrative chore that doesn't require the project manager's authority or broad knowledge of the project; it can be accomplished effectively by team members. Everyone on the team needs to respect the controls and follow the rules, but unless the responsibility is specifically assigned, the controls may not be fully implemented or their value fully realized.

### CHANGE CONTROL IS ESSENTIAL FOR MANAGING EXPECTATIONS

While you are carrying out all these change control activities, don't forget that the ultimate goal of change control is to maintain realistic expectations. Too often, the project manager and customer will sign off on every $1,000 change, never considering that all the changes together are adding $100,000 to the project. Change control is more than recording the cost-schedule-quality impact of each potential change; its purpose is to keep the overall cost-schedule-quality equilibrium realistic and desirable.

### END POINT

Clear goals and controlled scope are two of our project success factors. It's easy to understand that keeping track of changes is important and even easier to understand that there will be changes throughout the project.

Change control is the process of monitoring changes to specifications and scope and ensuring that these changes and their associated cost and schedule impacts are understood before they are approved.

Configuration management means keeping track of the decisions and deliverables created during the project. If we allow a change to a specification, it is equally important to communicate that change.

The best project managers pay special attention to developing these processes and habits. For change control and configuration management, success is in the details.

### FAST FOUNDATION IN PROJECT MANAGEMENT

Controlling changes to scope, schedule and cost should be a systematic process. The *change log* and *change request* provide structure to keep track of the many proposed and accepted changes on the project. The Issues Log creates a simple, structured method for keeping an eye on all known problems that have not been resolved.

These templates are available for download at www.versatile company.com/FFMBAinPM. Use these documents as the foundation of your own project management standards.

## PMP Exam Prep Questions

1. The project to roll out tablets for use in a 500-bed hospital is going well, except for a minor problem in the MRI area, where the wireless access isn't working as expected. What documentation should be used to track and manage this problem?

   a. Stakeholder register

   b. Stakeholder management plan

   c. Issue log

   d. Charter

2. The customer has requested a five-week delay on the project while they rebuild a warehouse used for manufacturing a key piece of the project. This delay wasn't planned, but the project couldn't continue without it. The company is limited on available resources. This delay will be best shown in what?

   a. Network diagram

   b. Responsibility assignment matrix

   c. Work breakdown structure (WBS)

   d. Budget

3. Which of the following statements regarding issues and risks is most correct?

   a. Issues and risks are the same

   b. Issues and risks can be the same

   c. Issues and risks are different and should be managed accordingly

   d. Issues and risks are the same, but should be managed differently

Answers to these questions can be found at www.VersatileCompany.com/FFMBAinPM.

# 16

# Measuring Progress

## INTRODUCTION

True or false? It becomes increasingly important to track progress as the deadline nears to see how close the project will be to finishing on time and on budget.

False! This is a pretty easy question to answer if you've read the previous chapters. By the end of the project it doesn't matter how close you are because you have almost no ability to change your cost and schedule performance. The key to *finishing* on time and on budget is to *start out* that way and stay on track throughout the project.

When projects start with challenging schedules, if they fall behind, even by a little, they spend the rest of the project trying to catch up. Other projects, however, seem to have a self-correcting process built into them; if they fall behind a little, the problem is quickly identified and dealt with immediately. The best project managers find problems early and solve them without overtime. They make the project look easy.

Progress measurements are the tools we use to identify problems when they are small—when there is still time to catch up. Since cost and schedule progress comprise two-thirds of the cost-schedule-quality equilibrium, they are the primary focus of progress measurement.

 **MEASURING SCHEDULE PERFORMANCE**

Each work package in the plan is a measurable unit of progress. Each has start and finish dates. The smaller the work packages, the more progress points you can refer to, and therefore the more accurate your schedule progress will be. (Work package size guidelines are covered in Chapter 8.) The following story highlights the importance of breaking down a project into small, measurable units.

A software project manager responsible for a major release of a flagship product was trying to ascertain the schedule status. Several of the development managers had broken their work down into only a few tasks that were six months long. All were reporting that they were "on schedule" four and a half months into their work. The project manager's gut feeling was that the developers really had no idea where they were. She also felt that they were not likely to recognize a schedule problem for at least three more weeks—and that they wouldn't admit to it even at that point. To find the truth, she sat down with each development manager and said, "We've got six weeks until your deadline. Can you give me a week-by-week description of the work you have left to do?" During these meetings, three of the four managers had to admit they were dangerously behind schedule. Although they were 75 percent through the project schedule, the managers were able to finish their portion on time by turning all their developers onto this project.

This near-disaster illustrates the importance of questioning schedule status when the work is not broken down into small, detailed tasks. The primary tool for illustrating a schedule is also good for displaying schedule status. Figure 16.1 is a Gantt chart showing schedule progress.

Notice that the focus here is on *displaying* schedule status. You will use project status meetings, as described in Chapter 14, for capturing actual task completion status. The real truth about schedule status is often elusive because it is hard to pin down what proportion of a project is really complete. The following tips are commonsense ways to get the most accurate picture possible of a project's progress.

### Use the 0-50-100 Rule

A project manager should always be suspicious of work package status that is reported in detailed increments, such as 12 percent, 35 percent, or 87 percent, unless there is empirical basis for this amount of detail. When possible, use the 0-50-100 rule for recording schedule completion of tasks that span no more than two reporting periods.

- 0 percent complete: The task has not begun.
- 50 percent complete: The task has been started but not finished.
- 100 percent complete: The task is complete.

Using this method, as long as the work packages are small, no task will have 50 percent completion for two status meetings in a row (because the maximum time to complete each task is no more than two reporting periods).

### Take Completion Criteria Seriously

Every work package is supposed to have completion criteria (see Chapter 8) and should not be considered 100 percent complete until it

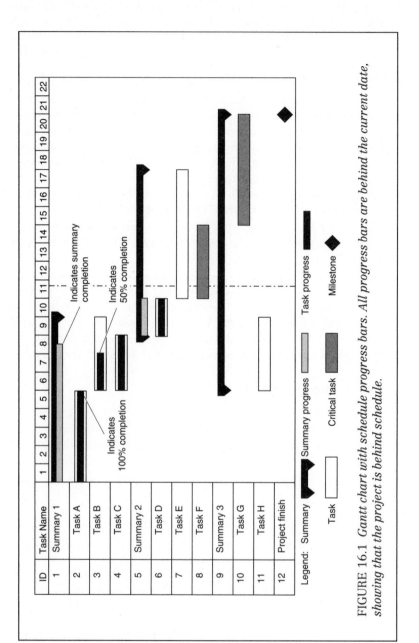

FIGURE 16.1 *Gantt chart with schedule progress bars. All progress bars are behind the current date, showing that the project is behind schedule.*

meets these criteria. You need to be rigid about this—if tasks are consistently allowed to register as complete before all the final details are taken care of, the project might fall far behind, even though the official status reports it as being on schedule.

### Schedule Performance Measures Accomplishment

Schedule completion measures accomplishment, not effort expended. Just because you've used up 50 percent of your labor budget doesn't mean you've accomplished 50 percent of the project. Schedule status is a measure of whether you've accomplished as much to date as you had planned to.

### The Dangers of Management by Exception

Management by exception is a seductive method for keeping the project on schedule that, in many cases, can actually increase schedule problems. Management by exception focuses on keeping critical path tasks on schedule while ignoring noncritical tasks that fall behind their scheduled start or end dates. Although it may be true that tasks that have float can continue to be delayed until they run out of float and become critical, these delays can lead to a resource crisis at the end of the project—which is the worst time to try to accomplish extra work. The people poured onto the project at the end will have had little or no experience with the project. In addition, you will have increased your schedule risk, because a late completion of any one of the critical tasks can delay the project finish.

### Measuring Progress When There Are Many Similar Tasks

There is a way to measure schedule progress if your project contains many similar tasks. To begin, consider what these three projects have in common:

1. Driving hundreds of piles into marshy soil to form the foundation for a huge building.
2. Creating thousands of engineering drawings to produce a next-generation fighter aircraft.
3. Converting hundreds of computer programs originally written for one brand of hardware to run on another manufacturer's hardware.

In each case, the portion of the total number of piles, engineering drawings, or computer programs completed can produce a useful schedule status. Figure 16.2 shows an example of a simple graph

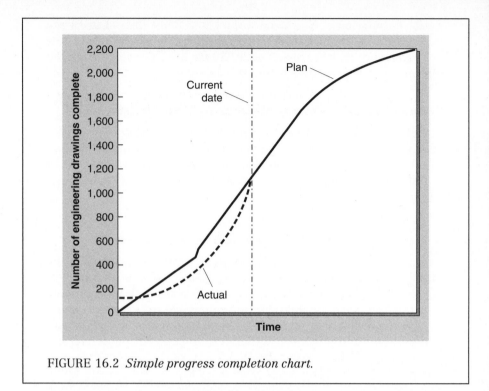

FIGURE 16.2 *Simple progress completion chart.*

that displays this type of status. This graph can be generated by simple spreadsheet programs or project management software. These graphs can be extremely useful, but they can be misleading because they don't differentiate between easy and difficult tasks. For example, if all the easy piles were driven first, or if all the easy drawings were created first, the projects might initially show progress ahead of schedule, only to fall behind later when the time comes to handle the difficult piles and drawings.

## MEASURING COST PERFORMANCE

**CONCEPT**    Measuring costs accurately is critical as a project progresses because cost measures productivity. Every work package has cost estimates for labor, equipment, and materials. As each one is executed, be sure to capture the actual costs; comparing planned and actual costs will tell you whether the project is progressing as planned (see Table 16.1).

### How to Gain Cooperation in Reporting Labor Hours

If project management is new to your firm, you may encounter plenty of resistance to tracking actual labor hours on tasks. Engineers,

### TABLE 16.1 Track Actual Costs for Each Work Package

| Task Name | Planned | | | Actual | | |
|---|---|---|---|---|---|---|
| | Labor | Equipment | Materials | Labor | Equipment | Materials |
| Task n | 40 hrs. | $1,000 | $1,500 | 50 hrs. | $1,200 | $1,500 |
| Task p | 30 hrs. | $200 | $100 | 25 hrs. | $200 | $150 |
| Task r | 60 hrs. | $0 | $0 | 55 hrs. | $0 | $0 |

programmers, scientists, and other knowledge workers often complain bitterly about the lost productive hours they must spend each week just writing down their labor for specific tasks (even though experience has shown that this rarely takes more than five minutes a day). Here are two approaches for overcoming their resistance. These methods concentrate on winning their cooperation rather than forcing their compliance:

1. Point out that there is a legitimate need to track actual labor hours. Being able to compare planned and actual labor provides early warning on cost problems—and will improve estimates on future projects. Help them to understand that they will benefit from both of these factors.

2. Make it easy for them to report by using the largest increments possible for reporting actual hours. For instance, a department in a software company that was introducing project management chose to estimate and report labor in increments of five hours. As long as the work packages were kept small, it was easy to report actual labor at every project status meeting. This might not have been quite as accurate as planning and reporting in hourly increments, but it was a great leap forward compared to what they did before (which was nothing).

### Problems Associated with Graphing Cost Performance

⬦ DANGER!

Graphing cost performance usually compares the projected expense over time to actual expenses (see Figure 16.3). That's useful information, but this kind of graph has some potential drawbacks:

- *The rate at which money is being spent doesn't indicate whether the work is getting done.* For example, the project in Figure 16.3

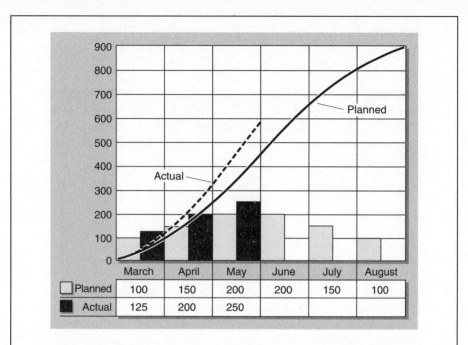

| | March | April | May | June | July | August |
|---|---|---|---|---|---|---|
| ☐ Planned | 100 | 150 | 200 | 200 | 150 | 100 |
| ■ Actual | 125 | 200 | 250 | | | |

FIGURE 16.3 *Planned versus actual cost over time. During the first three months, the project spent money faster than forecasted, but that isn't necessarily an indication the project will be over budget—it might be ahead of schedule.*

could show higher-than-planned expenditures because it is ahead of schedule.

- *Accounting lag times can make cost information arrive months late.* This kind of delay means that a project's cost performance might appear to be excellent all the way through the project—but after completion the bills just keep coming in.

## EARNED VALUE REPORTING

Comparing planned cash flow with actual cash flow has its uses, but it doesn't tell you whether the project will be over or under budget. To find the true picture of cost performance, the planned and actual costs for all completed tasks need to be compared. This is accomplished with a technique called *earned value reporting.* Earned value reporting uses cost data to give more accurate cost and schedule reports. It does this by combining cost and schedule status to provide a complete picture of the project. For example, projects can be ahead of

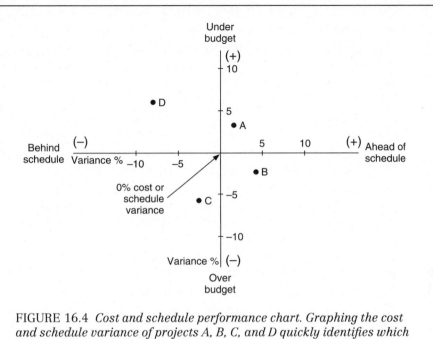

FIGURE 16.4 *Cost and schedule performance chart. Graphing the cost and schedule variance of projects A, B, C, and D quickly identifies which needs the most immediate attention.*

schedule (good), but over budget (bad). Or they can be ahead of schedule (good), and under budget (good). Altogether, there are five possible combinations when you include "on schedule and on budget" (see Figure 16.4). As this diagram shows, project managers who track only cost or only schedule are getting only half the picture and won't really know if their project is in trouble.

## Calculating the Cost Variance Using Earned Value

Tracking cost with earned value introduces some new terms:

- *Planned cost:* The planned (budgeted) cost of any or all tasks.
- *Budgeted cost of work performed (BCWP):* The planned (budgeted) cost of tasks that are complete. This is the actual earned value of the project to date, because it is the value of the work that has been completed. Tasks that are partially complete can claim some BCWP. A $100 task that is 50 percent complete has a BCWP of $50.
- *Actual cost of work performed (ACWP):* The actual cost of tasks that have been completed.

- *Cost variance (CV):* The cost variance is the difference between planned and actual costs for completed work. CV = BCWP – ACWP.

- *Cost variance percent (CV%):* The cost variance divided by the planned cost. A positive CV% is good; it means the work was performed under budget. A negative CV% is bad, because it means the work was over budget. CV% = CV/BCWP.

- *Cost performance index (CPI):* Earned value (BCWP) divided by actual cost (CPI > 1.0 = under budget; CPI < 1.0 = over budget).

- *Budget at completion (BAC):* The budget at the end of the project. This represents the approved budget for the project.

- *Estimate at completion (EAC):* This is a re-estimate of the total project budget. The original budget is multiplied by the ACWP and divided by BCWP. It's a way of saying that if the current cost performance trends continue, the final cost can be predicted.

- *Estimate to complete (ETC):* The budget amount needed to finish the project, based on the current CPI. ETC = EAC – AC.

- *Variance at completion (VAC)* The estimated difference, at the end of the project, between the budget and actual cost of the project. VAC = BAC - EAC.

Figure 16.5 shows an example of using earned value both to measure cost performance to date and to recalculate the budget.

### New Terminology: BCWS = PV, BCWP = EV, ACWP = AC

**DANGER!**

Not long ago, only the U.S. Department of Defense (DoD) used earned value to manage projects. Now the practice has spread to large and small commercial firms as well as the civilian agencies of the federal government. Through increased use, the terminology is beginning to change. Although international standards organizations still promote use of the preceding terms, the Project Management Institute (PMI), based in the United States, recommends substituting the following terms:

- Planned value (PV) *replaces* budgeted cost of work scheduled (BCWS).

- Earned value (EV) *replaces* budgeted cost of work performed (BCWP).

- Actual cost (AC) *replaces* actual cost of work performed (ACWP).

Firms that want to be aligned with PMI terminology and individuals studying for one of PMI's certification exams should take special note of these terms.

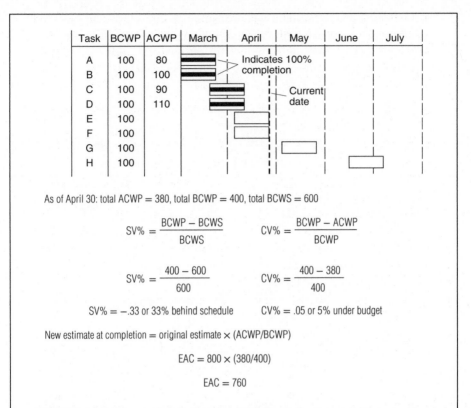

FIGURE 16.5 *Measuring cost and schedule performance with earned value.*

## Use the Cost Variance to Identify Problems Early

**DANGER!** Recalculating the estimated cost at completion using earned value implies the current trends will continue. But be careful not to assume that just because you are over budget now that you will be granted more budget. Instead, the cost variance should be used as a warning flag to help you identify problems early, when there is still time to get back on track.

## Calculating Schedule Variance Using Earned Value

Is the project on schedule? This is a question that all the stakeholders want answered. But it can be difficult to measure the degree to which a project is ahead or behind schedule. What if the majority of tasks are on schedule, but a few are ahead of schedule and others are behind? What is an accurate description of this project's schedule status? In this kind of situation, earned value calculations can help measure schedule variance just as they help in measuring cost variance. Calculating schedule variance uses some of the same concepts as the cost variance calculation. (Substitute PMI terminology here as well). These are:

- *Budgeted cost of work performed (BCWP):* The planned (budgeted) cost of tasks that are complete.

- *Budgeted cost of work scheduled (BCWS):* The planned (budgeted) cost of work that should have been completed to date.

- *Schedule variance (SV):* The schedule variance is the difference between the value of the work that was planned for completion and the value of the work that was actually completed. It uses cost values to measure schedule performance. SV = BCWP − BCWS. (The example in Figure 16.5 demonstrates how schedule variance works.)

- *Schedule variance percent (SV%):* The schedule variance divided by the planned cost to date. A positive SV% is good; it means more work has been performed to date than originally planned. A negative SV% is bad, because it means less work has been completed than the plan called for. SV% = SV/BCWS.

- *Schedule performance index (SPI):* BCWP divided by BCWS (SPI > 1.0 = ahead of schedule; SPI < 1.0 = behind schedule).

Using the cost figures as the basis for schedule measurement is useful because it takes into account the number and size of tasks that are behind schedule. That means if 10 concurrent tasks, each worth $10,000, are all one week behind schedule, the schedule variance will be larger than if only one of those tasks is one week behind schedule.

### Graphing Earned Value

There is no more accurate presentation of a project's cost and schedule performance than earned value charts. Not only do they show the cost and schedule status at any given date, but they also indicate performance trends. Figure 16.6 shows an earned value chart.

An executive with 10, or even 100, projects under his or her control can use the kind of graph shown in Figure 16.4 to pinpoint the cost and schedule performance of each one. This will help to determine which project demands the most attention.

**KEY**
**CONCEPT**

### Earned Value Relies on Disciplined Project Management

The example in Figure 16.5 shows how simple it can be to use earned value metrics to report progress. Unfortunately, many firms trying to

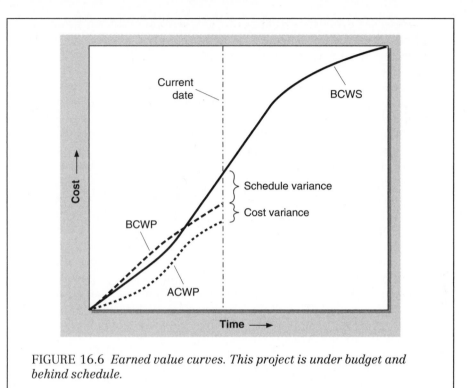

FIGURE 16.6 *Earned value curves. This project is under budget and behind schedule.*

apply earned value practices find it much more confusing. If you've read the previous chapters in this book and are practicing the discipline as it is described here, earned value metrics are practically free. In other words, if you have a detailed plan and capture actual performance data, the earned value calculations become easy. What follows here are some hard-won insights on applying the earned value reporting methods on projects.

### The Work Breakdown Structure Is Critical

The secret to making earned value work is in the work breakdown structure (WBS). Each task on the WBS must be a discrete task that meets these criteria:

- It must have defined start and finish dates.
- The task must produce a tangible outcome whose completion can be objectively assessed.
- Costs must be assigned to the task, even if they are only labor costs.

If you've applied the guidelines in Chapter 8, your WBS will probably enable easy earned value reporting. The problem occurs when the WBS contains one of these mistakes:

*WBS tasks should rarely represent an ongoing activity.* There will always be some tasks that are planned as *level of effort* (LOE) tasks, meaning that a function within the project requires some basic staffing level that runs throughout the project. Project management is an example of an LOE task—we expect a certain amount of labor cost each week to be spent on project management, and the total duration of this activity is dictated by the length of the project. A construction project that hires security services to monitor the site is also an example of a task where a weekly cost can be estimated, and the task duration depends on the project's duration. But these should be the exception within the WBS. The problem arises when a category of tasks is lumped together under a heading such as "Engineering." Rather than breaking all the engineering work into separate discrete tasks, the manager simply assigns people to the task for a period of time. The result is a WBS task like this: "'Engineering' will last four months, and we'll assign eight engineers." That produces a few problems:

- With this task description we can't track cost or schedule variance—as long as the task begins on time and doesn't use more than eight engineers, there is no cost or schedule variance.

- LOE tasks produce the illusion that the task is on schedule and on budget until the day that it doesn't finish on time—then every day after that we watch the costs and schedule variances increase.

- An LOE task that is understaffed actually sends the message that it is under budget because fewer people are working on the task than originally called for. Of course, since there is no objective way to track incremental schedule progress, the news might look very good until the day the task is supposed to be complete yet isn't.

*Keep the lowest level tasks small.* The size of work packages plays a big role in calculating cost and schedule variance accurately. When it comes to assessing schedule progress at the task level, you really know only two things: whether the task has started and whether it is finished. In between we are guessing if we report incremental progress. The simple method of assigning 50 percent of the BCWP to a task once it has begun and 100 percent of the BCWP when it is complete results in very accurate schedule variance calculations if the work packages are small. If the work packages are large, the variance is likely to be skewed, both positively and negatively, from week to week.

## Data Isn't Information

What does a CPI of 0.95 really mean? If my SPI is 1.1, what should I do? Although we've defined the basic terms of earned value analysis, we still need to make sense of the numbers in the context of our project.

*Trends are more useful than snapshots.* A CPI of 0.95 means the project is over budget. But if the CPI a month ago was 0.90, it means we may have figured out the problem behind the cost overrun. A major value of these metrics are their predictive capability—forecasting the total cost or schedule variance for the entire project based on variance early in the project. Focusing on trends tells us whether our management strategies are working. The graphing techniques shown in Figures 16.4 and 16.6 can show earned value data over time. (The graph in Figure 16.4 could be drawn for a single project, with each week's variance represented as a single point—connecting the dots tells a story.)

*Schedule variance doesn't tell the whole story.* Don't forget the importance of the critical path as you track schedule. Projects with many concurrent tasks benefit from tracking schedule variance, because with many tasks being simultaneously performed, many are bound to be ahead while others will be late. In this scenario, however, many noncritical tasks could be ahead of schedule while critical path tasks are falling behind—providing a positive schedule variance and false confidence. If critical path tasks are late, sooner or later the entire project will be held up. *Watch both the schedule variance and the critical path.*

**DANGER!**

## Size Increases Complexity for Earned Value

The projects that benefit most from earned value will have the greatest challenges implementing it. The larger the project, the more difficult it is to understand all the parts and to stay on top of cost and schedule variance. That's why these practices were invented—to manage huge defense programs. Putting the infrastructure in place to generate honest data on a routine basis is a formidable task on a major project or program—but the alternative is even worse.

**KEY CONCEPT**

## Escalation Thresholds

While the project team has the authority to solve certain problems, others need to be escalated to higher management or may even demand the direct attention of senior management. The determining factors for who handles a problem or approves a solution are its cost and schedule impacts. Escalation thresholds represent preset variances that signal the severity of a problem; these thresholds are

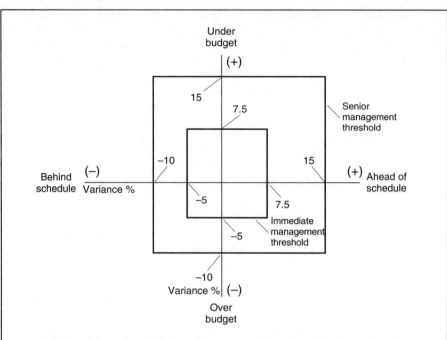

- Problems and changes beneath the immediate management threshold are left to the team to resolve.
- Any problem that can potentially cause a −10 percent cost or schedule variance will be immediately escalated to senior management.
- Changes that result in extremely positive variances will also be quickly escalated.
- Both midlevel and senior management will monitor the project on a routine basis while it is below their escalation thresholds, but they are less likely to actively intervene.

FIGURE 16.7  *Escalation thresholds.*

set during the planning process. The communication plan developed early in the project and described in Chapter 14 contains a description of the cost and schedule escalation thresholds (see Figure 16.7).

Thresholds accomplish several important functions:

- Change control thresholds separate the types of changes the project team can approve from those the change board must approve (see Chapter 15).

- Problem-resolution thresholds bring the proper level of attention to specific problems. When a problem is encountered that threatens project cost and schedule goals, it needs to be identified and raised to the proper level immediately, skipping the normal project status process. Any single problem that is big enough to cross an escalation threshold is big enough to demand immediate attention;

passing the problem from one level of management to the next using the normal status process of weekly or monthly status meetings would take much too long. The threshold shows exactly who needs to be involved in solving the problem.

- Overall project progress thresholds signal upper management that it is time to become actively involved in the project. The project may have fallen behind a little at a time, and the trend may have been apparent over several status periods, but at a certain point in this decline the escalation threshold will be crossed. This is the signal that management must intervene to solve the problems or set new cost and schedule goals.

## COST AND SCHEDULE BASELINES

**KEY CONCEPT**

A baseline is a comparison point. Cost and schedule baselines represent the original project plan as approved by the stakeholders. Ideally, a project should never vary from its original plan, so a comparison between actual performance and the baseline would show no variance. But in reality this zero variance never happens. Even though everything may not happen according to the plan, however, many projects do meet original cost and schedule goals. Keeping the baseline cost and schedule goals visible is one way of holding the focus on the original goals, even when changes start to happen. Earned value reporting, as shown in Figure 16.6, is one way of keeping this vital information visible, because it emphasizes variance from the baseline. A Gantt chart may be used to focus on schedule variance alone (see Figure 16.8).

The baseline is more than just a starting point; it also represents the accepted cost-schedule-quality equilibrium on the project. The project team is committed to meeting the baseline and should assume it will continue to be held to the baseline, unless otherwise directed by the project manager. Consider the following example.

The BoxBetter project had been stuck about two weeks behind schedule for a month. The project manager had tried several ways to catch up, but none of them were working. At this point, Terry and Madison, who spent about a quarter of their time on the project, gave up on bringing the schedule up-to-date and decided to turn their attention to other projects. Although the schedule for BoxBetter called for them to complete a task prior to the next status meeting, neither of them worked on the task. At the meeting, Terry and Madison were chagrined to learn that the other project team members had done extra duty to bring the project back on schedule. Their task was now the only one that was late—and others were waiting for them to complete it. In this case, Terry and Madison had mistakenly assumed that the baseline for the project had changed.

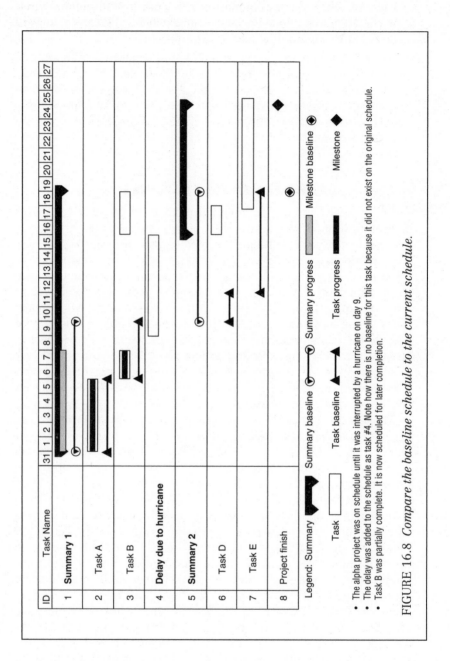

FIGURE 16.8 *Compare the baseline schedule to the current schedule.*

- The alpha project was on schedule until it was interrupted by a hurricane on day 9.
- The delay was added to the schedule as task #4. Note how there is no baseline for this task because it did not exist on the original schedule.
- Task B was partially complete. It is now scheduled for later completion.

Changing the baseline, however, is a big deal because it represents a new cost-schedule-quality equilibrium. This new equilibrium requires approval from all the stakeholders. If the justification for the change is good enough, meeting the new baseline might even be considered a success. Other times, however, it simply represents accepting a new reality. If all the evidence suggests that the project will miss the original cost and schedule goals, then it probably makes sense to change them. Maintaining unrealistic goals is rarely motivating. At the same time, however, the baseline must be changed cautiously and honestly, because it affects motivation if the baseline is changed over and over again. The new baseline should be as realistic as possible, reflecting the level of performance that led to the baseline change.

## END POINT

It's surprising how many projects never really know their status until they get close to the deadline, when they have no hope of finishing on time or on budget. There's no mystery to measuring progress accurately; all you need is a detailed project plan with cost and schedule estimates for each work package. But it does require disciplined, systematic attention to the details. It is this attention to the details that enables the project manager and team to spot the problems early, when they are still small and there are still good options for solving them.

The financial analysts on Wall Street wouldn't stand for companies releasing quarterly or annual results based on gut feelings; they demand hard data to show quantifiable results. It's time every project was held to the same standard.

## PMP Exam Prep Questions

1. Activity A is worth $400, is 100% complete, should have been done on day 1, and actually cost $400. Activity B is worth $150, is 90% complete, should have been done on day 2, and actually cost $240 so far. Activity C is worth $400, is 75% complete and should have been done on day 3, and has cost $350 so far. The total budget is $2,000. What is the planned value as of day 3?

   a. $950.00

   b. –$950.00

   c. $990.00

   d. –$990.00

2. Activity A is worth $800, is 100% complete, and actually cost $800. Activity B is worth $300, is 90% complete, and actually cost $480 so far. Activity C is worth $800, is 75% complete, and has cost $700 so far. The total budget is $4,000. What is the cost performance index for the project?

   a. 1.19

   b. 0.88

   c. 1.14

   d. 0.84

3. The project manager of the retooling project has been replaced by the company in an effort to finish the project within budget. The replacement project manager wants to determine the rate at which the project is progressing in comparison to the rate planned. What tool or technique can he use to make this determination?

   a. Schedule variance

   b. Schedule performance index

   c. Gantt chart

   d. Variance report

4. Of the following, which is the most comprehensive definition of monitoring and controlling?

   a. To monitor plan resources and make replacements as needed

   b. To check for variances from the plan and make appropriate adjustments when variances are encountered

   c. To control the activities needed to successfully complete the project

   d. To monitor the planned expenditures and to ensure controls are in place to conclude the project within budget

5. Project A is four months long, has four stakeholders, and has completed planning. Project B is 12 months long, has 10 stakeholders, and is in execution. Project C is 12 months long, has four stakeholders, and is in planning. Which project is most likely to experience scope creep?

   a. Project A

   b. Project B

   c. Project C

   d. Not enough Information

Answers to these questions can be found at www.VersatileCompany .com/FFMBAinPM.

# Solving Common Project Problems

## INTRODUCTION

The science of project management gives us the ability to calculate schedules, calculate budgets, forecast resource requirements, measure performance, estimate risk probabilities, and much more. Project management software is increasingly available to make the number crunching easier and to distribute the information faster. But computers don't manage projects, and estimates don't magically come true. The tools and techniques described in this book form a powerful tool set, but, as with any tools, they require a skilled hand to deliver a completed project. This chapter describes how this tool set will help you overcome problems that crop up on projects of any size, in any industry.

Each problem or challenge is accompanied by a strategy for using the tools we've discussed throughout this book. Many of the problems will sound familiar, and the proposed solutions may give you new insights. But don't stop with the answers you read here. The art of project management is applying the science to achieve your goals. With this chapter as a starting point, you can begin practicing the art of project management on the problems confronting your own projects.

## RESPONSIBILITY BEYOND YOUR AUTHORITY

When projects span organizational boundaries, you can suddenly find yourself relying on people over whom you have no authority. They work for neither you nor your sponsor. How will you enlist them as accountable, enthusiastic team members you can count on?

- *Charter.* Ask your sponsor to publish a charter for all the stake-holders. Make sure that it strongly designates your authority on this project.

- *Statement of work.* Explain the reason behind the project, and give them the background necessary to understand its importance to the organization.

- *Communication plan.* Involve them in setting up your primary means of communication. If they are outside your organization, you'll probably need a formal means of keeping them up-to-date. Make sure that this is a two-way medium so you'll know that they are up-to-date and involved.

- *Small work packages with strong completion criteria.* Make assignments easy to understand and track. Involve them in esti-mating the cost and duration of tasks and in defining completion criteria. The more they are involved in developing the plan, the more ownership and commitment they'll feel.

- *Network diagram.* Show them how they fit into the project; empha-size the importance of their input and the probable impact on the project if they fall behind on their schedule. If they have tasks with a lot of float, you can let them set their own schedules, but be sure to let them know that you expect them to meet the planned start and finish dates.

- *Project status meetings with an open task report.* Give them updates on the project, even during times when they aren't actively involved. Invite them to status meetings when their tasks are near enough to appear on the open task report. Hold them accountable to the schedule and to the rest of the project team.

- *Sponsor.* Develop a strong relationship with your sponsor by keeping him or her informed of your plans and your progress. You may need the sponsor's help in overcoming organizational obstacles.

## DISASTER RECOVERY

In this scenario, a project is off the rails in a big way. After missing several major schedule milestones, the project manager is removed. You are assigned to turn this project around. What do you do?

- *Statement of work.* Start at the beginning with this project. What are its goals? Prioritize the remaining scope and clarify the penalt-ies for missing the deadline or running over budget.

- *Project plan.* Using the work breakdown structure and critical path analysis, figure out the best possible schedule scenario, assuming infinite resources. This will give you the absolute shortest possible schedule. Next, negotiate for more resources, more time, or less scope (or all three) based on your plan. You can use your critical path schedule to show management which resources you will need to perform the project as fast as possible. If you do use more people, you shouldn't expect them to be productive immediately; you will need to allow for some learning time. There will be a lot of pressure on you to come up with a schedule that shows you will meet the deadline. At this point, resist this pressure and remember that an unrealistic schedule will benefit nobody. Because there is already recognition that this project wasn't being managed correctly, you are likely to persuade management to agree to a realistic schedule if you present your facts confidently. In a situation like this, the project team needs a leader with a firm resolve to stick to the discipline.

- *Work package estimates.* Use the actual performance so far to create realistic estimates, and include the team in the estimating process. You'll be dealing with an exhausted, frustrated team— don't alienate team members by ignoring their experience as you create the plan.

- *Project status meetings.* Frequent status meetings focused on completing near-term tasks will keep you on top of progress and allow you to solve problems early. Use the open task report to keep your meetings brief and productive. Graph the progress on the plan so it's plain to everyone, especially the team, that there is tangible progress. Celebrate the small victories.

## REDUCING THE TIME TO MARKET

Speed counts in your industry. The pace of change demands that your next release of a current product have a development time 20 percent less than that of the previous release. Between now and the deadline, you have to take your product through requirements, design, and construction, while building in the maximum functionality.

- *Statement of work.* Fast, focused performance demands a solid foundation. Getting agreement on authority, decision structures, and responsibilities among the participating groups will ensure that you don't waste time fighting organizational battles during the project.

- *Fixed-phase estimating.* Since you'll be working through the entire product development life cycle, there's no point in generating a detailed schedule from start to finish. Instead, choose several review points where you can reevaluate the functions of the product against the available resources and deadline. These review points constitute phase-end milestones. You can determine the duration of these phases using performance data from previous development efforts. You will need to stick to these review dates; for the team to meet the deadline, it must meet every phase-end milestone.

- *Project plan.* Develop a detailed plan for every phase. Using a network diagram, identify all possible concurrent tasks. The concurrent tasks are the opportunities for performing more work at the same time; these are the places where adding people to the project can compress the schedule. You can use this technique to determine the largest number of people who can work on the project productively. (Don't forget the resource-leveling guidelines, though.) Just remember that compressing the schedule by adding people may result in higher project costs.

- *Completion criteria.* Build quality checks into the project every step of the way. Although it may be tempting to skip some of the early quality-related activities in order to save time, you need to stay the course. It really is faster to do it right the first time.

- *Project status meetings.* Be clear about responsibilities and track schedule progress rigorously. Create a culture of schedule accountability by having strong completion criteria, and show clearly that falling behind, even by a little bit, is not acceptable. Build enthusiasm and a positive attitude by celebrating victories all along the way.

## WHEN THE CUSTOMER DELAYS THE PROJECT

Based on a good statement of work and solid project plan, you and your team are making steady progress and are right on schedule. At this point, however, you start encountering delays that are the fault of the *customer*. How can you stick to the schedule when the customer is causing the holdup?

- *Network diagram.* First look for other activities that the team can shift its attention to. The network diagram will show you what other tasks you can be pursuing while you are waiting for the customer. The network is also the tool for assessing the impact of the delay. Is the customer working on a critical path task? If not, how much float is there? Use the network to demonstrate the customer's impact on the schedule.

- *Change control.* Determine the cost and schedule impacts of the delay. Even if the customer isn't on the critical path, there may be costs associated with changing your plan. Document the reason for the delay as well as the cost and schedule impacts, and bring it to the customer's attention without delay. You can show the unexpected delay on the project plan by adding a task to the work breakdown structure called "Delay due to _____"; insert the delay in the network diagram, too. If the delay idles any of your team members, you can start assigning their hours to the delay task. Even though you must keep a positive attitude when working with the client to stay on schedule, these actions will send a clear message that the cause of the delay is well understood by all stakeholders.

## THE IMPOSSIBLE DREAM

You've been handed a deadline and budget that are impossible. When you tried to tell the managers that it was not realistic, they started talking about "can-do attitudes." How will you handle this situation?

- *Statement of work.* Be extremely clear about the project's purpose, scope, and deliverables. Make sure that the scope and deliverables are really necessary to accomplish the purpose. Learn all the schedule and cost penalties.

- *Project plan.* Putting on your best can-do attitude, develop at least three options for what can be done. You must be able to demonstrate the trade-offs available to the managers. Then recommend the option that seems to match their cost-schedule-quality priorities. Figure out the maximum number of people you can usefully apply to the project, using the network diagram and resource spreadsheet. Then look for the schedule adjustments that will bring the greatest cost reductions. Finally, use a crash table to analyze the most cost-effective tasks to compress.

- *Risk management.* Because this project will have risks that affect both cost and/or schedule, you will have to perform risk assessments at both the high level and the detail level to find your danger points. You can then take appropriate steps to mitigate the risk, including frequent monitoring and watching for new risks.

- *Status reports.* If you are attempting to meet a schedule that you believe is impossible, don't give up on changing your stakeholders' expectations. Let them know with every status report how diligently the team is striving to meet the goals and what the actual progress is. Raise the alarm frequently that, if early progress is an indicator, actual cost and schedule performance won't match the plan. They may not believe you the first time, but as the evidence builds that this is a well-managed project that was underestimated, they will be forced to come to terms with reality.

## FIGHTING FIRES

Your projects are always quick, high-intensity, and have little lead time. While the definition and planning activities sound great in theory, there just isn't any time for them.

- *Organizing for project management.* Rather than making the excuse that your projects are too fast or too fluid for these project management techniques, remember that a systematic method for using all of them will increase your ability to respond quickly to any situation. Fire department folks—who literally fight fires for a living—don't wing it. When their fire bell rings, they know all the right questions to ask to define the project, identify the risks, and make a plan. They don't call them project managers, but they have a designated leader whose job it is to monitor, coordinate, and communicate. So take a tip from the real firefighters: Get organized before the fire starts.

## MANAGING VOLUNTEERS

You are leading a project for a volunteer organization. No one disputes your leadership, but you must accomplish all the goals without having any authority over anyone on the team. What's the secret?

- *Statement of work.* Build enthusiasm and a common vision by focusing on the purpose and deliverables. Sharing the purpose engages team members emotionally, and focusing on the deliverables will keep the scope limited. (Controlling the scope is particularly important for a volunteer project around which it may be difficult to rally the team to spend extra hours.)
- *Small tasks with strong completion criteria.* Make it easy for each person to succeed by giving everyone clear direction and little latitude for straying from the task.
- *Project plan.* You must be extremely organized and very aware of the critical path and the float. People may procrastinate early in the project if they don't perceive any urgency. Volunteers are often very busy people, so you will need to do some resource analysis. Without it, you may end up with a few people trying to accomplish everything at once.
- *Communication plan.* Develop a method of staying in touch with everyone without a lot of effort or frequent meetings. They will want to spend their limited volunteer time getting things done, not attending meetings.
- *Status meetings.* Frequent status checks will keep you in touch with progress, but periodic status meetings provide opportunities

to energize the group, build relationships, and make project decisions. Celebrate the progress. Use good meeting management techniques to ensure that these are productive meetings that people will want to attend.

## Manage Professionals Like Volunteers

In a way, you are managing volunteers. Peter Drucker[1] likened managing professionals to managing volunteers, because they both want the same thing: interesting, meaningful work that is a good use of their time.[1] Ask yourself: If you viewed every project you lead as a volunteer project, would it change your management style? Would your team be more enthusiastic? Would you be more enthusiastic?

### END POINT

The art of project management is applying the science to achieve success. When you are armed with the basic tool set of techniques to define, plan, and control projects, you have the components of every successful project. This is a tool set, however, that is sharpened through use.

Practicing the art of project management begins not only with understanding the science of project management, but also by believing that it works. Learning the science is not terribly difficult. I sincerely hope that this book has revealed the techniques in a way that makes them simple and easy to understand. Unfortunately, no book can ever make them easy to apply.

Project management is hard work. It requires persistence, dedication, and a thick skin. You will encounter opposition from people who consider project definition and planning a waste of time. They will test your conviction, particularly if the cynic is your boss or customer. You must hold true to the discipline through any opposition. This will ultimately bring you success and the reputation of being a professional project manager.

# Advancing Your Practice of Project Management

There is always a new way to improve our project management ability. At a personal level, we can learn to use the technology that's been designed to apply the techniques presented in previous chapters, and we can pursue the Project Management Professional certification. Organizations can improve their project management ability by creating consistency in their approach to selecting and managing projects.

Part 5 contains five chapters that each address a different opportunity for individuals and organizations to extend and improve their practice of project management.

Chapter 18, on enterprise project management (EPM) presents a framework for organizing a project-driven organization. It contains the current practices that organizations use for managing multiple projects with shared resources. Chapter 18 also sets a context for Chapter 20.

Chapter 19 introduces requirements engineering, a discipline that is essential to project success. Failure in establishing and managing requirements undermines all the hard work done to define, plan, and control the project as described in the first four parts of this book.

Chapter 20 changes the perspective from effective management of projects, to viewing projects as investments. Project Portfolio Management views projects as a means to achieve strategic goals.

Passing the Project Management Institute's Project Management Professional exam is a milestone in a project manager's career. Chapter 21 provides advice on how to prepare for this challenging exam.

Microsoft Project is the most commonly used software application specifically designed for planning and managing projects. Entire books and training courses are available to learn about this tool. Combined with the techniques in Parts 3 and 4 and downloadable tutorials, the advice in Chapter 22 will help you get a strong start in using Microsoft Project.

## CHAPTER 18

# Enterprise Project Management: Coordinate All Projects and Project Resources in Your Organization

## INTRODUCTION

Project management techniques have been practiced for more than 50 years on projects around the world, but until the 1990s, they focused primarily on individual projects. With few exceptions, projects have been treated as organizational anomalies—each one was looked on as so unique that there seemed to be little value in changing organizational practices or policies to accommodate the special needs of managing them. Even the giant construction and engineering firms that worked exclusively on projects simply hired good project managers for each individual project instead of developing a corporate approach to managing projects.

A dramatic change has taken place since the mid-1990s. As companies restructure to strengthen their competitiveness, projects have become the focus, whether they are developing new products or delivering better service. Project-focused companies can't be dependent on heroes to pull off a miracle each time; the heroes get tired and there just aren't enough of them. These firms need a new paradigm. The frontier in modern project management is to take the lessons learned at the project level and apply them to the enterprise—whether the enterprise is a department or an entire corporation.

This chapter explores the most current questions and practices for institutionalizing the use of project management principles—what is becoming known as *enterprise project management* (EPM).[1] Unlike the concepts in previous chapters, many of these new practices have not been proven over decades, but instead are emerging as new trends. We will explore these trends and present the common wisdom for accomplishing the shift to EPM.

### Reading This Chapter

This chapter is designed to introduce enterprise project management. Let's begin by providing a path through the chapter, which is broken into three major parts:

1. It begins by defining what is meant by EPM and introduces the model showing how all the elements of EPM work together (Figure 18.1).

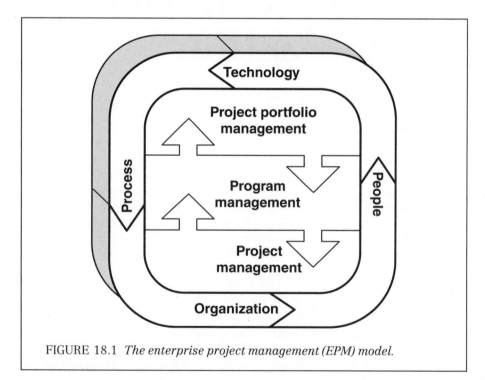

FIGURE 18.1 *The enterprise project management (EPM) model.*

2. Next we explain the three tiers of EPM, describing what function each tier serves.

3. In the third section we explore each of the four structural components that enable EPM.

## KEY CONCEPT — Benefits of Formalizing Project Management

Consider again the five project success factors:

1. *Agreement among the project team, customer, and management on the goals of the project*

2. *A plan that shows an overall path and clear responsibilities, which is also used to measure progress during the project*

3. *Constant, effective communication among everyone involved in the project*

4. *A controlled scope*

5. *Management support*

When all these factors are present in a project, the likelihood of success markedly increases. In fact, it would make excellent sense for a firm to institutionalize these factors in order to achieve them consistently. Indeed, a survey performed by the pci group of Troy, Michigan, determined that firms that have implemented the components of enterprise project management have significantly better rates of completing projects on time and on budget.[1]

Research organizations such as the Software Engineering Institute were the catalysts. These organizations discovered that the lessons of the quality movement apply to projects and project management. They have learned that consistent, defined processes are a launching pad for improving productivity and profitability.

Since the Software Engineering Institute first published its Capability Maturity Model in the early 1990s, many other frameworks have also been proposed, including the Project Management Institute's Organizational Project Management Maturity Model. All of these frameworks reinforce the movement toward enterprise project management.

## KEY CONCEPT — DEFINING ENTERPRISE PROJECT MANAGEMENT

*Enterprise project management* (EPM) is the conscious integration of processes, technology, organization structure, and people in order to align strategy with the execution of projects. Figure 18.1 illustrates all the components of EPM. The structural components of EPM enable the three tiers of management that is possible when EPM exists. We describe the model briefly here, then delve into each element in greater detail later in the chapter.

The three tiers of management in the EPM model form the link between project resources and organizational strategy. At the lowest level, *project management* focuses on the efficient execution of selected projects, the subject of all previous chapters. The next tier, *program and multi-project management*, serves to coordinate projects and the resources that all projects share—particularly the people. The highest tier, *project portfolio management*, connects the selection of projects and programs to the strategic goals of the organization.

The enabling components of the EPM model all work together (see Figure 18.1). Standardized *processes* are the accepted methods for managing projects and for management activities at the program and project portfolio levels. *Technology* consists of the information and telecommunication technology that enables people to follow the processes. A project management office, or PMO, is an *organization structure* with specific responsibility for implementing and maintaining the other elements of EPM. Finally, the *people* in the model are the people who both manage and work on projects. The skills of the people must be adequate to use the technology, follow the processes, and perform project work.

As we introduce the components of EPM we must also confront the term *enterprise* and be clear about where EPM can apply. In practice, an enterprise can range from an entire business to a department or product group. Small and midsize businesses that are project-driven, such as engineering or consulting firms, can include their entire operation within the scope of EPM. In large corporations or government agencies, an EPM initiative more often falls within specific departments, because the complexity of EPM increases dramatically when it is applied to loosely related groups.

## Enterprise Project Management Is an Enterprise Commitment

DANGER!

It should be obvious from this brief introduction that EPM won't cause a ripple in your organization; it will cause a tidal wave. The shift to EPM requires far more than new software, training, or a project management methodology—although those are the tangible evidence of the shift. Gaining the benefits of EPM will require the cooperation of every person in the organization that touches projects. It is an enterprise-wide discipline that requires commitment from top to bottom. This chapter contains many guidelines for making the shift to EPM—none is more important than full commitment from the top.

## THREE TIERS OF MANAGEMENT WITHIN EPM

A major challenge of managing an organization filled with projects is the very nature of projects themselves. Each project is temporary and unique—some are quick, others stretch over years; some are routine, while others require special skills. As projects begin and end and staffing requirements go up and down, the kind of efficiency possible in managing a repetitive operation seems nearly impossible. The three tiers of EPM are a response to this challenge.

Project management comprises the practices used to define, plan, and control a single project. These have been described in detail throughout the rest of this book. The other two tiers are explained here in greater detail.

### Program Management

Keeping track of all current and potential projects causes confusion for many firms, particularly when they are spreading the same people across many projects. Program and multi-project management respond by providing visibility and coordination across projects. It should be noted that the term *program* has two separate, yet commonly accepted definitions. One definition refers to all the projects that support a related goal—such as capturing and performing a contract to design, build, and operate a telecommunications network. This is consistent with the Project Management Institute's definition of a program. A program in this sense contains functions that extend beyond the scope of EPM, with supplier management and operations management as only two examples. The other commonly used definition of *program* is simply the oversight of multiple projects within an organization. In this case, all the projects are related because they share broad organizational goals and draw on the same resources. Using either definition, program management strives to remove the chaos posed by many related projects with the following activities:

- *Deploying limited resources—particularly personnel—among many projects.* Among IT projects there are often tasks requiring a database analyst (DBA), yet many of these projects don't need one full-time. An energy company must assess and respond to the environmental impacts of its hydroelectric dams, and therefore has a staff of scientists, each with their own specialty, that all work on a variety of projects. In fact, most people working on internal projects for their employers are spread across many projects—and they also have operational duties to balance. Whether it's people with special skills, equipment, or even suppliers, the availability of project resources constrain the project schedule. The flip side of this challenge is that we also want all of our resources in steady use, with neither too much nor too little to do. In Chapter 9 we explored the techniques and rationale behind resource leveling on a single project. The problem is more complex and every bit as important when we are spreading resources across many projects. Matching limited resources to many projects must be done based on the priorities set by the project portfolio management tier. Without this linkage, a firm does not really have enterprise project management.

- *Tracking relationships among projects.* When several projects are launched to support an initiative they are likely to be interdependent, with the product of one providing a necessary input to another. Likewise, projects with unrelated goals may actually both affect the same part of an organization. Managing these kinds of relationships among projects is typically outside a project manager's control, yet these add complexity and risk to the project. Program management specifically attends to the interactions and overlaps that occur among projects.

- *Managing projects or tasks that add value across projects yet are onerous to any one project.* For example, selecting a supplier of equipment or services that will be used on many projects. The work associated with the selection could substantially increase the cost of any one project, and the results of the selection process will benefit many projects and create consistency among projects. Additionally, the choice will reflect the requirements of many projects rather than just one. This is one more way the program management tier strives to make the project management tier efficient.

The functions of program management are typically performed by a *project* (or *program*) *management office* (PMO). The various forms and responsibilities of the PMO are described later in this chapter, where we will see that PMO responsibilities typically extend beyond the program management activities described here.

## Project Portfolio Management

Improving the management of each project has its rewards, but a consistent project management framework isn't complete unless it includes processes for managing the project portfolio. Like a portfolio of stock and bond investments, managing a portfolio of project investments requires a systematic approach to selecting, monitoring, and canceling projects. This makes portfolio management the link between the limited resources of the firm and its strategic objectives.

Chapter 20 describes project portfolio management (PPM) and provides guidelines for putting this discipline in place. PPM makes the most important decisions in the EPM model because that is where projects are chosen and limited resources are deployed to accomplish organizational objectives.

### Project Portfolio Management Is Part of Strategic Planning

Strategic goals drive project portfolio management. The methods and discipline of setting these goals is far beyond the discipline of project management. We must also recognize that when we apply the term *portfolio management* to strategic planning, that portfolio will include far more than projects; it contains the budgets for all the operations of the firm. True portfolio management happens above the EPM level.

### The Three Tiers Work Together

Project, program, and portfolio management combine to align every resource on every project with the goals of the enterprise. Project execution is improved as resources are more consistently and realistically available. Management decisions to favor one project over another are based more on facts than assumptions. Consistent reporting and oversight identify projects that are straying from their cost and schedule goals. We see how these tiers make the entire project delivery system more effective. Now let's examine what enables these tiers to operate.

### THE FOUR COMPONENTS OF EPM

The three tiers of EPM that we just discussed can operate only when the four components are in place—processes, people, technology, and organization. In the model in Figure 18.1, these components form the structure of EPM. All four work together, so if your firm is moving toward EPM, include all four in your vision. In the following sections, we will examine each of the components to understand what contribution it makes to effective project delivery. We will also introduce some guidelines to consider as you develop each component.

### The EPM Structure Is Not the Goal

Enterprise project management means aligning your project resources to accomplish your organizational goals as efficiently as possible. The four components of EPM are the means for reaching the goal, but they are not themselves the goal. As we examine each of the

**411**

four components in greater detail in the following sections below, bear in mind that our organizations do not exist to fund EPM tools or processes—nor even to accomplish projects. It works the other way around. The tools, people, processes, and organization that form EPM within a firm exist to support the projects. The projects exist to support the goals of the firm. This warning may seem obvious, but too many organizations lose sight of this primary goal as they develop the infrastructure that enables EPM.

## ESTABLISH CONSISTENT EPM PROCESSES

Good project managers have a system—a method of understanding and organizing projects that they bring to every assignment. This method is distilled from their successes and failures, from all the lessons they've learned in the past. Bring two or three seasoned project managers together from the same firm and they'll compare their approaches and techniques in an effort to learn from each other's experiences. While this kind of informal sharing can benefit the individual managers, it doesn't really help their firm. Their knowledge and experience stay with each of them, and if they leave the firm, their knowledge leaves with them. Enterprise project management creates a framework for the firm to build expertise in project management—which carries the added benefit of building better project managers. This portion of the chapter describes the *process* component of EPM, describing the contribution of defined EPM processes and guidelines for putting them in place.

Consistent process is necessary at the program and portfolio levels for EPM to function, but the most essential processes—which have also been the most difficult to define—have been those at the project level. Despite the abundance of project management methodologies available, many firms struggle to build practical guidelines for managing projects, so we will examine this level in detail first.

Using common status reports and risk assessments are obvious examples of consistent project management practices, but consistent practices are more than just standard formats for project management deliverables. In this part of the chapter we'll also see that clear responsibilities and decision points also make up a process description.

### KEY CONCEPT   The Project Life Cycle Defines the Project Process

All process improvement efforts begin by establishing the boundaries of the process, then move on to breaking the process down into smaller units in an attempt to improve the whole by improving the individual parts. When it comes to project management, the *process* is the project life cycle. Therefore, the creation of consistent project management practices begins by defining the phases in the life cycle of a project, then determining the most appropriate practices for each phase.

### KEY CONCEPT — Create Standard Deliverables and Approvals for Each Project Phase

Just as every work package on a work breakdown structure has a deliverable and completion criteria, every phase of a project life cycle has deliverables and approval processes. The approvals constitute the boundaries between project phases (the approval gates). The deliverables represent the various activities described in this book, such as a statement of work, communication plan, risk log, or change management process. Table 18.1 lists potential standard deliverables by project phase. The downloadable forms described in previous chapters are a starting point for creating standard deliverables.

### KEY CONCEPT — Separate Project Management Practices from Development Practices

Recall the distinction made throughout this book between a project life cycle and a development life cycle: The *project life cycle* reflects the activity required to *manage* the work (such as building a detailed plan or communicating status), whereas the *development life cycle* contains the actual description of how to *perform* the work (such as standards for design documents or testing procedures). This distinction should be maintained when establishing project management practices. An effective organization will have standards for both project management and product development, but it also recognizes that different kinds of projects exist, so a universal, one-methodology-for-all projects approach isn't practical. Allow the standards for establishing requirements, designing the product, building it, and so on to be developed independently of the standards for managing the project. True, both product and project methodologies should mesh, but they'll both work better if they are designed to be separate but complementary. (See more on this topic in Chapter 3.)

### KEY CONCEPT — Different Kinds of Projects Deserve Different Project Management Practices

Why does a company have to develop project management standards? Why can't it just buy a set from a project management consulting firm or use the downloadable forms from the website?

**TABLE 18.1   Potential Standard Deliverables by Project Phase**

**Definition**

- Charter
- Statement of work
- Responsibility matrix
- Communication plan
- Order-of-magnitude estimating guidelines

**Plan**

- Risk profiles
- Risk log
- Risk management plan
- Work breakdown structure
- Guidelines for task size
- Network diagram (PERT)
- Gantt chart
- Cost-estimating worksheet

**Execution**

- Status reports for different audiences
- Cost and schedule tracking charts
- Meeting agendas, including open task reports
- Cost-tracking guidelines
- Issues log
- Change request form
- Change log

**Closeout**

- Post-project review agenda and guidelines
- Post-project review report
- Client satisfaction assessment
- Project history file guidelines
- Project summary report

Or better yet, why can't we all agree on a single best way to manage projects? The obvious answer is that not every project has the same management requirements. The differences between projects make it impossible to use a one-size-fits-all approach. There may be several different types of projects within an organization and each type will require different management standards. The downloadable forms on the website are meant to provide a starting point for a firm's project management standards, but they'll have to be customized to reach their full potential.

For example, one department came up with three project types:

1. *Small:* Projects requiring less than 100 labor hours.
2. *Internal:* Projects in which the department had complete control of the people and decisions.
3. *External:* Projects in which the department was delivering a service outside its boundaries—and therefore required a good deal more coordination and communication.

For each project type, department staff devised templates and guidelines for creating a statement of work, project plans, status reports, and other project management deliverables. Since each type of project was progressively more complex to manage (small projects were easier to manage than external projects), each set of standards was progressively more thorough. That added much more structure to the larger projects with external customers, but the simplest projects weren't weighted down with excessive management requirements.

### KEY CONCEPT — Establish a Consistent Approach to Project Management

A common approach for managing every project establishes the basis for process improvement. Project managers will know what is expected of them, and they will be able to add lessons from their projects to the project management standards. These two factors will increase the performance of all project managers.

## TECHNOLOGY ENABLES EPM PROCESSES

The science of project management is the foundation for the art of leadership—a theme that's been stressed in every chapter. The science of project management relies heavily on our ability to assemble and maintain accurate information. In the case of enterprise project management it is even more important. EPM requires a broader scope within an organization, and the only way to manage that broader scope is with accurate, up-to-date information.

In the previous section we looked at the process component of EPM. In this section we describe how technology contributes to our EPM goals. In addition, we provide guidelines for achieving successful implementation of EPM technology.

## EPM Technology Capability

EPM has a broad scope, which includes successfully managing individual projects, understanding relationships among projects, and selecting and monitoring projects based on their fit with strategic goals. The following list categorizes eight common capabilities of EPM technology as they relate to the discipline of project management.

1. *Project management.* From the work breakdown structure to the resource-leveled project schedule, individual projects need a detailed plan that integrates cost, schedule, scope, and resource constraints and can be used to measure progress against these goals. The diagrams found in Chapters 8, 9, 11, and 16 show example output from software used at the project level.

2. *Team communication and collaboration.* Organizing project documentation, tracking issues and risks, and reporting individual progress against assignments are all necessary within projects. Internet- and network-based technology enables teams to consistently and efficiently share this information, whether team members share office space or are spread around the world.

3. *Visibility of inter-project dependencies.* When projects share personnel, or when one project is waiting for another project to reach a key milestone, coordination of multiple projects requires visibility of their relationships. Systems that store all project information in a common database provide an integrated view of all projects.

4. *Visibility of resource use across all projects.* As people are assigned to projects, we try to avoid overloading some people and under-assigning others. The complexity of this problem grows when people work part-time on many projects. The capability to see availability or over-allocation of personnel across many projects has become one of the driving factors for implementing EPM technology.

5. *Project portfolio summary.* Managers responsible for many projects benefit when they are able to see accurate summary status for all their projects. Figure 18.2 shows how an executive could organize all projects within his or her span of control, with access to detailed project information by selecting any project. Again,

| Category and Project Name | Approved Budget $ | $ Cost Variance | % Cost Variance | % Complete | % Schedule Variance |
|---|---|---|---|---|---|
| Proposed | 9,850,000 | 0 | 0 | 0 | 0 |
| Region Expansion | 9,850,000 | 0 | 0 | 0 | 0 |
| Auto | 319,000 | 1,962 | | | |
| LAN Upgrade | 89,000 | (2,315) | +1% | 77% | +2% |
| ★ ARM Calculator | 230,000 | 4,277 | -18% | 8% | -1% |
| Home Mortgage | 377,500 | 245 | | | |
| Branch 23 Remodel | 245,000 | 1,255 | -2% | 33% | +3% |
| Branch 33 Security | 37,500 | (1,010) | +3% | 90% | -5% |
| AIPA Training | 95,000 | 0 | 0% | 70% | 0% |
| Financial Services | 1,957,000 | 8,265 | | | |
| ★ Credit Card | 677,000 | 24,300 | -9% | 44% | -3% |
| ★ IRRP Extension | 1,215,000 | (16,440) | +2% | 68% | -14% |
| Utility Web | 65,000 | 405 | -2% | 25% | +1% |

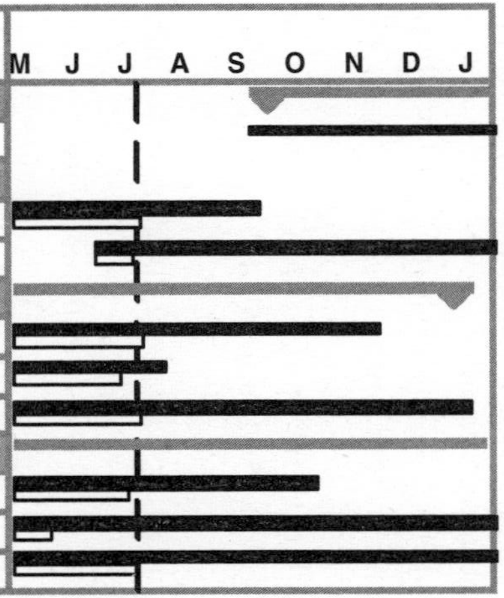

An example of the way EPM technology enables a bank executive to view summary information about all active and proposed projects. The summary schedule bars show the baseline schedule and the percentage complete against the baseline. The first column identifies projects with a significant cost or schedule variance. (Cost variance and schedule variance are described in Chapter 16.) EPM technology typically allows an executive broad flexibility in creating such summary information.

FIGURE 18.2 *Project portfolio information.*

this is typically the product of a system that stores all project information in a common database.

6. *Project status reporting.* Project status consists of both hard data, such as cost performance, and verbal descriptions of project events (both the good and the bad). EPM technology enables both types of information to be merged in a consistent format so that management gets a common, reliable view of progress across all projects.

7. *Cost accounting.* Aligning resources and goals is pretty theoretical if we can't capture and analyze costs. Costs are typically incurred at the project level, but useful cost analysis includes categorizing costs that span projects. The fundamental task of recording time (labor) spent on projects is increasingly fulfilled by EPM technology.

8. *Interfaces to complementary systems.* EPM doesn't cover every business process. The ability of the EPM system to interface with accounting and portfolio management systems decreases the work required to keep project accounting—particularly timekeeping for individual project team members—synchronized with the overall accounting system.

### Most of the Solution Already Exists

Many off-the-shelf software packages are designed for enterprise project management—both managing projects and summarizing information above the project level—and they do their job well. They are available in a range of costs, capabilities, and architectures. Or you can keep it simple with a system you build yourself (very simple!). Either way, choosing your tool and implementing it successfully should follow the common wisdom of any information system implementation.

### Off-the-Shelf Technology Must Be Configured

EPM technology is designed around proven EPM concepts. Although those concepts may apply universally, your organization is unique. When you purchase an EPM software application, it must be configured as well as installed. Installation means loading the software and making sure it runs on your network. Configuration means setting all the variables within the system to reflect the way that you want to manage projects. A simple example is found in Figure 18.2, which shows what an executive might see looking at all the projects under his or her span of control. The projects are grouped by categories—categories that were chosen and entered into the technology as part of the configuration. The more powerful the tool, the more configuration options you have.

Configuration should be distinguished from customization. As powerful as EPM tools can be, you may still find some functionality that is important to your organization but not included in the tool. In that case, you'll develop some unique interface or add-on to the EPM tool. That is customization.

### EPM Technology Is Ready

Technology has been a driving force behind the growth of project management. Prior to the advent of PCs, few projects could afford the software that simply calculated a critical path schedule or produced reports showing personnel assignments within a project. Many people believed in the project management theory but just didn't have the tools to put it into practice. Now it is the reverse. With every passing year, technology designed for project management increases in power and capability. Reliable products now exist to perform every capability described in this chapter. We are no longer waiting for technology that enables firms to efficiently put EPM theory into practice; the obstacle has now become our ability as an organization to change.

### THE PEOPLE WHO DELIVER PROJECTS

In our focus on the processes and technology of EPM, we dare not lose sight of the reality that the purpose of our organization is to deliver projects, and those projects are delivered by people. In nearly every field, no matter what the maturity of the firm's tools and processes, when difficult projects loom, management turns to its proven leaders to bring these projects home successfully. In short, the best projects are performed by the best people.

The best projects are performed by the best people. That might seem to argue against our focus on standardized tools and processes—just hire better people! However, when we examine these challenging projects that are delivered successfully, we find that the best project leaders consistently use the best practices. Listening to stories of project success is how we derived the five project success factors referenced throughout this book. In fact, successful project leaders are usually the greatest advocates for institutionalizing the project management discipline because that has been the source of their own effectiveness.

The best people use the best practices. If we believe that, the question becomes: How do we get more people to use the best practices? Our tools and processes represent the practices we want our project leaders to use, so institutionalizing these practices through our EPM initiative is the best way to develop the project leaders of the future. Training is certainly part of the answer, because we want people to be able to understand and use the best practices of the firm. But beyond classroom training, our people will improve their project management ability through experience using our EPM tools and methods. Through day-to-day practice, they will reach the level of "unconscious competence"—doing it right without thinking about it— because project management has become a habit.

Institutionalizing the best project management practices creates an environment that teaches and reinforces project management skills to our project managers. But what about our other EPM stakeholders— the team, the sponsors, and the functional managers? Their situation is similar, only with a smaller learning curve. These stakeholders all have key roles to play if we are to have effective EPM. They need to be aware of how they fit into the big picture and know how to make their contribution. That's why training for these stakeholders typically includes a description of the goals and value of EPM and the overall EPM structure for the firm as well as the details of how they will be expected to perform.

### EPM Serves the People

It is not a question of whether people or processes make the difference—people, processes, and tools work together. When our EPM components are all present and effective, the contributions of every person bring a greater reward to the enterprise.

### SUPPORT PROJECT MANAGEMENT: THE PROJECT OFFICE

An undeniable reality of organizational behavior is *entropy*; this means that, if left to themselves, policies and processes will decompose and return to their natural state. It follows, then, that if nobody is responsible for project management practices, including portfolio management, the whole idea will likely fade away and be chalked up as one more management fad. The last component of our enterprise project management model, therefore, establishes responsibility for the continued support of the standards, practices, and technology that define project management for the organization. This role is increasingly known as the *project office*.

This section is broken into two parts: The first describes the forms of authority found in project offices, and the second part describes the possible duties a project office may fulfill.

### Project Office Goes by Many Different Names

**DANGER!**

The forms of project office are new and evolving, and the names for the different models are by no means standard. The names, however, are not as important as the concepts. If you focus on how the responsibilities and authority are handled in each model, the different names will assume less importance.

## The Spectrum of Project Office Models

**KEY CONCEPT**

Like any good idea, the concept of the project office may be implemented in a variety of ways. The two factors that govern a project office role are *responsibilities* and *authority*. This section describes the most common models for the project office in terms of responsibility, authority, and best application. (Table 18.2 is a matrix showing the spectrum of project office incarnations and their associated responsibilities.)

### Center of Excellence

The primary purpose of a center of excellence is to maintain the project management standards and promote their use in an organization. Although the staff is often called on to support project managers in a consultative capacity, they don't have a direct role in making project decisions. Instead, their authority in the organization comes almost entirely from their expertise in project management skills; this means that, in addition to their knowledge, they must also be skilled change agents, persuasively offering counsel to personnel at all levels of the organization.

### Project Support Office

In addition to maintaining and promoting project management standards and practices, the project support office (PSO) actively supports a variety of projects by handling the mechanical chores such as building and updating the project plan and budget. Staffed by planning analysts, the PSO can be compared to bookkeepers who are responsible for maintaining accurate accounts while having no responsibility for profit and loss decisions. Planning analysts often grow into project managers, which means that adding more project managers to the firm's talent pool is another benefit of project support offices.

### Project Management Office

A project management office (PMO) can supply schedule and budget support in the same way as the PSO. The major difference is that a PMO will supply project managers to projects all over the organization. A PMO thus becomes a long-term home in the organization for people who want to make a career out of project management. And, because it is populated by project managers, the PMO has the capacity to enforce project

***TABLE 18.2*** **Project Office Forms and Responsibilities**

| | Low | Authority to Influence Projects | | | High |
| | | Forms of the Project Office | | | |
|---|---|---|---|---|---|
| Responsibility | Center of Excellence | Project Support Office | Project Management Office | Program Management Office | Accountable Project Office |
| Maintain standards | • | • | • | • | ○ |
| Maintain history | ○ | • | • | • | • |
| Organize training | ○ | ○ | ○ | ○ | ○ |
| Mentoring and consulting support | ○ | • | • | • | • |
| Schedule and budget analysis | | ○ | • | • | • |
| EPM technology | | ○ | • | • | • |
| Multi-project coordination | | ○ | • | • | • |
| Project oversight | | ○ | ○ | • | • |
| Make project management decisions | | | | • | • |
| Supervise project managers | | | ○ | | • |
| Meet project objectives | | | ○ | ○ | • |
| Career growth for project managers | ○ | ○ | • | ○ | • |
| Supply project managers to the organization | | | ○ | | • |
| Participate in project portfolio management | ○ | ○ | ○ | • | • |

Legend:   • = Full responsibility
          ○ = Partial responsibility
          Blank = No responsibility

management standards. Although PMOs are responsible for managing the salaries and the career growth of their project managers, they are not responsible for project success or failure. That responsibility stays with the organization to which the project manager is loaned. On the other hand, if the firm develops a series of failed projects, the PMO would share the blame, because it is the source of the firm's project management expertise.

### Program Management Office

Programs are a series of related projects. For instance, when Boeing develops a new model aircraft, the effort—from customer support through procurement—is organized into a program. Programs have many similarities to projects; the most obvious are that they produce a unique product and that they have a beginning and an end. (The primary difference is that programs are so large and last so long that they develop some ongoing operations within them.) The role of the program management office is to supply project management expertise to the entire program, thus linking all the projects together. A large program management office will contain teams that perform many of the project management functions, such as schedule, budget, and risk management. Like a project support office, a program management office is not directly responsible for meeting schedules and budgets; its role is mainly to put good project management practices in place and support them. Unlike a project support office, the program management office does participate in program decision making, usually having an equal seat at the table with the other program leaders. (Figure 18.3 shows how the organizational structure of a program includes the program management office.) Finally, unlike any other form of project office, the program management office has a life span—it will be dismantled when the program is over.

### Accountable Project Office

The accountable project office is the oldest, but in some ways the most radical, incarnation of the project office models. Although it is commonly referred to simply as "the project office," we call it the *accountable* project office to distinguish it from the other forms of project office in this chapter. This traditional model is accountable because it bears complete responsibility for meeting quality, cost, and schedule objectives of the projects assigned to it. Like the project management office, it is a long-term home for project managers, providing them a career path and administrative management. Its staff includes both project managers and project support personnel.

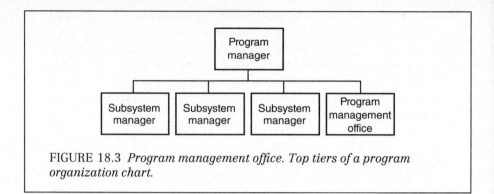

FIGURE 18.3 *Program management office. Top tiers of a program organization chart.*

The degree of influence wielded by the accountable project office depends on two factors:

1. *The degree to which the organizational structure favors projects.* When the accountable project office oversees a project-oriented organization, it sits at the top of the authority structure. More commonly, however, this office is responsible for cross-functional projects, resulting in a classic matrix organization.

2. *The degree to which the organization embraces consistent project management practices.* This most powerful form of project office is often given more authority over projects at the same time that the organization is resisting implementation of the EPM components described in this chapter. This paradox results from the outdated notion that project management is an individual skill set rather than an organizational ability. However, in firms that embrace project management as a discipline, the dual role of executing projects and maintaining the project management process makes the accountable project office extremely influential.

 **Possible Project Office Responsibilities**

There is a large range of responsibilities that a project office can assume. (The first column of Table 18.2 lists a range of possible responsibilities.) Let's look at the possible range and what is involved in performing each of these various responsibilities.

### *Maintaining Project Management Standards*

This includes documenting, promoting, and updating the best practices for project management. For example, a project office might make standards available via intranets or attend post-project reviews to look for improvements in the current standards.

### Maintaining Project History

The collective experience of the enterprise is far more useful when it is maintained and organized for future retrieval. A project office can provide the structure and guidelines for storing and retrieving project history.

### Organizing Training

Project office personnel may establish training objectives for project managers and teams and administer a training program to accomplish these objectives. The training program may be developed and delivered by the project office or brought in from an outside vendor. Given the range of skills required to manage a project, a project management training curriculum can be complex to build and administer. Because of this, many project offices share this responsibility with a functional training department.

### Mentoring and Consulting Support

Because the acknowledged experts in project management techniques are in the project office, projects across the organization will look to this office for hands-on support of their project managers. Project office personnel will participate in planning sessions, phase reviews, and turnaround efforts. Even though the project office may simply be acting as a consultant and not running the project, there are still some activities, such as performing a risk assessment, where the expertise of project office personnel might make them the natural leaders. The advantage of this advisory role is that the expertise of the project office can be leveraged across many projects, without the burden of the day-to-day duties of project leadership.

### Schedule Analysis and Budget Analysis

Perhaps the most common role of a project office is that of supplying planning analysts to assist project managers; these analysts help to build and maintain the detailed project cost and schedule information. They are well versed in the science of project management, and the project manager relies on them for accurate information and even recommendations. This, however, is where their responsibility ends; analysts do not make project management decisions.

### Enterprise Project Management Technology

If the firm chooses to implement EPM technology, every form of project office will participate in this to some degree. At the lowest level of involvement, the center of excellence will determine the system requirements and design, but will have no role in collecting or consolidating project information. Both the project support office and project management office models will assist in development and operation of the system. In fact, the need for such information is often the catalyst for forming a PSO or PMO. The program management office and accountable project office will each have complete authority over generation and consolidation of project information within their respective spans of control.

### Multi-Project Coordination

The program management functions of cross-project resource leveling and monitoring relationships among projects will be practiced by every form of the project office except the center of excellence. These activities must be performed routinely with the cooperation of all the project managers and functional managers. If they perform this function well, it leads to the project office having greater influence within the organization.

### Project Oversight

Creating and consolidating a consistent view of project status so that management can usefully monitor all projects is a responsibility of many forms of the project office. If state-of-the-art EPM technology is in place, this job is simplified, but the project office is still responsible for making it happen. In addition, the project office will usually participate in analyzing the information, using its expertise to identify a problem before it becomes a crisis.

### Making Project Management Decisions

Here is where the strong line of authority and responsibility is drawn. Only the program management office and accountable project office will participate in managing a project.

### Supervising Project Managers in Their Project Responsibilities

Only the accountable project office is actively involved in supervising project managers as they perform their jobs. A program management office can raise alarms if it sees problems and can use its influence with the program manager to bring about changes on particular projects, but project managers do not report to this office. A good PMO will also be proactive in mentoring its project managers, even though the project reporting structure doesn't include them.

### Meeting Quality, Cost, and Schedule Objectives

Accountability for project success lies directly with the accountable project office. However, the roles of both the project management office and the program management office also bind them tightly to project success or failure. A string of project failures will bring scrutiny to a project management office, and a program management office will share much of the glory or blame for the end result of a program.

### Career Growth for Project Managers

To some degree, all forms of the project office are responsible for the career growth and opportunities of project managers within the firm. At the very least, the training programs will provide a path to gain skills in project management. In addition, any of the models that employ planning analysts provide a potential source for future project managers. However, only the project management office and accountable project office models have complete responsibility for developing project managers and creating opportunities for them.

### Supply Project Managers to the Organization

Only two of the models provide an ongoing source for people with the ability to manage projects and a place for project managers to call home between projects: the project management office and the accountable project office.

### Participate in Project Portfolio Management

Each form of project office can have different levels of influence on project portfolio management, ranging from no involvement to an equal seat at the table. At the very least, staff from a project office may participate because their expert opinions and judgments carry weight. The PSO or PMO that consolidates and presents project information can add to its expert authority with the value of its data. And finally, just as they participate in managing projects, the program management office and accountable project office are likely to have an equal vote in decisions to initiate or cancel projects.

### All Forms of the Project Office Have Value

**KEY CONCEPT**

It would be a mistake to consider the various forms of project offices as a progression that all firms should follow. This would suggest that a center of excellence is just the beginning and that the natural and correct evolution will always lead to the accountable project office with responsibility for managing all projects. This is the mistake of the fervent disciple—that if some is good, more is necessarily better. Instead, the project office should reflect the organizational structure

**427**

and the location of projects within the firm. For instance, a Fortune 500 corporation that has been steadily increasing its project management focus for two decades uses both the weakest and the strongest models. It has a center of excellence located within its corporate information technology (IT) group to maintain corporate best practices and organize training. In addition, within the separate business units of the corporation, some IT directors have created an accountable project office responsible for managing all IT projects. The accountable project office at the business unit relies on the standards and training from the center of excellence and even uses them for consulting support on occasion. This firm has succeeded in matching the strength of each model to different needs within the corporation.

### Scale the PMO to the Projects

Our discussion of PMOs so far implies full-time staffing to accomplish the many responsibilities of even a center of excellence–style PMO. Organizations with many complex projects probably do need to have people assigned full-time to handle PMO activities. But smaller organizations with smaller projects can accomplish the same activities with less formality. For example, a department with 10 project managers overseeing about 50 projects assigned all the project managers the task of creating their own standards and tools to accomplish project management, program management, and project portfolio management. These project leaders worked as a team, supported by the various functional managers to whom they reported. Without a spot on the organization chart, they were still able to act as a virtual PMO.

The mere presence of a project office, in any of its forms, is a commitment to improving project management. The most successful project offices serve as both experts in the science of project management and evangelists—untiring advocates of its value.

### END POINT

For project-driven organizations to mature, they must shift from the perspective that each project is unique and should be managed independently. The new perspective is to view all projects as related because they all support the organization's goals and they all share the same pool of limited resources.

The term emerging to describe the cohesive management of all projects and resources is *enterprise project management* (EPM), which is the conscious integration of processes, technology, organization structure, and people in order to align company strategy with the execution of projects. EPM recognizes the need to manage all the projects at three different levels:

1. The *project* tier represents the tools and methods for managing individual projects.
2. The *project portfolio* tier is responsible for the selection of projects and prioritization of resource deployment across projects.
3. The *program tier* operates between the other two, overseeing the relationships among projects, assembling the information necessary for portfolio decisions, and coordinating the deployment of resources across projects.

To enable these three levels of management, four components form the structure of EPM:

1. *Processes* are described for each tier of management, describing what should be done and who should do it.
2. *EPM technology* enables the processes—putting the application of project management theory in practical reach of the people performing the work.
3. The *people* who select, manage, and work on projects have the skills and knowledge to use the tools and processes.
4. A *project office* has responsibility for the EPM structure. Without some entity taking responsibility for EPM, it cannot endure. In addition to the project office, the organization may restructure lines of authority to streamline the communications and decisions taking place at the three levels of EPM.

The project management tool set has been in development for more than 50 years, driven by the belief that rational decisions based on accurate information will lead us to higher levels of productivity. Applying that tool set at the enterprise level not only has the potential for still greater productivity gains, but also helps to build the foundation for developing the next generation of project managers.

## *Stellar Performer: Bill & Melinda Gates Foundation*
# Enterprise Project Management Office

The Bill & Melinda Gates Foundation, guided by the belief that every life has equal value, works with partners around the globe in the areas of health, education, and poverty. The Foundation issued nearly $4 billion in grants in 2014 and that number grows every year. Approximately 1,200 people work at the Foundation headquarters in Seattle, Washington, setting the strategy and interacting with partners in four major program areas:

- *Global Development:* Working to help the world's poorest people lift themselves out of hunger and poverty.

- *Global Health:* Harness advances in science and technology to save lives in developing countries.

- *The United States Division:* Improve U.S. high school and postsecondary education and support vulnerable children and families in Washington State.

- *Global Policy and Advocacy:* Build strategic relationships and promote policies that will help advance the work of the Foundation.

In 2006, Warren Buffett pledged over $30 billion and joined Bill and Melinda Gates as a trustee of the Foundation. It is now the largest private foundation in the world.

The Foundation is infused with the type of results-oriented culture that is familiar to veterans of the software industry. *Stewardship* and *impact* are guiding principles, emphasizing the importance to accomplish as much as possible with the funds available. This focus on results and efficiency, paired with aggressive goals creates a natural need for enterprise project management.

In 2012, the Foundation's executive leadership recognized the need for a centralized Enterprise Project Management Office. Employee surveys found that people were increasingly feeling overloaded. Executives could see that the number of projects and programs was growing, and that many of these had dependencies among them. The growing trend in corporate America to have an EPMO seemed appropriate for this business-like nonprofit as well.

### EPMO LEADER: CHANGE AGENT, VISIONARY, AND PROJECT MANAGEMENT EXPERT

Don Kingsberry joined the Bill & Melinda Gates Foundation in July 2013 with the express charter to build an Enterprise Project Management Office, work he had done several times before at much larger organizations in the computer, bio-tech/pharmaceutical, and consumer products industries.

By choosing Don Kingsberry, the Foundation followed a key success factor for starting an EPMO: choose a leader who is an expert in project management and is accomplished at leading organizational change. Kingsberry's previous successes equipped him to quickly assess the work of the Foundation and propose a vision for implementing project and portfolio management standards.

## EPMO ROLE AND SCOPE

The primary purpose of the EPMO is promoting structure and standards for project management and project portfolio management. Most projects, large and small, are embedded in the functions of the organization, so project managers will continue to report into these departments rather than move to the PMO. The staff of five is capable of promoting their desired practices across the enterprise. As with most organizations, however, the EPMO is taking responsibility for some of the larger, mostly cross-functional projects.

Projects affected by the EPMO are primarily operational, the kind you'd find in any business. The four major program areas accomplish most of their work through external partners, and not every grant is a project.

Over a three-year period, the EPMO has set its target to address standardization in how projects are managed, create more rigor in project selection to ensure the right work is happening, and to build the skills and culture of project management across the enterprise.

These are not small goals, and Kingsberry is very aware that his team is changing the way people work, which is always a risk. Fortunately, the EPMO enjoys the sponsorship of the Chief Operating Officer and the Chief Financial Officer, another critical success factor for an EPMO in any organization.

## ESTABLISH PROJECT MANAGEMENT STANDARDS

With decades of project management experience, Kingsberry knew he didn't need to reinvent the wheel for the Gates Foundation. The standards, as shown in Figure 18.4, are familiar and could easily apply to most organizations. Ask him about the standards and he is quick to point out the four that make the biggest impact.

First, he cites the Intake phase as essential. "Why is this project worthwhile? Why are we doing it?"

After Intake, he likes the project charter. "There is something about a sponsor's signature on that document, after the sponsor and project manager have created it together."

Like many seasoned project managers, Kingsberry values a project plan. He emphasizes that a plan has multiple critical elements: the WBS, key milestones, a critical path schedule, and a baseline.

His fourth favorite shows why he has been effective at building EPMO's in the past. He values organizational change management. "Change management is hugely important. Projects make changes."

Standards for managing projects include a common definition of what constitutes a project, practical standards for different levels of project complexity, and a project life cycle with common deliverables.

The basic definition of a project is drawn from the Project Management Institute: "a temporary endeavor undertaken to create a unique product, service, or result." To be subject to project management standards, the work must also meet two or more of the following criteria:

- Greater than four weeks in duration
- Require more than 60 hours of effort
- Cost over $25,000
- Require more than two people
- Have at least 20 individual tasks.

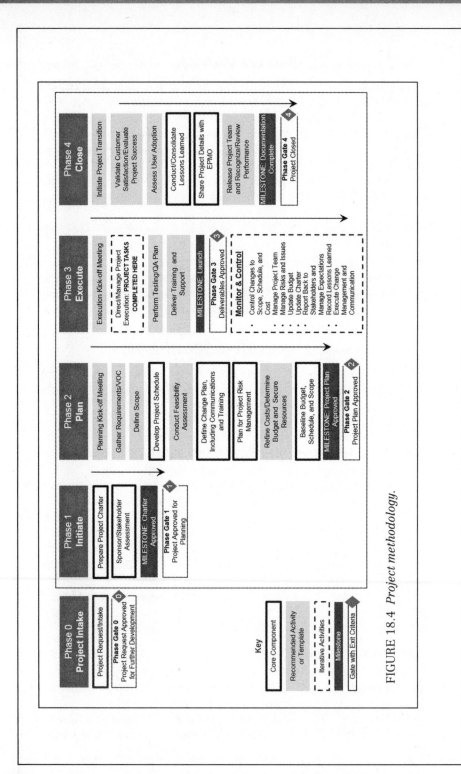

FIGURE 18.4 *Project methodology.*

In addition to defining this minimum threshold for applying project management rigor, there are three tiers of projects, each requiring a higher level of oversight. The EPMO established these tiers so that they could take on the biggest, most strategic projects first. Tier 1 projects received their initial attention. These projects have the highest visibility and are the top priorities of the executive leadership team. The project tiers also factored into which projects would be included in the portfolio management activities. Over time, all projects will appear in the project portfolio. Initially, however, only Tier 1 and Tier 2 projects were subject to portfolio scrutiny, which is described later in this article. Tier 2 projects are not as large as Tier 1, but they do tend to be cross-functional. Tier 3 projects are primarily managed within a function or department.

When discussing the standard project lifecycle, Kingsberry makes another point about reducing project risk: "Experience has shown that the larger the project, the greater the risk. So if our projects are big we break them down and manage them as multiple projects. We try to avoid projects that last multiple years."

## PROJECT PORTFOLIO MANAGEMENT OPTIMIZES RESOURCES AND LIMITS DAMAGE

The EPMO is also adding rigor to project selection. "Once you define what a project is, and then gather the inventory of all the projects, the next thing that is apparent is that they are not all equal and must be categorized."

As with most organization, the trend is that a larger proportion of work is accomplished by projects. That was leading to another common phenomenon, people were becoming overwhelmed. Kingsberry lays out three goals for portfolio management: strategic alignment, prioritization and sequencing. He emphasizes sequencing because some projects are dependent on others, projects share resources, and he wants to avoid drowning parts of the organization in too much change.

## PROJECT SELECTION CRITERIA AND PORTFOLIO VISIBILITY

The EPMO does not make decisions about which projects should be approved. Instead, they promote a consistent project scoring method and facilitate the prioritization discussion.

Table 18.3 shows the ten factors that determine the rank of projects in the portfolio. Projects that have completed their Intake phase are scored by their sponsor and project manager. During annual planning and monthly and quarterly reviews, new projects are presented by their sponsor to the executive leadership team. Many projects have merit, but the Foundation is trying to be careful not to overcommit, preferring to focus on better performance of fewer projects.

Prior to the prioritization meetings, the EPMO team enters the scores into a spreadsheet that produces a portfolio bubble chart, similar to that shown in Figure 18.5. "The big conversations happen about projects in the yellow boxes," explains Kingsberry. "Can a project's risk be reduced or its benefits improved?" The ten selection factors can also be weighted, which will change where the projects fall on the grid. It also allows the grid to be sensitive to the goals of top executives, "We can present different portfolio scenarios depending on the current strategic focus."

The EPMO also shines a light on organizational change. One of the EPMO dashboards measures the amount of change that different parts of the Foundation will experience as a result of projects.

**TABLE 18.3  Portfolio Valuation Criteria**

| Benefits | Description | 1–Poor | 4–Marginal | 7–Good | 10–Excellent |
|---|---|---|---|---|---|
| **Impact** — Programmatic Impact and Alignment | Degree to which the project aligns/impacts a BMGF program strategy | Is not aligned with any programmatic initiatives | Somewhat aligns with one or more program initiatives | Aligns with at least one program initiative | Aligns with multiple program initiatives |
| Effectiveness | Increases effectiveness or ability to have impact through our work | Unknown or negative effectiveness potential | Small net effectiveness gains | Medium net effectiveness gains | Significantly increases net effectiveness |
| **Stewardship** — Grantee/Partner Experience | Degree to which the project sustains or improves grantee or partner experience | Does not sustain or improve grantee or partner experience | Somewhat sustains or improves grantee or partner experience | Sustains or improves grantee or partner experience | Significantly sustains or improves grantee or partner experience |
| Efficiency | Degree to which the project reduces complexity, costs, or time to perform essential business functions | Unknown or negative efficiency potential | Produces small net efficiency gains | Medium net efficiency gains | Significantly increases net efficiency |
| Payback Period | Speed at which the project generates a positive return on investment | Unknown period or greater than four years | Greater than two years | Greater than one year | Less than one year |

| Risks | Description | 1–Low | 4–Medium | 7–High | 10–Extreme |
|---|---|---|---|---|---|
| **Risks** — Change Management Impact Risk | Degree to which amount of change, voice of the customer, and necessary adoption supports are understood by sponsors, and key decision makers willing and able to act as visible champions of change | Amount of change/change impact is well understood, and sponsors and key stakeholders are engaged | Amount of change and impact is understood, and sponsors and key stakeholders are moderately engaged | Amount of change and impact is not well understood, and there are some barriers to engaging sponsors and key stakeholders | Amount of change and impact is not well understood, and there are significant barriers to engaging sponsors and key stakeholders |
| Requirements Risk | Degree to which project need or requirements are understood and degree to which they are stable | Project requirements well understood | Project need/requirements understood and stable | Project need/requirement speculated, but basis justifiable | Project need/requirements not well understood or stable |
| Dependency/Coordination Risk | Degree to which the project is dependent on activities outside of its control or requires cross-functional, cross-cultural, or cross-regulatory coordination | No known dependencies or little to no coordination required | Minor dependencies, but dependencies well understood, monitored and mitigation planned | Major dependencies, but dependencies well understood, monitored and mitigation planned | Major dependencies outside of project team's control, and dependencies not well understood, monitored or mitigation planned |
| Schedule Risk | Degree to which the project may require additional time and resources and/or degree to which timing/urgency is a critical factor, e.g., fix to a critical system | Project schedule based on identical project with known actuals. Timing/urgency is not critical | Project scheduled based on similar tools and functional estimates. Timing/urgency is somewhat critical | Project schedule based on *available* dates instead of *need* dates with little slack. No history on which to validate estimates | No detailed schedule or schedule based on perfect execution with no slack |
| Capacity Risk | Degree to which the project requires overcommitted resources | Team has access to all resources at the time they are needed | Team has access to all of the resources, but needs to closely manage timing | Team does not have access to all of the resources, but has a plan to address capacity issue | Team does not have access to all of the resources, and has no plan to address capacity issue |

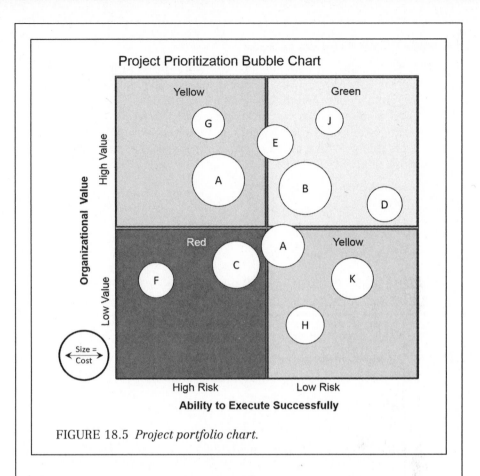

FIGURE 18.5 *Project portfolio chart.*

They look at the size of the expected change impact (small, medium, or large), at when the change is expected to start and end (different from the project start/end dates), and which groups and specific roles will be impacted by the planned changes.

The EPMO actively engages across the organization to help departments do a better job of project management and oversight. EPMO staff facilitate quarterly project reviews for departments and at the top levels in the organization.

## ACHIEVING MAXIMUM IMPACT AND STEWARDSHIP

There is a sense of awe and deep responsibility for those working at the Bill & Melinda Gates Foundation. They are the stewards of an immense endowment. The Foundation has demonstrated it can make significant progress on many health and poverty issues. And the work to be done remains enormous.

The team in the Enterprise Project Management Office takes satisfaction in knowing that they play a part in achieving the Foundation's mission, and that their work increases the impact of every project.

Sources: Interview with Don Kingsberry, February 2015, and www.gatesfoundation.org.

### PMP Exam Prep Questions

1. The company has been plagued by disorganized projects that are not in alignment with business goals, and not focused on interactivity between the projects where applicable. They want to have a better focus on grouping related projects together by business unit and product lines to help maximize efficiency and profitability. Which of the following best describes what they are trying to accomplish?

   a. Management by objectives

   b. Portfolio management

   c. Project management

   d. Operations management

2. What organization could audit projects in an organization to help ensure the health of the project and offer suggestions for improvement if needed?

   a. Projectized organization

   b. Balanced matrix organization

   c. Tight matrix organization

   d. Project management office

3. The international metallurgy company has a large project management office (PMO) due to the number of projects it pursues each year. Of the following, which is the best description of the areas a PMO typically controls?

   a. A PMO typically controls project funding, project documentation, project managers, and project policies

   b. A PMO typically controls project policies, project documentation, and project managers

   c. A PMO typically controls project policies, project documentation, and project selection

   d. A PMO typically controls project documentation, project policies, and project reporting

Answers to these questions can be found at www.VersatileCompany.com/FFMBAinPM.

# 19

# Requirements Engineering: The Key to Building the Right Product

**James Rivera and Eric Verzuh**

James Rivera has more than 20 years experience as a business analyst and project manager in the manufacturing and high-tech industries. He has authored requirements engineering courses and taught them in both university and business settings.

## INTRODUCTION

Project success—delivering the right product at the right time for the promised cost—is intimately tied to developing a clear agreement about the features and performance of the product or service being produced. Equally important is maintaining agreement on this product vision throughout the project and actually delivering it. The techniques and processes associated with developing this shared product vision and delivering on that promise comprise *requirements engineering*.

Despite this intimate relationship, requirements engineering is rarely considered within the scope of project management. Rather, it is its own discipline that can be completely understood only in the context of what's being produced. For example, the exact processes and techniques for documenting the desired features and performance of an office building will differ from those associated with developing an accounting software package or a space shuttle.

Certain requirements engineering principles transcend industries, so the framework in this chapter should be useful to everyone. However, since the projects that most consistently suffer from requirements failure are information technology and software development, the examples and techniques in this chapter are directed at these projects.

Requirements engineering is a large topic and the subject of entire books. The goal of this chapter is to introduce readers to the discipline; you'll understand what it is, why it is important, and be able to identify possible steps for improving your requirements engineering activities.

## ◆KEY CONCEPT REQUIREMENTS ENGINEERING AND PROJECT MANAGEMENT ARE INTIMATELY CONNECTED

When and where do these two disciplines intersect? In every phase of the project.

At the most basic level, customer satisfaction (or better yet, customer *delight*) is rooted in producing a product or service that fulfills the customer's purpose in an ideal fashion. Although we've previously stated that the quality component of the triple constraints is defined by requirements, in truth, the cost and schedule elements are also a function of completely understanding the customer's ideal project outcome. Requirements form a key component of a project proposal because they describe the ideal outcome of the project and because they drive the project scope. To the extent that requirements are uncertain or to be determined, the cost and schedule estimates lose their accuracy.

It seems more than obvious that the project stakeholders must have agreement on the requirements if the project is to be a success. Consequently, one could assume there would be an intense focus by all involved to accurately document and manage requirements and that cursory attention to requirements, vague requirements, or undocumented requirements would be as rare as rain in the desert. Unfortunately, that is not true. The incidence of project failure that is directly related to failed requirements engineering is staggering. In fact, it's safe to say that every person who has worked on projects for more than a few years has personally experienced the pain of requirements failures. And how painful that can be! At a minimum, discovering that requirements were incorrectly understood causes rework. It can take 10 to 1,000 times as much effort to fix a problem as it would have taken to accurately understand the requirement![1]

If a 1:10 or 1:1,000 cost factor seems hard to believe, just consider that getting a requirement wrong leads to an error in design, which will lead to an error in building the product, which may not be caught until the customer is testing it for acceptance. It could get even worse: The error might not be detected until it is encountered after the product has been released and is in use. In that case, the cost of the error includes disruption to operations. The longer it takes to detect the error, the greater the rework. When a requirements error generates errors for customers, it costs revenue and reputation.

### The Business Analyst Plays a Key Role

Who is responsible for interacting with customers and other stakeholders to extract and document requirements? This key role is filled in different ways depending on the kind of project. For residential and commercial construction, architects fulfill this role. For software and information technology projects, an old role is gaining new attention: the business analyst. Proof of this is the newly formed International Institute for Business Analysis (IIBA). Formed in 2003, the IIBA provides a focal point for developing standards for gathering, documenting, and managing requirements for software development and IT projects. Every project manager would do well to make sure whoever fulfills this key role is experienced and understands his or her own industry's best practices for requirements engineering.

## REQUIREMENT TYPES ILLUSTRATE THE EVOLVING PRODUCT VISION

It is appropriate at this point to more precisely define *requirement*. This term itself has been defined in many ways, but the IIBA definition should suit any project (IIBA 1.6, p. 9). A requirement is:

1. A condition or capability needed by a stakeholder to solve a problem or achieve an objective.
2. A condition or capability that must be met or possessed by a system or system component to satisfy a contract, standard, specification, or other formally imposed documents.
3. A documented representation of a condition or capability as in (1) or (2).

Requirements form as the vision for the product evolves from an abstract understanding of a problem or an opportunity to a specific feature set. At each stage of evolution, the requirements serve a different purpose and can take a different form. Figure 19.1 illustrates this evolution. The product development process should contain methods for documenting each of the following types of requirements.

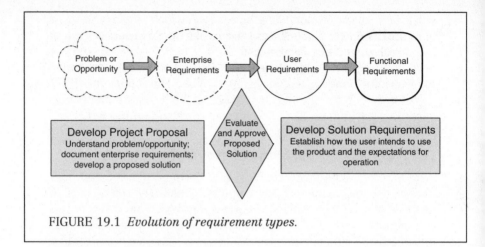

FIGURE 19.1 *Evolution of requirement types.*

## Enterprise Requirements

Also known as *business requirements* or *mission requirements*, these requirements form the justification for the project and are included in the project proposal. They describe the problem being solved and the difference between the current state and the desired future state. For example, why even *have* a space shuttle? What services do we expect it to perform for us? If a kitchenware retail store wants to change the way it manages inventory, what new inventory management capabilities do the owners want?

Enterprise requirements are necessarily too high a level and too abstract for building a specific product. Their purpose is to establish the ultimate goals for the product: If the project teams can meet these requirements, then the product will have succeeded. They form the *what;* subsequent requirements will establish the *how*. Notice that in the product evolution process in Figure 19.1, the enterprise requirements form the basis for evaluating possible solutions to the original problem or opportunity.

## User Requirements

User requirements describe the solution from the perspective of the end user. User requirements document everyday tasks performed by the end user as features to be provided by the solution. For example, an online course registration system at a community college might include the features "register for class" and "manage student grades," among others.

A common method for documenting user requirements is *use case specification*. Use cases are effective in documenting user tasks because they use a natural language style to describe the user tasks as a series of

**TABLE 19.1  User Requirements Compared to Functional Requirements**

| Use Case Statement (User Requirement) | Declarative Statement (Functional Requirement) |
|---|---|
| The system provides the student the option to create a new schedule, modify a schedule, copy a schedule, and delete a schedule. The student chooses to create a new schedule. | The system must allow the user to create an existing schedule. The system must allow the user to modify an existing schedule. The system must allow the user to copy an existing schedule. The system must allow the user to delete an existing schedule. |

steps performed in reaching a prescribed goal. When effectively written, a use case linguistically simulates the user performing a task and allows the end user to experience successfully achieving a desired goal by reading the use case.

## Functional Requirements

Functional requirements describe the solution from the perspective of the system. Functional requirements are documented as capabilities the system is required to provide to allow the user to perform a user task. For example, the feature for course registration may have the following functions: login, search, add course, delete course, copy course, submit payment, logout. Unlike user requirements that are written in a natural language, functional requirements are written in the form of declarative statements. Also, functional requirements are not written in a conversational form like user requirements; instead, functional requirements are written like a list of demands. For example, a comparison of user requirements to functional requirements can be seen in Table 19.1.

## REQUIREMENTS ENGINEERING SCOPE AND PROCESSES

Requirements engineering can generally be broken into two major groups of activities: requirements development and requirements management. Table 19.2 places these activities in the context of product development phases. The simple product development life cycle we introduced in Chapter 2 used four phases: requirements, design, construct, and operate. (As we noted in Chapter 2, this model

**TABLE 19.2  Requirements Engineering Activities in the Product Development Life Cycle**

| | Product Development Phase | | | |
|---|---|---|---|---|
| | **Requirements** | **Design** | **Construct** | **Operate** |
| Requirements development activities | 1. Scope definition<br>2. Product vision<br>3. Stakeholder identification<br>4. Elicitation<br>5. Analysis<br>6. Specification<br>7. Requirements validation | 1. Develop test cases | 1. Requirements verification | 1. User acceptance |
| Requirements management activities | 1. Define document types<br>2. Define requirement types<br>3. Develop requirements attributes<br>4. Define requirements reports<br>5. Develop requirements plan<br>6. Requirements baseline | 1. Define testing strategy | 1. Change control<br>2. Perform requirements traceability<br>3. Monitor requirements performance | 1. Project closeout |

represents a high level of abstraction—and would be broken into more specific phases for many kinds of product development efforts.) That simplistic view of a development life cycle rightly begins with a focus on requirements. Table 19.2, however, points out how requirements engineering activities continue to drive development all the way through product acceptance.

## Iterative Development Changes the Paradigm

CONCEPT    The linear product development model shown in Table 19.2 is applied on some IT projects, but many others have evolved to iterative development methodologies. These methods don't assume that all requirements can be known up front, before design commences. Rather, they repeat the cycle of requirements-design-construct over and over, discovering new requirements as they develop the architecture and features of the new product. Using iterative development methods does not mean requirements engineering won't work—-in fact, it makes it all the more challenging because new requirements are added over and over again.

## REQUIREMENTS DEVELOPMENT ACTIVITIES

CONCEPT    The reason requirements failures occur is that the process of gathering requirements is complicated by several factors:

- Requirements are not known by the end-user or the customer. The project team (more specifically, the business analyst) may be asking for information the user just doesn't have or hasn't considered.

- There is not agreement on the proper way to document requirements, so it is easier to just charge ahead, designing and building the obvious product.

- Generating and documenting requirements is hard work, expensive, and abstract, and just doesn't feel like progress to some people. It's tempting to get on with the "real work" of building the product.

- In requirements engineering, change is the only constant. Changing requirements are a way of life, and many organizations are not equipped to deal with this frequent need for realignment of product vision with business needs.

- Software is inherently intangible, immaterial, and very difficult to conceptualize in a written form.

Breaking down the process of requirements development will shed light on how to overcome some of these challenges.

### Elicitation: Collecting Information

Customers live in a symptomatic world and sometimes cannot distinguish between the symptoms of the perceived issues and the real cause of their pain. As a result, elicitation can be more art than science, demanding business analysts to be adept at wading through the white noise to get to the nuggets of requirements.

Elicitation includes identifying sources of requirements and collecting requirements information from project stakeholders. During elicitation, the business analyst discovers and collects information from multiple sources and includes stakeholder needs, user requirements, constraints, risks, performance goals, and success criteria.

The most common techniques for requirements elicitation range from one-on-one interviews to group elicitation sessions such as joint application development (JAD) workshops and focus groups. Other techniques rely on existing sources such as benchmarks of existing processes or products, observing users performing real-time business tasks, or reviewing existing documentation.

### Analysis: Transforming Information into Requirements

Analysis is a process that involves studying, examining, investigating, and dissecting the elicitation results to discern the true requirements. To perform this analysis, the business analyst must be skilled in abstract thinking, problem solving, communication, and data analysis. Modeling plays a key role in analysis.

Modeling techniques visually represent and analyze the requirements and become the means of communicating abstract ideas in a concrete form. Modeling includes process flow diagrams for mapping existing processes and identifying potential gaps and bottlenecks, system diagramming to visually represent the interfaces between people and systems and capture the information that flows between them, and data flow diagrams to visually translate information flow into its component data parts.

### Specification: Documentation for Communicating and Managing Requirements

Specification produces the requirements in a format that enables stakeholders to review, modify, and approve them. The precise format of the specification varies depending on the purpose and audience (i.e., user requirements take a different form than enterprise requirements).

### Validation and Verification: Did We Build the Right Thing and Did We Build the Thing Right?

Well-written requirements provide the basis for testing whether the product was correctly built. But how do we test the requirements? *Validation* and *verification* are the terms we use for making sure the requirements are correct and that the product meets requirements.

Validation is primarily focused on ensuring the requirements deliverables are correct and complete. During the requirements analysis phase the requirements are reviewed with the stakeholders using a static review process such as an inspection, walk-through, or ad hoc review. Several dynamic approaches to validating (during the requirements analysis phase) are prototyping, demonstrations, or conducting a pilot—which validate the requirements against a product simulation or partially functioning product.

Verification is primarily focused on ensuring that the product was built correctly and is functioning as designed. Verification is typically performed during the construction phase through testing. These activities are typically performed by the analyst, designers, developers, and testers.

### KEY CONCEPT — REQUIREMENTS MANAGEMENT ACTIVITIES

Once a common vision for the product has been established, the work transitions to maintaining that vision and ensuring that downstream work is performed in accordance with that vision. For example, despite everyone's best efforts to get it right the first time, the requirements will change. As that happens, it's necessary to know how those changes will affect other requirements or previous design decisions. (In Chapter 15 we referred to this as *change control* and *configuration management.*) In addition, the product design process and the product acceptance process must include methods for ensuring that all requirements have been met.

Requirements management activities are most successful when they are intentional and consistent—planned in advance and performed systematically following organizational standards. If every project team is required to invent its own requirements management processes, none will ever reach maturity. The three examples that follow demonstrate how much energy and discipline it takes to manage requirements.

### Baseline Requirements and Manage Changes

A baseline is a snapshot of the set of requirements documentation at a specific point in time for a given solution. For a baseline to be valid, the requirements artifacts must be verified as accurate and complete, approved by all stakeholders, and placed under version control in a requirements repository. An example set of requirements artifacts for a software project includes use cases, software requirements specifications, infrastructure requirements specifications, application designs, infrastructure designs, test cases, project schedule, change requests, and user documentation.

Managing change means maintaining a stable and consistent baseline over time. To achieve this, the business analysts must consistently monitor the product's progress against the baseline and proactively determine when change has occurred. For any product, there may be more than one baseline, each representing a particular stage of product development.

As mentioned earlier, a common practice in software engineering is iterative development, where multiple phases of the project progress simultaneously. While the developers are coding the application for release one requirements, the architects are completing the design specifications for release two. This approach requires very disciplined processes for creating and managing stable baselines, because it is expected that frequent change will occur.

### Maintain Traceability

Traceability enables the team to assess the impact of a change against the baseline. It means that we should be able to trace every requirement to design elements, to test cases, to other requirements, and to the code that produces the feature fulfilling the requirement. Traceability is important because changes from defects, scope reductions, or enhancement requests have a ripple effect and typically require updates to one or more dependent requirement artifacts. For example, adding a new type of acceptable payment method to an online bookstore requires updated use cases, interface diagrams, design specifications, user documentation, test cases, and schedule. Traceability examines the baseline and identifies these dependencies as "links" between the requirements artifacts.

In traceability, the baseline is tracked in a requirements database, and these links are documented as attributes assigned to each requirement artifact. The links between requirements are complex, many-to-many relationships and represent a web; therefore, managing the traceability links becomes even more challenging as the project experiences frequent change. Requirements management software is designed to keep track of these myriad relationships and is essential on large projects.

### Manage Requirements Performance

To manage the requirements engineering process requires effective measurement, and a common measure is requirements stability.

Requirements stability measures requirements change over time and how frequently the baseline is updated. Requirements stability assumes that a certain variance is acceptable on a periodic basis. For example, in a requirements baseline with 100 requirements artifacts, it is acceptable to have five requirements added, removed, or changed on a weekly basis.

Monitoring requirements stability provides an early warning mechanism, revealing problems with the initial requirements gathering and documenting processes. Unstable conditions are an indication that the quality of the final product may be in jeopardy. This is just one example of establishing metrics for managing the requirements process.

## REQUIREMENTS DOCUMENTATION TECHNIQUES

Since the very first computer programs were written, users have complained that the results have not met requirements. As a result, many different requirements documentation techniques have been proposed. Some have caught on and matured. All reflect the challenge of trying to document the detailed rules and logic that describe an activity that will eventually be performed by a computer.

There is such a variety of requirements documentation techniques that introducing them is beyond the scope of this chapter. However, it must be emphasized that a common characteristic of any technique is the blending of graphic models to illustrate the relationships of system components and detailed text to describe the rules for a specific component. These graphics and text combine to create complex models that represent proposed systems. It takes education and practice to effectively apply these techniques.

## KEY CONCEPT — REQUIREMENTS ENGINEERING DEMANDS DISCIPLINE

This chapter has provided an overview of the discipline of requirements engineering. It should be clear by now that having a thorough understanding of requirements is essential and far from easy to accomplish. Here are some first steps for getting serious about this discipline:

*Train business analysts.* Good business analysts understand the software development process, can use modeling techniques to lead a group to solve business problems, and can communicate effectively with end users and developers. They can write test cases, establish traceability systems, and document, baseline, and manage changes to requirements. These are all skills that are developed through training and practice. *Business analyst* is every bit as much a profession and skill set as is project management.

*Formalize requirements engineering.* Techniques like process modeling, use cases, and context diagrams exist in a variety of forms. That means every firm needs to standardize a specific set of modeling techniques. Further, distinguishing between enterprise requirements, user requirements, and functional requirements requires using a consistent format for documenting these as well. Review Table 4.2 and realize there are many processes and techniques that provide an opportunity for standardization.

*Match the requirements techniques to your development approach.* The classic waterfall system development life cycle is still appropriate on some kinds of projects. But other development methods are equally appropriate and well established, namely, incremental and iterative methods. Each of these approaches changes the requirements-design-code relationship, which means the methods of requirements elicitation, documentation, and requirements management change as well. Recognizing that requirements techniques should change depending on the development approach is consistent with our assertion at the beginning of this chapter: Requirements engineering is necessary no matter what is being built—buildings, telephones, highways, or software—and the methods for documenting requirements are driven by the product being built.

*Consider automating requirements management.* Generating and tracking requirements means managing lots of detailed information. Software applications designed for requirements engineering improve the integrity of the requirements. These products are databases designed specifically for managing requirements. They encourage consistency in recording the requirements, and they make it possible to establish traceability and monitor stability. Without a requirements management application, the activities associated with baselining and tracking requirements become far too complex for all but the simplest projects.

---

Building a requirements engineering capability has many facets. Ivy Hooks and Kristin Farry have developed a 12-point checklist to use as a guideline for building your requirements capability. Consider it the verification plan for a requirements process:

Does your current process . . .

- Eliminate inconsistencies between requirements?
- Uncover requirements for the product's entire life cycle?
- Reveal gaps in the requirements?
- Produce clear, unambiguous requirements?
- Reveal assumptions underlying requirements?

- Remove unnecessary requirements?
- Ensure verifiable requirements?
- Help you locate specific requirements?
- Minimize requirement changes after baseline?
- Adapt to changes in requirements and resources?
- Assess requirements change impact?
- Improve the process?

*Source:* Ivy Hooks and Kristin Farry, *Customer-Centered Products: Creating Successful Products through Smart Requirements Management* (New York: American Management Association, 2001).

## END POINT

Project success means delivering the right product when the customer expects it and for the promised cost. Delivering the *right* product relies on the project team and the customer having a clear, common vision of that product. Requirements engineering is the discipline that provides the techniques and processes for discerning and documenting the product vision, and then managing the updates and changes to that vision as it is built.

Requirements engineering complements project management; both are necessary to develop solid estimates and to manage changes. Every project, no matter what industry, must have a reliable process for understanding requirements and integrating those requirements into the product development process.

Information technology and software development projects have been particularly challenged with establishing and managing requirements. These projects too often have requirements that are difficult to discern, and their complexity is difficult to manage. Many methods have been developed to address this challenge, including software development approaches that allow for discovery of requirements as the software is developed. All of these techniques have one thing in common: They require disciplined practice.

*20*

# Project Portfolio Management: Align Project Resources with Business Strategy

**Ralph Kliem and Eric Verzuh**

Ralph Kliem has more than twenty-five years of experience as a project management leader for a Fortune 100 firm, including developing and implementing a project portfolio management process for a major business unit within that Fortune 100 firm. He is the author of several books, including *Tools and Tips for Today's Project Manager* (PMI) and *Project Communications Management* (CRC Press).

## INTRODUCTION

Projects are the means for achieving strategic goals. Entering new markets, driving down costs, delivering innovation—all are achieved through projects. There is a seemingly infinite supply of worthwhile initiatives, but clearly a limited supply of the people and resources needed to perform projects. Further, just about every project management think tank has found that far too many projects don't deliver their promised benefits. All these factors underscore that it is absolutely critical to view projects as investments that must be carefully chosen and regularly monitored. Project portfolio management (PPM) is the means for doing so.

## Project Portfolio Management Aligns Resources with Strategy

Project portfolio management (PPM) ensures that projects and programs promote organizational strategies and goals. It accomplishes that by avoiding the common trap of trying to do all projects in the midst of limited resources. It requires disciplined decisions driven by agreed-upon priorities.

Project portfolio management has three principal purposes:

1. Align project selection with strategy.
2. Assign limited resources based on priorities.
3. Optimize deployment of resources across projects.

PPM is a holistic approach for investing in a categorized collection of projects that support business strategies and goals. The idea is similar to creating and maintaining a 401(k) investment. The investor seeks a balanced approach using limited resources to maximize gains and minimize losses. Projects and programs, like other investments, require a balanced perspective, with some projects having a potential for a higher return, others having less risk with a lower return, and others providing a safe but modest return.

## Benefits of Project Portfolio Management

Perhaps the best way to appreciate the benefits of PPM is to identify the symptoms of not having it in place. These symptoms include investing in projects that do not support any strategy or priority, having a cacophony of projects reflecting an imbalance between risk and reward, lacking control over investments in projects, pouring good money into bad projects, and deploying resources inefficiently and ineffectively.

The benefits of PPM can be summarized as follows:

- Balancing all project investments according to risk and reward.
- Encouraging a focus on meaningful results directly supporting strategic goals.
- Investing in the right projects with enough resources to accomplish them.
- Using strategic priorities to be the guide for resource allocation.

In short, PPM provides the right mix of projects. This discipline is gaining attention among project management office (PMO) leaders and executives with many projects under their control.

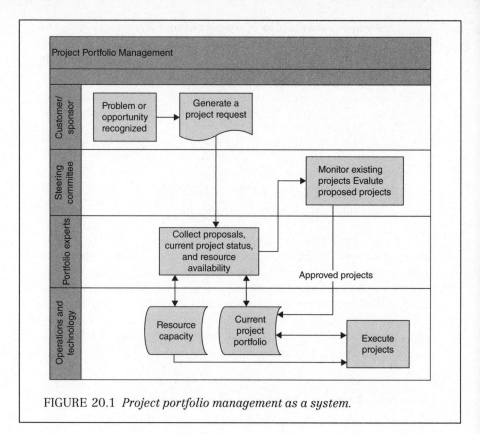

FIGURE 20.1 *Project portfolio management as a system.*

For PPM to accomplish its goals, an organization needs to have certain people, information, and processes in place. Figure 20.1 illustrates the components of a portfolio management system. The goal of this chapter is to introduce PPM by describing how these components work together.

### *Strategy Planning Is Beyond the Scope of PPM*

One critical input to PPM that is not included in this chapter is establishing strategic goals. For the purposes of this chapter we assume the organization's executive team can articulate strategy for the enterprise, whether that is a single department or the entire company.

**THE SCOPE AND GOALS OF THE PORTFOLIO**

View PPM as a system, and it is clear that the system needs a purpose and some boundaries.

As you determine the scope of the portfolio, ask some questions to set the boundary. Will it contain only certain types of projects or programs? Will the portfolio include the entire organization? Or will it focus on specific groups such as the human resources department or a sales region?

Identify potential stakeholders. These include the executives who will sponsor or champion the projects and the people or organizations that will provide input into portfolio decisions. Stakeholders also include those affected by PPM, such as customers and the groups that actually execute projects.

As the goals and boundaries are set, maintain a systemic view of the environment. Look at business conditions, current organizational performance, and culture. Try to find key performance indicators already in place for the organization. These factors set the context for the portfolio.

## Portfolio Categories

Projects fulfill a number of purposes within an organization. The categories within a portfolio make clear which purposes the projects serve. Examples include mandatory growth, cost-cutting, and sustaining projects. For example, a sustaining project could include preventive maintenance projects for current manufacturing equipment. Growth versus cost-cutting distinguishes projects that generate new revenue from projects that make the operation more efficient. Strategic goals also become portfolio categories when multiple projects become tied to each goal.

Establishing portfolio categories provides a framework for allocating resources and risk. Just as a 401(k) establishes investment proportions, such as 40 percent fixed income and 60 percent equities, a project portfolio uses the categories to allocate the organization's cash and personnel at a high level (see Figure 20.2).

Whenever the steering committee reviews the portfolio, the first focus should be to review the categories and the allocation among the categories to ensure that they continue to reflect the goals of the organization's strategy. Due to changing contextual conditions, this may require altering weights, recalculating scores, and adjusting the portfolio accordingly.

## KEY CONCEPT: STAKEHOLDERS: ROLES IN PROJECT PORTFOLIO MANAGEMENT

The people involved in PPM provide the authority and expertise for PPM to function. The following roles must exist in some form, even if some people end up fulfilling multiple roles.

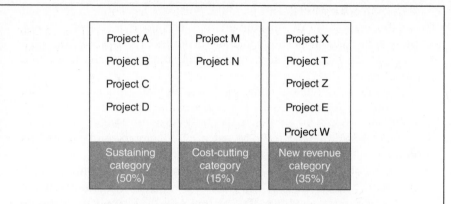

| Project A | Project M | Project X |
| Project B | Project N | Project T |
| Project C | | Project Z |
| Project D | | Project E |
| | | Project W |
| Sustaining category (50%) | Cost-cutting category (15%) | New revenue category (35%) |

FIGURE 20.2 *Project portfolio. A portfolio is made up of different categories, each of which can represent a different proportion of the overall portfolio. Within each category, projects are ranked.*

## Steering Committee or Review Board

This committee must link the enterprise's strategy and operations to ensure that the portfolio adds value to the organization. It has representatives from several areas:

- *Customers.* This group understands the benefits of each project better than anybody. Customers are appropriate on the steering committee if the project portfolio being evaluated supports an internal department—such as information technology (IT) projects for a corporate human resources (HR) department.

- *Representatives from technology and operations management.* The organizations that will actually deliver the projects bring a reality factor to estimates and resource availability. They also benefit from hearing why the projects were selected.

- *Senior executives.* These members set the overall strategy and are accountable for investing organizational resources into projects that will accomplish the strategy. They have the authority to make portfolio decisions.

- *Managers of the processes supporting PPM.* Don't overlook this critical group. They won't have authority for approving projects, but they need to understand the factors driving portfolio decisions. If they are involved in the steering committee, then the PPM processes will probably work better.

## Portfolio Experts

Also known as portfolio managers, these people possess the expertise in PPM to maintain the necessary processes, compile the information, and keep stakeholders abreast of the content in the portfolio. The people with this expertise typically reside in a project management office (PMO). Chapter 18 contains more information on the purposes and responsibilities of a PMO.

## Project Sponsors

These executives champion the projects being proposed to the PPM steering committee. Every proposed and approved project or program should have a sponsor—an executive who will be accountable for its success.

## Business Analysts

This role is filled by those who perform the initial analysis that leads to a project proposal. The title of *business analyst* is common on projects with an information technology component, but the role can be played by anyone with the skills to analyze the problem or opportunity and write the proposal. One often overlooked but critical contribution of a good analyst is to help project requestors refine their understanding of a potential project. With skilled analysis, a project's direction may be refined or the requestor may recognize that the project is not sufficiently worthwhile to pursue. This up-front work makes the job of the review board a little easier because they'll be reviewing fewer proposals and the proposals will be of higher quality.

## The PPM Sponsor

View PPM as a system and we must have a system owner, or sponsor. For PPM, it is the executive willing to fund the people and technology that keep the system working smoothly. Like any sponsor, this executive will champion the need for PPM and generate cooperation across the enterprise.

## PPM INFORMATION SUPPORTS DECISIONS

Project portfolio management is intended to be a data-driven decision process. A critical success factor for PPM is the capability to provide, as one PMO manager called it, "a single source of truth." Although PPM decisions will always be subjective—even political—accurate information that everyone can trust increases the quality of the discussions and decisions.

PPM information generally consists of a list of all active and proposed projects, specific information for each project, and information about the limited resources that are being spread across the projects. The information supports both portfolio selection and portfolio monitoring.

The list of all projects is critical during selection to avoid redundant projects. Portfolio monitoring information tends to include the following for every active project:

- The approved budget and the current forecast cost at completion.
- The approved completion date and the current forecast completion data.
- Updates to the criteria used for portfolio selection that describe strategic fit, risk, and return on investment.

In addition to project-specific information, PPM typically requires an understanding of resource constraints that will affect the portfolio. At a minimum, this would include the cash flow available to fund projects. Recent technology advances also make it easier and more practical to include personnel availability forecasts. These forecasts prevent a firm or department from taking on more projects than its staff can handle, while scheduling projects so that all staff members are kept busy.

## PROJECT SELECTION AND PRIORITIZATION

It has been said that you can't compare apples and oranges. It is a saying that characterizes a choice between two options with different benefits and disadvantages. Choosing between potential projects frequently presents that same dilemma.

A seasoned executive can justifiably rely on her or his intuition and judgment to choose between two projects, even if they are an apple and an orange. That won't work for project portfolios. The range of projects that confront a portfolio steering committee can turn the "apples versus oranges" dilemma into a fruit salad. Consistent proposals and selection criteria put a decision-making framework in place.

Project proposals are the input to the selection process. It may seem obvious that a portfolio steering committee expects consistent information for project proposals, but without formal project portfolio management processes, that is often not the case. The proposal format will directly address all of the project selection criteria. Chapter 4 described some basic proposal content.

### Stakeholders Agree on Selection Criteria

Work with the steering committee to gain agreement on weighting the categories within the portfolio. Within each category, quantitative and qualitative criteria are used for ranking projects. Although criteria may change between categories, some factors are common to most portfolio ranking processes:

*Mandatory.* Certain projects must be done, such as those needed for Sarbanes-Oxley compliance. If a project is mandatory, the question is not whether to do it, but whether the scope can be minimized.

*Quantitative benefits versus cost comparison.* This comparison is made using a return on investment formula that quantifies the expected benefit (increased revenue or decreased costs) with the expected project and life cycle costs. Using a consistent quantitative formula makes it possible to compare projects that are otherwise quite different.

*Subjective.* Factors such as strategic fit, customer satisfaction, and risk should all play a role. These factors can be assigned a score— such as 1 to 5—to make them easier to compare.

*External.* What factors outside your control—such as exchange rate or market trends—should affect project selection? A car manufacturer that is comparing potential new models might have a variable that reflects the effect of the price of gasoline on the demand for proposed vehicles.

Not all of these factors will count equally, which is part of the "apples versus oranges" challenge. Once the criteria are chosen, it is common to use a weighting formula that recognizes the relative importance of each factor.

One goal of creating a project selection model is to gain the approval of the sponsors for the portfolio and minimize resistance by other stakeholders. Establishing the criteria exposes the different values executives use to choose projects. Expect the process to be somewhat contentious, but the give-and-take required to refine the criteria will build support for the PPM process.

### Create Portfolio Options and Select the Best

All together, the common factors and weighting formulas provide the framework for making quantitative comparisons among projects. PPM analysis usually includes tables and graphics that help illustrate the variables. Figure 20.3 shows a classic portfolio bubble chart. These charts are able to show four variables by using the vertical and horizontal axis and the size and color of the bubbles.

As long as selection factors are subjective, the selection process is far more than just a math problem worked out on a spreadsheet. The categories and rankings are models that allow us to adjust our

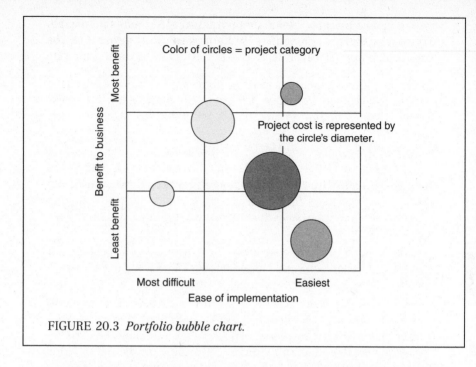

FIGURE 20.3 *Portfolio bubble chart.*

variables to consider different scenarios. As you adjust these variables, also watch the effect on resource allocation and expenditures.

### Personnel Capacity Management Is a Major Benefit of PPM

PPM information systems are increasingly able to tie personnel requirements to projects, which allows personnel utilization to be a factor in project selection. Integrating personnel limitations into the process yields three major benefits.

1. *Avoid overloading the people who deliver the projects.* When people spread their time between ongoing operations and multiple projects, it is easy to assign them far more work than they can realistically accomplish.

2. *Available skills can change priority ranking.* Money is fungible, but people are not. If one project is taking the majority of electrical engineers, another equally high-priority project that also needs electrical engineers might have to be put on hold while a lower-priority project that uses available mechanical engineers gets the green light.

3. *Tie staffing plans to strategic goals.* The projects in a portfolio line up to strategic goals. Staffing can be projected based on the

forecasted projects, identifying particular skill areas that need to grow or that are overstaffed. With this resource forecast, it can be possible to increase or decrease staffing at a more deliberate rate that is more cost-effective.

Whether it's cash flow or personnel, organizations are faced with limited resources. When a PPM system sheds light on the resource constraints, the true cost of pet projects becomes more evident as we see the other projects that won't be performed.

### Selection Culminates in Project Charters and Sponsors

The complex work of project selection is not complete until the selected projects are formally chartered and have a sponsor assigned.

## ONGOING PORTFOLIO MANAGEMENT

Ongoing portfolio management has many similarities to monitoring and control of a project. Both rely on goals and plans to be in place, and both portfolio and project monitoring are watching for signs of trouble as the projects progress toward their goals. Both recognize that plans and proposals are full of assumptions, so both expect the information used to select and launch the project to be updated systematically.

### Regularly Scheduled Portfolio Review Meetings

Portfolio planning and review should take place at regular intervals. The duration of the interval will reflect the size of projects within the portfolio. As an example, if an information technology portfolio contains many projects lasting two to four months, it makes sense that the portfolio should be evaluated at least quarterly. Other factors affecting the frequency will be contextual factors such as economic conditions, strategy, and customer priorities.

During portfolio review meetings, the steering committee will verify the overall strategic fit, reward, and balance. Their other duty is to review the performance of individual projects. Projects that are exceeding cost or schedule targets may be canceled. Successful projects might have their scopes expanded or schedules accelerated. When PPM is really working, even projects that show every sign of success might be delayed or canceled to make room for projects that will provide better results using the same project resources.

One distinction can usefully be made at this point between project portfolio management and the project oversight often performed by a PMO. The project progress information required for portfolio monitoring can be used by the PMO to monitor for signs of trouble on a project

**459**

and to initiate upper-management intervention if necessary. That oversight is more tactical and needs to be more frequent than portfolio monitoring. In addition, conversations about resolving specific project problems should happen outside of portfolio review meetings, resulting in specific recommendations to the portfolio steering committee.

### Phase Gate Approach

**TIP**

The phase gate approach described in Chapter 3 is very appropriate for PPM. Phase gates cover the entire life cycle of a project. Each gate serves as a checkpoint to determine whether to proceed with or to kill a project. PPM benefits from this approach because, as projects progress, the original assumptions about cost, schedule, scope, benefits, and risk change. Each project that hits a phase gate should be reevaluated against other potential projects, given the limited resources of the portfolio.

## KEY CONCEPT — MONITOR THE RESULTS OF PROJECTS AND THE PORTFOLIO

*Benefits realization* is the current term for monitoring the intended result of a completed project. It seems obvious that we'd want to know whether a project generated the cost savings or revenue gains projected in the proposal. But project teams are often disbanded before the benefits of their efforts begin to materialize. That's why monitoring benefits realization is a part of PPM.

The frequency of benefit review points should be consistent for all projects. For example, an IT PPM may monitor results at three months, six months, and one year.

Recording the final cost and schedule performance of a project is also related to benefits realization. After all, financial metrics such as net present value or payback period can be calculated only if the cost basis is accurate.

One obstacle to monitoring the benefits is the effort required. If additional work is required just to monitor results, then it is less likely it will be done. That's something to consider during the project proposal or project execution phase. When success metrics are required in the proposal, it increases the ability to monitor and increases the likelihood that the project will actually deliver results.

### The Portfolio Supports Strategic Goals

The original intent of PPM is to align organizational resources with strategic goals. This is another link between PPM and strategic planning. In addition to monitoring the results of individual projects,

PPM can monitor the cumulative results that projects contribute to the strategic goals.

To return to our 401(k) example, each investment within a portfolio has objectives and is monitored. Each contributes to the overall return.

### The Portfolio Changes with the Enterprise

Expect the content of the portfolio to change over time, because the business climate changes. An inflexible portfolio can spell its death as a useful tool. That means the team that is actively supporting PPM will do well to make sure the PPM processes and data continue to be driven by organizational strategy.

## CULTURE CHANGE

We've just reviewed the people, information, and processes that enable PPM. Even with all of these in place, PPM can still fail if there is one essential component missing: the discipline to follow the process. Nowhere is this discipline more difficult and more apparent than in the ability to cancel existing projects and to reject projects requested by customers. Canceling projects that have already made progress and have already consumed resources is the sign that a rigorous decision process is in place.

Information technology departments are finding that customer education and inclusion are critical to establishing PPM. If the departments they serve have never had a limit, refusing a project request can cause a shock. What both sides need to realize is that PPM is the joint effort to provide all the customers the most benefit. Including customers in the steering committee engages them in the discipline of PPM.

## END POINT

In an era of limited resources, project portfolio management plays an essential role in executing the strategies and goals of an organization. PPM requires a disciplined system that includes decision makers with sufficient authority to select and cancel projects, up-to-date data about current projects in the portfolio and the resources required to execute them, and rules for balancing the portfolio and ranking projects. Although the benefits to the enterprise are clear, establishing this system is potentially contentious because it will have a big impact on how organizational resources are deployed.

PPM represents an investment strategy of the organization. As with any investment strategy, the discipline to follow the process will be at the heart of its success or failure.

# PMP Exam Preparation

**Tony Johnson**

Tony Johnson, MBA, CSP, PMP, PgMP, is the CEO of Crosswind PM Inc. and has more than 20 years of experience as a program and project manager in various industries. The PMP® Exam Success Series products he has authored are used in 72 countries and Project Management Institute (PMI) chapters worldwide.

## INTRODUCTION

The Project Management Institute (PMI), founded in 1969, is committed to promoting the profession of project management. One of its most visible contributions to the profession is its Project Management Professional (PMP) certification. Held by more than 600,000 people worldwide, this is the most commonly recognized project management certification in the United States.

Earning the PMP demonstrates a commitment to professionalism in project management. It requires you to do more than just manage projects; you must pass an exam and maintain your certification by continuing your professional development through education and contributions to the profession.

In 1990, fewer than 1,500 individuals had earned their PMP. Why has that number multiplied so rapidly? Because employers—including the federal government—have increasingly required their project managers to demonstrate that they have been educated in standard project management techniques. Though other certifications exist from professional associations, colleges, and universities, the PMP has emerged as the most widely known and recognized. This chapter is designed to acquaint you with the requirements for earning the PMP and includes study tips to help you pass its rigorous exam.

## REQUIREMENTS TO EARN THE PMP

Earning the PMP requires experience and successful completion of the PMP Exam. Here are a few insights for understanding the PMP experience requirements:

**Minimum education requirements**—A completed bachelor's degree or high school diploma (or equivalent). If your bachelor's degree is not complete, you fit into the high school diploma criteria.

**Secondary degree**—A minimum of five years (sixty months) of project management experience of which at least 7,500 hours were actually spent leading a project. This experience must have taken place with the last eight years.

**Bachelor's degree**—A minimum of three years (thirty-six months) of project management experience of which at least 4,500 hours were actually spent leading a project. This experience must have taken place with the last eight years.

It should be noted that if you worked on overlapping projects, you cannot claim both toward the duration requirement but you can claim both toward the hours requirement. For example, if you were spending twenty hours per week leading project A, from January 1 through June 30, and also spending twenty hours per week leading project B, from January 1 through June 30 you have accrued six months and approximately 1000 hours experience.

**Project management training hours**—All applicants are required to attend a minimum of thirty-five hours of training in subjects directly related to project management.

## KEY CONCEPT — TOP 10 STUDY TIPS FOR THE PMP EXAM

1. *Use a proven study approach and products. They can minimize uncertainty and build confidence.* Today, a variety of study approaches and products exist in the market. When selecting the best approach, ensure that the material aligns with the exam as based on the current *PMBOK® Guide*. Ultimately, you are preparing for an exam, so it is a must that the approach you choose offers an exam simulation. Work the questions to the point where you can tear them apart fairly quickly and recognize the best answer. To prepare for the marathon of the four hours, run through a complete 200-question test at least three times before taking the real exam.

2. *Be familiar with differences between PMI's approach to project management and how you manage projects at your job. Failing to recognize differences can make you vulnerable on the exam.* One of the two biggest differences between what the typical project manager does at work and what is on the PMP exam is the project management approach your company takes compared to the approach described in the *PMBOK® Guide*. The other big difference is terminology usage. You might have to consider some of the views and terms as "PMI theory" to recognize them for the exam. If your workplace takes a different approach, know the difference.

3. *Study with another person or a group, if possible. Group study and feedback can help you stay on track and keep everyone accountable.* Studying together helps create accountability for yourself and others. As you study with others, assign content to one another and become the expert on your assigned content so you can mentor the others. After all, the best ways to learn are to do and to teach. As the test date approaches, wind down the group study a bit so group members can study on their own and focus more on their specific preparation needs.

4. *Set a date for the exam and work to that date. Sticking to a date will help you stay focused.* Procrastination can be your worst enemy in getting ready for the exam. Set a date for the test. Work to that date. Keep the exam a priority. Focus on it. Establish a study window, a time period during which all that you read and research remains fresh in your mind. This period is in the range of three to six weeks, depending on your own capabilities. Whatever the period, your goal is to focus on the material and retain the concepts fresh in your memory just before the exam.

5. *Become familiar with the process inputs, tools and techniques, and outputs.* PMI's *A Guide to the Project Management Body of Knowledge (PMBOK® Guide)* describes project management as comprising nine knowledge areas, each of which is a process with inputs, tools and techniques, and outputs (ITTOs).

It isn't critical to memorize every ITTO for every process. In fact, mere memorization may leave you hanging when it comes to taking the exam. The most valuable action you can take with regard to ITTOs is to understand how they fit into the processes, when, and to what end. There is a certain flow to ITTOs that make sense when you grasp the logic and reason behind their use and application. Just as planning comes before execution, certain inputs to some process are not possible unless they have already started life as outputs from another.

Envisioning outputs and inputs in their own right can give you another view on how the processes themselves function, on how activities follow one another, precede one another, or run concurrently.

6. *Don't overanalyze questions. Keep in mind that three years' experience is the minimum needed to qualify for the exam.* Some project managers with years of experience overanalyze questions to the point where they actually select the wrong answer. Answer questions based on three years of experience, the minimum needed to qualify for the exam, instead of 20 years' experience (or however much you have). Don't assume a question is a trick question just because its answer seems too obvious. Don't apply too much specific industry experience, such as information technology (IT) or construction, to questions. In other words, assume you know nothing about the specific industry in the question and focus on the project management piece of the question.

7. *Break the exam into manageable pieces (25-question chunks). This breakdown makes the exam less overwhelming.* Just as you use the work breakdown structure to break project work into manageable pieces, do the same with the exam. The first 10 questions let you know you are in the exam, and during the next four hours, you and the exam will do battle. Your goal is to come out the winner, so break down the exam into battle chunks you can overcome. After getting through the first 10 questions, move up to question 25 with the knowledge that you are one-eighth complete. Then continue through the exam in 25-question chunks. Breaking the exam into smaller pieces helps you stay focused and prevents the exam from intimidating you.

8. *Don't be shaken up by a few questions that you feel you don't recognize. Remain confident. Attitude goes a long way on the exam.* The PMP exam is ever evolving. It doesn't simply test your knowledge of the *PMBOK® Guide*. It tests any potential subject used in modern project management. Very likely, there will be a few questions you just don't recognize no matter how familiar you are with project management. You are trying to pass the exam, not get a perfect score, so stay focused on the end result (passing) and continue onward through the exam.

9. *Understand the value and substance of the ethics and conduct standards behind professional and social responsibility.* Successful responses to questions on professional and social responsibility come from a solid foundation in values and ethics, standards that extend beyond your work as a project management professional. You must be willing and prepared to do what is proper and principled in every facet of your life, personally and professionally, whether at work or at home. The ideology behind professional and social responsibility focuses on honesty, fairness, truthfulness, and conscientious conduct.

With regard to professional and social responsibility, exam questions may deal with how to advance project management as a profession. It is the responsibility of every project management professional to build on and advance project management as a profession, through personal conduct and support of others. It is important to enlighten others about project management and its benefits, whether those others are within an entire industry or at your company. It is important that you mentor others and provide guidance to help them gain positive experience and knowledge.

Exam questions may also explore adherence to policies and law as well as your duty to report any violations. Reporting violations is a key aspect of professional and social responsibility. If something wrong is going on, you are obligated to report it, whether at the company, government, or legal level. Reporting of violations extends to truthful and accurate reporting as it applies to PMI certification and the certification process. PMI expects its member to comply with its governances regarding ethics violations.

An important element of professional and social responsibility is respect. If you have respect for others and for policies, everything else falls into place. You honor intellectual property rights, including copyrights, patents, and trademarked information. You honor agreements, including nondisclosure agreements. You recognize others, their values, and their differences, especially cultural differences. You listen and learn to gain an understanding of various points of view and diverse perspectives. You hold yourself to high principles, conducting yourself professionally and dealing with conflict or disagreement in a positive, direct approach, affirming your standing as a constructive and trusted project management professional. You negotiate in good faith and avoid taking advantage of others. You establish a productive environment that fosters mutual cooperation to ultimately build trust, confidence, and performance excellence.

Another important element is fairness, a standard that governs how you make decisions without prejudice or favoritism and how you interact with others with equity and sincerity. You should set your own interests aside and open opportunities equally for all candidates and suggestions that advance the project toward its goal. The standards behind professional and social responsibility touch on how to avoid real and perceived conflicts of interest.

A final important element is honesty, a standard that encourages truthfulness in both communications and conduct. You must report information accurately and in a timely manner, without withholding any details that impact the outcome. When you commit to something, do so in good faith. You also need to nurture a safe environment that invites frank communication and candor.

10. *Take time to learn about other PMI resources and standards.* PMI makes a wealth of information available about certification and project management itself. Some of this information relates to tools for increasing project management knowledge. Other information documents various standards.

**eReads and Reference**—eReads and Reference is an online book repository for PMI members. Its catalog of web-based books covers topics both vital and useful to project management professionals.

**Global Standards and Practice Standards**—PMI is publishing a series of standards and guideline publications. These publications attempt to pull commonly recognized practices together in order to establish a common perspective and vocabulary in the industry. Examples include *Practice Standard for WBS, Standard for Program Management, Standard for Scheduling, Standard for Earned Value*, and *Standard for Estimating*. These standards do not yet have the widespread recognition and acceptance of PMI's *Guide to the Project Management Body of Knowledge*, but they are useful for every student of project management.

**END POINT**

Preparing for the PMP exam is more than just a cram session. Most professionals studying for the exam—no matter how much experience they have—report that in preparing for the exam they gain new knowledge that they can apply to their current job. The requirements for maintaining certification encourage continuing education in the field. All of these factors work together to make the PMP a consistent standard of professionalism.

---

The study questions throughout this book have been contributed by Crosswind Project Management, Inc. The answers to the study questions are available at www.versatilecompany.com/FFMBAinPM. Crosswind Project Management specializes in developing educational materials for all the PMI certifications. The company's books, CDs, flash cards, and training classes have helped thousands to pass these exams. To find Crosswind's full set of products, visit the company website at www.crosswindpm.com.

# 22

# Microsoft Project: Guidelines for Effective Use

## INTRODUCTION

Microsoft Project is an enormously popular software package. It has millions of users around the world, and among them are both fierce opponents and ardent proponents. That's to be expected when you consider how central a role Project plays in the actual practice of project management. It's used in every industry and on projects of all sizes, including some worth hundreds of millions of dollars. It can be used as informally as a whiteboard in a meeting room or it can be the official repository of cost data used for paying project vendors.

Whether Project is the best project management software tool is certainly subject to debate—there are many, many excellent competitive offerings. Suffice it to say that Microsoft has successfully leveraged its market share of desktop applications to make Project the most commonly used project management software in the world. This chapter is included for all readers who are trying to get the greatest value from Microsoft Project while minimizing the time spent entering and updating the data. As an adjunct to this chapter, owners of this book are entitled to view several tutorials for using Project, and these may be found at www.VersatileCompany.com/FFMBAinPM.

## PROJECT MANAGEMENT SOFTWARE SUPPORTS THE DISCIPLINE

If you've read the previous chapters of this book, you know that managing a project involves keeping track of a lot of data and making calculations—both excellent tasks for computers. Project management software is designed specifically to apply project management principles. If you are committed to practicing project management, you'll want to master some project management software tool.

One of the primary benefits of using a project management software tool consistently is that it both enables you and requires you to be disciplined in the way you collect and present project management information. Consistency builds habits and eventually leads to a culture that rigorously practices project management.

The challenge is that all project management software requires data—both initial planning data and project control data such as task completion reporting. The amount of data can seem overwhelming when you consider that on projects, the plan can change every day. In practice, however, the amount of data is not the real obstacle; people struggle with Microsoft Project because they just don't understand how it works! The amount of effort required to use Project drops dramatically when it is used properly. The intent of this chapter is to make sure you know enough to make Project a practical tool.

### Conventions for Navigating Project Used in This Chapter

This chapter does not contain any step-by-step instructions for using Microsoft Project. However, it does reference specific navigation, both in the text and in the figures. These references are all in bold. Project 2010 uses a ribbon for navigation that references tabs and command groups. For example, the instruction **Project > Properties > Change Working Time** is instructing you to select the **Project** tab on the top of the ribbon and then in the command group **Properties** find and select **Change Working Time**. This is the method for navigating to the Project Calendar view found in Figure 22.1.

## LOOKING UNDER THE HOOD: THE DESIGN OF PROJECT

Project is a powerful software application, and because of that it is also complex. The many features and options can make this tool seem daunting and far from intuitive. However, understanding a few basics about its design can remove a lot of the mystery.

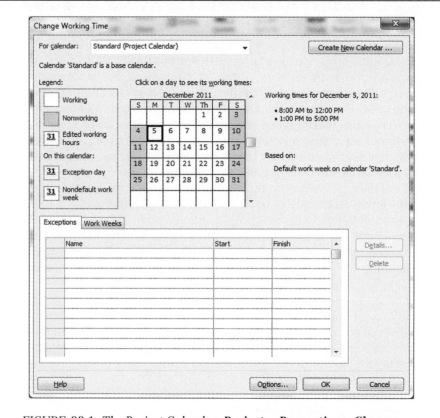

FIGURE 22.1 *The Project Calendar.* **Project > Properties > Change Working Time**.

Project is essentially a database with charting tools. As a database, it stores information about tasks, information about resources, and assignments—which connect tasks and resources. All of the various charts available just present different combinations of task information, resource information, or both.

*Task* information includes dates (start, actual start, baseline start, etc.); costs; and relationships to other tasks, such as which task is a predecessor (necessary to make a network diagram).

*Resource* information can apply to human resources as well as equipment and consumable materials (like lumber or gasoline). We can know the name of a resource, several kinds of costs (standard rate and overtime rate), and the availability of the resource.

Of course, combining task and resource information is incredibly useful. We can know who is working on tasks or how many hours a week some people are working. The foundation of all the features of

Project consists of collecting and presenting data about tasks and resources.

## SET UP THE PROJECT FIRST

**CONCEPT**    If you are planning a project, you can save a lot of keystrokes by making some basic decisions before you begin to enter task or resource data. Project will make many calculations for you, but you need to make sure the calculations are based on the right assumptions. Here are two settings to enter for each project so you don't risk having the default settings work against you.

1. *Establish calendars.* When Project calculates a schedule, it won't make you work on weekends or holidays (unless you want to). To achieve this, Project relies on some calendars that are established for each project and for some project resources. When you set up your project, start by opening the Project Calendar (see Figure 22.1). Use the project calendar to establish working and nonworking days and to set the number of work hours per day. These two parameters will affect all the tasks on the project. If you have some team members whose working days or work hours per day must be different from the standard, make a resource calendar for them. For example, if part of your team works Saturday through Wednesday so you have seven-day-a-week coverage, set up a resource calendar to reflect that. Then, whenever that crew is scheduled, tasks will occur on Saturdays and Sundays but not on Thursdays or Fridays. Resource calendars trump project calendars for all scheduling calculations.

2. *Set the project's start date.* Just about the only precise date you should enter into Project is the project start date. Project will use this as the beginning and calculate all other task dates from here. This enables you to enter the start date, link all tasks (establish predecessor relationships), and have Project determine all task start and finish dates. If the project start gets delayed or accelerated, you change that one date, and all other dates are recalculated. (To set the Project's Start Date, **Project > Properties > Project Information**).

## FOLLOW THE PLANNING MODEL IN THIS BOOK

**CONCEPT**    If you've read and understood Chapters 8, 9, 11, and 16 of this book, you already have the conceptual understanding necessary to build and manage a plan in Project. All of the advice from those chapters applies when using project management software. What follows are additional tips and strategies for hitting that sweet spot where the effort of plan upkeep is minimized and the value of information is maximized.

### Summary Task Rules

In Chapter 8, we established the difference between summary tasks and work packages. (Project refers to them as summary tasks and tasks.) Project allows you to treat summary tasks the same as regular tasks—by assigning people, work, and predecessor relationships to them. *Don't do it.* The only values you should assign to summary tasks are notes in the task description. Every other value for a summary task should be calculated by Project. Assigning a person to a summary task may duplicate work assigned to that person in the same time period. Assigning predecessor-successor relationships to summary tasks can cause a variety of problems, including unnecessarily extending the project schedule.

### The WBS Is Your Communication Plan

The levels of the work breakdown structure (WBS) can be collapsed so that only certain levels of detail are exposed. As you develop the WBS, collapse it so only tier-one tasks are visible: Is this a meaningful view of the project to somebody important? If not, reconsider your tier-one task names, or break up some of these tasks. Do the same exercise for all tier-two tasks.

Be sure to view the WBS Formatting tutorial for more tips.

### Network Diagrams: Establishing Task Relationships

One of the most important reasons to use project management software is to be able to set the predecessor-successor relationships between tasks. Once entered, these act as constraints. In the Gantt view and Network Diagram view, you can see how predecessor relationships drive the schedule. View the Network Diagram tutorial for tips on formatting.

### Estimating Task Cost and Duration

The guidelines for estimating task cost and duration that were presented in Chapters 9 and 11 still apply when using Project. Understanding the difference between fixed duration, fixed units, and fixed work is important for entering estimates. That topic is covered in the next section.

### Critical Path and Float Analysis

Obviously, this is one powerful feature of Project that you want to leverage. If you've entered tasks, linked them (established predecessors), and entered a duration for each task, Project will have established a schedule, including the float and critical path. Once you've reached this point, you can analyze the schedule you've built using a Gantt chart or the Network view. If you use the Gantt, it is easy and useful to display float: Use the **Format** tab and **Box Styles** command group, or simply right-click in the Gantt chart to format the bar styles. Add a bar for float that begins on the Early Start and ends on the Late Finish.

## **KEY CONCEPT** TASK TYPES: FIX THE DURATION, WORK, OR RESOURCE LEVEL

In Chapter 9 we saw how our assumptions about resources can affect the duration of a project. As an example, if an analyst is working 50 percent on one project, it will take two weeks to accomplish a 40-hour task. Increase that analyst to full time and the task can be performed in one week. Project takes these variables into account using the following formula:

$$Work = Duration \times Units$$

where Work = total hours of labor on a task
Duration = the number of calendar days for the task
Units = how many resource hours per day will be applied to the task

For example, if you have a person working 50 percent (4 hours per day) on a task for five days, for a total of 20 hours, all three variables have been set. If the task changes, you can change one of the variables and Project will recalculate one of the other -variables—but one of them is held constant. The task type determines which one is held constant.

Figure 22.2 shows the task dialog box, one place to set the task type. *It is essential to understand how Project uses the task type setting.* Table 22.1 explains how fixing one variable will affect the other two.

### Set the Default Task Type

Every task you add to your project is one of the three task types. If you expect most of your tasks to fall in one category, then set that as the default task type (**File > Options > Schedule**). You can always change the task type for individual tasks, but using the right default will save you a lot of clicks.

## **KEY CONCEPT** ASSIGNING RESOURCES TO A PROJECT

Resources are the people, equipment, and materials used to accomplish tasks. The best approach to adding these to

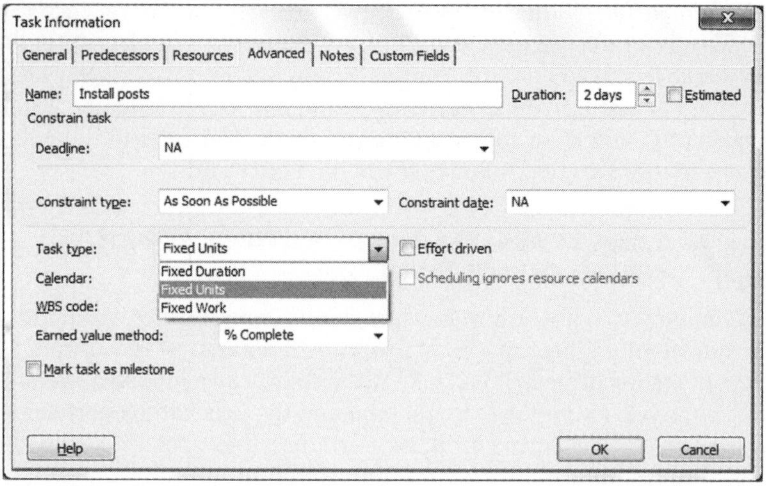

FIGURE 22.2  *The task dialog box. One of several places to set the task type.*

your project is to first put all expected resources in the Resource Spreadsheet and then assign them to specific tasks.

### Adding Resources

The Resource Spreadsheet view is shown in Figure 22.3. Add each resource here. You'll have to make a decision at this point whether

**TABLE 22.1  Task Types Affect the Way Project Responds to User Changes**

| | How Will Project Respond to a User Change? | | |
| | **User Changes** | **User Changes** | **User Changes** |
| **Task Type** | **Units** | **Duration** | **Work** |
|---|---|---|---|
| Fixed-units task | Project recalculates duration | Project recalculates work | Project recalculates duration |
| Fixed-work task | Project recalculates duration | Project recalculates units | Project recalculates duration |
| Fixed-duration task | Project recalculates work | Project recalculates work | Project recalculates units |

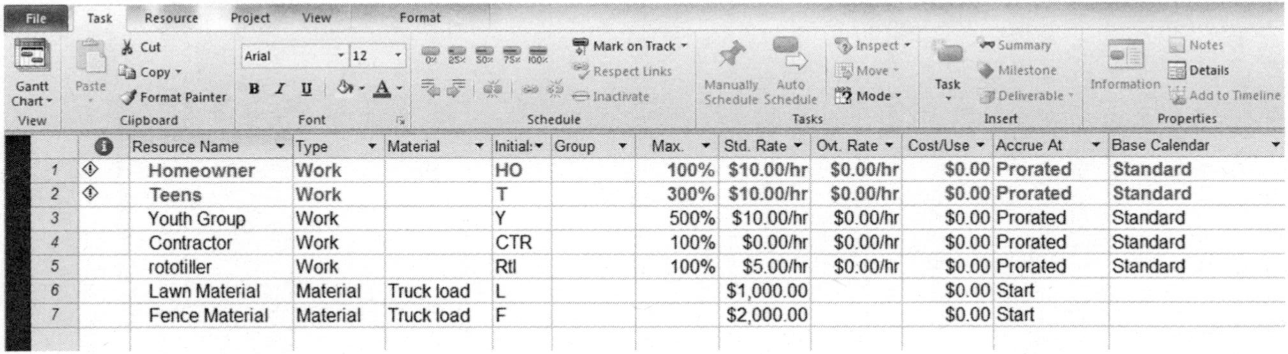

| | Resource Name | Type | Material | Initials | Group | Max. | Std. Rate | Ovt. Rate | Cost/Use | Accrue At | Base Calendar |
|---|---|---|---|---|---|---|---|---|---|---|---|
| 1 | Homeowner | Work | | HO | | 100% | $10.00/hr | $0.00/hr | $0.00 | Prorated | Standard |
| 2 | Teens | Work | | T | | 300% | $10.00/hr | $0.00/hr | $0.00 | Prorated | Standard |
| 3 | Youth Group | Work | | Y | | 500% | $10.00/hr | $0.00/hr | $0.00 | Prorated | Standard |
| 4 | Contractor | Work | | CTR | | 100% | $0.00/hr | $0.00/hr | $0.00 | Prorated | Standard |
| 5 | rototiller | Work | | Rtl | | 100% | $5.00/hr | $0.00/hr | $0.00 | Prorated | Standard |
| 6 | Lawn Material | Material | Truck load | L | | | $1,000.00 | | $0.00 | Start | |
| 7 | Fence Material | Material | Truck load | F | | | $2,000.00 | | $0.00 | Start | |

FIGURE 22.3 *The Resource Spreadsheet. Two resource types are highlighted because they are over-allocated.*

you are going to use generic resources, specific resources, or a combination. For example, if your team members are pretty interchangeable, such as the number of painters on a commercial tenant improvement project, you could just add "painter" as a resource name. In this case "painter" is a generic resource. But if you are running the painting company and want to know where all your people will be working, you'll have to put the individual painters in as specific resources and assign each of them to the tasks. In practice, you may use both: entering in a generic resource to plan a project before your team is assigned, then changing assignments to specific resources when you have people assigned to your project.

### All Human Resources Have Costs

Project allows many types of costs to be entered into the Resource Spreadsheet, not all of which apply to your projects. There is one cost that you should use for every human resource: standard rate. Too many Project users leave all these cost fields blank, either because each project manager doesn't know the cost or because the human resource is a salaried employee and thus thought to be free to the project. Whether we have salaried employees or not, when the project is under way we'll want to know whether we are spending more or fewer hours than originally planned. Several report formats are available within Project that track cost, including earned value—if the cost of resources is zero, there will be no variance. Therefore at least set the standard rate for every human resource at $1 per hour.

### Assign a Resource to a Task

You don't need to have resources entered into your Resource Spreadsheet before assigning them to a task, but it is the recommended practice. After that, you can assign one or more resources to any task. Figure 22.4 shows two resources assigned to a task. Note that the homeowner will be working full-time (eight hours per day) for two days on this task. The materials needed for the lawn have been calculated as one truckload that will total $1,000.

### RESOURCE LEVELING YOUR SCHEDULE

Chapter 9 provided the explanation of what resource leveling is and why it's so important. Project can assist you in this process using several features.

First, recognize that when you start to level resources within the schedule, you are using the power of the tool to do some what-if analysis. For example, what if we change some task relationships and have more concurrent tasks? What if we assign fewer people to a task

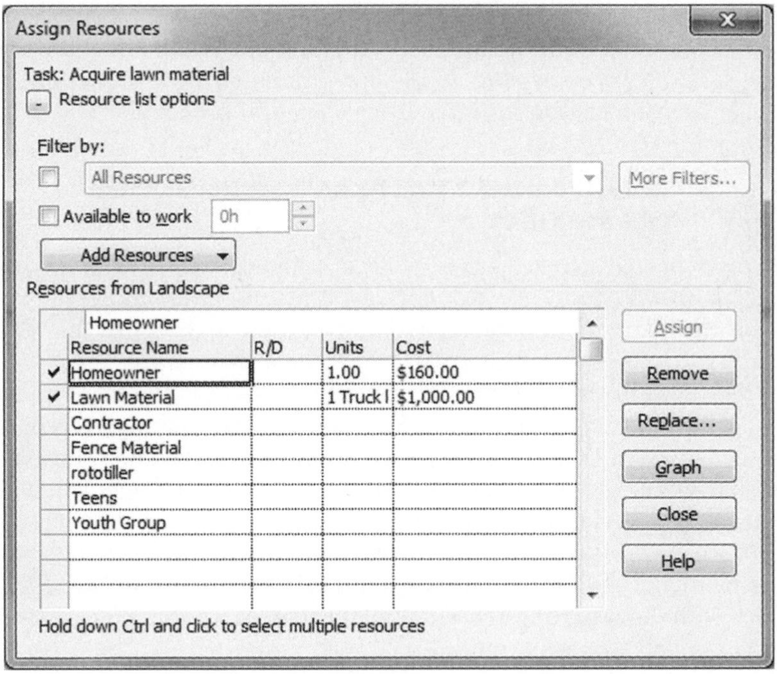

FIGURE 22.4 *Assign resources dialog box.*

but let the duration expand? What if we take Sue off one task and replace her with Ivan? In each case, you need a before-and-after picture so you understand the effect of the change.

## Use a Copy of Your Project for What-If Analysis

When you are ready to start the what-if analysis, save your project file, make a copy of it, and make the changes to the copy. This allows you to make lots of changes without corrupting your original plan.

## The Level Resources Feature

Project actually has a one-click method of leveling your project resources. **Resource > Level > Level All** will analyze your project, and for every resource over-allocation found, Project will add delay to one or more tasks until the over-allocation is removed. Sometimes adding delay to tasks is the right strategy for leveling resources, but not always. If enough delay is added, it could change the completion date of the project. To get the most from this feature, be sure to use the

Leveling Gantt view before and after leveling. It shows the amount of float and delay for every task.

It is often necessary to manually level a project schedule. View the tutorial, Resource Leveling, to see a combination view that makes it easier to visualize the resource over-allocation problem.

## MAINTAINING THE PLAN THROUGHOUT THE PROJECT

A lot of people use Project to build a schedule, but after the work begins, they abandon Project because it just takes too much time to keep the plan up-to-date. The time invested in keeping the plan current can be minimized if you follow these guidelines.

First, establish regular reporting -periods—when the team members are expected to report in and when the project manager needs to report upward. Accept that no matter how often you update it, the plan will always be out-of-date, but it can still be a useful management tool. Pick update periods such as every week or once a month when the plan will be brought up-to-date. These should be frequent enough that the plan is useful for managing even if it is not completely accurate. Stick with the reporting process until it becomes a habit. It gets easier with regular practice.

### Remaining Work Is the Key Variable

The plan contains work (hours of labor) for every task. When recording progress against these tasks, enter actual work first, and then change the remaining work field. If a task goes more quickly than you'd expected, you'll decrease the remaining work field. If a task is going to take more effort than originally expected, then increase remaining work. Project will use the actual work and remaining work to calculate the Percent Complete for the task.

The best advice for minimizing your ongoing effort to keep the plan up-to-date is to not let it get too far out-of-date. Part of the value of project management software is that by keeping it up-to-date, it keeps you in touch with the details of the project.

### Baselines Are Essential

In Chapter 16, we discussed the value of a baseline—it is a record of our original plan. Progress compared to the baseline tells us whether work is going according to plan. Project allows you to set the baseline for all task data (cost and schedule) as a basis for comparison to actual performance. Just remember the following guidelines about setting the baseline.

- Set the baseline before you start to track! The baseline is the target at which your team will be aiming. Once work begins, the plan starts to move and it becomes too late to record the real baseline.
- When a new task is added to the plan, you can baseline just that task without having to baseline the entire project.

View the tutorial Setting a Baseline to learn about the options associated with baselines in Project.

### Allow Team Members to Update the Plan

Wouldn't it make sense for team members to update their own tasks, rather than making the project manager perform all that data entry? Project Professional, Project Server, and Project Web App make that possible. Microsoft's enterprise project management solution is explained in greater detail at the end of this chapter.

### Earned Value Requirements for Project

Chapter 16 explained why so many firms want to use earned value reporting. There are only a few things you need to know to have Project support earned value on your project. First, tasks must have resources applied to them, and second, those resources must have a cost applied (even if it is only $1 per hour!) so that every task has a cost. If your WBS follows our guidelines for small work packages with clear completion criteria, just baseline the plan and enter actual hours and Project will calculate earned value.

### PROJECT SERVER AND PROJECT WEB APP

Microsoft has developed its own enterprise project management solution based on Project. The company has added two products that work with Project and extend the capability of Project in two important ways:

1. *Resource visibility and management is available across multiple projects.* All of the resource analysis we have performed for individual projects can now be performed for the enterprise. For people assigned to more than one project, a manager can see if their workload is too big or too small. Resource forecasts for particular skill types, such as technical writer, painter, or software engineer, can be developed across all projects that are being planned into the future.

2. *Communication among the project manager, team, and resource managers (functional managers) is streamlined.* Team members can see their specific assignments within the plan and provide their own task updates, reducing the effort required by the project manager to maintain an accurate plan. Resource managers can more easily see what their people are working on and collaborate with project managers to build project teams with the best available people. All stakeholders gain increased visibility on risks and issues.

These two capabilities are added when organizations use Project Professional, Project Server, and Project Web App. Project Professional is the version of Project that is designed to interface with the other two products. Project Server is a database product. When individual project plans are saved to the database, all the task and resource data of each project become available to qualified users. Project Web App is a browser-based application that enables team members, resource managers, and executives to read and update the data in the database.

## END POINT

The practice of project management has benefited immensely from the constant evolution of project management software applications. Microsoft Project makes it far easier to develop and maintain detailed plans with cost, schedule, and resource information. The many features of Project can make it confusing to learn. This chapter has pointed out some of the most important practices for using Project correctly. With these best practices, as well as the tutorials available at www.VersatileCompany.com/FFMBAinPM, you will be able to leverage this popular tool more efficiently.

# The Detailed Planning Model

**I**n Chapters 8, 9, and 11 we explored a six-step model for developing a detailed project plan. The example for this model, the home landscape project, was spread over these three chapters. To make it easier to see the steps of planning, the home landscape project example is repeated here, beginning with the detailed planning model in Figure A.1 and following the stages through to completion (Figures A.2 through A.6).

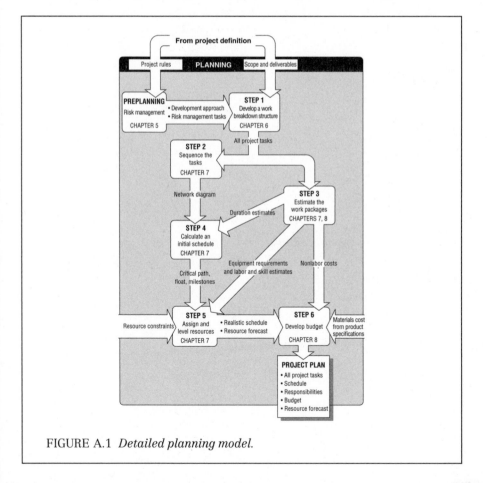

FIGURE A.1 *Detailed planning model.*

| ID | Task Name | Predecessors | Duration | Labor Hours | Resource Names |
|----|-----------|--------------|----------|-------------|----------------|
| 1 | Design home landscape | | 5 days | 80 hrs. | Homeowner [0.5], Teens [1.5]* |
| 2 | Put in lawn | | | | |
| 3 | Acquire lawn materials | 1 | 2 days | 64 hrs. | Homeowner, Teens [3] |
| 4 | Install sprinkler system | | | | |
| 5 | Identify sprinkler locations | 1 | 1 day | Fixed fee, 8 hrs. | Contractor, Homeowner |
| 6 | Dig trenches | 5, 11 | 2 days | Fixed fee | Contractor |
| 7 | Install pipe and hardware | 6 | 3 days | Fixed fee | Contractor |
| 8 | Cover sprinkler system | 7 | 1 day | Fixed fee | Contractor |
| 9 | Plant grass | | | | |
| 10 | Remove debris | | 4 days | 256 hrs. | Teens [3], Youth Group [5] |
| 11 | Prepare soil | 10, 3 | 4 days | 96 hrs. | Teens [3], Rototiller |
| 12 | Plant lawn seed | 8 | 1 day | 16 hrs. | Teens [2] |
| 13 | Plant shrubs | 10, 1 | 6 days | 96 hrs. | Teens [2] |
| 14 | Build fence | | | | |
| 15 | Acquire fence material | 1 | 2 days | 16 hrs. | Homeowner |
| 16 | Install fence | | | | |
| 17 | Mark fence line | 1 | 1 day | 32 hrs. | Homeowner, Teens [3] |
| 18 | Install posts | 17, 15 | 5 days | 80 hrs. | Teens [2] |
| 19 | Install fencing and gates | 18 | 6 days | 144 hrs. | Teens [3] |
| 20 | Paint/stain fence and gates | 19 | 3 days | 72 hrs. | Teens [3] |

* On task 1, both the homeowner and teens are working 4 hours per day.

FIGURE A.2 *Develop a work breakdown structure, sequence the tasks, and estimate the work packages.*

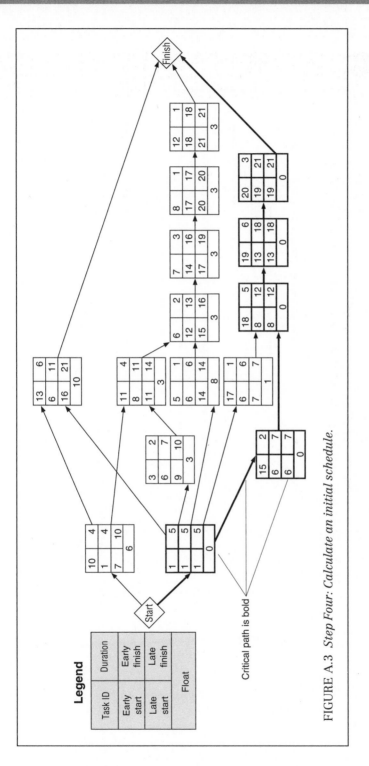

FIGURE A.3 *Step Four: Calculate an initial schedule.*

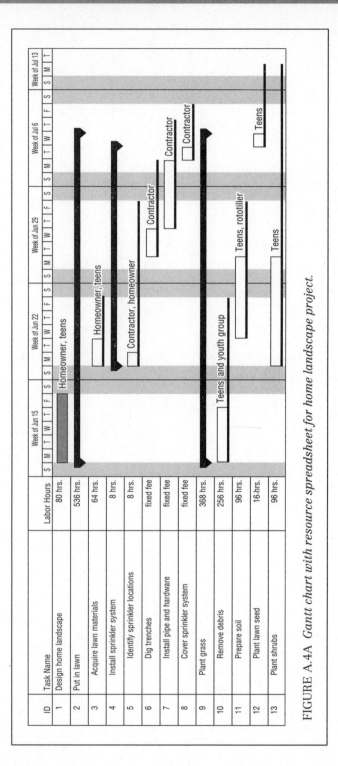

FIGURE A.4A *Gantt chart with resource spreadsheet for home landscape project.*

| ID | Task Name | Labor Hours |
|----|-----------|-------------|
| 14 | Build fence | 344 hrs. |
| 15 | Acquire fence material | 16 hrs. |
| 16 | Install fence | 328 hrs. |
| 17 | Mark fence line | 32 hrs. |
| 18 | Install posts | 80 hrs. |
| 19 | Install fencing and gates | 144 hrs. |
| 20 | Paint/stain fence and gates | 72 hrs. |

*(Gantt chart bars)* Homeowner · Homeowner, teens · Teens · Teens · Teens

**Legend**

- Critical
- Noncritical
- Float
- Summary

Resource spreadsheet (days shown S M T W T F S per week):

| ID | Resource Name | Week of Jun 15 | Week of Jun 22 | Week of Jun 29 | Week of Jul 6 | Week of Jul 13 |
|----|---------------|----------------|----------------|----------------|---------------|----------------|
| 1 | *Homeowner* | 4 4 4 4 4 | 32 16 | 56 16 24 24 | 24 24 40 24 24 | 24 |
| 2 | *Teens* | 36 36 36 36 12 | 64 40 56 56 56 | 8 8 8 8 | 8 8 | |
| 3 | Contractor | | 8 | 8 | | |
| 4 | Youth group | 40 40 40 40 | | | | |
| 5 | Rototiller | | 8 8 8 | 8 | | |

*Hours per day*

- The resource spreadsheet shows the labor hours per day for each resource. Overallocated resources are in italics.
- The family has three teenagers working on the project, for a total of 24 hours each day (3 teens @ 8 hours).
- There is only one homeowner, who is available for 8 hours a day.
- Given this initial schedule, with all tasks beginning on their early start dates, both the homeowner and teens are overscheduled during much of the project.

FIGURE A.4B *(Continued)*

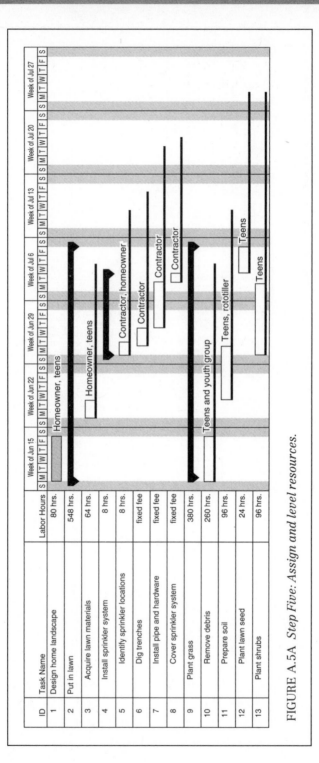

FIGURE A.5A *Step Five: Assign and level resources.*

| ID | Task Name | Labor Hours | Week of Jun 15 S M T W T F S | Week of Jun 22 S M T W T F S | Week of Jun 29 S M T W T F S | Week of Jul 6 S M T W T F S | Week of Jul 13 S M T W T F S | Week of Jul 20 S M T W T F S | Week of Jul 27 S M T W T F S |
|----|-----------|-------------|---|---|---|---|---|---|---|
| 14 | Build fence | 344 hrs. | | | | | | | |
| 15 | Acquire fence material | 16 hrs. | | | Homeowner | | | | |
| 16 | Install fence | 328 hrs. | | | | Homeowner, teens | | | |
| 17 | Mark fence line | 32 hrs. | | | | Homeowner | | | |
| 18 | Install posts | 80 hrs. | | | | | Teens | | |
| 19 | Install fencing and gates | 144 hrs. | | | | | | Teens | |
| 20 | Paint/stain fence and gates | 72 hrs. | | | | | | | Teens |

Legend

Critical

Noncritical

Float

Summary

| ID | Resource Name | Week of Jun 15 S M T W T F S | Week of Jun 22 S M T W T F S | Week of Jun 29 S M T W T F S | Week of Jul 6 S M T W T F S | Week of Jul 13 S M T W T F S | Week of Jul 20 S M T W T F S | Week of Jul 27 S M T W T F S |
|----|---------------|---|---|---|---|---|---|---|
| 1 | Homeowner | 4 4 4 4 | 8 8 | 8 8 8 8 | 8 | | | |
| 2 | Teens | 24 24 24 24 | 24 24 24 24 | 24 24 24 24 | 24 24 24 24 | 16 16 24 24 | 24 24 24 24 | 24 |
| 3 | Contractor | | | 8 8 8 8 8 | 8 8 | | | |
| 4 | Youth group | 40 40 40 40 | 8 8 8 | | | | | |
| 5 | Rototiller | | | 8 | | | | |

Hours per day

The leveled schedule has eliminated the task overlaps, which caused unrealistic work hours for the teens and homeowner.

• *Task 5*—Delayed 5 days to level homeowner while keeping the sprinkler contractor on schedule.
• *Task 10*—Reduced teens to 4 hours per day (each) so they can participate in design home landscape at the same time. (Design home landscape also calls for each teen to work 4 hours per day.) Added on additional day for the youth group to work on the task. This changed the task duration from 4 to 5 days and the total labor from 256 hours to 260 hours.
• *Task 12*—Changed the task from two teens for one day (16 hours' labor) to one teen for 3 days (24 hours' labor). One teen working on the task alone won't be as efficient, but now the other two teens can work on Task 18 at the same time.
• *Tasks 13, 15, and 17*—Delayed these tasks to level the project and their successor tasks were delayed as well.
• The new schedule is 10 workdays longer, but neither the teens nor the homeowner are overallocated on any day.

FIGURE A.5B *(Continued)*

**487**

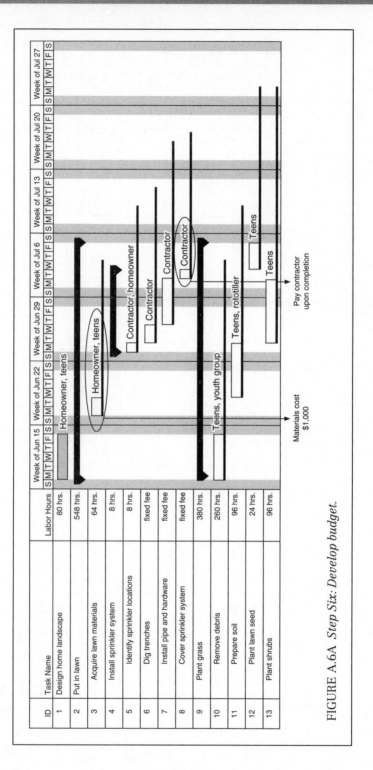

FIGURE A.6A *Step Six: Develop budget.*

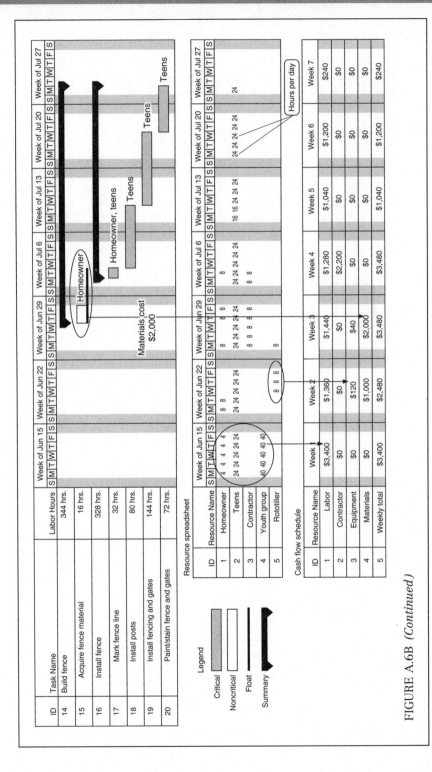

FIGURE A.6B *(Continued)*

# Downloadable Form Samples

The downloadable forms shown on the following pages comprise The Fast Foundation in Project Management. Owners of this book are entitled to download these forms from HYPERLINK "http://www .VersatileCompany.com/FFMBAinPM" www.VersatileCompany.com/ FFMBAinPM. Users have the right to modify these forms in any way that makes them useful to the reader including using them to create organizational project management standards. Modifying and reselling these forms for profit is prohibited.

Whenever a document has multiple pages, only the first page is shown here.

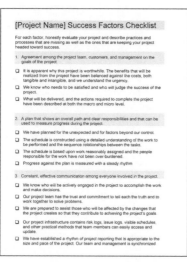

**Checklist for Successful Projects**

**Project Proposal**

## [Project Name] Stakeholder Analysis

Project Manager

**Stakeholder Role Profile**
These questions will encourage the project team to consider a wide variety of stakeholders. Use these questions to identify as many stakeholders as possible. After generating the list, you may decide some of the stakeholders are represented by other stakeholders or will have so little involvement in the project that you don't need to consider them and you may remove them from your list.

**This list is a starting point**
Add questions to this list that fit your project environment. If you miss an important stakeholder on one project, add a question to this list that will cause the next project team to identify that stakeholder.

For each of the questions below answer the question: "Who...?"

| | Question | All stakeholders that apply. Use people's names whenever possible. |
|---|---|---|
| 1. | Approves funding for this project? | |
| 2. | Approves functional requirements? | |
| 3. | Approves technical requirements? | |
| 4. | Approves design decisions? | |
| 5. | Approves changes to requirements? | |
| 6. | Approves changes affecting schedule? | |
| 7. | Approves changes affecting cost? | |
| 8. | Will use the product or service produced by the project? | |
| 9. | Set the organizational goals that drive the necessity of this project? | |
| 10. | Will assign people to the project team and determine the hours per day they work on the project? | |
| 11. | Approves contracts for suppliers? | |
| 12. | Is the manager or executive sponsoring this project (will use their authority on behalf of the project team to overcome organizational obstacles)? | |
| 13. | Will manage the project (provide leadership to assure tasks are assigned and completed on time, cost and schedule are monitored, issues are identified and resolved)? | |
| 14. | Represents organization policies governing this project? | |
| 15. | Represents regulations or laws affecting this project? | |
| 16. | Will have their work disrupted by this project? | |

**Stakeholder Analysis**

**Project Charter**

## [Project Name] Statement of Work

Project Manager:  Sponsor:
Date Last Updated: mm/dd/yy

**Purpose**

**Scope**
 Major project activities
 1.
 2.
 Out of scope activities that are critical to the success of the project
 1.
 2.

**Deliverables**
 1.
 2.

**Cost Estimates**

| Cost Type | Amount |
|---|---|
| Labor hours | |
| External costs | |
| Labor (consultants, contract labor) | |
| Equipment, hardware or software | |
| List other costs such as travel & training | |

**Schedule Overview**

| Estimated Project Completion Date: [mm/dd/yy] |
|---|
| Major Milestones |
| [Milestone name]   mm/dd/yy |
| External Milestones Affecting the Project |
| [Milestone name]   mm/dd/yy |
| Impact of Late Delivery |
| [Describe] |

**Measures of Success**
 1.
 2.

**Statement of Work**

## [Project Name] Statement of Work

Project Manager:  Sponsor:  Date: [mm/dd/yy]

**Revision History**

| Revision date | Revised by | Approved by | Description of change |
|---|---|---|---|
| | | | |

**Purpose**

**Scope**

All project tasks

| Task description | Who is responsible | Due date |
|---|---|---|
| 1 | | |
| 2 | | |

Out of scope activities that are critical to the success of the project

| 1 |
|---|
| 2 |

**Deliverables**

| 1 |
|---|
| 2 |

**Cost Estimates**

| Cost Type | Amount |
|---|---|
| Labor hours | |
| External costs | |
| Labor (consultants, contract labor) | |
| Equipment, hardware or software | |
| List other costs such as travel & training | |

**Schedule Overview**

| Estimated Project Completion Date: [mm/dd/yy] |
|---|
| Impact of Late Delivery |

**Measures of Success**

The project will be judged complete and successful when:

| 1 |
|---|
| 2 |

**Small Project Statement of Work**

## [Project Name] Definition Checklist
**Project Manager**

**Stakeholder Analysis**

- ❏ The project sponsor is known and actively involved in supporting the project.
- ❏ The project sponsor has sufficient authority within the project environment to effectively champion the project team.
- ❏ Functional managers supplying personnel or other resources to the project have been identified and are ready to supply the required resources.
- ❏ The people who will approve requirements & specifications, changes to requirements & specifications, and who will accept the final product are identified and have agreed to the process for these approvals.
- ❏ The people who will approve funding and changes to funding are known and a process exists for approving changes to funding.
- ❏ Stakeholders inside and outside the firm that will have veto power over any decision in the project are known and are identified in the responsibility matrix and communication plan.
- ❏ All contributors necessary to complete the project have been identified and understand their role on the project.
- ❏ The stakeholders that will receive and operate the outcome of the project are included in the responsibility matrix.
- ❏ Stakeholders who will be affected by the outcomes of the project are known, their stake is understood, and there is a strategy for managing them to benefit the project.
- ❏ A project charter that clearly identifies and shows management support for the project manager has been published.

**Project Proposal**

- ❏ A project proposal has been prepared and approved.
- ❏ The project manager has received and understands the proposal.
- ❏ Any future milestones requiring an updated proposal and renewed approval have been identified.

**Definition Checklist**

## [Project Name] Planning Checklist
**Project Manager**

**Risk Management**

- ❏ The project team has invested time and energy into identifying project risks.
- ❏ A risk response strategy has been developed for all risks that have a significant impact or probability.
- ❏ Contingency funds or time have been allocated by management.
- ❏ Funds to account for unexpected problems have been set aside as Management Reserve.
- ❏ A risk log has been developed to manage known risks and is accessible to all project team members.
- ❏ Every risk in the log has someone responsible for managing it.
- ❏ There is a plan in place for continuously identifying and responding to new risks.

**Work Breakdown Structure**

- ❏ Tasks have been identified to produce every deliverable in the statement of work.
- ❏ The work breakdown structure for the project is consistent with standard WBS guidelines and/or templates for similar projects.
- ❏ The project team participated in building the WBS or has reviewed and approved it.
- ❏ Every task on the WBS has a strong, descriptive name that includes a noun and a verb.
- ❏ Every task on the WBS has a beginning, an end, and clear completion criteria.
- ❏ Project management tasks are included on the WBS.
- ❏ Tasks have been broken down to a level that enables clear responsibility to be assigned.
- ❏ The WBS follows the rules for creating a top-down decomposition.
- ❏ The structure of the WBS has been evaluated to ensure the summary tasks are meaningful to stakeholders that require high-level understanding of the project.

**Planning Checklist**

## [Project Name] Kick-Off Checklist
**Project Manager**

**Stakeholder Participation**

- ❏ The project sponsor has clearly communicated the project goal to the project team.
- ❏ The project goal is understood and accepted by the project team.
- ❏ The project team understands how the project fits into the overall goals of the organization.
- ❏ Team members understand their specific assignments and how they fit into the overall project.
- ❏ Part-time team members and support organizations within the firm understand their contribution to the project and have agreed to this role.
- ❏ Functional managers who contribute personnel to the project understand the work required from their personnel and have committed to support these people in fulfilling their project duties.
- ❏ The customer is represented and has agreed to a regular plan for communication.

**Project Process**

- ❏ The project plan has a baseline budget and schedule.
- ❏ The project plan shows specific tasks and responsibilities and is easily accessible to all project team members.
- ❏ There is an accepted process for team members to record progress against their task assignments.
- ❏ There is a change management process in place.
- ❏ An issue log has been established and it is easily accessible to all project team members.
- ❏ A configuration management plan has established the location of all project documents, naming conventions, and version control.
- ❏ Management has agreed to a format and frequency for reporting status.
- ❏ There is a schedule established for project team meetings.

**Kickoff Checklist**

## [Project Name] Meeting Agenda & Minutes

| Meeting Date | Meeting Time | Location |
|---|---|---|
| [mm/dd/yy] | hh:mm – hh:mm | [location] |

**Meeting Leader** [Meeting Leader Name]
**Meeting Purpose** [Describe meeting purpose]
**Project Purpose** [Purpose description from statement of work]

**Participant Names**
[participant names]

| Agenda Item | Who's Responsible | Time Allotted |
|---|---|---|
| 1. [topic description] | | |
| [topic discussion] | | |
| [topic resolution] | | |
| 2. [topic description] | | |
| [topic discussion] | | |
| [topic resolution] | | |
| 3. [topic description] | | |
| [topic discussion] | | |
| [topic resolution] | | |

**Meeting Agenda**

## [Project Name] Status Report

Project Manager          Sponsor

Status Date [mm/dd/yy]

| Cost performance | [cost variance] % under/over budget |
|---|---|
| Planned cost to date | |
| Actual cost to date | |
| Approved project cost baseline | |
| Estimated cost at completion | |

Schedule performance    [schedule variance] % ahead/behind schedule
attach a tier 1 Gantt chart with baseline and current schedule

Issues requiring management attention
1
2

Changes to scope, schedule, cost during this period
1
2

Major problems encountered and planned action to resolve
1
2

Issues identified this period and required action
1
2

Major accomplishments in the past week
1
2

Major accomplishments scheduled for next week
1
2

**Status Report**

## [Project Name] Control Checklist

Project Manager

*Use this evaluation on an on-going basis throughout the project.*

**Stakeholder Participation**

❑ The project sponsor is fully aware of the state of the project, including revised schedule and budget estimates.

❑ The customer is fully aware of the state of the project, including revised schedule and budget estimates.

❑ The project team is fully aware of the state of the project, including revised schedule and budget estimates.

❑ Team members understand their specific assignments and how they fit into the overall project.

❑ Part-time team members and support organizations within the firm understand their contribution to the project. These expectations are clearly communicated both well in advance and again just prior to their involvement in order to give them the opportunity to plan to meet these expectations.

❑ The responsibility matrix is accurate.

❑ All stakeholders who need to be informed of project progress have adequate access to project information.

**Project Process**

❑ The project plan is routinely updated to reflect the near term action plan

❑ Progress against the baseline budget and schedule is recorded and understood by the team.

❑ The baseline budget and schedule continue to be realistic.

❑ An issue log has been established and it is being used to track issues.

❑ Continuous risk management activities reveal new risks, which are evaluated and assigned to team members

❑ Known risks are monitored and, where possible, mitigation strategies are followed to reduce the probability or impact.

❑ The project team meets on a regular basis to discuss accomplishments, plan for near-term activities, and share new information about the project.

**Control Checklist**

## [Project Name] Closure Report

Project Manager: [Name]
Sponsor: [Name]

**Project Goal**

**Project Objectives & Results**

| Objectives from Statement of Work | Results |
|---|---|
| 1 | |
| 2 | |

**Scope Comparison**
Additional scope
Decreased scope

**Cost Performance**

| Cost Categories | Approved | Actual |
|---|---|---|
| Internal Labor hours | | |
| External costs | | |
| Labor (consultants, contract labor) | | |
| Equipment, hardware or software | | |
| List other costs such as travel & training | | |
| Explanation of cost variance | | |

**Schedule Performance**

| | Approved | Actual |
|---|---|---|
| Project completion date | | |
| Explanation of schedule variance | | |

**Major Obstacles Encountered**
1
2

**Lessons Learned that are Relevant to Other Projects**
1
2

**Closure Report**

## [Project Name] Change Request

| Change Name | [short description] | | |
|---|---|---|---|
| Date | [mm/dd/yy] | Change Request | [####] |
| Submitted | | Number | |

Requested by   [Name of person requesting change]
Submitted by   [Name of person writing this request]

**Detailed Description of Change**

| Impact Analysis | |
|---|---|
| Schedule | |
| Cost | |
| Related impact to other projects or parts of this project | |

**Decision and Rationale**

Approval:          [signature]

Approved by:     [name]

Approval date:   [mm/dd/yy]

**Change Request**

493

## [Project Name] Risk Log

Project Manager:

Last updated [mm/dd/yy]

| Risk ID | WBS | Rank | Date Found | Assigned | Description | Strategy | Status | Close-Out Date |
|---------|-----|------|------------|----------|-------------|----------|--------|----------------|
| | | | | | | | | |
| | | | | | | | | |
| | | | | | | | | |

**Description of fields:**

**Risk Id:** A unique identifier

**WBS:** WBS number of the task(s) related to this risk.

**Rank:** How important is this risk relative to others? Prioritize from 1 to 5 with 1 = highest.

**Date found:** Date risk became known. mm/dd/yy

**Assigned to:** Person who is assigned to manage this risk

**Description:** High level description of risk event, impact and probability

**Strategy:** What will be done to reduce the probability, impact, or both?

**Status:** On-going log of changes to risk, in order from most recent to oldest. Format: mm/dd/yy – action/update

**Close-Out date:** When did the risk probability go to zero? Describe in the final status.

**Risk Log**

## [Project Name] Change Log

Project Manager:

Last updated [mm/dd/yy]

| Change ID | Date Submitted | Requested by | Description | Cost/Schedule Impact | Status |
|-----------|----------------|--------------|-------------|----------------------|--------|
| | | | | | |
| | | | | | |
| | | | | | |

**Description of fields:**

**Change Id:** A unique identifier

**Date Submitted:** Date issue became known. mm/dd/yy

**Requested by:** Person who is requesting the change

**Description:** Describe the change being requested.

**Impact:** Describe the impact to cost or schedule.

**Status:** Approved or Pending or Rejected and date.

**Change Log**

## [Project Name] Issues Log

Project Manager: [Name]

Last updated [mm/dd/yy]

| Issue ID | Priority | Date Found | Assigned | Description | Status | Close-Out Date |
|----------|----------|------------|----------|-------------|--------|----------------|
| | | | | | | |
| | | | | | | |
| | | | | | | |

**Description of fields:**

**Issue Id:** A unique identifier

**Priority:** High, medium, or low indicates the urgency to resolve.

**Date found:** Date issue became known. Format: mm/dd/yy

**Assigned:** Person who is assigned to resolve this issue

**Description:** What is the problem or what action needs to be taken?

**Status:** On-going log of changes to issue, in order from most recent to oldest. Format: mm/dd/yy – action/update

**Close-Out date:** When did the issue get resolved? Format: mm/dd/yy

**Issues Log**

## CHAPTER 1

1. Clayton Christensen, *The Innovators Dilemma: The Revolutionary Book That Will Change the Way You Do Business*. (New York: HarperBusiness, 2011).

## CHAPTER 3

1. Tim Brown, *Change by Design*. (New York, NY: HarperCollins, 2009)
2. Mark C. Paulk, Charles V. Weber, Bill Curtis, and Mary Beth Chrissis, *Capability Maturity Model for Software*. CMU/SEI-91-TR-24. (Pittsburgh, PA: Carnegie Mellon University, Software Engineering Institute, 1991).
3. Bruce Brown and Scott Anthony, "How P&G Tripled Its Innovation Success Rate." *Harvard Business Review*, June 2011, 66.
4. Eric Ries, *The Lean Startup: How Today's Entrepreneurs Use Continuous Innovation to Create Radically Successful Businesses*. (New York, Crown Business, 2011).

## CHAPTER 4

1. Tim Brown, *Change by Design*. (New York, NY: HarperCollins, 2009), 18. See also, www.IDEO.com for these three factors.

## CHAPTER 5

1. Robert Miller and Stephen Heiman describe this decision-maker in their book, *Strategic Selling*. (New York: Warner Books, 1985). While theirs is primarily a book about selling, any project manager promoting organizational change will benefit from understanding the decision-making processes outlined in their book.

## CHAPTER 8

1. Michael A. Cusumano. "How Microsoft Makes Large Teams Work Like Small Teams." *Sloan Management Review*, Fall 1997, 13.
2. Steve McConnell, *Rapid Development: Taming Wild Software Schedules*. (Redmond, WA: Microsoft Press, 1996), 72.
3. Stephen R. Covey, *The Seven Habits of Highly Effective People: Restoring the Character Ethic*. (New York: Fireside, 1989).

## CHAPTER 11

1. Fred Magness, *Fundamentals of Project Management*. (Washington, DC: Qualitech Systems, 1990).

## CHAPTER 12

1. Fred Brooks, *The Mythical Man-Month*. (Reading, MA: Addison-Wesley, 1995).
2. Project Management Institute, *A Guide to the Project Management Body of Knowledge* (Newtown Square, PA: PMI, 1996), 68, 162;

Harold Kerzner, *Project Management: A Systems Approach to Planning, Scheduling and Controlling*, 4th ed. (New York: Van Nostrand Reinhold), 1992), 684–688.

3. Tom DeMarco and Timothy Lister, *Peopleware: Productive Projects and Teams.* (New York: Dorset House, 1987), 15–16.
4. Philip B. Crosby, *Quality Is Free.* (New York: McGraw- Hill, 1979).

## CHAPTER 13

1. David P. Hanna, *Designing Organizations for High Performance.* (New York: Prentice Hall, 1988).
2. Kristin Arnold, "Making Team Decisions," in Elaine Biech (ed.), *The Pfeiffer Book of Successful Team Building Tools.* (San Francisco: Pfeiffer, 2001), 157.
3. The responses to conflict have been written about widely. The original reference on this topic is R. R. Blake and J. S. Mouton, *The Managerial Grid.* (Houston: Gulf Publishing, 1964).
4. Roger Fisher and William L. Ury, *Getting to Yes: Negotiating Agreement Without Giving In.* (New York: Penguin Books, 1991). To some degree, all the guidelines for working through conflict are expressed in this useful book. In particular, guideline 4 comes directly from Chapter 3.
5. John C. Redding, *The Radical Team Handbook.* (San Francisco: Jossey-Bass Business & Management Series, 2000), 64–65.
6. Ibid., 89–90.
7. Ibid., 103.
8. Peter Senge, *The Fifth Discipline: The Art and Practice of the Learning Organization.* (New York: Doubleday, 1990). Also *The Fifth Discipline Fieldbook: Strategies and Tools for Building a Learning Organization.* (New York: Doubleday, 1994).
9. An excellent reference on the topic of high- performance teams is Peter R. Scholtes, Brian L. Joiner, and Barbara J. Streibel, *The Team Handbook.* (Madison, WI: Oriel Inc., 1996).

## CHAPTER 14

1. Fred Magness, *Fundamentals of Project Management.* (Washington, DC: Qualitech Systems, 1990).

## CHAPTER 17

1. Peter F. Drucker, "Management's New Paradigms," *Forbes*, October 5, 1998, 152–177.

## CHAPTER 18

1. Denis Couture, "Enterprise Project Management," in Eric Verzuh (ed.), *The Portable MBA in Project Management.* (Hoboken, NJ: John Wiley & Sons, 2003), 349.

## CHAPTER 19

1. Barry W. Boehm, *Software Engineering Economics.* (Englewood Cliffs, NJ: Prentice- Hall, 1981).

Page references followed by *fig* indicate an illustrated figure; followed by *t* indicate a table